IN THE LIGHT OF NAPLES
THE ART OF FRANCESCO DE MURA

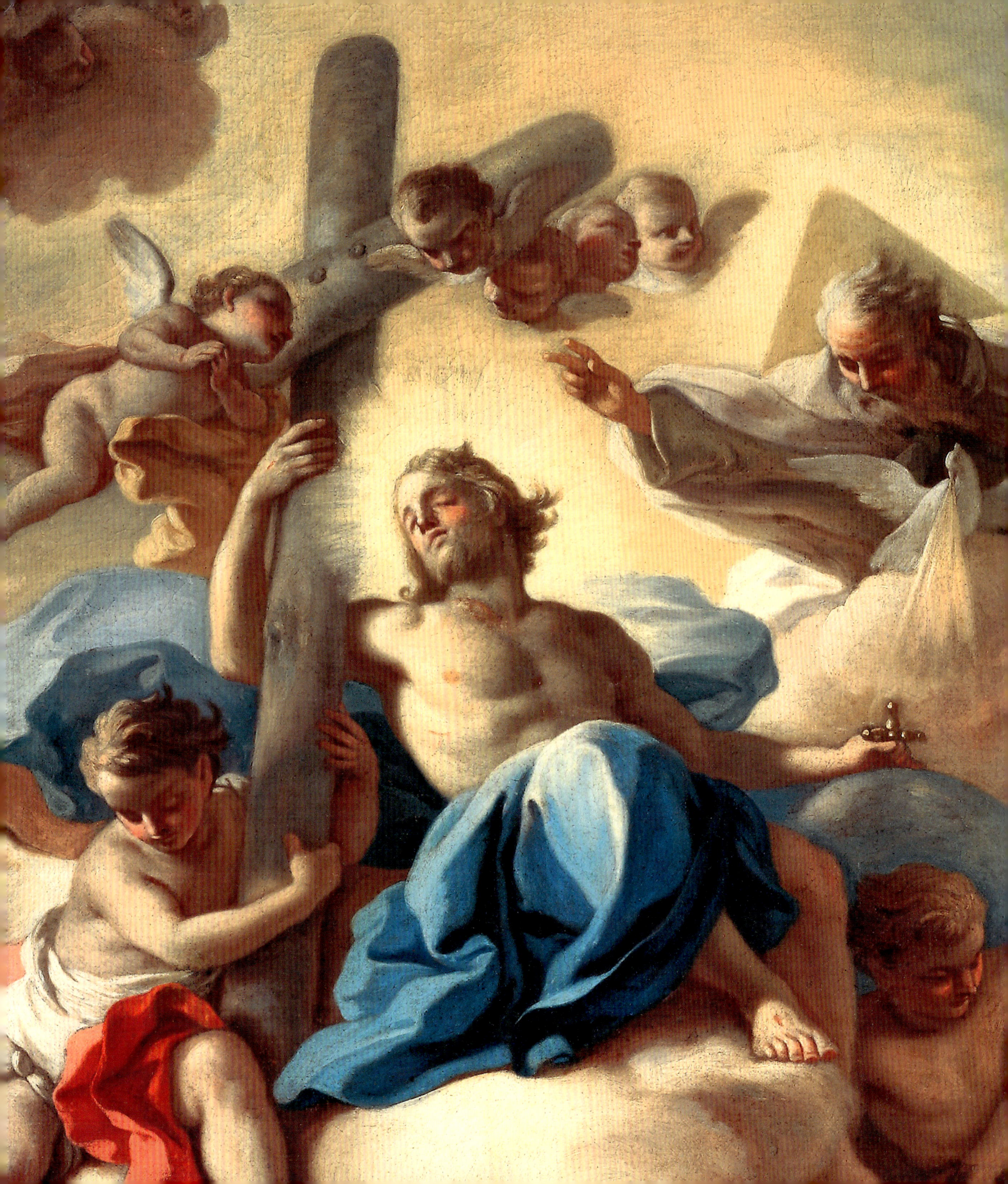

IN THE LIGHT OF NAPLES

THE ART OF FRANCESCO DE MURA

Arthur R. Blumenthal

Contributing essays by
Nicola Spinosa
David Nolta
Loredana Gazzara
Maria Grazia Leonetti Rodinò

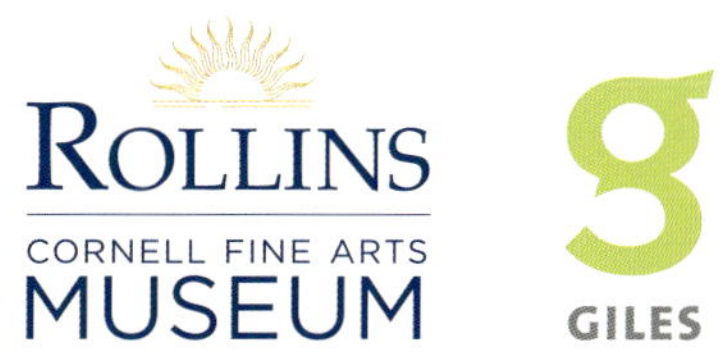

The Cornell Fine Arts Museum, Rollins College, Winter Park, Florida
in association with D Giles Limited, London

As organizing institution of the exhibition and its national tour, the Cornell Fine Arts Museum gratefully acknowledges the following generous donors:

Catalogue/Principal Sponsor
Bruce and Dolores Douglas

Exhibition Sponsor
The Steward's Fund

Exhibition Patrons
Mark Mahan and Kathryn Saugstad
June and Jack Nelson
PNC Foundation
The Cornell Fine Arts Museum Board of Visitors

Contributors
Anonymous
Mark and Laura Cosgrove

Members of the Director's Circle at the Cornell Fine Arts Museum
Jacqueline Bradley
John and Kelly Burrus
Mark and Laura Cosgrove
Carl and Ann Croft
Barbara and Gary DeVane
Bruce and Dolores Douglas
Chad Holloway
Marc and Henrietta Katzen
Jeremy Lang
June Nelson
Margery Pabst-Steinmetz and Chuck Steinmetz
Alexander Read
Pat and Randy Robertson
Leila E. Trismen

Lenders to the Exhibition

The Art Institute of Chicago
Chicago, Illinois

Bob Jones University Museum and
Gallery, Inc.
Greenville, South Carolina

Federico Castelluccio
New Jersey

Chazen Museum of Art
University of Wisconsin–Madison

Cooper-Hewitt, Smithsonian Design
Museum
New York City

Cornell Fine Arts Museum
Rollins College
Winter Park, Florida

Davis Museum, Wellesley College
Wellesley, Massachusetts

The Fitzwilliam Museum,
University of Cambridge
Cambridge, United Kingdom

Frances Lehman Loeb Art Center,
Vassar College
Poughkeepsie, New York

Hearst Castle
San Simeon, California

Myron Laskin, Jr.
Malibu, California

The Metropolitan Museum of Art
New York City

The Minneapolis Institute of Art
Minneapolis, Minnesota

The Morgan Library & Museum
New York City

Museo de Arte de Ponce
Ponce, Puerto Rico

Museo e Gallerie Nazionali di
Capodimonte
Naples, Italy

Museum of Fine Arts
Boston, Massachusetts

National Gallery of Art
Washington, D.C.

Philbrook Museum of Art
Tulsa, Oklahoma

Pio Monte della Misericordia
Naples, Italy

Frank and Demi Rogozienski
San Diego, California

John and Mable Ringling Museum of
Art, FSU
Sarasota, Florida

Seattle Art Museum
Seattle, Washington

Snite Museum of Art
University of Notre Dame
Notre Dame, Indiana

Walters Art Museum
Baltimore, Maryland

Bob and Teresa Wilson
Greenville, South Carolina

Mr. and Mrs. Clovis Whitfield
London, United Kingdom

Anonymous collector

This catalogue was published in conjunction with the exhibition *In the Light of Naples: The Art of Francesco de Mura*, organized by the Cornell Fine Arts Museum at Rollins College in Winter Park, Florida, and held there from September 17 through December 18, 2016. It then traveled to the Chazen Museum of Art at the University of Wisconsin–Madison from January 20 through April 2, 2017 and to the Frances Lehman Loeb Art Center at Vassar College from April 21 through July 2, 2017.

In the Light of Naples: The Art of Francesco de Mura was curated by Arthur R. Blumenthal.

Library of Congress
Cataloging-in-Publication Data

Names: Blumenthal, Arthur R. | Gazzara, Loredana. | Leonetti Rodinò, Maria Grazia. | Nolta, David Derbin. | Spinosa, Nicola. | Mura, Francesco de, 1696-1782. | George D. and Harriet W. Cornell Fine Arts Museum, organizer, host institution.
Title: In the light of Naples : the art of Francesco de Mura / Arthur R. Blumenthal; Contributing essays by Nicola Spinosa, David Nolta, Loredana Gazzara, Maria Grazia Leonetti Rodinò.
Description: Winter Park, Florida : D Giles Limited, 2016. | Includes bibliographical references.
Identifiers: LCCN 2016018122| ISBN 9781907804854 (hardback) | ISBN 9780979228018 (paperback)
Subjects: LCSH: Mura, Francesco de, 1696-1782--Exhibitions. | BISAC: ART / Individual Artists / General. | ART / History / Baroque & Rococo. | ART / Collections, Catalogs, Exhibitions / General. | ART / Subjects & Themes / Religious.
Classification: LCC ND623.M925 A4 2016 | DDC 759.6--dc23
LC record available at https://lccn.loc.gov/2016018122

First published in 2016 by GILES
An imprint of D Giles Limited
4 Crescent Stables
139 Upper Richmond Road
London, SW15 2TN, UK
www.gilesltd.com

ISBN (hardcover): 978-1-907804-85-4
ISBN (paperback): 978-0-9792280-1-8

For the Cornell Fine Arts Museum,
Rollins College
Volume Editor: Arthur R. Blumenthal

For D Giles Limited
Copyedited and proofread by
Jodi Simpson
Designed by Alfonso Iacurci
Produced by GILES, an imprint
of D Giles Limited, London
Printed and bound in China

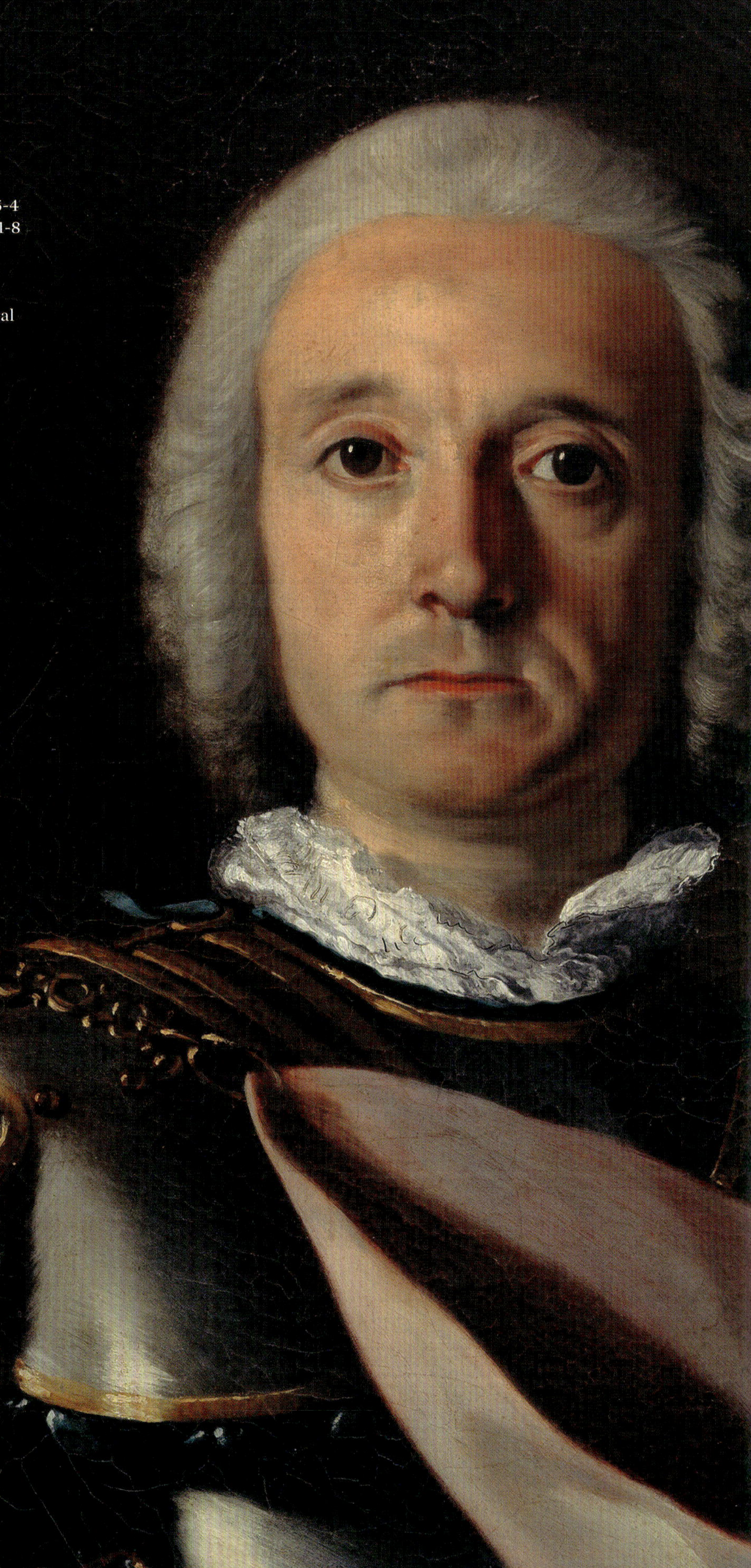

Contents

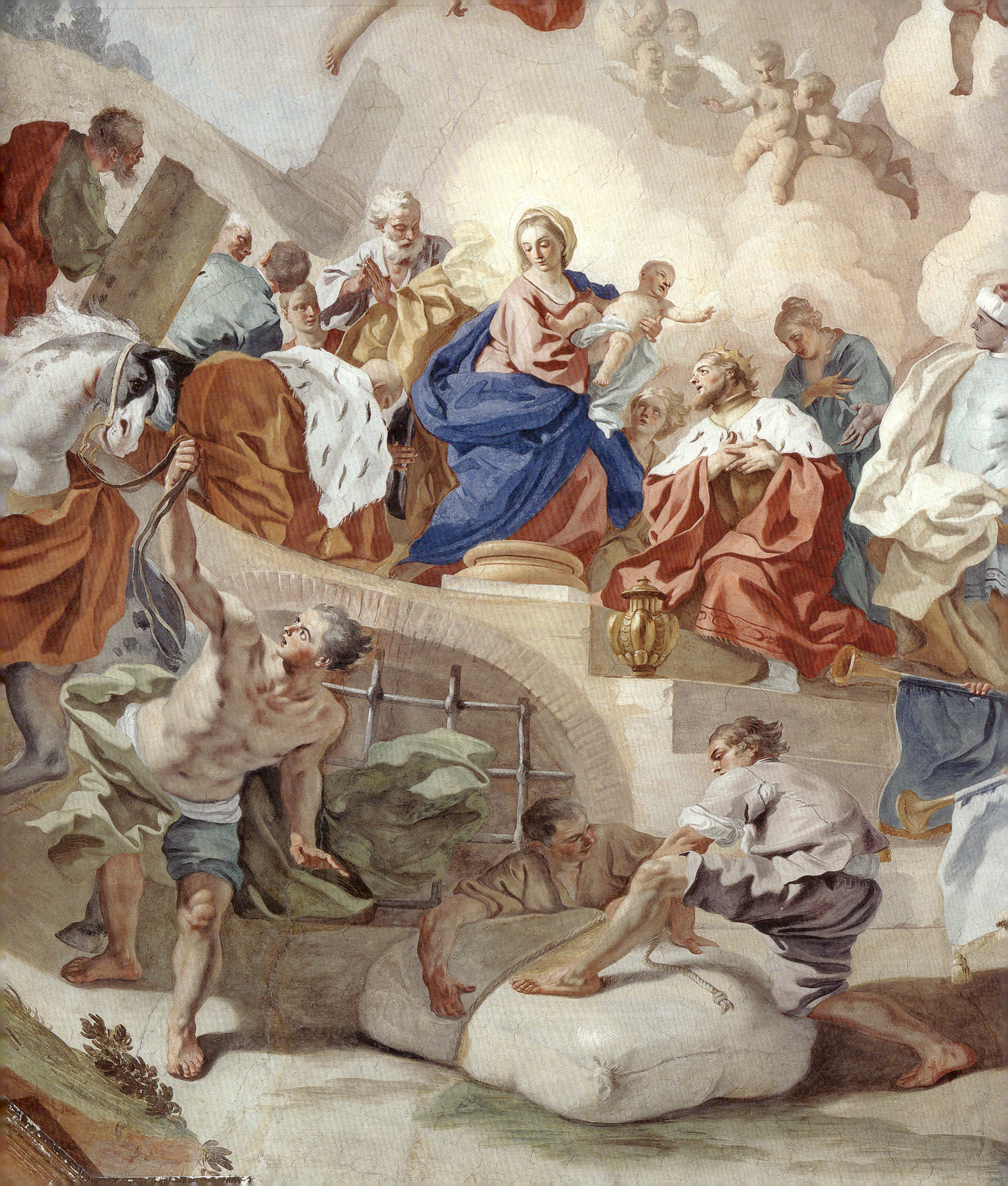

From the Consul General of Italy in Miami

In the Light of Naples: The Art of Francesco de Mura is the first-ever public display of the works of a richly deserving Neapolitan artist, considered the greatest painter of Naples' Golden Age and one of the last of the Baroque old masters.

De Mura, the favorite painter of the Bourbon King Charles VII of Naples, is celebrated for his refined and elegant compositions; his superb artistry rivals that of his famous Venetian contemporary Giambattista Tiepolo. De Mura's works, with their exquisite, light, and airy colors, heralded the Rococo in Naples, and his later classicist style led to Neoclassicism. This exhibition shows De Mura in his rightful place as a leader of the Neapolitan School, assigning to his many works the reputation they justly deserve in the art world.

In the Light of Naples is the culmination of a long journey. This journey began in 2006 when Dr. Arthur Blumenthal started his comprehensive research into De Mura, inspecting both private and public collections, and in 2010 giving a lecture on De Mura at the Italian Cultural Institute of New York, followed by another in 2012 at Pio Monte della Misericordia in Naples.

The exhibition features more than 40 works by the great painter, lent by The Metropolitan Museum of Art, New York; the Art Institute of Chicago; the Minneapolis Institute of Art; the National Gallery of Art, Washington, D.C.; Museo e Gallerie Nazionali di Capodimonte, Naples; and Pio Monte della Misericordia, Naples, as well as other public and private collections. Spearheaded by the Cornell Fine Arts Museum at Rollins College, which owns *The Visitation*, a major painting by De Mura, the exhibition will travel in 2017 to the Chazen Museum of Art at the University of Wisconsin–Madison and the Frances Lehman Loeb Art Center at Vassar College.

I am very pleased that so many institutions from different countries have collaborated to share peacefully the vision and the beauty of art—a testimony to the unparalleled power of culture to bring people together.

Gloria Marina Bellelli
Consul General
Consulate General of Italy In Miami
Honorary High Patron

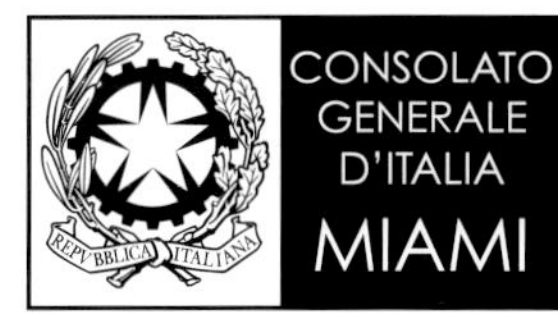

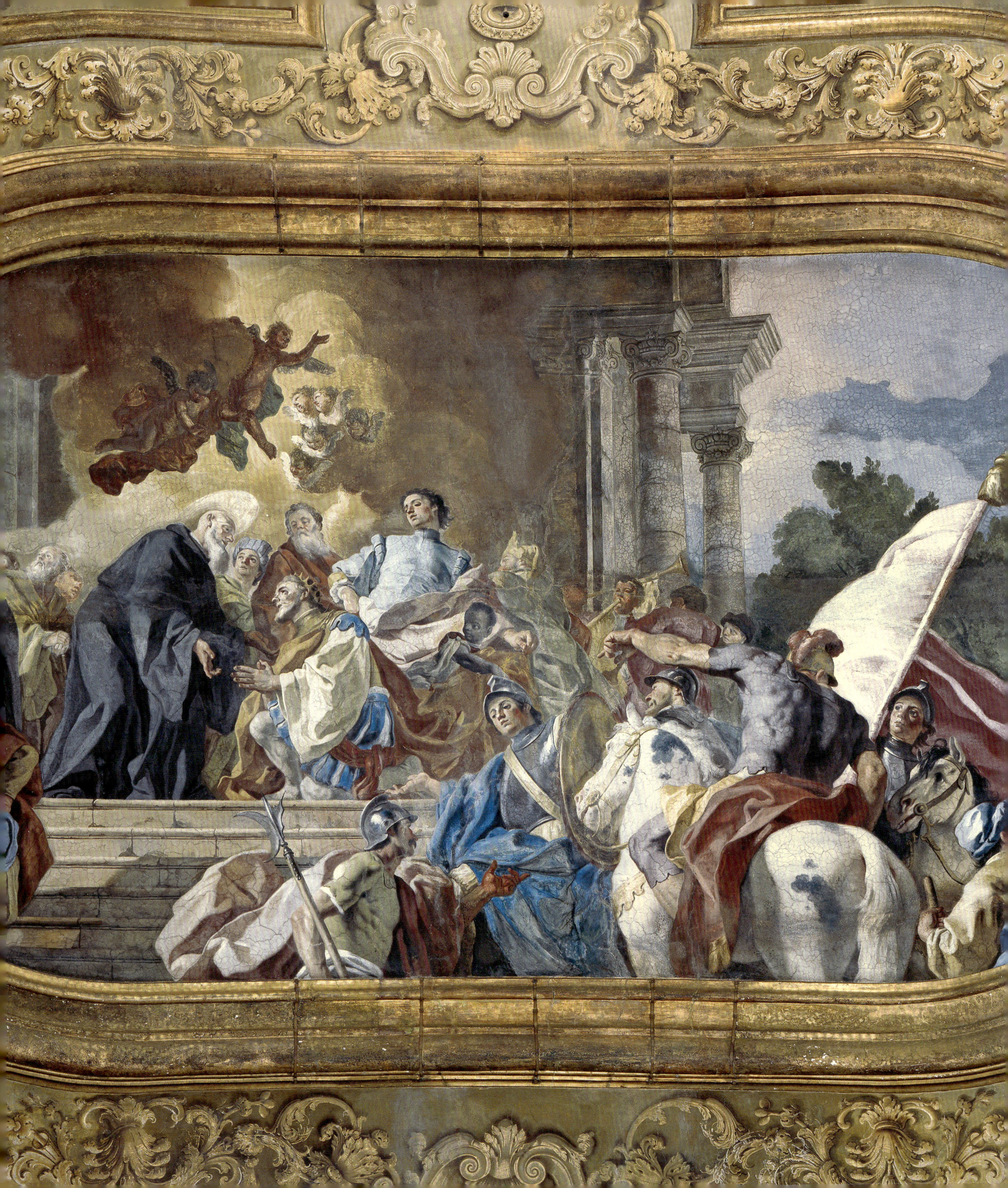

Directors' Foreword

For specialists and casual visitors alike, museum exhibitions delight the most when they include an element of discovery. It may be looking at a well-known artist in a new light, or connecting works in unexpected ways. It may be the discovery of a new artist, a style, even a medium. Or—and this is the case with the exhibition *In the Light of Naples: The Art of Francesco de Mura*—it can be the rediscovery of an artist once famous yet long forgotten. It is also redressing the artist's ill-fated art historical destiny.

Francesco de Mura (1696–1782), a leader of the Neapolitan School, was perhaps the most sought-after painter of his day. His robust yet elegant compositions placed him among lauded Baroque masters, while his lighter palette heralded the Rococo style. Among his many prestigious commissions were frescoes for several Neapolitan churches, the Palazzo Reale in Turin, and the abbey of Monte Cassino. History, however, was not kind to De Mura: a third of his *œuvre* was completely destroyed in the Allied bombing of Naples during World War II. The fresco cycle at Monte Cassino, perhaps the crowning achievement of a long career, was tragically lost. That loss may well explain why modern art history has paid so little attention to Francesco de Mura.

The exhibition *In the Light of Naples: The Art of Francesco de Mura*, the first ever dedicated to the artist, hopes to correct that state of affairs, and to demonstrate the significant place held by De Mura in eighteenth-century Neapolitan, and more generally Italian, painting. As directors of academic art museums, we are particularly pleased to host this exhibition that teaches our students not only about the evolution of painting from Baroque to Rococo to Neoclassicism, but also about the vagaries of history and how they influence the critical fortune of artists. Finally, as we look back with regret at the destruction caused by war, we reflect upon the price of freedom and how it affects the knowledge of future generations.

We are grateful to Dr. Arthur Blumenthal, director emeritus of the Cornell Fine Arts Museum, for organizing this landmark exhibition, to the leadership of our schools for their support, and to our staffs for making the exhibition a success at each venue.

Ena Heller
Bruce A. Beal Director
Cornell Fine Arts Museum, Rollins College

James Mundy
Anne Hendricks Bass Director
The Frances Lehman Loeb Art Center, Vassar College

Russell Panczenko
Director
Chazen Museum of Art, University of Wisconsin–Madison

Acknowledgments

Organizing *In the Light of Naples: The Art of Francesco de Mura* has been a testament to the magnificence of numerous individuals—to their belief in this exhibition and to their extraordinary generosity. Early on, I was told an exhibition of Francesco de Mura's art could never happen—yet it has. From its inception as an idea in 2006 to its execution a decade later, this "impossible" exhibition has unfolded in a serendipitous, nearly miraculous manner. So, let me acknowledge the heavenly power that channels extraordinary beauty through geniuses like De Mura, whose splendid achievements live on, transcending the horrors of war.

This exhibition's earthly supporters are many. I am indebted to a number of people who recognized De Mura's brilliance long ago. The first is David Nolta, professor of the history of art at Massachusetts College of Art and Design, who twenty-seven years ago wrote his powerful doctoral dissertation at Yale on "Francesco de Mura: Lives and Works" and in 2016 authored an essay for this catalogue. We both looked to Nicola Spinosa—the celebrated Neapolitan art expert who was former director of Naples' Museo di Capodimonte and head of Naples' museums—for his incredible scholarship on and familiarity with De Mura. Professor Spinosa has been a great adviser to this show, pointing us toward newly identified works, and freely offering his knowledge and support, as well as contributing an essay to this catalogue.

I am greatly indebted to our wonderful Neapolitan friends who have worked tirelessly for this exhibition. Maria Grazia Leonetti Rodinò, former *Governatore* of Naples' Pio Monte della Misericordia and its first female director (*direttrice*), is one of this show's many angels, opening many doors, including access to the frescoes in the Nunziatella and elsewhere; a complete *ammiratrice* of De Mura, she has written an illuminating essay for this catalogue. Many thanks, also, to the generous Leonetti family for their assistance: Lisi and Piera and their brother Gianpaolo, now director of Pio Monte. I thank the gracious and hard-working Loredana Gazzara, curator of the Picture Gallery (*Quadreria*) at Pio Monte, for her help and her excellent essay that reveals much about the dispersal of De Mura's works. Words do not adequately express my gratitude to Federico Castelluccio, the actor/artist/art connoisseur who owns the largest collection of De Muras outside of Italy; he offered constant encouragement, donated time for fundraising, and acquired artworks for this show.

More encouragement came from dear friends Dr. Mark Mahan and his wife, Kathryn Saugstad, through their seed donation that allowed this show to get off the ground; ten years ago, Mark traveled to Naples with us, fell in love with De Mura, and has since played "art detective" in his travels, searching for De Muras in American museums. I am also hugely grateful to Gary and Kay Rupp, cherished fellow art-lovers, for many years of friendship and for spiritual/financial support of this show. Thanks also go to the Board of Visitors of the Cornell Fine Arts Museum, who backed this project from the beginning. Board member Bruce Douglas and his wife, Dolores, principal sponsors, generously gave specifically for the publication of this catalogue. Longtime board member June Nelson and her late husband, Jack, kindly became patrons of this show. Our thanks go to The Steward's Fund, the exhibition sponsor, and PNC Foundation, an exhibition patron. Other contributors include Mark and Laura Cosgrove and an anonymous donor. And we thank the generous members of the Director's Circle of the Cornell Museum.

Rollins College awarded me a Petters International Initiative Award in 2006–7 that allowed me to travel to Italy and conduct research on De Mura. Great appreciation goes to the staff of the Cornell Fine Arts Museum, all of whom took on the extra burden of this challenging project: Dr. Ena Heller for giving me the opportunity to organize this exhibition; Austin Reeves for brilliantly juggling the myriad details of this show, allowing things to run smoothly; Dana Thomas for coordinating fundraising; Sandy Todd for handling complex grants and budgets; Louise Buyo for educational programming; and for their assistance, Amy Galpin, Dina Mack, and Adam Lavigne. Thanks to Devon Massot, director of grants at Rollins, for her help with proposals, and to Edward Borsoi, professor emeritus, and Samuel Gallacher, for their fine translations from the Italian.

I thank Stephen Borys, former curator at the John and Mable Ringling Museum of Art (now director of the Winnipeg Art Gallery), and John Wettenhall, former Ringling director (now director of the George Washington University Museum), for their early support of the initial exhibition groundwork, including the winning of a Samuel H. Kress Foundation exhibition preparation grant.

My gratitude goes to Alberto Manai, former director of the Italian Cultural Institute at the Italian Embassy in Washington, D.C., for hosting my talk on De Mura there in 2011. A similar lecture was given in 2010 at the Italian Cultural Institute at the Italian Consulate in New York, for which I thank the staff and Renato Miracco, its former director; I also thank Pio Monte della Misericordia for kindly hosting my talk there (in Italian) in 2012. We owe a debt of gratitude to the Honorable John Mica, congressman of Florida's seventh district, for his assistance in reaching out to possible donors and his enthusiasm in promoting the show.

We thank all the generous lenders (listed on page 5), who expressed confidence in this exhibition by parting with their treasures. Special appreciation to the private collectors from New York, New Jersey, California, South Carolina, and London for lending to this show. To all the museums willing to lend their works, I express deep gratitude, as well as to their staffs, especially: Martha Wolff, Art Institute of Chicago; John Nolan, Bob Jones University Museum and Gallery; Maria Saffiotti Dale and Russell Panczenko, Chazen Museum of Art (gratitude also for the Chazen's venue-sharing of this show); Caitlin Condell, Cooper-Hewitt, Smithsonian Design Museum; Eve Straussman-Planzer, Davis Museum at Wellesley College; Tim Knox, The Fitzwilliam Museum; James Mundy, The Frances Lehman Loeb Art Center at Vassar College (gratitude also for the Loeb's venue-sharing of this show); Mary Levkoff, Hearst Castle; Tanya Paul, Milwaukee Art Museum; George Goldner, former

curator of prints and drawings at The Metropolitan Museum of Art; Patrick Noon, The Minneapolis Institute of Art; Jennifer Tonkovich, The Morgan Library & Museum; Pablo Pérez d'Ors, Museo de Arte de Ponce; David Brown, National Gallery of Art, for his kind assistance with international loans; Sylvain Bellenger, Museo e Gallerie Nazionali di Capodimonte; Frederick Ilchman, Museum of Fine Arts, Boston; Christine Kallenberger, formerly at the Philbrook Museum of Art; Steven High, John and Mable Ringling Museum of Art; Chiyo Ishikawa, Seattle Art Museum; Charles Loving, Snite Museum of Art; and Joaneath Spicer, Walters Art Museum.

For images of De Mura's two paintings of *St. Bertharius* in the Molinari Pradelli collection, I acknowledge the gracious signora Bianca Maria Radaelli Molinari and her daughter, signora Carla Bianchi, who generously donated these images, as well as the cost of re-photographing the paintings by Carlo Vannini and L. Landi. Special appreciation goes to Irene and Gerald Stoffer and to Yvonne Maria Schaefer for taking beautiful photos of De Mura's paintings in the Palazzo Reale in Turin. Thanks also to Luciano Pedicini in Naples for quickly supplying numerous images. Thanks to Emma Kronman at Christie's and Christopher Apostle at Sotheby's. To Pat Barylski and the staff at D Giles Limited in London, many thanks for their patience and support in creating this beautiful catalogue, which was expertly designed by Alfonso Iacurci.

This exhibition is dedicated to Kären Love Blumenthal '14. Her unwavering belief in its possibility and her loving, indefatigable work brought it to fruition. *Grazie molto, mia moglie bellissima!*

We are grateful to Gloria Marina Bellelli, Consul General of Italy in Miami, for her honorary patronage of this exhibition.

E finalmente, al maestro Francesco de Mura, molto grazie a voi—thank you for creating, in the light of Naples, the magnificent art that reveals your heart, your faith, and your soul's expression. Even the horrors of war could not extinguish a light as bright as yours.

Arthur R. Blumenthal
Director Emeritus and Guest Curator
Cornell Fine Arts Museum

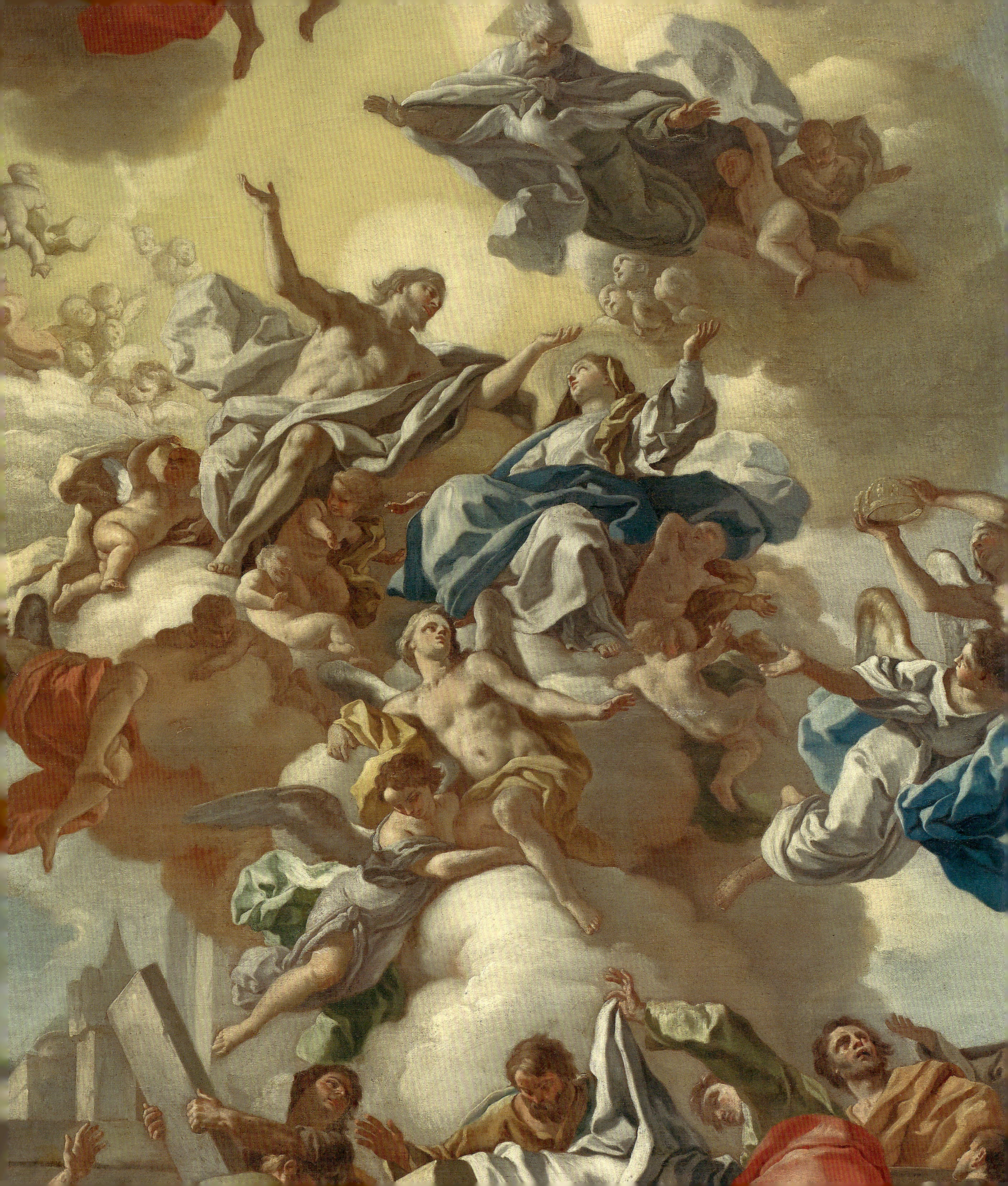

Introduction

Arthur R. Blumenthal

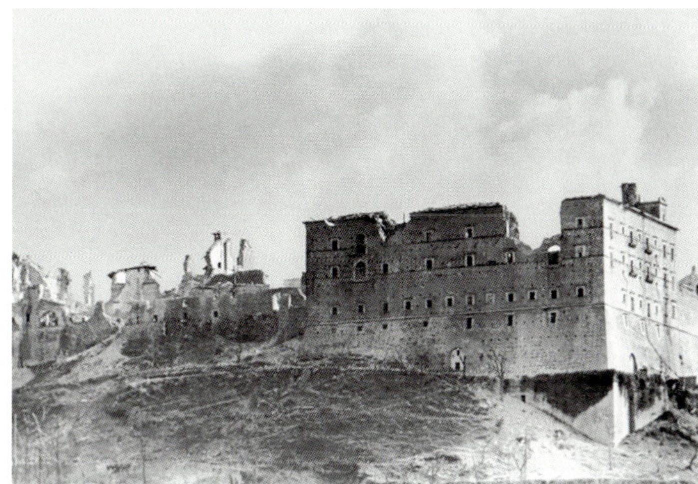

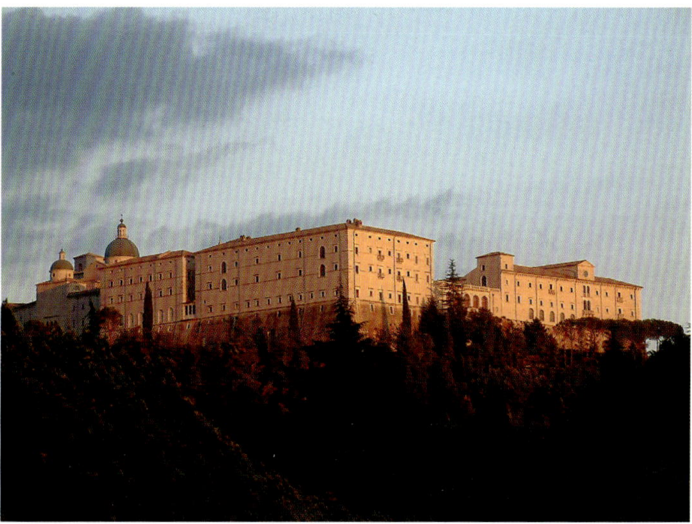

Fig. 1 (top)
Abbey of Monte Cassino after the Allied bombing of 1944

Fig. 2 (above)
Abbey of Monte Cassino as reconstructed in the 1950s and 1960s

The horrific destruction of Italy's abbey of Monte Cassino in February 1944 (figs. 1–2), executed in large part by American bombs, destroyed irreplaceable paintings, sculpture, books, and manuscripts, detailing all that is good in human nature by countless artists and writers. Among the art destroyed was one-third of the works of Francesco de Mura (1696–1782), a brilliant Neapolitan artist of Naples' Golden Age. We are mounting this historic exhibition, *In the Light of Naples: The Art of Francesco de Mura*, to atone in part for this loss and to restore this artist to his rightful place in history. Simply put, Francesco de Mura's art is impossibly beautiful, a contemplation on the magnificent. On those fateful winter days, De Mura's splendid ceilings and paintings turned to ash, as did our memory of the artist. Time forgot the virtuoso De Mura ... until now. It is our hope this exhibition, in some small measure, will heal this terrible cultural wound.

To appreciate De Mura, we must enter his eighteenth-century Neapolitan world. The city of Naples—splendid, chaotic, secretive—has barely changed since the artist walked its cobblestone streets in the 1700s. Nestled by the spectacular Bay of Naples, Mount

Vesuvius in the distance, the city is often bathed in a near-spiritual light (fig. 3). During the Bourbon rule (1734–99), the light of Naples drew artists to it—artists who saw its blues and shimmering roses and golds, where sky and water meet in a heavenly confluence. Today, forgotten, unseen art overflows Naples' countless churches; Baroque treasures wait under lock and key to be discovered again. Nothing is lovelier than hearing the creak of an ancient door, then peering into the darkness to discover the light of a De Mura ceiling fresco filled with flying angels against clouds as delicate as mist. To stand transfixed is to enter the heart of the Neapolitan Baroque.

Francesco de Mura showed extraordinary artistic talent at a young age. He entered the prestigious studio of Francesco Solimena (1657–1747) when he was just twelve years old. There, a father-son relationship blossomed with the master artist, one that kept De Mura in Solimena's studio into his early thirties, long past the age when young men ventured out on their own. The young De Mura experienced daily encounters with beauty: great paintings by Luca Giordano (see fig. 6) were everywhere. A short walk away, Caravaggio's magnificent *Seven Acts of Mercy* glowed above the main altar at Pio Monte della Misericordia (see fig. 24), the charitable institution to which he would eventually bequeath his art. De Mura listened to the keyboard sonatas of Domenico Scarlatti and saw the classical plays of Pietro Metastasio. He relished opera at the Bourbons' Real Teatro di San Carlo, which opened in 1737 with Domenico Sarro's *Achille in Sciro*. De Mura, a person of faith, probably worshipped in the cathedral of San Gennaro, where shimmering candlelight, music, and incense fired his young imagination. In the churches and palaces, he observed energetic and beautifully carved *presepio* figurines (see fig. 90) that reflected Naples' street life. De Mura embraced these cultural impulses, and brought them to his art in Solimena's studio and afterwards. In his teens, he began to create canvases and splendid frescoes that echoed Solimena's style so closely he was soon known as "the young Solimena."

The more than forty paintings and drawings in this show narrate the life of De Mura. His essence lives in his art, and it is there we must look for him, since few of his words survive in letters and documents. In De Mura's art, we sense an affinity for Neapolitan light, for the city's music and theater that pulse like a heartbeat. We also see a single-minded intensity and discipline. De Mura felt a deep respect for the long line of geniuses who preceded him—from Caravaggio to Giordano to Solimena. Thus, through this exhibition, we see how De Mura "lived" his art and how he lived *for* his art. We can imagine the sheer physical effort and backbreaking hours De Mura poured into his painting—something barely imaginable today. We cannot envision, without heartbreak, the wiry De Mura, sprawled on scaffolding in the abbey of Monte Cassino creating his glorious paintings, knowing that, two hundred years later, Allied bombs would destroy it all. *In the Light of Naples* is not only the first exhibition of De Mura's art; it is a revelation of the broadness and fullness of his creative vision. For the first time, we see where De Mura came from, the artist he developed into, and what he left behind. We discover the soul of the man.

That soul is evident in De Mura's extensive palette. In this show, we view up close one of history's most extraordinary colorists. Even the highest resolution photograph cannot capture the vitality and depth of De Mura's brilliant colors. We must observe them in person, standing before the painting, feeling their energy reach into us. On the exhibition walls, we perceive not just his color virtuosity and shifts in style, but we witness the growth of De Mura's skills, particularly in the meticulous draftsmanship (*disegno*) of his naturalistic figures. Beyond his expertise as a composer of narratives,

Fig. 3
Joseph Vernet (1714–1789), *View of Naples with Mount Vesuvius*, oil on canvas, 39 × 77½ in. (99 × 197 cm), Musée du Louvre, Paris

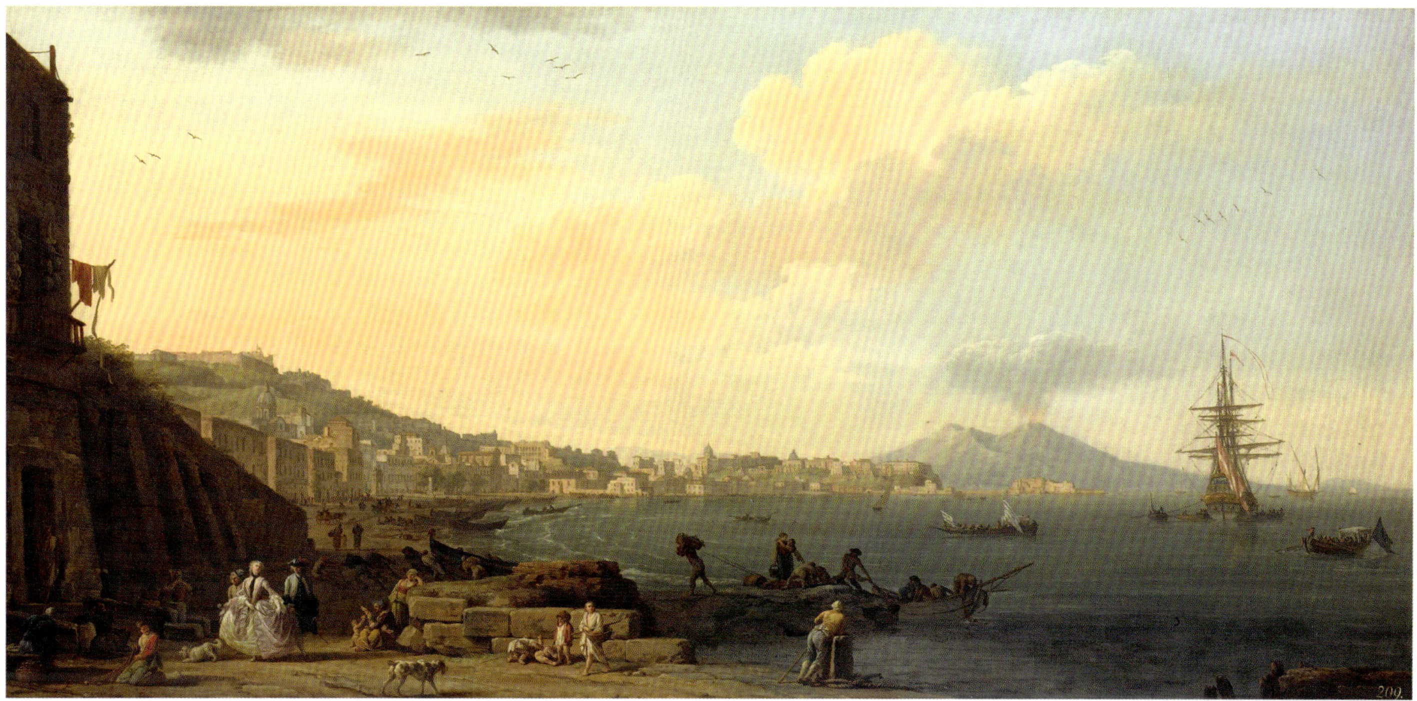

De Mura also proves himself a powerful portraitist, one who conveys an emotional depth in the eyes and hands and in the physicality of the pose. This empathy, coupled with superb artistic discipline, drew a multitude of royal, aristocratic, and ecclesiastical commissions. De Mura has left us a wide-ranging "documentary" of the city of Naples in the mid-1700s. We see a city where a special light shone in the skies and sparkled on the water—*and* in the color-saturated frescoes in the vaults of churches (as in the Nunziatella; see fig. 65). After all, De Mura's soul reflected Naples; he epitomized the city itself.

More than a salute to Francesco de Mura, this exhibition illuminates the flow of artistic style from the late 1600s to the 1700s and beyond. In his early career, De Mura's talent for the Baroque outshone his contemporaries and his work was barely distinguishable from Solimena's. In 1732 in the Nunziatella's frescoes, he lightened his palette to a remarkable degree. We see him rapidly develop into a brighter Rococo style in the ceiling frescoes and overdoors of the sumptuous Palazzo Reale in Turin, suggesting a French influence. In this show, we trace De Mura's progress from the Baroque into the Rococo, and then his final effort, in late age, to adapt to the simplicity and sculptural quality of the burgeoning Neoclassicism. The arc of his story is there: Francesco de Mura begins painting in the early 1700s, succeeds to an incredible degree in the mid-1700s, and then, in the late 1700s, anticipates the artistic style of the even-later 1700s and early 1800s. If we consider Rococo as a late extension of the Baroque, then De Mura was among the very last Baroque artists, alive and still working when the United States of America was founded. The full sweep of a century's artistic style is seen in these forty-five works of art.

As we reacquaint ourselves with De Mura, the heart of the artist and the scope of his contribution come into clear focus. The exhibition is blessed with an abundance of generous loans of artworks from museums and private collections in North America—more than three-quarters of the objects in the show. The Cornell Fine Arts Museum owns two major works in the exhibition, De Mura's *Visitation* (cat. no. 23, the *raison d'être* for this exhibition), and Solimena's *St. Francis Xavier* (cat. no. 41), specially acquired for the show. Fortunately, both participating museums have lent at least one painting: the Chazen's De Mura and Solimena (cat. nos. 18 and 42) and the Loeb Center at Vassar's Giaquinto (cat. no. 44). Most of the works from abroad have never been seen on this continent. We are fortunate to exhibit oil sketches (*bozzetti*) for works tragically destroyed at Monte Cassino or lost over time. The miracle, of course, is gathering these treasures into one exhibition, under one roof. Today, a visit to Naples in search of De Mura paintings and ceilings would take months. We would have to traverse the museums and churches and dusty storerooms and spend endless hours trying to gain entry. But today, these examples come together for a joyous reunion.

Of these works, seven have never been included in any publication and are here published for the first time. A number of works were unknown before now and others hidden in storerooms. For example, several works generously lent by the Museo di Capodimonte in Naples are normally not on view. Many of the show's paintings and all drawings will return to storage at the close of this exhibition. In addition, the show juxtaposes De Mura's works (and those by his master, followers, and students) in such a way as to gain insights into their dating, subject matter, and more. The very act of hanging De Mura's artworks next to each other informs all of them.

The exhibition also allows us to redate or re-attribute a number of artworks newly identified. For example, Nicola Spinosa, a contributor to this catalogue, has redated the best-known work by De Mura, the *Allegory of the Arts* (see fig. 23) at the Louvre in Paris from about 1743 to about 1758–62, and the new dating is published here for the first time. This show sparked a new interest, a new energy from several private collectors, who acquired De Mura works after the original loan agreements had been signed for their earlier acquisition. And works surfaced from collectors in New York, New Jersey, London, and Malibu. There are also De Mura works that have been retitled, and several have been assigned entirely new titles because we discovered that the subject was different than originally believed. It is a testament to De Mura's art that so many distinguished museums around the world own works by him, and were so generous in lending them.

Why is so little known about Francesco de Mura? A major reason, of course, is the loss of one-third of his art in the 1944 bombing. But other forces conspired against him as well. For example, his master, Solimena, who lived into his nineties, cast an immense shadow throughout De Mura's life. With Solimena's death in 1747, De Mura finally came into his own, becoming the most admired painter in Naples. But while he enjoyed fame in Naples, De Mura rarely traveled out of his region (except for a few years in Turin), thus was virtually unknown in Europe's art capitals, except perhaps in parts of Spain. While Naples was a teeming art center, Venice and Rome enjoyed higher status. Lastly, the French dominated the Rococo (and Neoclassicism) art scene, eclipsing even the brightest of Italians as the Baroque fell out of fashion.

Our knowledge of this fine artist has been severely limited for other reasons as well. Perhaps most significant is that many surviving De Mura works have not been accessible to the public. An example is De Mura's dazzling ceiling frescoes in the church of the Nunziatella, which is now a military school and closed to the public.

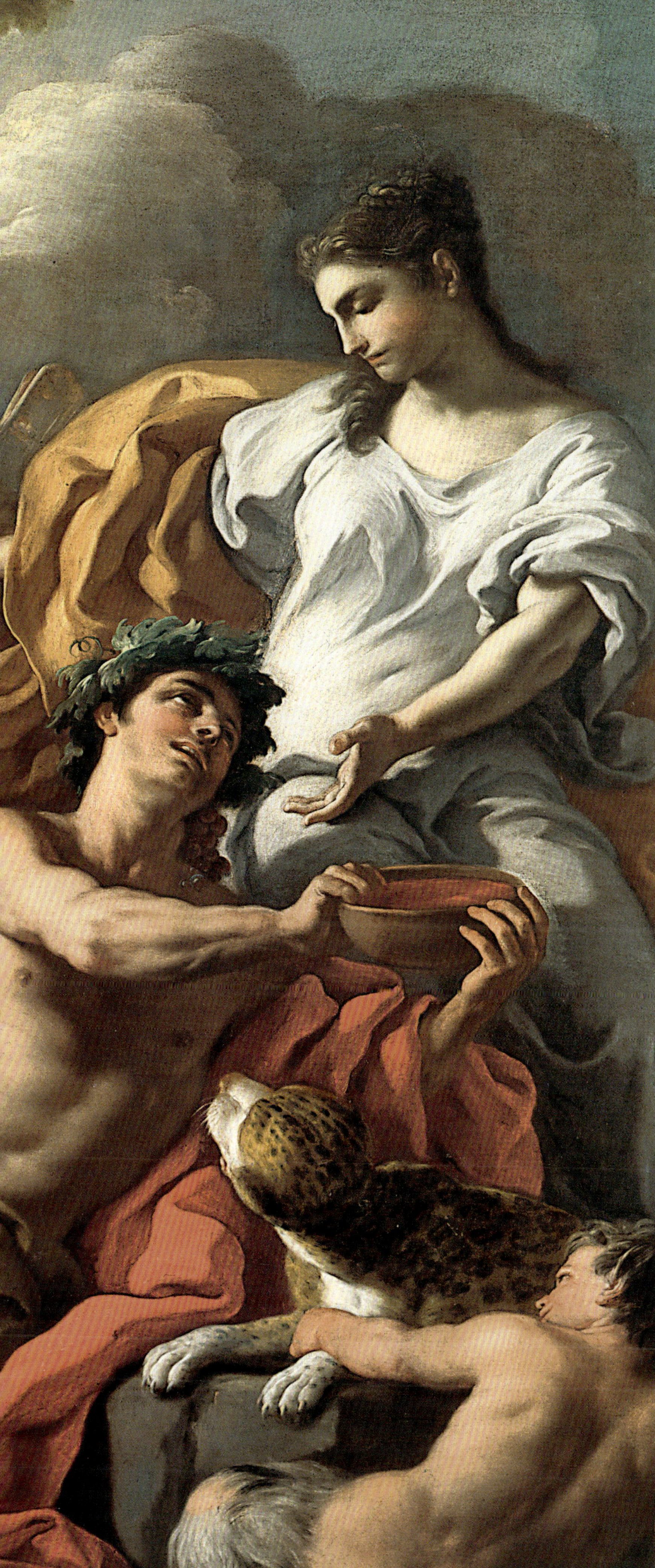

Cat. 37 (detail)

And even though Pio Monte della Misericordia is blessed with the vast collection of De Mura's art (since 1782), the Picture Gallery only opened to the public in 1972. The artist's generous bequest to Pio Monte reflects his spiritual connection there. Pio Monte has returned the favor by lovingly caring for his works. Scholars and art lovers owe a debt to Pio Monte for opening their doors so that De Mura's works can be studied and appreciated. We hope this exhibition brings the once-forgotten De Mura to the forefront of art history.

Professor Nicola Spinosa—former director of the Museo di Capodimonte/supervisor of Neapolitan museums and the leading world expert on Neapolitan art—has contributed a scholarly essay to this catalogue that sheds exciting new light to the work of De Mura and his transition from a classicist style into the Rococo, through tracing De Mura's entire career. David Nolta, professor of the history of art, Massachusetts College of Art and Design and the author of "Francesco de Mura: Lives and Works," has not only written a fine essay comparing De Mura with his contemporary Tiepolo, but also has compiled a brief biography of De Mura just for this catalogue. Two wonderful officials of Pio Monte della Misericordia, Countess Maria Grazia Leonetti Rodinò, former director of Pio Monte, and Loredana Gazzara, curator of Pio Monte's Picture Gallery, have each written about the dispersal of De Mura's works to the United States and beyond.

During its one-year tour (September 2016 through July 2017) to three university art museums, *In the Light of Naples: The Art of Francesco de Mura* will create the largest gathering of De Mura's art in one place in the world. The artist's love of beauty for the sake of beauty radiates a welcome light into our dark world. Now, 233 years after his death, we have the great pleasure of finally giving Francesco de Mura his due.

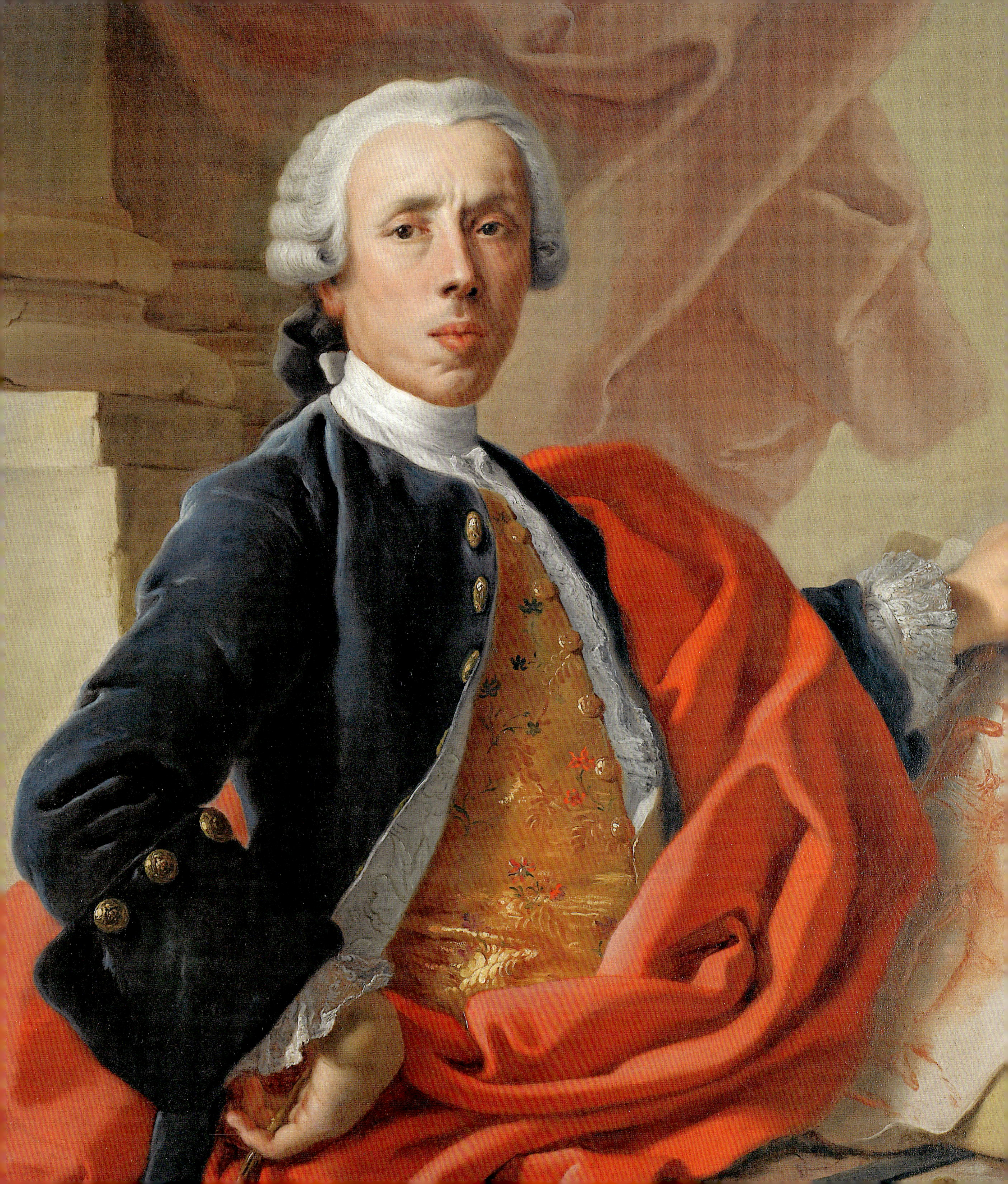

The Life of Francesco de Mura

David Nolta

Francesco de Mura was born in Naples in 1696 and died there in 1782. He was, then, the contemporary of Giambattista Tiepolo (1696–1770), William Hogarth (1697–1764), and François Boucher (1703–70). Like these better-known artists, De Mura is strongly, justifiably identified with his native place, to the extent that his art can be said to represent that place in his time. Among these and other eighteenth-century artists, De Mura can also be said to have a particularly rich stylistic trajectory; as a Neapolitan living and working in the wake of the great Luca Giordano (1634–1705), De Mura displays a range of artistic interests and capabilities and a pictorial repertory worthy of the great artistic legacy of his hometown.

Trained first, and very briefly, in the studio of the little-known Domenico Viola, De Mura transferred at age twelve to the workshop of Francesco Solimena (1657–1747; fig. 4), who was the most famous artist in—as well as the most sought-after Neapolitan artist outside—Naples following the death of Giordano in 1705. The first phase of De Mura's career marks him as the best of Solimena's pupils (see cat. no. 1), his superiority

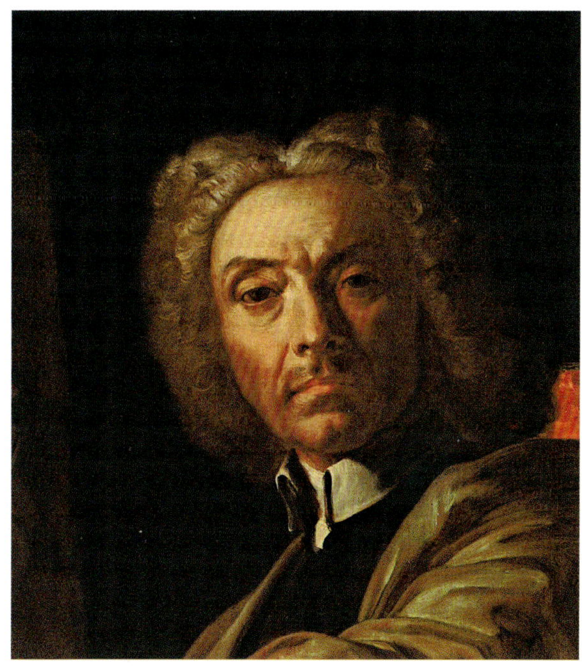

Fig. 4
Francesco Solimena, *Self-Portrait* (detail, see also p. 130)

proclaimed by the master himself and judged, in keeping with accepted criteria of the time, by the pupil's ability to copy the works of his teacher-employer. According to contemporaries, De Mura impressed Solimena and his peers above all with his talented draftsmanship; such testimonials to his early mastery of *disegno* set the young painter within the conservative, academic camp, with its essentially southern Italian blend of classicizing and Baroque traditions. The approbation of Solimena, whose art gravitated increasingly toward a grand classical manner after his experience in Rome in 1702, was clearly the key to De Mura's immediate future, resulting in his first large-scale commissions in the 1720s, often for important works outside of Naples (five works for the cathedral at Capua; three, including a ceiling fresco, for the church of the Annunziata at Airola (see fig. 63). Through these commissions, De Mura helped to disseminate the Solimenesque mode, but they also allowed him the opportunity to experiment with and develop his longstanding inclinations toward a wider-ranging, and especially a lighter, chromatic scale, more animated figures, and a larger, more atmospheric view of their surroundings and the world.

By the 1730s, De Mura was on his own, establishing, in works such as the light-filled and ebullient Nunziatella apse fresco of *The Adoration of the Magi* (see fig. 49), an original artistic presence in Naples. His successes there and elsewhere led him into a long and mutually satisfying affiliation with the motherhouse of Western monasticism, the Benedictine abbey of Monte Cassino, for which, between 1731 and 1738, the artist provided over thirty oil paintings and frescoes, all virtually destroyed by the Allied bombing in 1944. The success of these undertakings is confirmed by the fact that by the end of the decade, De Mura was painting a monumental ceiling fresco of *The Glory of the Princes* (see cat. no. 35 and fig. 81) for King Charles of Bourbon's Royal Palace in Naples, as well as beginning the decoration of the vast vault of the much-rebuilt Neapolitan church of Santi Severino e Sossio (see fig. 53). The centerpiece of nine large and numerous subsidiary images, *The Vision of St. Benedict* (cat. no. 15) is signed and dated 1740. With its luminous palette and its operatic composition of solidly conceived figures in graceful and richly varied poses, all made visible and real by a cascade of light over ephemeral cloud, this work survives as one of the masterpieces of De Mura and of the age.

The subsequent decade, certainly the busiest of the artist's long career, opened with a trip to Turin at the request of King Charles Emmanuel III of Savoy. For eighteen months, till his return in the winter of 1743, De Mura worked on no fewer than six ceiling frescoes in

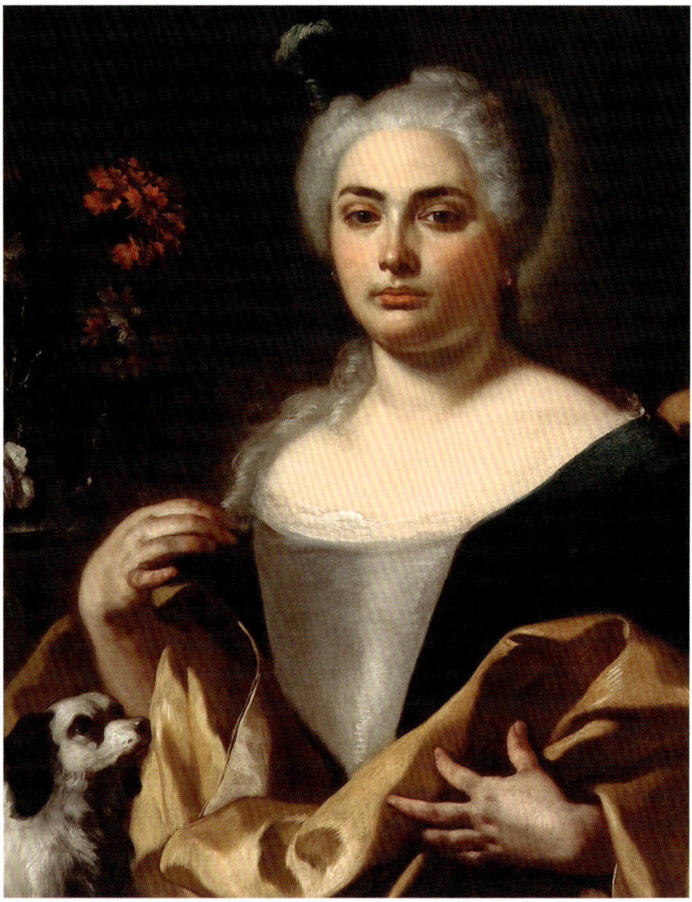

Fig. 5
Francesco de Mura, *Portrait of the Artist's Wife, Anna d'Ebreù* (detail, see also p. 130)

the Palazzo Reale (see cat. no. 18), and received numerous other commissions as well. Many of these were for classical scenes to fill the *sovrapporte* (overdoors) of the Palazzo Reale and other palaces (see cat. no. 19); the artist was still filling orders for these as late as 1758 (see fig. 86). One of the most commonly overlooked strengths of De Mura was his skill as a portraitist, and numerous exercises in the genre begin to appear in his *œuvre* in the 1740s (see cat.

nos. 17, 25, and 27), outstanding among them being the portrait presumed to be a *Prince of the House of Savoy* still to be found in the Palazzo Reale in Turin. Likewise, few painters surpass De Mura in the conception and execution of single-figure allegories, many of the finest created for his northern patrons. The Louvre's *Allegory of the Arts* is undoubtedly De Mura's best-known and most often reproduced picture (see fig. 23).

The allegories in the Louvre and elsewhere, the series of lively and engaging portraits (including a rather daunting, but also haunting, self-portrait, cat. no. 17), myriad histories, and religious scenes from the middle years of De Mura's life—all inevitably attest to the profound effects of his working stay in the cultural crucible of Turin, where he was exposed to the artistry of the Venetian Giovanni Battista Crosato (1686–1758) and the French painter Carle van Loo (1705–65), as well as to the dramatic colorism of his southern (Apulian) colleague, Corrado Giaquinto (1703–66; cat. nos. 44–45). It was in Turin that De Mura's instinctively light palette found its final confirmation, and it was in the years immediately after his return to Naples that he most confidently exhibited his unique synthesis—really, syntheses—of Rococo lightness and dynamism and well-grounded classical forms. When successful, the result of these pictorial experiments was charm, and it can be found in the best of even his largest and most imposing works of the 1750s and 1760s, such as his supreme effort *The Assumption of the Virgin*, frescoed on the vault of the Nunziatella in 1751 (see cat. nos. 20–21; fig. 65), and the *Annunciation* for the altarpiece of the eponymous church in the Forcella district, completed ten years later. Charm is also to be found in so many of his smaller works: the Certosa *Annunciation* (see fig. 66), the *Visitation* (see fig. 68), and the *Assumption* of 1757, in *Bacchus and Ceres* (cat. no. 37), and in *Christ and the Samaritan Woman* (cat. no. 24), two of many highlights in the present exhibition.

De Mura's final years in Naples were not without honors. He was invited to Madrid, to resume the patronage of Charles of Bourbon, now king of Spain, but declined for reasons that are not entirely clear. As teacher to an entire generation of southern Italian artists, including Giacinto Diano (1731–1803; see cat. no. 43), Fedele Fischetti (1732–92), Jacopo Cestaro (1718–78; see fig. 43), Domenico Mondo (1723–1806), and Alfonso di Spigna (1697–1785), he was recognized by an appointment to co-direct the Neapolitan Accademia di Belle Arti in 1766. De Mura stepped down from this post four years later, though he continued to receive and fulfill important commissions. In his ninth decade, he executed a series of overdoors for the spectacular new royal residence at Caserta; his application for payment is dated 1782, the year of his death. He was buried, at his request, in the Alcantarine church of San Pasquale a Chiaia, anonymously and perhaps, like the brothers, sitting up.

A Baroque artist with a Rococo bent (or at least palette), a classical artist with a light heart, at times a proto-Romantic, at other times as academic as they come, Francesco de Mura remains one of the great elusive masters of the Western tradition.

A Chronology

Arthur R. Blumenthal

1696
April 21 — Francesco de Mura born in Naples to Giuseppe de Mura and Anna Linguito.

1707
Attends workshop of Domenico Viola for about a year.

1708
Placed in studio of Francesco Solimena, where he remains until 1729.

1713
Copies Solimena's *Archangel St. Michael*; paints his own *Christ on the Cross*.

1718–20
Madonna Presenting St. Dominic with the Rosary (fig. 33).

1726–27
Ecce Homo (cat. nos. 2–3) for Collegiata dell'Assunta at Castel di Sangro in Abruzzo (fig. 35).

1727
June — Four *Patron Saints of Naples* (compare cat. no. 5); also, *Sacrifice of Iphigenia*, now in RISD Museum.

November — Marries Anna d'Ebreù; *Portrait of the Artist's Wife* (figs. 5 and 57), also a *Pietà* for Airola (fig. 36).

1727–28
Adoration of the Magi and eleven paintings for church of Santa Maria Donnarómita (figs. 11 and 48); works for chapel of San Nicola di Bari.

1729
Leaves Solimena to set up his own studio; creates illustrations for Cammarota's *Le tragedie cristiane*.

1730
September — Commissioned to do fifteen paintings of *Stories of Christ and the Virgin* for church of the Nativity in the Holy Sepulcher in Jerusalem (figs. 37, 41, and 46).

1731
Appears in the *Abecedario pittorico*, which was "dedicated to Francesco de Mura, excellent and magnificent Neapolitan painter"; listing of his paintings executed to that point.

1731–45
Abbey of Monte Cassino commissions many works to decorate chapels (cat. nos. 8, 10, and 11), choir, etc.

1732
Adoration of Magi for apse of the Nunziatella with its light and transparent colors (fig. 49 and cat. no. 12).

1733
Fresco of *St. Nicholas of Bari* (fig. 50) for cupola of San Nicola di Bari.

1738
Paints ceiling of Palazzo Reale in Naples with *Allegory of the Virtues of Charles Bourbon and Maria Amalia*.

1739–41
Ceiling frescoes of *Christ Receiving St. Joseph into Heaven with the Madonna and Saints* (cat. no. 13) for San Giuseppe dei Ruffi; *Christ as a Boy, Disputing with Scholars in the Temple* in Certosa di San Martino.

1740–41
Paints vault of ceiling of Santi Severino e Sossio with *Life of St. Benedict* (fig. 53 and cat. nos. 14–15).

1741
Ceiling frescoes of mythological *Stories of Achilles* (cat. no. 18; figs. 60–61) for Palazzo Reale in Turin.

1743
De Dominici writes about De Mura for his *Lives of the Artists*; lists De Mura's major works executed up to then.

1743–48
Sends allegorical figures, such as *Allegory of Charity* (cat. no. 19), to Palazzo Reale in Turin.

1745–47
Paints original (first official) *Self-Portrait* (cat. no. 17), which he replicated a number of times.

1747
May 3 — Solimena dies and De Mura becomes "*il primo dipintore oggidì in Napoli.*"

Before June: Paints superb *Portrait of Count James Joseph O'Mahoney* (cat. no. 25) during Neapolitan sojourn of Pierre Subleyras, who paints *Portrait of Countess Anna Giustiniani O'Mahoney* (fig. 70).

1750–51
Ceiling fresco of *Assumption of the Virgin* (cat. nos. 20–21; fig. 65) in the church of the Nunziatella.

1751–52
The Visitation for the church of San Nicola alla Carità (*bozzetto* at Cornell Museum, cat. no. 23; fig. 67).

1756
May 20 — *Portrait of Cardinal Antonio Sersale* (cat. no. 27), one of his finest.

1758
Monumental *Virgin in Glory Receiving St. Luigi Gonzaga* for Gesù Vecchio in Naples (cat. no. 28; fig. 73).

1759
Allegory of Spring (cat. no. 33) for Palazzo Reale in Naples.

1758–62
Stunning *Allegory of the Arts* (fig. 23), now in the Louvre.

1760
April 15–June 13 — Great French artist Fragonard visits Naples and draws images of workers.

1764
Plague returns to Naples—30,000 die; eruptions of Mount Vesuvius.

1767
October 14–20 — More eruptions of Mount Vesuvius.

1768
June 20 — De Mura's wife, Anna, dies (buried in the Nunziatella).

1770
Resigns from directorship of Royal Academy of the Study of the Nude after only four years.

1771
Multiplication of the Loaves in the cathedral of Foggia, his last major work.

1782
August 19 — De Mura dies, during a heatwave, in palace of Prince of Turin; buried in church in the convent of San Pasquale; bequeaths 55,454 ducats—in addition to 192 paintings, silver, carriages, and certificates of credit—to Pio Monte della Misericordia.

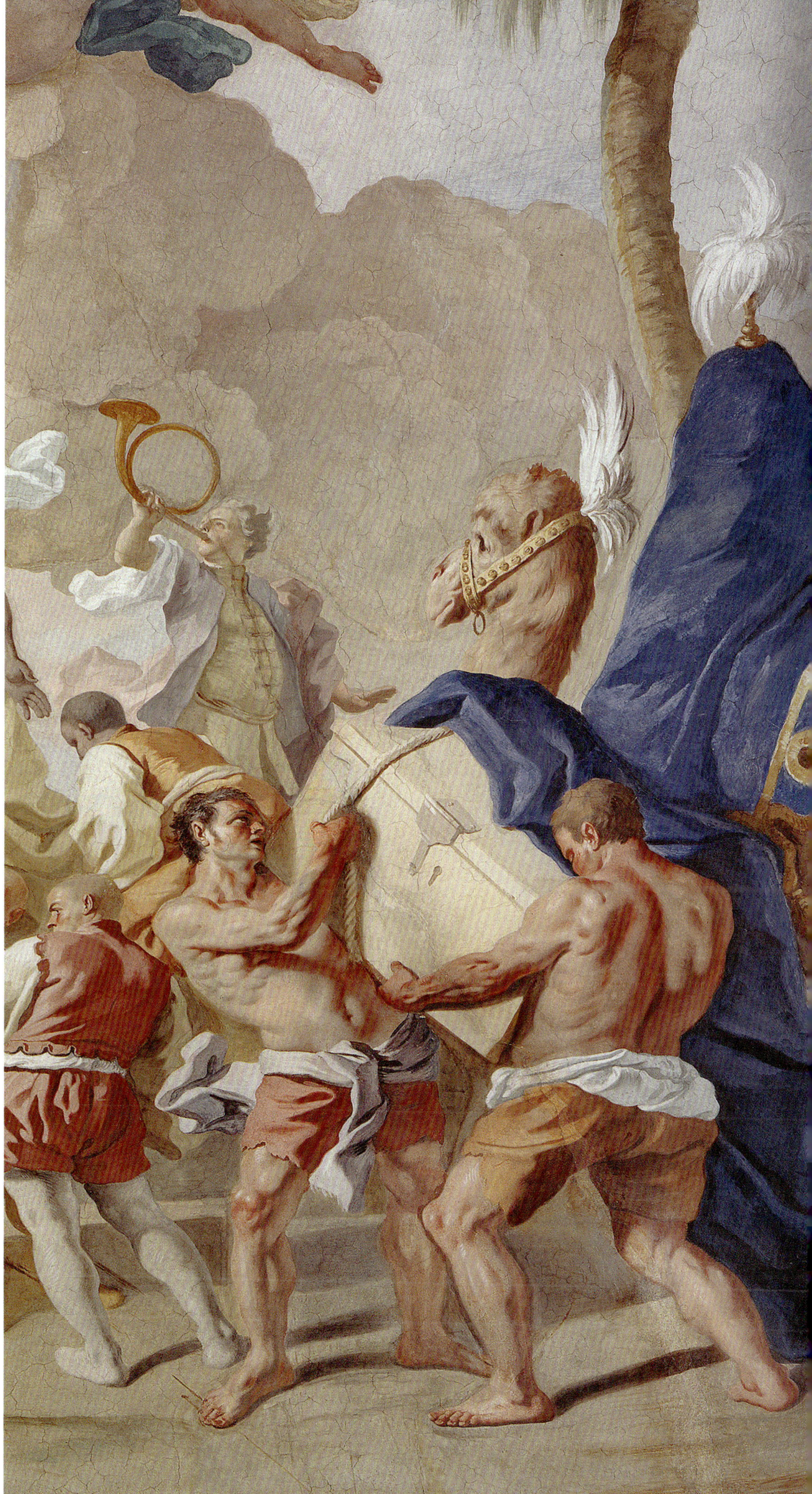

Fig. 49 (detail)

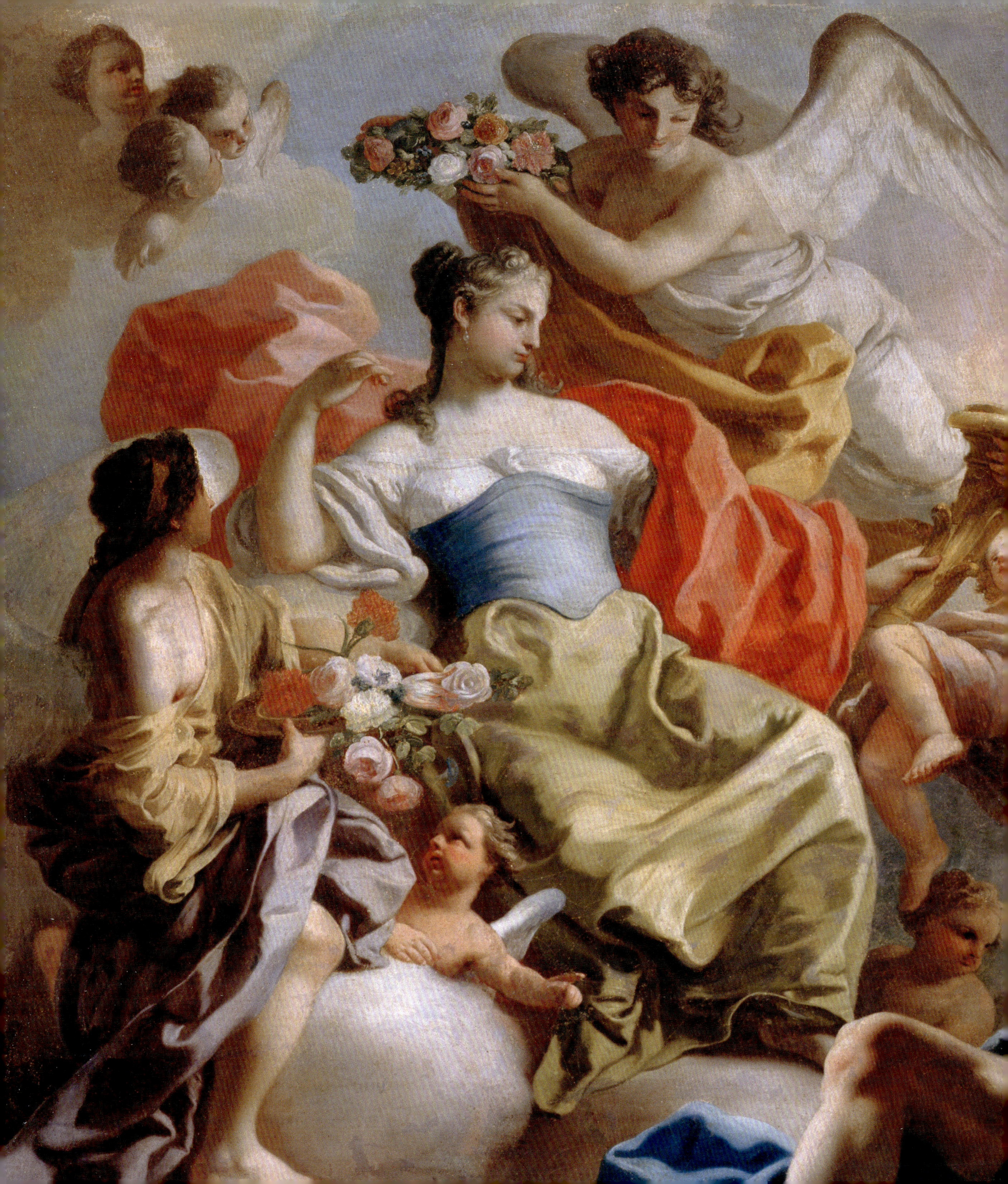

Francesco de Mura and Eighteenth-Century Neapolitan Painting: Between Classicism and Rococo

Nicola Spinosa

The formative years of Francesco de Mura (1696–1782) were spent in the studio of Francesco Solimena (1657–1747), after a brief and irrelevant period working in the workshop of Domenico Viola (ca. 1610–96).[1] His first paintings (see cat. nos. 1, 2, and 3) are dated around 1713 to 1728,[2] thus coinciding with moderate anti-Baroque and classical trends in Neapolitan art. These trends found a concrete application in painting, although with different outcomes, as can be seen in the work of Solimena from 1700, and that of Paolo de Matteis (1662–1728) during his first sojourn in Paris from 1703 to 1705.[3]

In Naples, such a revision of (if not a real dispute with) the illusionary Baroque tendencies of the greater part of its artistic production of the mid-1600s found, by the end of the 1600s, a theoretical foundation in the literary works of Giovan Vincenzo Gravina (1664–1718) and Pietro Giannone (1676–1748).[4] The reasons behind this revisionism can be found in the new cultural atmosphere and aesthetic tastes, which were aligned, on one hand, with moderate rationalism, and, on the other, with the traditions of the sixteenth century. Together they emphasized the new classical and anti-Baroque trends. Regarding poetry, this revisionism was already happening in Rome with Queen Christina of Sweden (1626–89), and soon after it came to Naples, expressed itself through the numerous works of the ardent followers of the "Arcadian" movement, in which we note the compositions of one particular adherent: Francesco Solimena.[5]

Meanwhile, Luca Giordano (1634–1705), who had returned to Naples from Spain in 1702, was reaffirming in 1704—the year before his death—his choice to remain faithful to the Baroque tradition, widening his approach in "neo-Berninian" terms, as seen in the ceiling frescoes of the Gallery in the Palazzo Medici Riccardi in Florence (1684–85), by filling the space in the small cupola of the Certosa di San Martino's Treasury Chapel (fig. 6) with colored images freely floating on a seemingly endless sky in order to give the illusion of an enlarged space. Instead, Solimena, from one side, and Paolo de Matteis, from the other, were already experimenting with new inventions to create artworks with clearer compositions and formal definitions, and with less expressive content. With Solimena, this is evident in the first canvases of

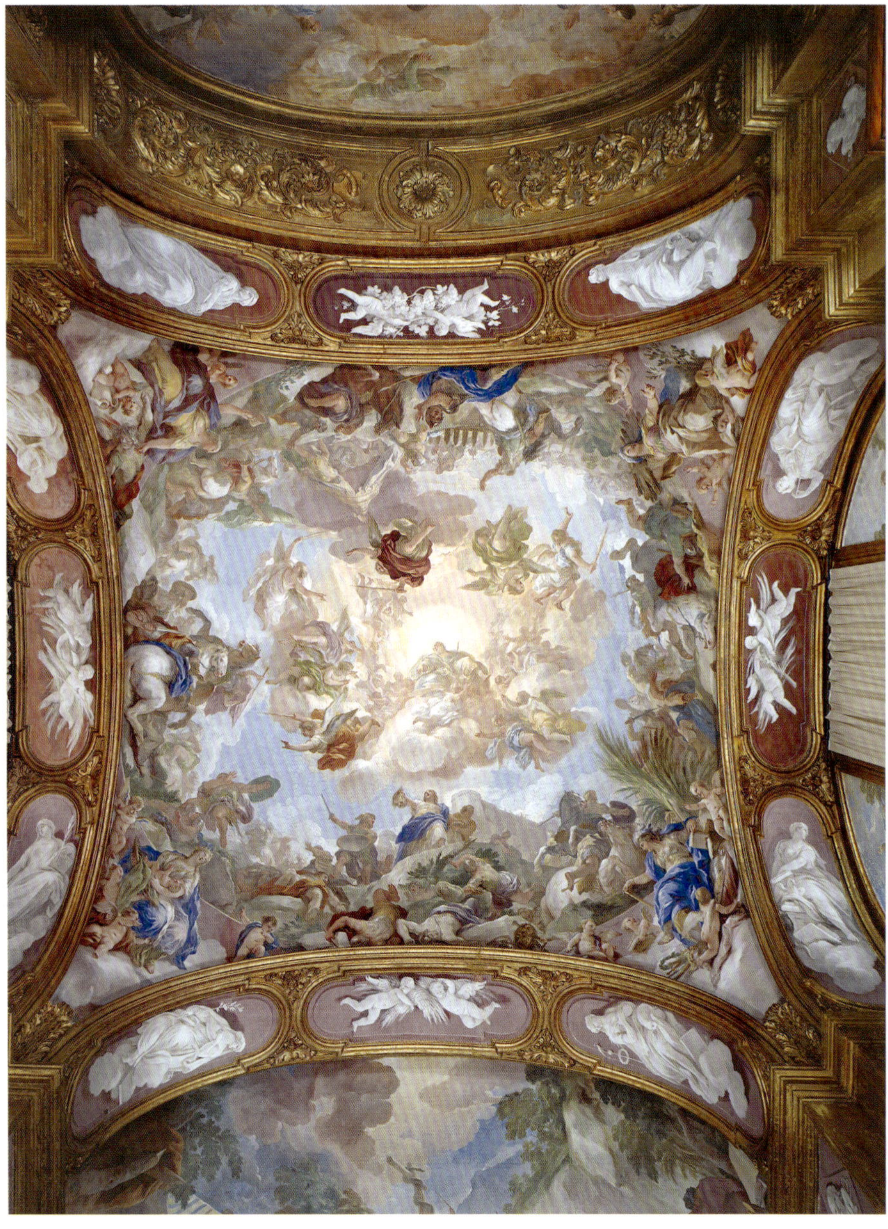

Fig. 6
Luca Giordano, *Triumph of Judith*, 1704, fresco, ceiling of the cupola, Treasury Chapel, Certosa di San Martino, Naples

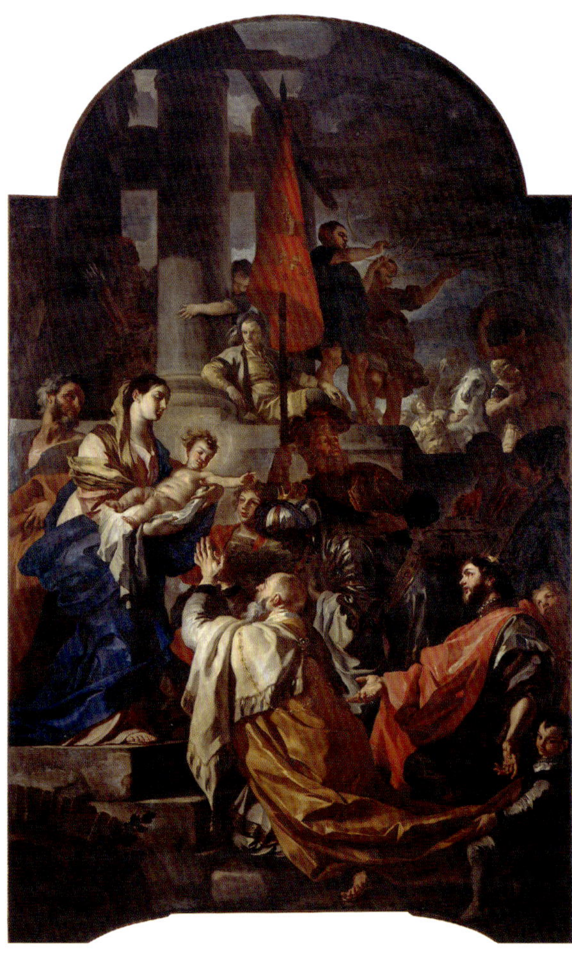

Fig. 7
Francesco Solimena, *Adoration of the Magi*, ca. 1700, oil on canvas, 158¼ × 94 in. (402 × 238 cm), transept, church of Santa Maria Donnalbina, Naples

the 1700s for the transept of the Neapolitan church of Santa Maria Donnalbina (fig.7). This also is true in the numerous paintings Solimena executed from about 1710, which display, through particular aspects and models, the influence of the Roman classicism of Carlo Maratta (1625–1713). Perhaps Solimena also knew about the prints, circulating between Rome and Naples, that were made by the French painters who were decorating the Palace of Versailles.[6] Already, before 1700, De Matteis had been able to reconcile aspects of Giordano's Baroque with the classical approaches of Maratta and his followers in Rome. We see this in De Matteis' fresco in the Pharmacy of the Certosa di San Martino (1699; fig. 8), and in the many painting series done after his stay in Paris (1702–5).[7] Immediate success followed for both artists, not only in Naples, but also throughout Europe, although, in the case of Solimena, fame was more consistent and extensive.

Against the classicism of Solimena and De Matteis, we find effective and brilliant attempts to create an alternative to their approach. We see this happening in the work of Domenico Antonio Vaccaro (1678–1745)—in his painting, but also more drawn out and more evident in his architecture and sculpture (such as those done for the *apparati* for festivals and public ceremonies); in the work of Giacomo del Po (1654–1726); and in the work of the largely unknown Francesco Peresi (ca. 1690?–1743), who decorated churches and palaces with brilliant anti-classical inventions, just at the beginning of the Rococo style. In the case of Vaccaro (fig. 9), he crisscrossed between the recovery and re-elaboration of the models of the late *maniera* in painting and the monumental style of sculptor Cosimo Fanzago (1591–1678) by reviving more recent approaches to art. This was also the case for Del Po (fig. 10) after he had returned to Naples; his style drew upon different aspects of Baroque decoration (as developed by Genoese painters active in Rome)

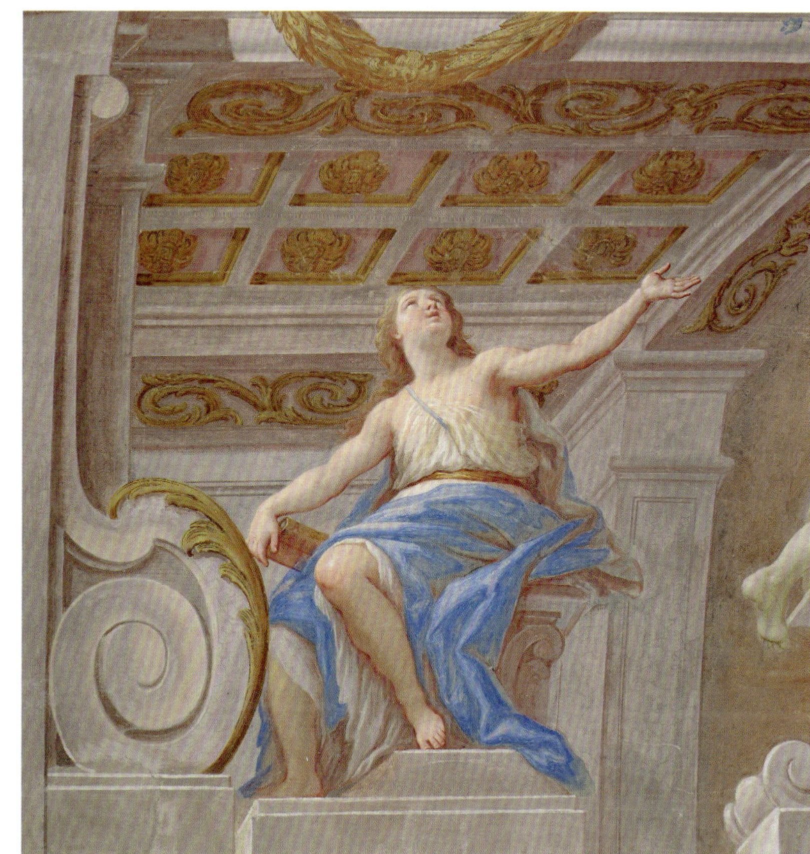

Fig. 8
Paolo de Matteis, *Allegory of Kindness*, 1699, fresco, Pharmacy, Certosa di San Martino, Naples

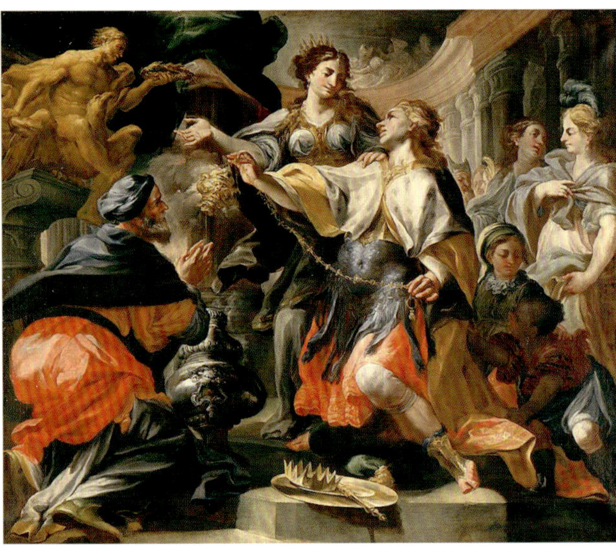

Fig. 9
Domenico Antonio Vaccaro,
*Solomon Worshiping the
Pagan Gods*, ca. 1695–1700,
oil on canvas, 71⅝ × 82⅜ in.
(182 × 209.3 cm), Detroit
Institute of Arts

Fig. 10
Giacomo del Po, *Allegory of
Glory*, 1723, fresco, Castello
di Opocno, Bohemia (now
Czech Republic)

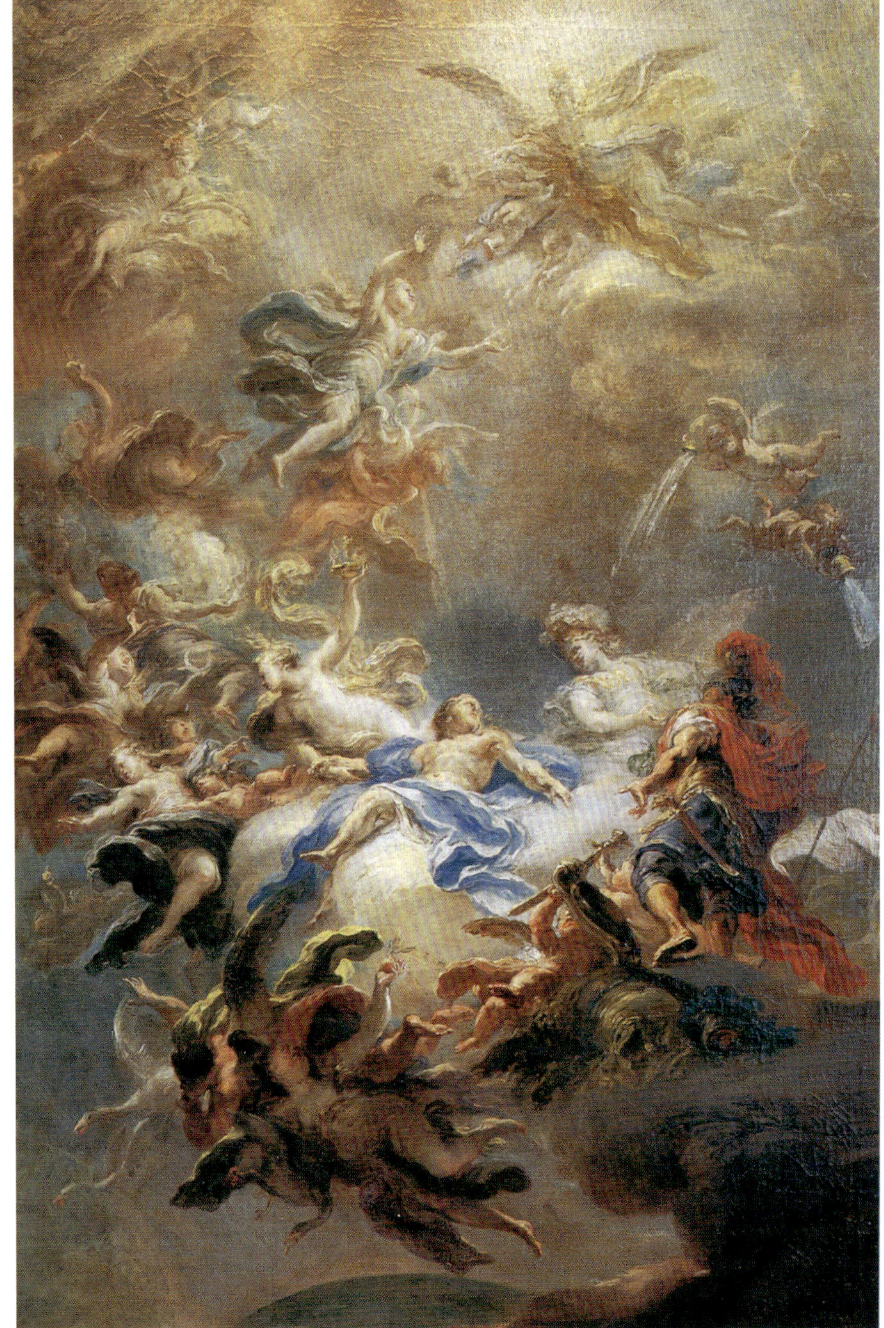

Fig. 11
Francesco de Mura, *Adoration of the Magi* (detail, see also p. 109)

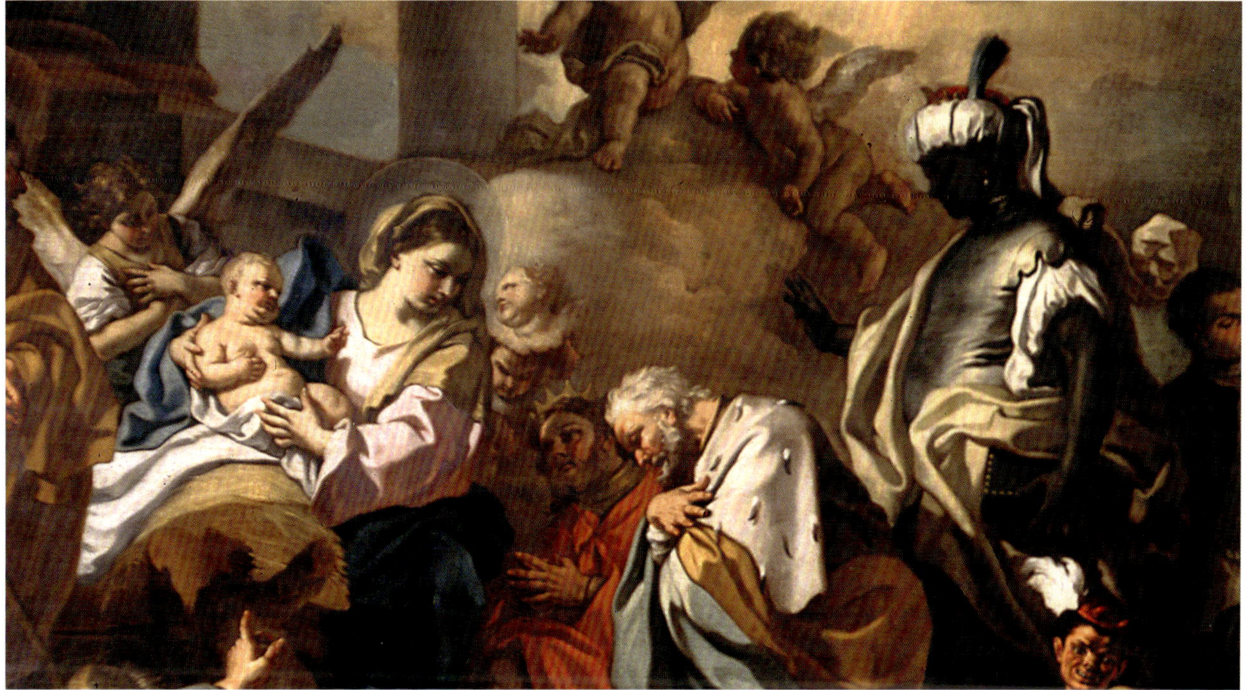

and the works of Giordano. As a result, these painters all produced impressionistic renderings of aerial spaces, above all when executed as small paintings on copper or on canvas, such as those made between 1713 and 1724 by Peresi, whom De Matteis trained at the start of the eighteenth century.[8] Clearly, many artists were also educated in Solimena's studio in the early 1700s, including, among many others, Francesco de Mura, and notably, Nicola Maria Rossi (1690–1752).[9] De Mura and Rossi worked hard to imitate various paintings by Solimena—on fresco and canvas, depicting both sacred and profane subjects—until they were able to copy, either in whole or in part, Solimena's ornate models, compositions, expressive solutions, and chromatic choices.

We can trace this dependence upon Solimena's examples (in the period from around 1705–10 to a little after 1730) in all of De Mura's production, not only in

his early work, but also in his mature style, towards the end of the 1720s. This was also the time when De Mura was appreciated not only by his master, but also by the publisher Angelo Vocola. Vocola dedicated to De Mura his 1731 reprint (edited with Roviglione) of Antonio Pellegrino Orlandi's *Abecedario pittorico* (Bologna, 1704), a publication of fundamental importance. Vocola also published a notable edition of *Vite de' pittori, scultori ed architetti napoletani*, written by Bernardo de Dominici (1683–1759) and published in 1743–45.[10] We can find examples of the constant references to Solimena in De Mura's mature work—for example, in the two almost identical treatments on canvas and in fresco of the *Adoration of the Magi*, for the churches of Santa Maria Donnarómita (1728; fig. 11, detail, and fig. 48) and for the Nunziatella (see cat. no. 12 and fig. 49),[11] as well as for part of the apse in the church of San Francesco

Saverio (1731–32).[12] Further examples of De Mura's varied Solimena quotations include the large series of canvases depicting episodes in the Life of Christ and the Life of the Virgin, done between 1729 and 1730, for the church of the Holy Sepulcher in Jerusalem (see figs. 37, 41, and 46),[13] and the first works executed for the various annexes of the abbey of Monte Cassino—in particular, the chapels of San Bertario (1730–31; see figs. 39 and 42) and of San Carlomanno (1734–35; cat. no. 8).[14] But even after 1730—when De Mura is thought to have reached his mature style—we still find compositional references back to Solimena. Examples of this are the work in the chapel of San Gregorio Magno (1737), again at Monte Cassino;[15] the decorative paintings done in the Palazzo Reale in Naples (1737–38)[16] for the wedding of Carlo di Borbone (Charles Bourbon, reigning as Charles VII of Naples, and in 1759, King Charles III of Spain) and Princess Maria Amalia of Saxony; and, following soon after, the frescoes on the ceiling of the church of Santi Severino e Sossio (1739–40; see figs. 19, 53, cat. no. 15) and in the cupola of San Giuseppe dei Ruffi in Naples (see cat. no. 13).[17]

Although the references to Solimena are also relevant in De Mura's paintings after 1725–28, and remain so until the painter's sojourn in Turin in 1741–43 (see figs. 60 and 61, cat. no. 18), De Mura's artistic production (both frescoes and canvases) in this period gradually became less influenced by the strict rules of his elderly master. Signs of a growing divergence in approach appear even more accentuated after 1734, when Solimena changed his own approach to a more rigorous "purism" in both form and composition, characteristic of his earlier work in the late seventeenth century, vigorously Baroque and "neo-Pretian" (fig. 12).[18]

One break, in particular, from Solimena's neo-Baroque style was De Mura's use of much more delicate chromatic layers of light and brilliant tonalities, contrasting with Solimena's return (in the years after 1730–32) to the dense "spots" of incandescent and bituminous colors, which Solimena used with greater ardor and creativity than in the past. De Mura's compositional approach of using a light layer of bright color began around 1730, and he used it with increasing frequency in the following years as he sought to loosen himself from Solimena's rigid inclinations, instead firmly keeping the physical appearance and emotional response of the subject matter. This exemplifies both the resolution and rigor behind the characters' existential choices in the composition of sacred subjects over that of profane subjects: these characters exist within an eternal sequence that superbly combines history and myth, reality and fantasy, past and present—just as we find in the "heroic" and dramatic Baroque theater.

De Mura's intention was to transfer into painting— against the nobility and solemnity of his old master and his pursuit of the "heroic" dimension in the interpretation of the protagonists in his sumptuous "theatrical scenes"—a re-emerging, refined tendency towards measured and discreet gestures, a studied attitude and poise in order to cultivate fragile affectations and controlled emotions.

Even in the final phase of Solimena's return to a Baroque, neo-Pretian style, monumental and expressive as it was, De Mura still maintained an awareness of his master's work. From Solimena, De Mura gained inspiration for colors suitable for the classical direction of his art, probably drawn from the canvases made for the church of Donnalbina or from those done in the first decade of the eighteenth century, or, in particular, for those made for buyers in Venice and outside of Italy.[19] As such, it is not improbable that some significant attention may have revolved around the artistic style elaborated by Paolo de Matteis between the end of the 1600s and the beginning of the 1700s, combining enlightened classicism with Rococo content. De Mura may also, by

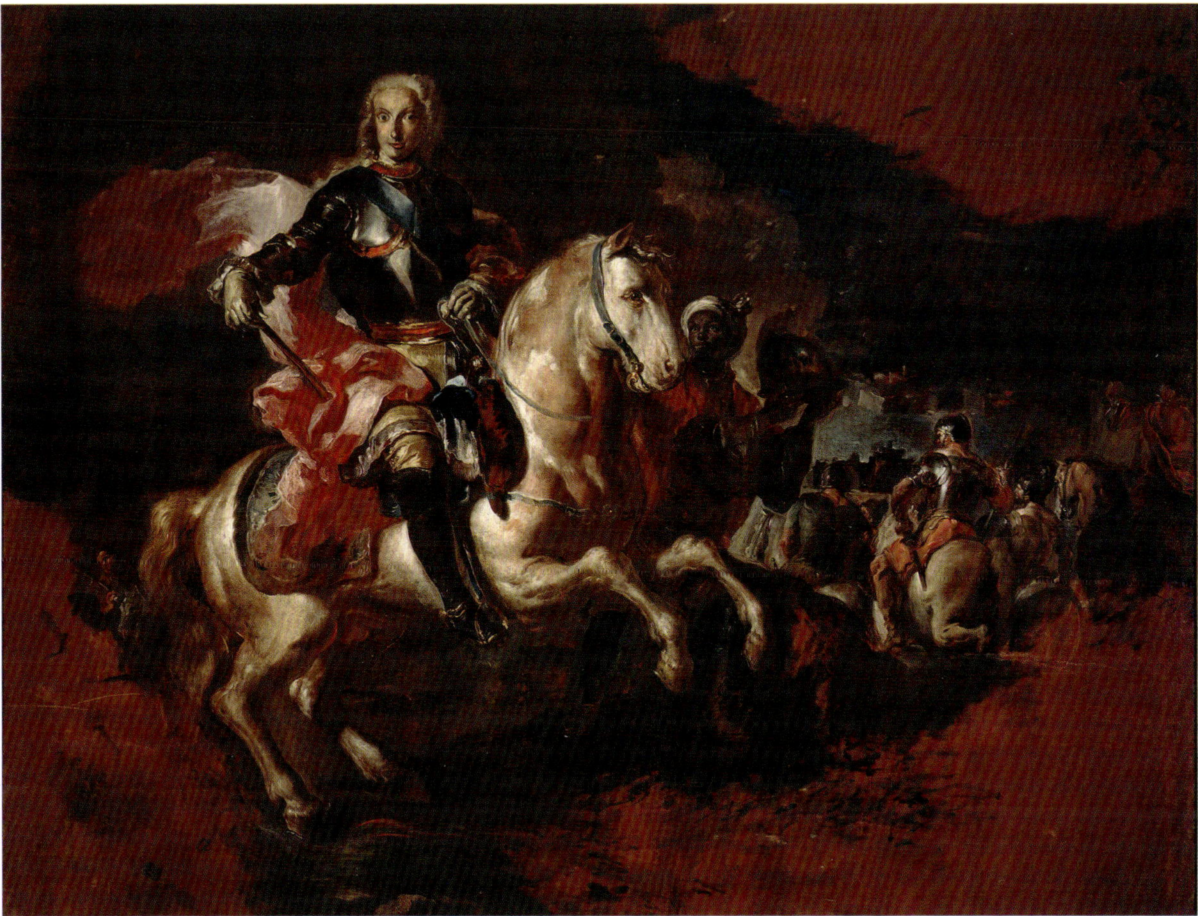

Fig. 12
Francesco Solimena, *Triumph of Charles VII Bourbon of Naples at the Battle of Gaeta, August 6, 1734*, ca. 1735, oil on canvas (replica?), 55⅛ × 73⅝ in. (140 × 187 cm), Palazzo Reale, Caserta

some means (e.g., a hypothetical journey to Rome or the presence of works in Naples), have found examples of tempered classicism "in the style of Carlo Maratta" in the early works of Sebastiano Conca (1680–1764), or in the light and embellished approach in a moderately classical direction and deliciously *rocaille* (Rococo) style of the young Corrado Giaquinto (1703–65), who had met with success during his years in Rome.[20] As later works would further exemplify, it is probable that, from about 1730, De Mura, while still making reference to his old master's models, felt the need to lighten his approach and his palette, both chromatically and formally, against Solimena's sumptuous and solemn style. In this period, De Mura's approach translated into painting the cultural and ideological tastes that were, by the mid-eighteenth century (though such classical tendencies had existed before in Arcadian poetry), starting to provide a new

expressive form for an educated and refined contemporary society, not only in Rome and in Turin, but also in Vienna, Paris, Madrid, and Prague.

By around 1730, this cultural movement had already encouraged the commission of paintings that demonstrated new ways to create elegant and ornate designs, with reasoned and clearly planned compositions of content that politely manifested the states of the soul and sentimental responses. The new style opposed the fantastic "libertarian" Baroque of Luca Giordano, but also offered an alternative to the noble, sumptuous, "heroic" and monumental approach of Francesco Solimena. In the same years, the anti-Baroque theater was under similar pressure to conform and concretely translate the new style into their work, as in the anti-heroic melodrama of Pietro Metastasio (1698–1782). In a close succession of theatrical works, Metastasio (a poet and dramatist with

Neapolitan connections) extended the concepts of the European Neoclassical movement into not only a themed identity and subject for the stage, but also something that could be translated into painting. As any single argument could be dealt with in a theatrical production—through the arrangement and composition of the scenes on stage, or the attitudes and expressions portrayed by the respective actors and protagonists—so, too, could an artist arrange a "scene." From about 1730, and especially in the years after, we find in De Mura's work a much more secure connection in his visual aesthetics to these broader cultural ideas than Solimena, and the other Neapolitan artists trained in his studio, had ever engaged in.[21]

Thus, from about 1730, De Mura showed signs of greater creative independence from the approach of Solimena, though he still referred to the models and formulas of his old master, as seen in his paintings of this period. Examples include the works for the chapel of San Gregorio Magno at Monte Cassino and the decoration, conducted together with other Neapolitan painters, of the *piano nobile* (principal floor) of the Palazzo Reale in Naples (see fig. 81 and cat. no. 35), work made necessary by the wedding of Charles VII of Naples and Maria Amalia of Saxony. Other examples are the partial use of compositional elements taken from Solimena in the vast fresco of the *Vision of St. Benedict* (see figs. 19 and 53), in the vault of the church of Santi Severino e Sossio, and, similarly, in the *Christ Receiving St. Joseph* (cat. no. 13), in the cupola of the church of San Giuseppe dei Ruffi.

In the Palazzo Reale, De Mura—influenced by both Solimena, who had decorated the same spaces, and by the preferences expressed by the Court—painted in fresco and with oils various allegories related to the forthcoming event of the royal marriage. This work was completed with characteristic results: lightened chromatic layers by the use of studied luminosity in the composition; an elegant and ornate subject; and graceful

gestures, manners, and expressive reactions in those portrayed in every scene. That this amount of work can seem less evident than one would expect is perhaps due to De Mura's mixed techniques of oil and tempera, as seen in the *Allegory of the Virtue of Charles and Maria Amalia of Bourbon*, still present in the vault of the first antechamber of the royal apartments.

De Mura's technique is more evident in some surviving *bozzetti* (or in autographed replicas, in the opinion of D'Alessio) of the different allegories that De Mura sent to Spain for the attention of Charles' parents, Philip V of Bourbon and Elizabeth Farnese. Thanks to the extraordinary technique of De Mura's execution and their state of preservation, we can experience their ornate elegance and rendering of chromatic light that draws upon both moderate classicism and delicately embellished *rocailles*. An example of this is the canvas depicting *The Glory of the Princes* or *Allegory of the Virtues of King Carlo di Borbone* (see fig. 81; cat. no. 35) for the decoration of the vault of the first antechamber; a more accentuated stately finesse and coloring can be seen in the works of the *Four Parts of the World* and the *Seasons*, painted in monochrome on the sides of the same vaulted ceiling, through the squared-off markings of Vincenzo Re (1695–1762), or, in the case of the destroyed frescoes representing the *Seasons*, around Solimena's painting in the vaulted ceiling of the sovereign's bedchamber, such as the *Allegory of Peace and Abundance* and *Ceres Giving Fruit to the Siren Parthenope by the River Sebeto* in the *passetti* (passageways) under the frescoes by Vaccaro.[22]

From 1741 to 1743, De Mura—having completed works at Monte Cassino, at the Palazzo Reale, and on the ceiling of the church of Santi Severino e Sossio—was in Turin to decorate, in fresco and on canvas, some spaces in the *piano nobile* of the Palazzo Reale (according to the designs and under the direction of Filippo Juvarra, 1678–1736). While in Turin, he was in direct contact with the work of other artists who were busy undertaking great projects of furnishing and decorating the same palace, who, albeit from diverse places and artistic educations, were all generally inclined toward the *rocaille* (Rococo style). This group included the painter Corrado Giaquinto, already successfully established in Rome, and the Venetian Giovanni Battista Crosato (1686–1758).[23] These artists likely influenced De Mura's earlier tendencies to change his approach and become lighter and more harmonious, rather than to continue with Solimena's sumptuous tones and "heroic" representation of the sacred and profane. We see this in the frescoes and the first canvases realized for the Savoyard court, adding further demarcation between his youthful and his mature style and a major step towards a more elevated artistic quality in his work.[24]

This advancement of De Mura's style is documented not only in the decorative frescoes in the vaulted ceilings (the quality of which is best understood through the surviving drawings), but also in the series of canvases executed for the churches and palaces of Naples, and for other patrons by the Neapolitan artist after his return from the royal residence of the Savoy in Turin to Naples in 1743. These works were all rendered with a new brilliance—the outcome of his contact with the painters who had worked before him and with him at the Savoyard court. As such, the experience managed to push De Mura into his definitive mature style that shared the ideals and cultural sensitivity—already found in his earlier production of paintings—with the theatrical/melodramatic style and inclinations of Pietro Metastasio. Instead of the epic and heroic style championed by Solimena, De Mura's depiction of the legends and mythological "histories" of Theseus, Aeneas, Achilles (cat. no. 18), and Ulysses, or of Alexander the Great (cat. no. 38) and Julius Caesar, were, through cultural tones and refinements, transformed into subtly evocative, elegiacal "pastoral fairytales" (see cat. nos. 36–37).

The stylistic separation of De Mura from Solimena, beyond the points raised above, may be explained also as the direct and immediate consequence of his relationships, during his sojourn in Turin, with the established painters of the time who were orientated towards the *rocaille*—in particular, Crosato and Giaquinto. These artists developed a brilliant opposition to the academic style of Carle van Loo (1705–65) and Conca, as well as to the Solimanesque Baroque style of Claudio Francesco Beaumont (1694–1766).[25] De Mura's attention fell on the examples of Crosato in the "luminous spell" of the Venetian Sebastiano Ricci (1659–1734) at the start of the century, and to Giaquinto—in particular, his ability to be precise and lighten his work by using moderate classicism and the finesse of the Rococo—who was most likely already known in Naples when Giaquinto was apprenticed in the studios of Rossi and of Solimena between 1720 and 1732 (though he perhaps also sent works from Rome to Neapolitan collections). De Mura was innovative in recovering aspects of others in his approach to the modern. De Mura's frescoes demonstrate these adaptations, for example, by rendering the beauty of sunlight in the way Luca Giordano painted in the last years of his life in the Treasury Chapel in the Certosa di San Martino (fig. 6). All the same, De Mura was moving away from the still-Baroque influences of Giordano, thanks not only to his time spent in Turin, but also to the "mediation" of Crosato and Giaquinto (see cat. nos. 44 and 45), who influenced De Mura to make brilliant inventions stylistically situated between controlled classicism and embellished Rococo.[26] These inventions were completing the translation of the same fragile content, expressive "tenderness," and delicate colors from porcelain figurines, which were also mostly contemporary with De Mura. From 1742 to 1743, these figurines were modeled—above all by the able Giuseppe Gricci (ca. 1715?–70)—at the Real Fabbrica (Royal Factory) of Capodimonte, or were produced

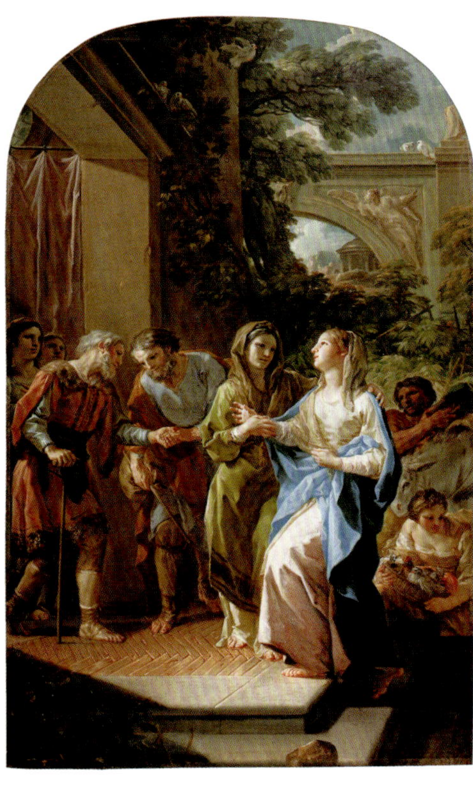

by Meissen and Sèvres, which had already been established for some years as the manufacturers of precious furnishings and ornaments for some of the sumptuous Neapolitan homes of rich, cultured, and refined patricians.

All of De Mura's work, on canvas and in fresco—not only in the late 1740s, but also in the 1750s, and the following decade, too—shows how he was interested in finding solutions between classicism and Rococo in the fashion of Giaquinto, but also in the style of some French painters then active in Rome. It is not without significance that these qualities persist—still noticeable in the canvases dated between 1763 and 1768 (although in more controlled terms)—in touching upon known points of *"barocchetto"* (little Baroque) exemplars. They coincided with several of the paintings by the elderly Giaquinto (having returned to Naples after a successful decade spent in the service of the Spanish court), who was, until his death in 1765, busy with the architects Luigi Vanvitelli (1700–1773) and Ferdinando Fuga (1699–1782) in some prestigious projects for the church of San Luigi di Palazzo, such as *The Visitation*, now in Montreal (fig. 13), and for the Neapolitan tapestry workshop (compare cat. no. 38).[27]

Predominating also in De Mura's work after his return from Turin were themes and subjects taken from antique myths, from Homeric poetry, from the *Aeneid* of Virgil, from the life of Alexander the Great (see cat. no. 38), and, more rarely, from Roman "histories" of Torquato Tasso's *Gerusalemme liberata*—although his output was also on the same level of quality, if we compare his vast productions to similar works made at the same time with sacred, celebratory, or allegorical subjects.

A quality between classicism and Rococo occurs, for example, in the canvases sent from Naples to Turin at various times and that were destined to decorate other rooms in the Palazzo Reale or to serve as pictorial models for the Savoyard tapestry workshop. Further examples include the three *sovrapporte* (overdoors) with allegorical subjects, the surviving elements of the five works commissioned for the Sala delle Macchine and realized between 1743 and 1745 (the now separated *Allegory of the Arts* [or *Allegory of Education*] in the Louvre [see fig. 23] I now date between 1758 and 1762);[28] the nine overdoors, parts of two diverse series on the *History of Alexander the Great* and the *History of Julius Caesar* along with various *Heroines of Roman Antiquity*, painted in 1750 and destined for the second floor of the Palazzo Reale, also with evident signs of a not unimportant interest in the proto-classicism of Pierre Subleyras (1699–1749; see fig. 70) and of those French painters then resident in Rome;[29] and the four surviving paintings of the series originally intended to be eight elements portraying the *Story of Dido and Aeneas* that were sent to Turin in 1768 to be made into cartoons for the tapestries that were to be woven at the local Manifattura Reale.[30]

In the same continuous stylistic vein are the various paintings sent over a period of more than twenty years to Turin, where they were gathered together with others, including the warm-colored *Procession of Bacchus* (1759), today in the Gemäldegalerie, Staatliche Museen, in Berlin (see fig. 77.);[31] the festive tarantella placed allusively in the *Allegory of Spring*, executed in 1759 for Carlo di Borbone (Charles of Bourbon) and now in the Toledo (Ohio) Museum of Art (cat. no. 33);[32] the models for two of the destroyed frescoes in the Palazzo Reale in Naples, depicting the *Glory of the Princes* (cat. no. 35) and *Aurora, Goddess of the Dawn, and Her Husband, Tithonus, Prince of Troy* (ca. 1763–64; cat. no. 36);[33] and the large canvas and *bozzetto* depicting *Hymen Unveiling Modesty* (now hanging in the Palazzo Reale in Caserta) that were pictorial models for a tapestry series alluding to the conjugal virtues of Ferdinand IV of Bourbon, destined to decorate the royal bedchamber of the young sovereign, again in the Palazzo Reale of Naples, in preparation for his marriage to one of the daughters of Maria Teresa of Austria.[34]

In the two decades after his Turin sojourn, De Mura's consistent inclination to elaborate is demonstrated by his expressive inventions of refined taste and "worldliness," studied compositional clarity, a knowledge of the precise composure of elegant forms and graceful attitudes, and the expressive rendering of a subject in relation to both the soul and to emotions. This style appears with similar outcomes in his vast production of sacred works, this time with protagonists such as images of Christ, the Madonna, and saints, or allegorical figures of the theological and cardinal virtues. This production, at least at the end of his active years, rarely can be characterized by irresolute inventions, or by diffuse and consolidated conventions between the generic tones of devotion or piety, such as one sees in the work of other painters. I include in this list the likes of Paolo de Maio (1703–84) and Giuseppe Bonito (1707–89), who were also trained, like De Mura, in Solimena's studio, and who continued to make artworks

that accentuated and perpetuated dependency on the early-eighteenth-century examples of the old Solimena, which were stylistically situated between academic classicism and ornate "purism."[35]

The result was that, in the paintings depicting Dido and Aeneas, Achilles and Deianira, or Alexander and Roxanne, the protagonists refer not only to the subject's identity, but also to the refined inventions of the melodramatic theater of Pietro Metastasio (see cat. no. 38, figs. 86–87). This was also true of the canvases and frescoes depicting biblical scenes, ecstatic visions, or episodes from the lives of the saints. As in *teatro sacro* (sacred theater), these works communicate by displaying a harmonious combination of the cultural and the popular. Indeed, this was being realized in those same years in the complex and crowded *presepi* (Nativity scenes) that made for an impressive visual effect—the result of informed compositional choices and sensitive scenographic inventions.

The connection between the sacred theater and *presepio* Nativity scenes appears, in the case of De Mura, in the now-destroyed canvases (known only from drawings) for the church of Santa Chiara in Naples: the *Adoration of the Eucharist* (1746), which was much admired in later years by Cochin and Fragonard; *Solomon Directing the Construction of the Temple* (the 1746 *bozzetto* or replica, formerly in the Chrysler collection, and at one time on view in the Chrysler Museum of Art, Norfolk, Virginia); and *St. Clare Forcing the Saracens to Flee* (1746).[36] The harmony that appears also in the vast decorative projects, in fresco and on canvas, for the ceiling of the nave and between the large windows of the church of the Nunziatella (1750–52; see fig. 65 and cat. nos. 20–21);[37] in the luminous models for the destroyed fresco in the Sedile di Porto, depicting *St. Januarius Exiting the Furnace Unharmed* (1755–57);[38] and, still more, and already showing new signs of classicism, in the canvases for the Casa della Missione ai Vergini and for the church of the Real Casa Santa dell'Annunziata in Naples (1760–61), for which the drawings are preserved.[39] Also identical in their ornate qualities and expressive renderings are the refined "portraits" completed at the same time and depicting *St. Charles Borromeo at Prayer, The Penitent Mary Magdalene*, and, above all, *The Blessed Francesco de' Gerolamo*.[40]

With regards to De Mura's portraits—in particular, this time, of "historic" personages and diverse characters of his own time, which were painted at various moments during his career—it is significant that this genre in Naples was, by the end of the seventeenth century, a long-established tradition, one that De Mura was able to master in only a few years during and after his time in Turin, as is evident in his distancing himself from the superb examples of portraiture by Francesco Solimena, such as the *Portrait of Ferdinando Vincenzo Spinelli* (fig. 14). This decision to change approach can also be seen in the refined inventions adapted by Bonito after 1740, and by Francesco Liani (1712–80) after 1750, in a large series of royal portraits and portraits of numerous aristocratic Neapolitans,[41] as well as the approach discernibly orientated towards the formula of the "state portrait," as elaborated by Anton Raphael Mengs (1728–79).[42] The progressive development in the noble, imperial, sumptuous, and superb style of "official" portraits by Solimena before and after 1730—such as that shown in the embellished pictorial style of Bonito and Liani, and followed by De Mura to better represent the personages being portrayed—did not repudiate the hallmarks of the elite social class. The preference of the time was to be represented on canvas in the correct attitude, meaning in a polite style with a calm and serene expression, portrayed with elegance, but, more important, with those cultural and social markers of refined and sophisticated taste, all the while without displaying emotional tension

and ambition, and without the concrete appearance or ephemeral inclinations to the heroic or moral, all of which De Mura's portraits would achieve.

There is some value in comparing portraits by De Mura done in the mid-1730s—executed rigorously in the recent style of Solimanesque portraiture (such as the realistic and almost "cruel" *Portrait of Father Ildefonso dal Verme* in the abbey of Monte Cassino, dated to 1735, or the sumptuous and superb *Portrait of the Artist's Wife* (see figs. 5 and 57) of about the same time that exudes Mediterranean beauty (in the Picture Gallery of Pio Monte della Misericordia)[43]—with those portraits painted in Turin and Naples in the 1740s, and with those from the mid-1750s. These later works include two similar *Self-Portraits* in the Uffizi Gallery in Florence and in the Minneapolis Institute of Art (cat. no. 17); the sumptuous but uplifting *Portrait of Count James Joseph O'Mahoney* (cat. no. 25) in the Fitzwilliam Museum in Cambridge, significantly, executed at the same time as Pierre Subleyras' painting of the sitter's wife, *Portrait of Countess Anna Giustiniani O'Mahoney* (see fig. 70), done in Naples between 1747 and 1748, demonstrating, with their common orientation between moderate classicism and fine *rocaille*, that De Mura was certainly in close communication with Subleyras and was both influencing and influenced by him; and, finally, the remarkably refined and elegant *Portrait of Cardinal Antonio Sersale* (see cat. no. 27), dated to 1756, in a private American collection (but on extended loan to the Milwaukee Art Museum).[44]

Even before the departure of Carlo di Borbone (Charles of Bourbon) for Spain in 1759, the court and other sections of Neapolitan society were developing an ever more concrete preference for new and different classical inventions. These inventions were also different from the shared approaches of architects Vanvitelli and Fuga, who propagated, not only in architecture, the transmission of the sixteenth-century classical inheritance

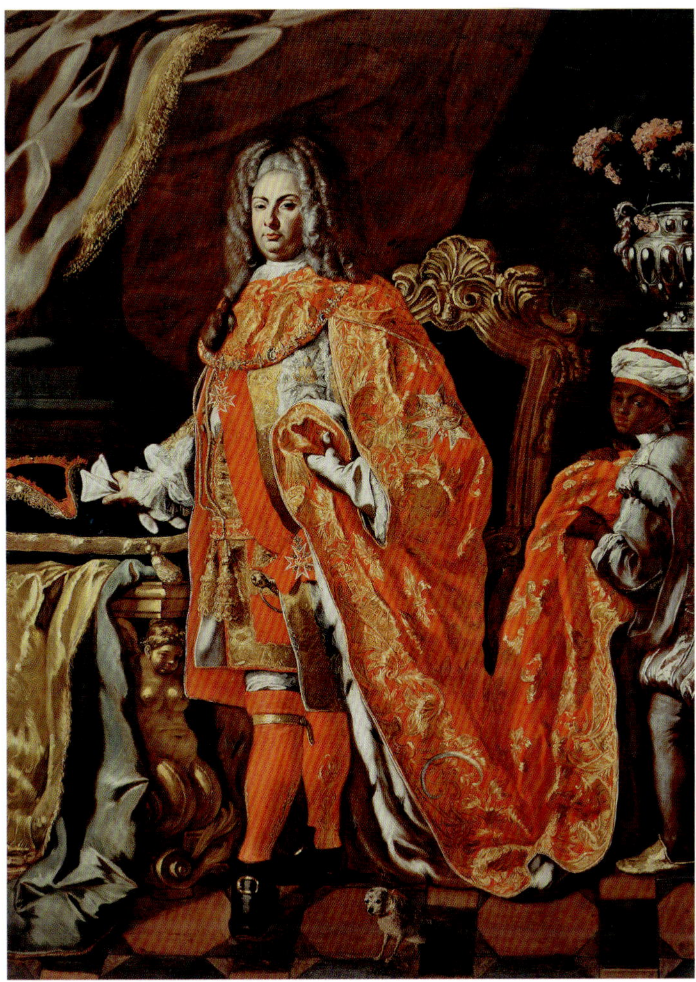

Fig. 14
Francesco Solimena, *Portrait of Ferdinando Vincenzo Spinelli, Prince of Tarsia*, ca. 1741, oil on canvas, 98 × 66 in. (250 × 168 cm), Museo e Gallerie Nazionali di Capodimonte, Naples

to influence the illusionary styles of the Baroque.[45] After having initially favored the rather eclectic and ever more tired Sebastiano Conca, the taste at court was consistent with that of Vanvitelli and Fuga, and also with Anton Raphael Mengs, Pompeo Girolamo Batoni (1708–87), and Stefano Pozzi (1707–68). In the face of these preferences, De Mura attempted—after 1760, and in greater evidence in his late works in the 1770s—to conform to these new aesthetic modes by renewing his own interest in the classical antique, consistent with the excavations underway at Pompeii and Herculanuem and the "rediscovery" of the Greek temples at Paestum. Unfortunately for De Mura, this new direction resulted, in short, in marginal, inconsistent, and above all, unrealizable projects. In the end, De Mura decided, around 1760, to progressively dilute and soften as much as was still discernible of his

late Baroque and moderate *rocaille* (Rococo) styles, as we see in the production of those years, and most evidently in the years after. His style of art was finishing just as the Neoclassical "season" was rising. The subsequent output—although not lacking in ornate elegance and composition or pleasant coloring, and always showing ability and knowledge—was ever more wearily "manipulated" for the academy, rather than drawing inspiration from the fertile traditions of the past.[46] Also, while De Mura was becoming increasingly culturally tired and disheartened, gradually losing his prestige and the quality in his paintings, a brilliant and ephemeral alternative to the modern approach to the decorative arts, such as De Mura's intense pictorial and figurative beauty, was lost to the contemporary rising of the Neoclassical in painting, having been promulgated by some exponents from the younger generation of Neapolitans.

This was the generation of Jacopo Cestaro (1718–78; see figs. 43–44) and Domenico Mondo (1723–1806), keen to prolong the spirit of the last works of Francesco Solimena's neo-Baroque. Giovan Battista Rossi (1730–82) and Francesco Celebrano (1729–1814; more noted as a sculptor) translated with new finesse the forms and colors in the vein of Giaquinto, or of Fedele Fischetti (1732–92), who cultivated the inheritance of the past into an elegant and refined *barocchetto* (little Baroque). But it was also the generation of Francesco Narici (1719–85), originally from Genoa, and above all, of Giacinto Diano (1731–1803; cat. no. 43) and Pietro Bardellino (1728–1819), who were educated in the 1750s in Francesco de Mura's studio, and whose example they would continue; in a short while, they would end the long and illustrious tradition of the *grande decorazione* in Naples that drew together the Baroque, the classical, and the Rococo, and used the same colors, delicate pastel tones, and precious mother-of-pearl that layer the Mediterranean sunset.[47]

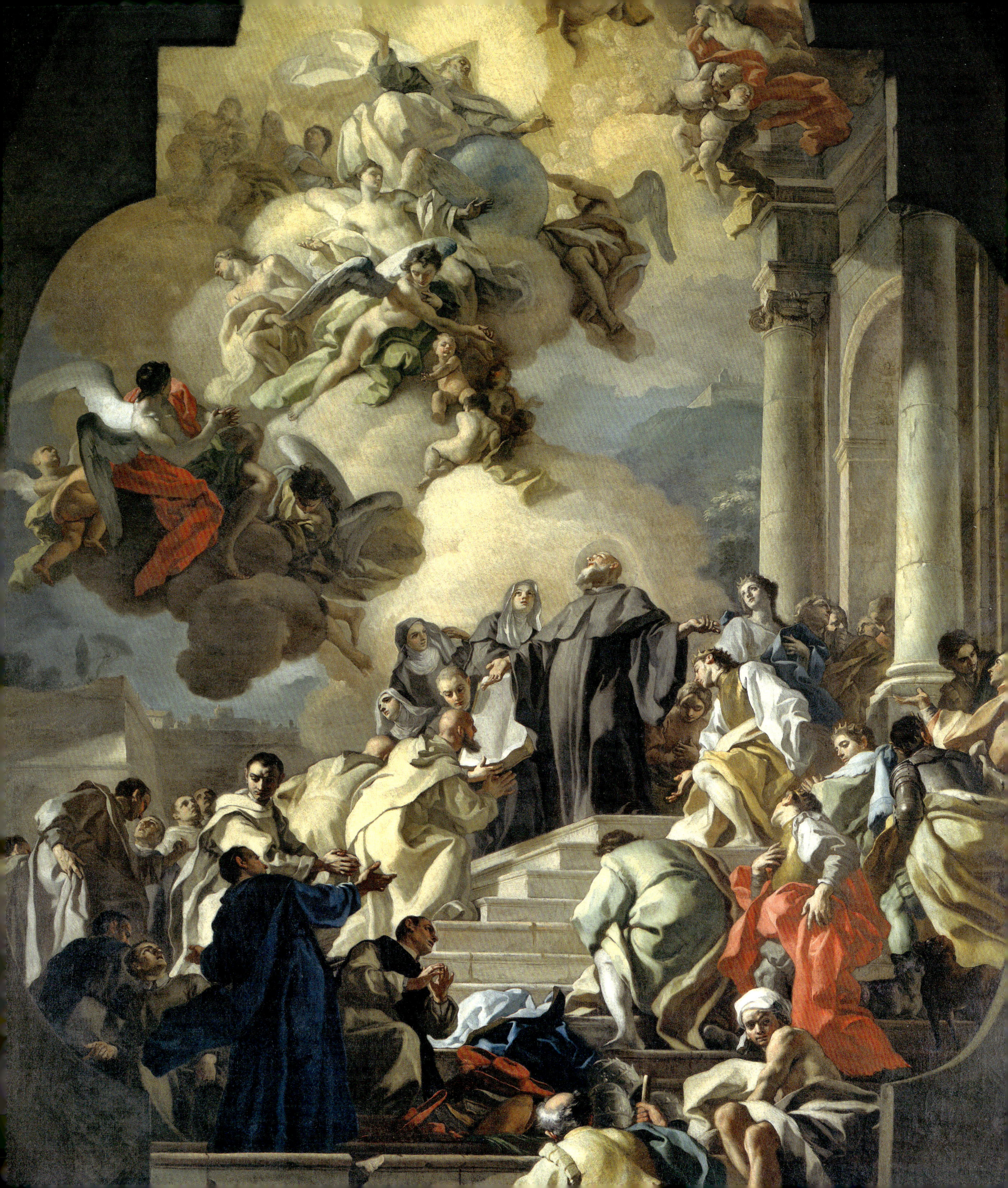

Notes

1. Domenico Viola (active in Naples in the second half of the seventeenth century) is noted for some paintings of sacred subjects, and above all, in the style of *"bamboccianti"* (foreigners in Rome in the early 1600s) and "genre scenes" (market and domestic scenes), and of figures with reduced dimensions, painted with a *grisaille* color palette; see Nicola Spinosa, *Da Mattia Preti a Luca Giordano: Natura in posa*, vol. 2, *Pittura del Seicento a Napoli* (Naples: Arte'm, 2011), 245.

2. On the education and early mature style of De Mura, see Vincenzo Rizzo, "L'opera giovanile di Francesco de Mura," *Napoli Nobilissima* 17: (1978), 110–111; Gino D'Alessio, "Nuove osservazioni sulle committenze reali per Francesco de Mura tra Napoli, Torino e Madrid," *Prospettiva*, no. 69 (1993): 70–87.

3. For Solimena around 1700, see in particular the canvases portraying "Episodes of the Life of Mary" in the transept of the church of Santa Maria Donnalbina: Ferdinando Bologna, *Francesco Solimena* (Naples: L'Arte tipografica, 1958), 84–87ff; Spinosa, *Da Mattia Preti a Luca Giordano*, 2:233 (also bibliography). For De Matteis before his sojourn in Parigi and his frescoes in the Pharmacy of the Certosa di San Martino, in particular the painting of the *Allegory of Virtues* that already shows elements between classicism and Rococo, see Spinosa, *Da Mattia Preti a Luca Giordano*, 2:160–61 (also bibliography).

4. For the role of Giovan Vincenzo Gravina and of Pietro Giannone in Neapolitan culture at the end of the seventeenth century, and for their respective anti-Baroque positions, recovery of the modern style, and with regards literature and the figurative arts of the *cinquencentesque* classicism, see Bologna, *Francesco Solimena*, 77–78, 123, 135; Ferdinando Bologna, "La dimensione europea della cultura artistica napoletana nel XVIII secolo," in *Arti e Civiltà del Settecento a Napoli*, exhib. cat., (Rome-Bari, 1982), 74, note 52; Nicola Spinosa, *Pittura napoletana del Settecento*, vol. 1, *Dal barocco al rococò* (Naples: Electa Napoli, 1986), 17–20. On Arcadia in Naples, including the involvement of Solimena, see Armedeo Quondam, *Dal barocco all'Arcadia*, in *Storia di Napoli*, vol. 6, pt. 2 (Naples: Societa editrice Storia di Napoli, 1970), 809–1094 (also bibliography).

5. For the connection between Arcadian classicism and moderate rationalism at the end of the 1600s—as well as the progressive choices made by Solimena from around 1700 in the direction of classicism, revising his former preferences for the Baroque of the early Luca Giordano and Pietro da Cortona, then of Mattia Preti—see the bibliography and argument in Nicola Spinosa, *Pittura napoletana del Settecento*, vol. 1, *Dal barocco al rococò* (Naples: Electa Napoli, 1986).

6. On possible influences, direct or indirect, with regards to the examples of the French painters busy at Versailles and on some aspects of Solimena's classical inventions at the beginning of the eighteenth century, or for the classical inclination towards the *rocaille* of Paolo de Matteis after his time in Paris, see Ferdinando Bologna, "La dimensione europea della cultura artistica napoletana del XVIII secolo, in Carlo di Borbone da Napoli a Madrid," in *Aspetti e problemi della civiltà artistica del Settecento*, ed. Cesare De Seta, conference proceedings, Naples, May 12–14, 1980 (Bari: Laterza, 1982), 38–72.

7. On the sojourn of De Matteis in Paris and its influence on his artistic development between the Rococo and classicism, see Spinosa, *Pittura napoletana del Settecento*, 1:31ff.

8. On the painters Domenico Antonio Vaccaro, Giacomo del Po, and Francesco Peresi, see Spinosa *Pittura napoletana del Settecento*; see also the catalogue entries for the respective paintings in *Settecento napoletano: Sulle ali dell'aquila imperiale, 1707–1734*, exhib. cat. (Naples: Electa Napoli, 1994), 170ff.

9. Nicola Maria Rossi became part of the large circle of students around Solimena in 1706; Citti Siracusano, "Nicola Maria Rossi e la cultura artistica napoletana del primo Settecento," *Quaderni di storia dell'arte medievale e moderna* 4 (1980): 47–56.

10. In the two editions of the text of Orlandi dedicated to De Mura and then to Solimena, favorable judgment was expressed initially by the master towards his young student and imitator, cited by Bernardo de Dominici in his *Vite dei pittori, scultori ed architetti napoletani* (Naples, 1743), ed. Fiorelli Sricchia Santoro and Andrea Zezza (Naples: Paparo Edizioni, 2008); see also D'Alessio, "Nuove osservazioni," 70 (also bibliography).

11. At this moment, there are two identified canvases depicting the *Sacrifice of Iphigenia*: one in the Rhode Island School of Design Museum, Providence, R.I., and one in a private Neapolitan collection (Spinosa, entry no. 15 in *Settecento napoletano*, 162–63); two canvases of *Ecce Homo* (see cat. nos. 2 and 3 in this volume); and *Christ Carrying the Cross with St. Veronica* of the Collegiata dell'Assunta in Castel di Sangro, of which there are also the respective preparatory *bozzetti* in the Molinari Pradelli collection in Marano di Castenaso (see fig. 34 in this volume; see also Spinosa, *Pittura napoletana del Settecento*, 1:156, no. 239, figs. 284 and 286).

12. For the first project of De Mura in the church of the Nunziatella and the corresponding drawings in the Picture Gallery of the Pio Monte della Miserecordia, see Robert Engass, "Francesco de Mura alla Nunziatella," *Bollettino d'Arte* 49 (1964): 133–48. For more information about this and other paintings of the main holding (including drawings models, finished works, and portraits) left in the bequest to Pio Monte della Misericordia, where today they are still exhibited, and also for a critical approach to the entire holding of De Mura's works in the collection, see Nicola Spinosa, "Francesco de Mura al Pio Monte della Misericordia," *FMR*, no. 29 (2009): 23–48.

13. For the twenty-two canvases destined for the Holy Sepulcher in Jerusalem, commissioned from De Mura a little before 1730 by the General Commission of the Holy Land in Naples, the Franciscan Giovanni Antonio Yepes (the remaining eight survivors), see Vincenzo Rizzo, essay in *Trésor du Saint-Sépulcre: Présents des cours royales européennes à Jérusalem*, by Bernard Degout and Jacques Charles-Gaffiot, exhib. cat. (Cinisello Balsamo, Milan: Silvana, 2013); Nicola Spinosa, "The Presence of Neapolitan Painting in the Holy Land," in *Baroque Art from the Holy Sepulchre: The Image of Jerusalem in the Pre-Alps*, ed. Manuela Kahn-Rossi and Chiara Naldi, exhib. cat. (Lugano: Galerie Canesso, 2014), 59–73, and entries by Chiara Naldi at 90–97.

14. On the first interventions at the abbey of Monte Cassino, and on the responding preparatory drawings, see Robert Engass, "Additions to De Mura: Four New *Bozzetti*," *The Burlington Magazine*, 121, no. 913 (April 1979): 243–47; Spinosa, *Pittura napoletana del Settecento*, 1:156, no. 244.

15. For the second involvement of De Mura at Monte Cassino (works in the chapel of San Gregorio Magno, since destroyed; of this project, a single drawing survives of a painting of San Simplicio: one of two such canvases depicting this subject are in the Molinari Pradelli collection at Marano di Castenaso), see D'Alessio "Nuove osservazioni," 84, note 43. See also cat. no. 10 in this volume.

16. For De Mura's work in the Palazzo Reale in Naples on the occasion of Charles Bourbon's wedding to Maria Amalia of Saxony, see D'Alessio "Nuove osservazioni," 70–73; D'Alessio proposes from his archival research that the related surviving drawings signed by De Mura were presentation copies for Charles' parents in Spain. Contemporaneously, also busy with the decoration in fresco and on canvas of the *piano nobile* of the Palazzo Reale were Francesco Solimena, Domenico Antonio Vaccaro, Nicola Maria Rossi, Leonardo Coccorante (overdoors depicting ruins and landscapes), and Vincenzo Re (decorations and *quadratura* [illusionistic ceiling paintings]); see D'Alessio, "Nuove osservazioni" (also bibliography), and Ferdinando Bologna, "Solimena al Palazzo Reale di Napoli per le nozze di Carlo di Borbone," *Prospettiva*, no. 16 (1979): 53–67.

17. On the first projects in the church of Santi Severino e Sossio, with the related *bozzetti* in the Museo di Capodimonte and the Picture Gallery of the Pio Monte della Misericordia in Naples, as well as for the initial work for the decoration of the cupola of San Giuseppe dei Ruffi (completed after De Mura's return from Turin), for which the study is in the Picture Gallery of the Pio Monte della Misericordia (cat. no. 13 in this volume), see Katia Fiorentino, entry in *Ritorno al barocco: Da Caravaggio a Vanvitelli*, ed. Nicola Spinosa, exhib. cat. (Naples: Electa Napoli, 2009).

18. For Solimena's vigorous return to the neo-Baroque after the years 1733–34, see Bologna, *Francesco Solimena*, 118ff; Spinosa, *Pittura napoletana del Settecento*, 1:51–55.

19. For these paintings by Solimena in the church of Donnalbina, and for some works intended for other patrons and collectors resident in Venice, see Bologna, *Francesco Solimena*, 163ff; Ferdinando Bologna and W. Prohaska, essay in *Settecento napoletano*, 200–214.

20. For an up-to-date bibliography on Corrado Giaquinto in Rome, see Michaela Scolaro, ed., *Corrado Giaquinto: Il cielo e la terra*, exhib. cat. (Bologna: Minerva, 2005).

21. On the possible connections between the work of De Mura and the melodramatic theater of Pietro Metastasio, the influence of which can already be found in his paintings around 1730 and above all in the following years, see Spinosa, *Pittura napoletana del Settecento*, 1:50–51, 55–57.

22. For the paintings of De Mura in the Palazzo Reale and some of the sketches or surviving autograph replicas, such as for the involvement of Solimena, Vaccaro, and Rossi, see note 16 above; see also D'Alessio "Nuove osservazioni," 70–73.

23. On the projects to decorate the apartments in the *piano nobile* of the Palazzo Reale in Turin, see Andreina Griseri and Vittorio Viale, eds., *Mostra del barocco piemontese*, exhib. cat. (Turin: Città di Torino, 1963); Andreina Griseri, *Le metamorfosi del barocco* (Turin: Einaudi, 1976).

24. For the involvement of De Mura in the *piano nobile* of the Palazzo Reale in Turin, see note 23; see also D'Alessio, "Nuove osservazioni," 73–76.

25. The Venetian Crosato (who also received paintings by De Mura created after 1760 for the tapestry workshop in Turin) was working in Turin in 1733 at the Palazzo Reale, the Villa della Regina, and the Palazzina di Caccia di Stupinigi in 1740–43, as well as at the sanctuary of the Consolata and the church of the Visitazione in Pinerolo. Giaquinto was in Turin for the first time in 1733, when he painted frescoes with Crosato at the Villa della Regina and painted a series of canvases on the *History of Aeneas* for the Castello di Moncalieri (transferred to Palazzo del Quirinale, Rome, in the nineteenth century), and for a second time from 1740 to 1742 (when he surely also met De Mura) in order to paint the frescoes and the canvases in the church of Santa Teresa; see Griseri and Viale, *Mostra del barocco piemontese*, 76–77 (Giaquinto) and 79–81 (Crosato).

26. In order to understand the effect of De Mura's familiarity with the work of Giaquinto, whose own work also included influences of Giordano's last work in the church of San Martino, it is not insignificant that De Mura, following the desire of his wife, refused to leave Naples (the Spanish sovereigns having left Naples for Madrid in 1753), and as such, Corrado Giaquinto was called upon to replace him. On this, and also the two paintings sent by De Mura to the church of the Convento della Visitación in Madrid, see D'Alessio, "Nuove osservazioni," 76–77.

27. For the paintings done by Giaquinto in Naples after having left Spain, see Nicola Spinosa, *Pittura napoletana del Settecento*, vol. 2, *Dal rococò al classicismo* (Naples: Electa Napoli, 1987), 148–49 (also bibliography).

28. For the overdoors and the other paintings made by De Mura in Naples and sent to Turin in 1748, other than referring to the catalogue citations of the paintings in Griseri and Viale, *Mostra del barocco piemontese*, see D'Alessio, "Nuove osservazioni," 75ff. Among the *Allegories* for the Sala delle Macchine, De Mura also painted the *Allegory of the Arts* (or *Education*), now in the Louvre (fig. 23 in this volume); see D'Alessio, "Nuove osservazioni," 75. The *Allegory of the Arts* has, on more than one occasion, been identified with the *Allegory of Charity* (or *Maternal Love*), now in the Art Institute of Chicago (cat. no. 19 in this volume), as an element of this series of overdoors in Turin: first dated to 1755 (in 1975), then to around 1755 (in 1979), and finally to 1747–50. Responding to the doubt expressed by Stéphane Loire of the Louvre (in *Ritorno al barocco: Da Caravaggio a Vanvitelli*, ed. Nicola Spinosa, exhib. cat. [Naples: Electa Napoli, 2009], no. 1.172, 310–311), I was recently impelled to write in a letter to Loire (personal communication, August 13, 2015) that the *Allegory* in the Louvre should be dated instead to between 1758 and 1762. On this hypothesis, I later added that there is a resemblance in the form, composition, and pictorial effects between the painting in question and the four overdoors with the *Allegories of the Elements*, bought in 1972 by the Gallery of Gilberto Algranti in Milan and today dispersed to various collections (Spinosa, *Pittura napoletana del Settecento*, 1:164, no. 265). Moreover, the *Allegories* show stylistic similarities with the dimensions of the four *Allegories of the Parts of the World* painted by De Mura

in Naples for the Palazzo Chiablese in Turin between 1758 and 1762 (D'Alessio, "Nuove osservazioni," 80, figs. 27–30). Already in 1986, the *Allegories* were being tentatively identified with the overdoor depicting *Allegories of Air, Earth, Fire, and Water*, also executed by De Mura, again in the years between 1758 and 1762, and in the same Palazzo Chiablese, but have with time been lost. Significantly, De Mura used the same model for the personification of the Earth as he did for the personification of the Arts. To confirm this new hypothetical dating of the *Allegory* in the Louvre, it is no less evident that, in respect to the qualities of the overdoors sent in 1748 to Turin and still located on the second floor of the Palazzo Reale (displaying a harmonious combination of classicism and *rocaille*), the Louvre canvas presents instead a different compositional approach and a more studied and classical definition of form and composition, not to mention a more controlled expressive rendering, which confirms the inclinations of De Mura in the late 1750s to seek new solutions more accentuated by classicism, in accordance with and under the influence of his Roman contemporaries, Girolamo Pompeo Batoni and Antonio Raffaello Mengs, and their adaptations of the classical approach.

29. The two series of paintings were painted in Naples by De Mura for the Sala delle Udienze and the Sala del Terrazzo on the second floor of the Palazzo Reale in Turin, on the occasion of the wedding of Vittorio Amedeo of Savoy, the crown prince, to the daughter of the Spanish sovereign, Maria Antonietta Ferdinanda of Bourbon; see D'Alessio, "Nuove osservazioni," 76 and note 92. At the same time, or a little before, De Mura also made two canvases depicting *Stories of Achilles*, in the opinion of D'Alessio, or with *Stories of Aeneas*, according to Federico Zeri; see Spinosa, *Pittura napoletana del Settecento*, 1:160, no. 256.

30. The surviving sketches are today preserved in the Palazzo Reale in Turin, later having been attributed to Crosato and temporarily transfered to Venice. See Mercedes Viale Ferrero, "*Arazzi*," in Griseri and Viale, *Mostra del barocco piemontese*, 28, 99–102; D'Alessio, "Nuove osservazioni," 80.

31. Spinosa, *Pittura napoletana del Settecento*, 1:165, no. 274, fig. 331.

32. Signed and dated 1759 on the back of the

canvas, where a piece of paper was placed on which were written some verses on Spring, drawn from the first book of *Odes* by Horace (see cat. no. 33 in this volume): Spinosa, *Pittura napoletana del Settecento*, 1:165, no. 276, fig. 333; D'Alessio, "Nuove osservazioni," 78, figs. 21–22.

33. *Ibid.*, 82 (also bibliography).

34. For the pictorial models of large dimensions conserved in the Reggia di Caserta for the tapestry series woven at the Manifattura Reale of Naples, see M. Siniscalco, entry on De Mura in *Civiltà del '700 a Napoli*, ed. Nicola Spinosa, exhib. cat. (Florence: Centro Di, 1980), 101.

35. On the work of Paolo de Maio and for the early activities of Giuseppe Bonito, both active on the models of formal *purismo* and the compositional style of Solimena in the 1720s, see Spinosa, *Pittura napoletana del Settecento*, 1:27–31, 57–60 (also bibliography).

36. For the related *bozzetti*, see Spinosa, *Pittura napoletana del Settecento*, 1:161, no. 258.

37. On the painting realized by De Mura on the occasion of his second involvement in the church of the Nunziatella and for the related *bozzetti*, see Engass, "Francesco de Mura alla Nunziatella," and Spinosa, *Pittura napoletana del Settecento*, 1:161, no. 260.

38. The *bozzetto* for the fresco that, along with many paintings, was part of the painter's bequest to Pio Monte della Misericordia, was in 1976 sold at Colnaghi's in London, and since 1977 has been in the Staatsgalerie of Stuttgart: Gerhard Ewald, *Das Jahrhundert Tiepolos: Italianische Gemälde des 18. Jahrhunderts aus dem Besitz der Staatsgalerie*, exhib. cat. (Stuttgart: Staatsgalerie, 1977), 87–89, no. 41; Spinosa, *Pittura napoletana del Settecento*, 1:161, no. 261.

39. For the canvases in the Casa della Missione ai Vergini and for the church of the Real Casa Santa dell'Annunziata, with their drawings, see Spinosa, *Pittura napoletana del Settecento*, 1:161, 164–65, nos. 260 and 269.

40. *Ibid.*, 1:165, no. 270.

41. On the examples of portraiture by Solimena and on the portraits made after 1740 by Bonito and after 1750 by Liani (both originally from Emilia), see Bologna, *Francesco Solimena*; Bologna 1986; and Bologna 1987 or 1993. See also catalogue entries by Spinosa, Petrelli, and

Bile (also bibliography) on the respective works in Flavio Caroli, ed., *L'anima e il volto: Ritratto e fisiognomica da Leonardo a Bacon*, exhib. cat. (Milan: Electa, 1998); Spinosa, *Ritorno al barocco: Da Caravaggio a Vanvitelli*.

42. Steffi Röttgen in Spinosa, *Civiltà del '700 a Napoli*, 2:387–406.

43. See Spinosa, *Pittura napoletana del Settecento*, 1:160, no. 257.

44. For the portrait by Subleyras (fig. 70 in this volume) now in the Musée des Beaux-Arts at Caen, see Pierre Rosenberg, "Tre note napoletane," in *Arte e civiltà del Settecento a Napoli*, ed. Cesare De Seta (Bari: Laterza, 1982), 197–234. For the *Portrait of Cardinal Antonio Sersale* (cat. no. 27 in this volume), see Spinosa, *Pittura napoletana del Settecento*, 1:161, no. 263, pl. 64.

45. On the role of the architects Luigi Vanvitelli and Ferdinando Fuga in mid-eighteenth-century Naples, and on the influence of both in the field of art in favor of classical approaches in combination with the tradition of the sixteenth century, and of moderate Baroque and modern rational effects, see Spinosa, *Pittura napoletana del Settecento*, 2:17–21 (also bibliography); Nicola Spinosa, "Luigi Vanvitelli e i pittori attivi a Napoli nella seconda metà del Settecento: Lettere e documenti inediti," *Storia dell'Arte* 14 (1972): 193–214.

46. On the rare works of his last years of activity and on the approaches of the final productions of the painter, by now ever more tired and hardened in the re-elaboration of a "formula" between classicism and accademicism, see Spinosa, *Pittura napoletana del Settecento*, 1:57; D'Alessio, "Nuove osservazioni," 82–83. See also Spinosa, "Luigi Vanvitelli e i pittori attivi a Napoli," 74ff; Spinosa, "Francesco de Mura al Pio Monte della Misericordia," 42–48.

47. Regarding the late-eighteenth-century painters cited here, from Cestaro to Diano and Bardellino, see Spinosa, *Pittura napoletana del Settecento*, 2:13ff (also bibliography).

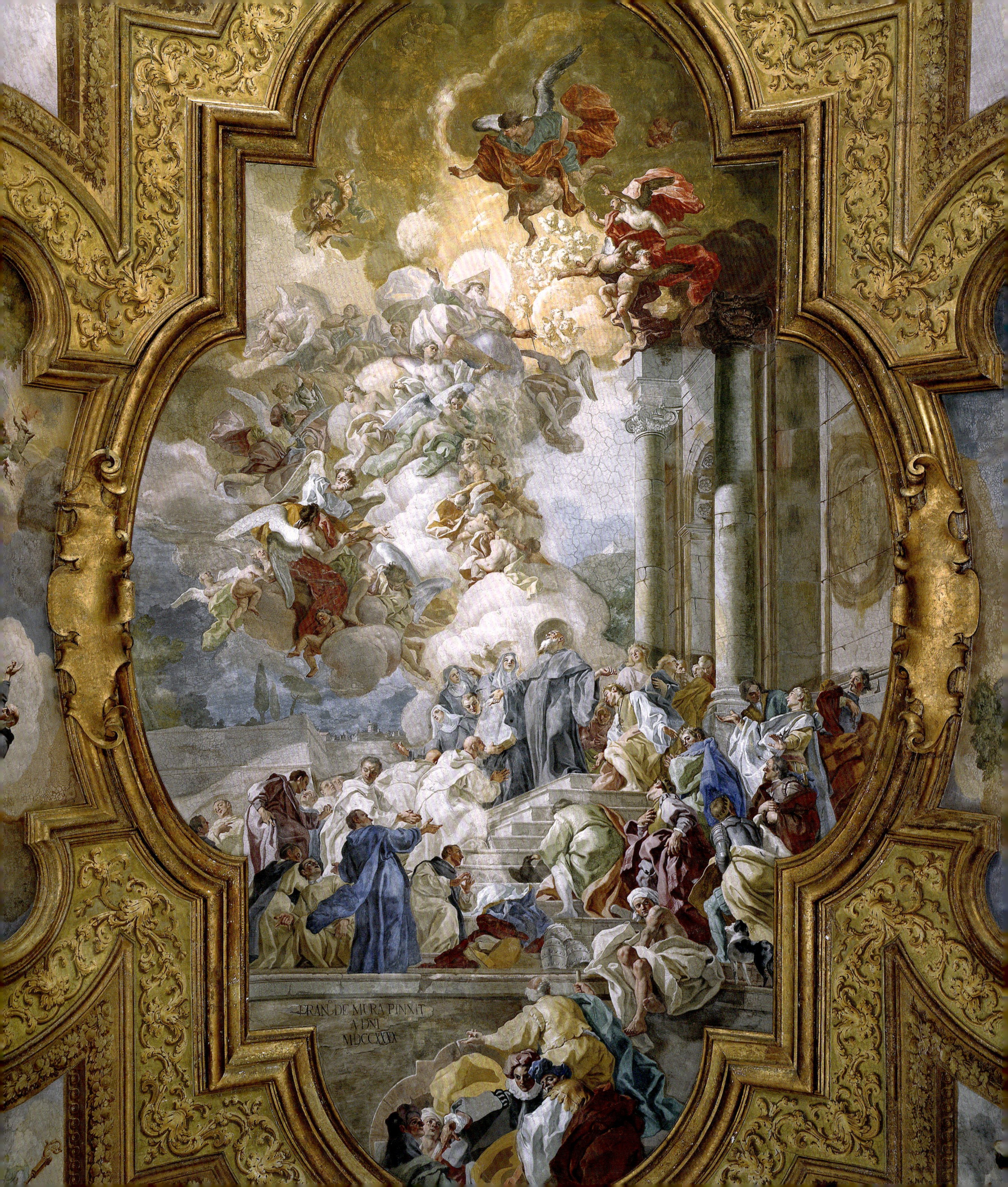
FRANC. DE MURA PINXIT
A. DNI
MDCCXXXX

Something—But Not the Same Thing—in the Air: De Mura, Tiepolo, and the Science of the Heavens

David Nolta

A bright graduate student in a Yale seminar on a completely unrelated topic once asked, pointedly and plaintively, "Why Raphael?" The student's question, as he went on to clarify, was a general one about the force of the arbitrary in determining the reputations, and especially the post-mortem reputations, of artists. Quality alone cannot explain the adulation that Raphael enjoyed during his own lifetime, and his subsequent deification, reaffirmed repeatedly, if not without debate, over the past five hundred years. Of course, the critical fortunes of artists as they are charted through the centuries speak at least as much about the attitudes and interests of the generations of scholars, connoisseurs, buyers and sellers and those sectors of the general public interested in art as about the artists themselves. So Caravaggio's virtual rediscovery in the early twentieth century, and his meteoric ascent to unprecedented popularity in the artistic pantheon of Western art, coincides appropriately with the loosening of sexual and gender taboos and the proliferation of explicit violence in images, especially photographic and cinematic, in our own place and time.

The present exhibition is the first ever to focus on the artistic ideas and output of one of the most prolific and uniquely talented painters at work in eighteenth-century Europe. As such, it inevitably raises a question, a corollary to the general one implied by the smart student above ("Why anybody?"): Why not Francesco de Mura? If De Mura was never extravagantly indulged by patrons and critics during his lifetime, he was nevertheless appreciated and preferred by artists and aristocrats and intellectuals within and well beyond the Kingdom of the Two Sicilies;[1] in any case, he was no *pictor ignotus*. At least not before his death, since when he has been more or less forgotten till now. By way of redressing this neglect, but even more in the interest of understanding it and our own perspective better, it seems worthwhile to identify what, in De Mura's art, might remain at odds with modern sensibilities or fail to answer to post-Enlightenment intellectual expectations. In this endeavor, it will prove helpful to consider De Mura in relation, not to a short-lived, mythically gifted Renaissance artist, but to one of the best, and best-known, artists of his own age, Giovanni Battista Tiepolo.

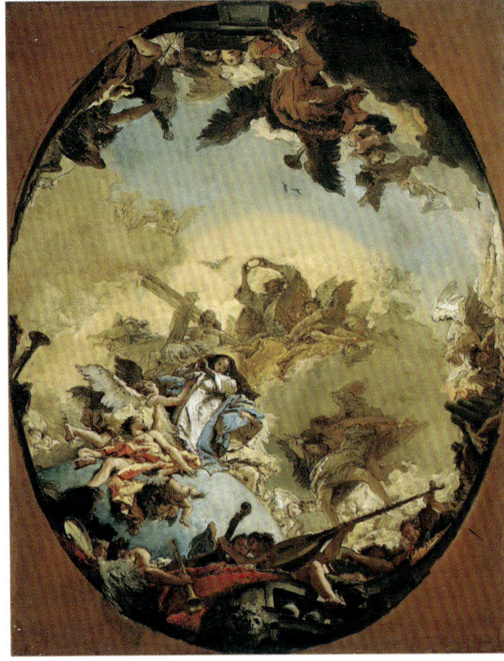

Fig. 15
Giambattista Tiepolo, *The Coronation of the Virgin*,
1754, oil on canvas, 40⅜ × 30⅜ in. (102.6 × 77.3 cm),
Kimbell Art Museum, Fort Worth, Texas

Tiepolo (1696–1770) was the last great master of Venetian large-scale mural decoration. De Mura (1696–1782) was his exact contemporary, occupying precisely the same niche in his native city of Naples. It is natural and illuminating to compare the careers, stylistic trajectories, and legacies of the constantly rediscovered and celebrated Tiepolo and the perpetually overlooked and underexposed De Mura. One particularly revealing point of comparison between the two artists—which not only offers suggestive reasons for their varying statures, but also opens up several interesting paths to future inquiry—has to do with their respective approaches to the representation of that most intangible but ubiquitous of pictorial subjects, air. Here, air is meant to signify everything from nothingness or empty space to the most meteorologically eventful, cloud-packed skies. Their very different treatment of the sky, above all in their large-scale ceiling frescoes, helps to locate the two artists relative to one another and to the larger intellectual currents of their time.

Ever since Andrea Mantegna, reviving ancient Roman decorative ideas, completed the ceiling of his famous *Camera Picta* in the Gonzaga Palace in Mantua, the open sky as subject has proven a particularly tempting challenge to artists, whose successful responses crown and confer greatness on some of the most memorable spaces in Western architecture. Whether the straightforward patch of blue with floating cloud puffs framed by a balustrade over the chamber by Mantegna, or the apocalyptic heavens opening to an explosive vision of salvation in Baciccia's ceiling of the church of the Gesù in Rome, or the vast airy setting for a tour de force of *trompe l'œil* architecture such as soars overhead in Andrea Pozzo's Sant'Ignazio in the same city, the illusionistic absence of the vault can invariably be counted on to seduce and delight the viewer. This is mainly because the sky, more succinctly and completely than anything else, represents the extreme of the illusion, the negation of the pictorial support, and, in so doing, calls into question the very notion of the solidity of finite form. The open sky represents unlimited space, and as we apprehend in it the infinite, it translates inescapably, if paradoxically, into time. Unlike Mantegna's illusionistic balustrade, or the mischievous putti perched along it, the painted sky is not three- but four-dimensional. The sky as treated by artists, though rarely the subject of comment beyond appreciative or critical remarks concerning the specific hues employed, is necessarily a powerful component of any pictorial representation that includes it.

By the end of the Baroque era, painted skies proliferated throughout the great ecclesiastical and secular buildings of Europe. De Mura and Tiepolo both belonged to that era to the extent that they benefitted from—in fact, depended upon and in any case actively participated in—the prolonging of the tradition of monumental architectural fresco decoration, a tradition that, in retrospect, had little future and no place in the modern-

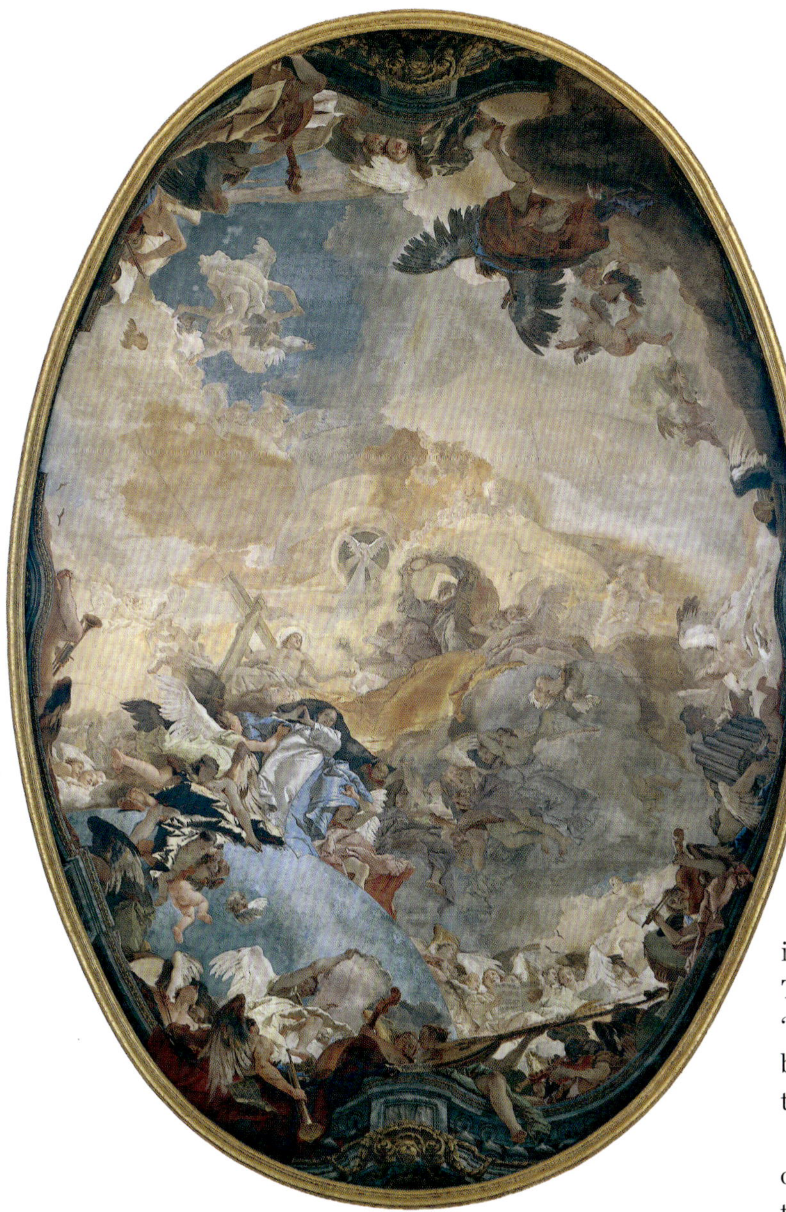

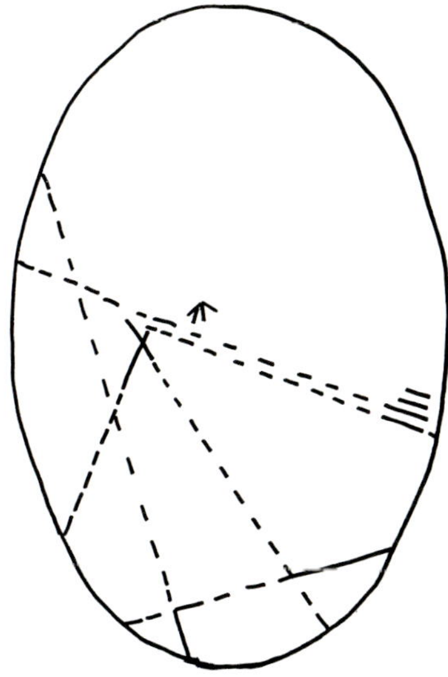

ist period. However we may strain to label De Mura and Tiepolo and their works in the usual terms—"Baroque," "Rococo," "Neoclassical," "proto-Romantic"—they are both Baroque in their roles as operatic transformers of the man-made environment.

How did De Mura and Tiepolo approach the subject of the sky, and the emptiness of space, in their respective works? Throughout the greater part of his career, Tiepolo seems to have conceived of the vault of heaven—and, by implication or extension, the extraterrestrial universe, beginning with what we see as sky—in terms of the oval, that is, as being viewed within or through an elliptical frame. Consider, among many more examples, his Palazzo Archinto ceiling (*Phaeton and Apollo*; now destroyed) in Milan, painted in the 1730s; the *Coronation of the Virgin* for the ceiling of the church of the Pietà in Venice (unveiled 1755; *bozzetto*, fig.15; fresco, fig. 16); and the ceiling he executed for the Palazzo Canossa (*Apotheosis of Hercules*) in Verona in 1761. Significantly, this conceptual preference for the oval is reaffirmed even when the artist adapts a finished composition to a predetermined, more or less rectangular architectural format, as, for example, in the preparatory study for the Palazzo Clerici ceiling in Milan (*The Rising of the Sun*, 1741, now in the Kimball Art Museum) and those extant oil studies (in the Accademia di Belle Arti in Venice, and in the British Rail Collection[2]) for the Scalzi ceiling in Venice of *The Holy House of Loreto* (1743–45). De Mura, on the other hand, seems rarely, if ever, to have imagined the oval as the aperture or underlying geometry of heaven, gravitating instead to the square and the rectangle, or the hybrid rectangle with curving ends, in large-scale decorative projects.[3] De Mura most assuredly does paint in the simple oval format—for example, in smaller-scale works like the *Dream of Jacob* in Pio Monte della Misericordia and the *Diana and Endymion* in the Certosa di San Martino, and even in subsidiary images for his vast *St. Benedict* cycle in Santi Severino e Sossio (see cat. no. 15; figs. 19, 53, and 55)—but the view through that simple oval is consistently frieze-like, lateral or more nearly lateral to the picture plane. For Tiepolo, the geometry of the ellipse is an opening to the infinite; for De Mura it is not.

There are implications in Tiepolo's preference for the ellipse as ingress to the infinite, and De Mura's comparative avoidance of the ellipse and his collateral avoidance of the dizzying *di sotto in su* (seen from below) visions for which his Venetian contemporary was so famous. Tiepolo's view of the infinite is upward and outward-tending; one effect of this is the diminution of the scale of the figures. There is simply more space in Tiepolo's work than in that of De Mura, who prioritizes, in a classicizing sense, the human figure over its context. This is easily seen when we compare two exactly contemporary works, Tiepolo's Gesuati ceiling (*St. Dominic Instituting the Rosary*, ca. 1737–39; fig. 18) and the

largest, central scene by De Mura for the vault of Santi Severino e Sossio (*The Vision of St. Benedict*, 1740; fig. 19, detail on p. 44, and fig. 53). Tiepolo's Gesuati ceiling is among the artist's most concentrated works, uncharacteristically respectful of its frame (though the figures at the bottom still overlap it), whereas De Mura's ceiling is among his most dynamic. De Mura always respects the boundary of the frame, whereas his northern counterpart, in the tradition of Baciccia, more often than not has figures tumbling out of it, as in the finished work at the Scalzi, the Treppenhaus and Kaisersaal ceilings at Würzburg, the ceiling of the Villa Pisani at Strà, and, at the very end of his career, in the throne room in the Palacio Real in Madrid.

It is interesting to consider Tiepolo's ellipses—if not their origins per se, then at least the context in which they occur. Such a consideration leads to an exploration of the internal geometries of his and De Mura's large-scale decorative commissions. At the outset, it is clear that these have little in common. A fruitful exercise in this regard is to compare the prominent, straight-edged geometrical armatures—those represented literally as architectural features as well as those indicated by and extrapolated from such accessories as crosses, spears, halberds, banner poles, etc.,[4] in the ceiling decorations of the two artists (figs. 17 and 20). The findings with regard to Tiepolo are especially intriguing, above all, since they can be seen to conjure up the artist's close affiliation, from 1743 onward, with his worldly, widely traveled compatriot, patron, and friend, Count Francesco Algarotti (1712–64). More specifically, the consonance between Tiepolo's architectonic substructures, with their recurring elliptical frames and their prominent, downward-opening, perpendicular angles, and numerous illustrations in early-eighteenth-century editions of the *Principia* of Sir Isaac Newton, one of whose greatest popularizers Algarotti was,[5] points suggestively, if only in

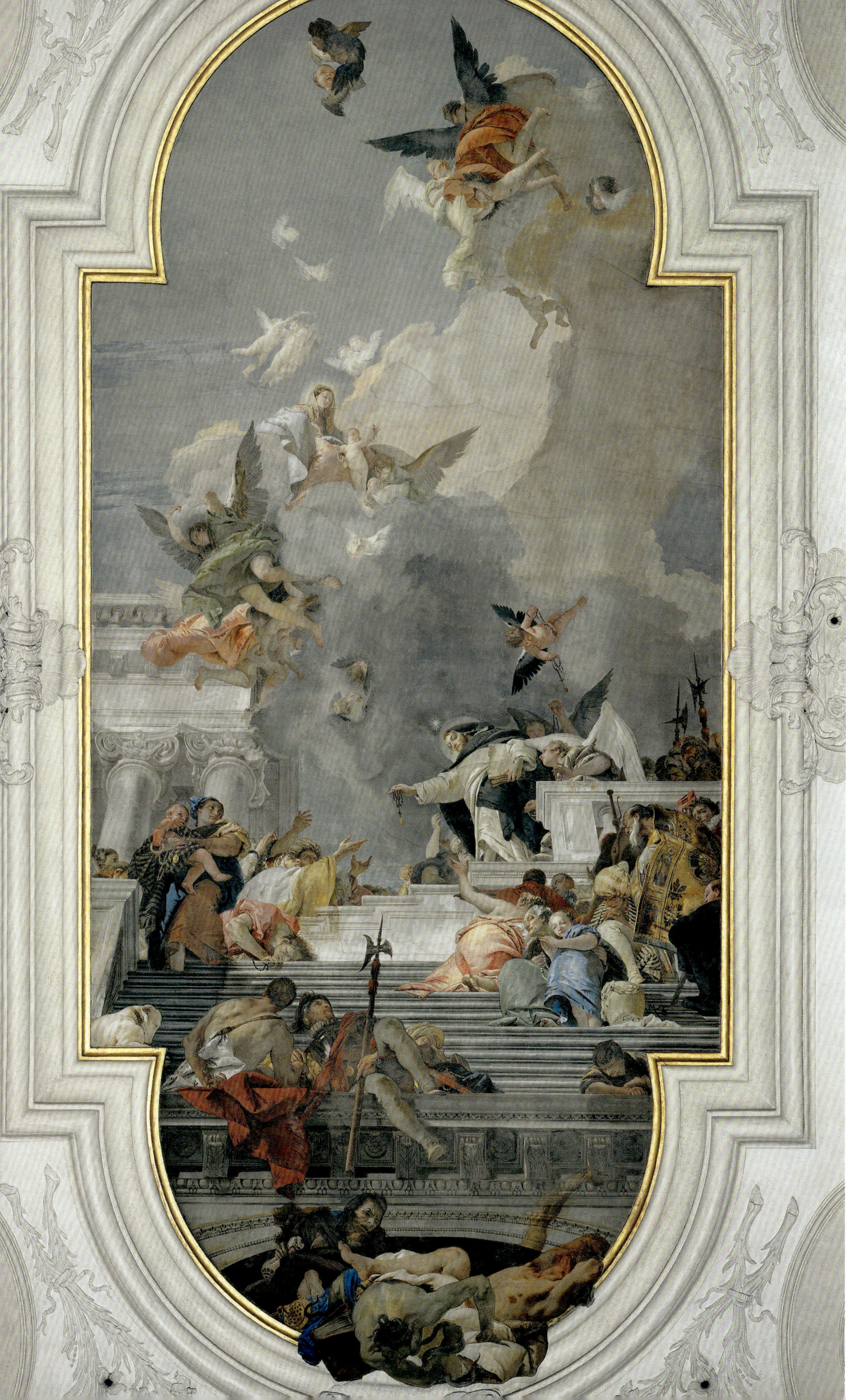

Fig. 18
Giambattista Tiepolo, *St. Dominic
Instituting the Rosary*, ca. 1737–39, fresco,
ceiling, church of the Gesuati, Venice

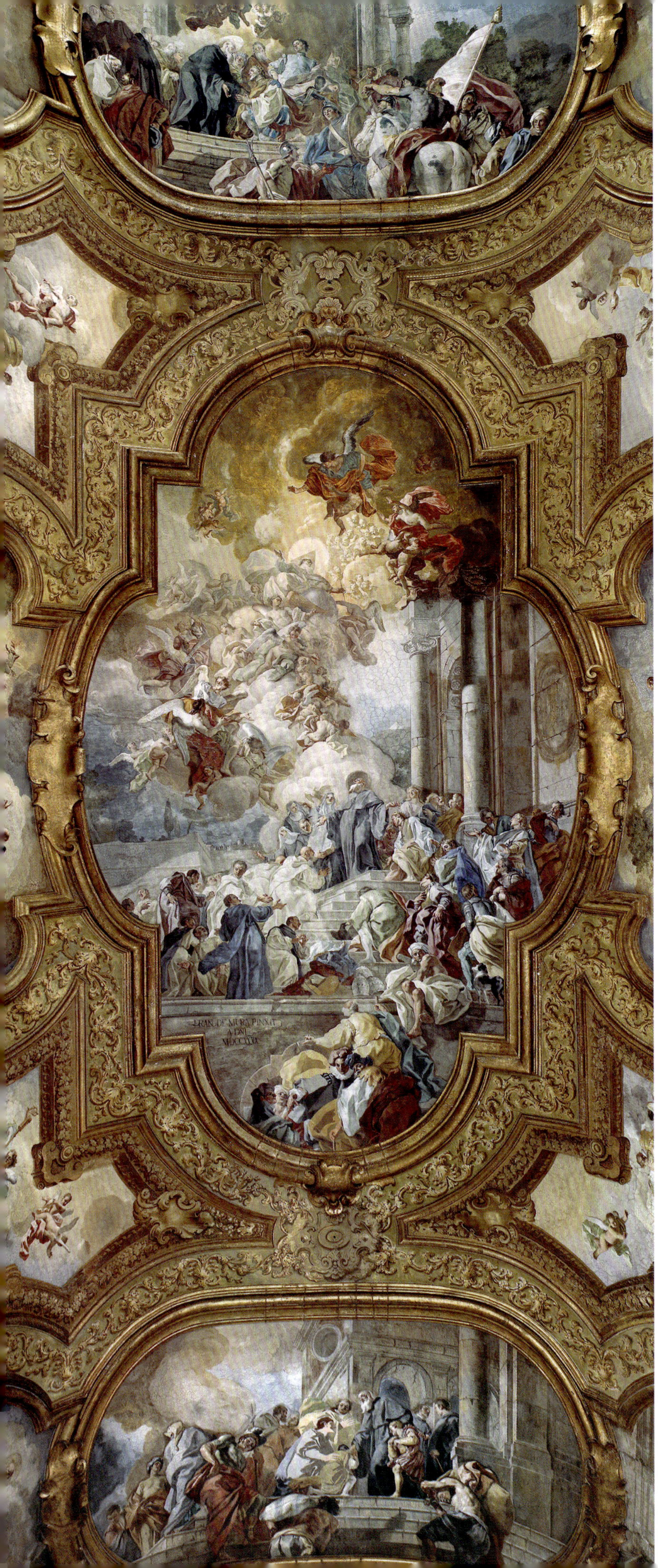

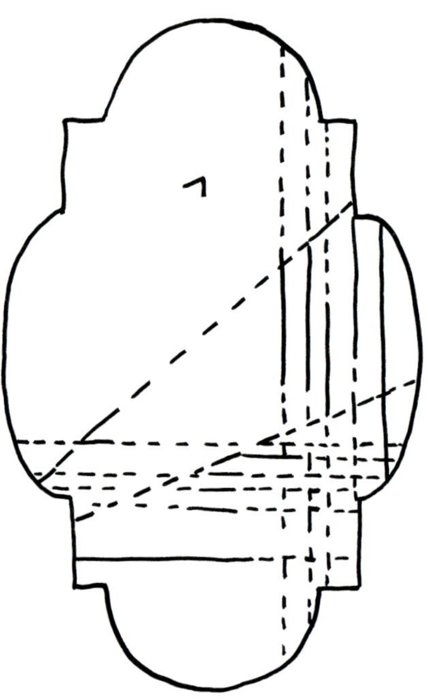

the most literal, formal sense, to the Venetian painter's familiarity with Newton's work.[6]

A pronounced, recurring, formal resemblance between the figures in Newton and the geometries in Tiepolo does not preclude similar analogies to the work of De Mura, and there are in fact also points of comparison to be made between De Mura's compositional formulae and illustrations in early- and mid-eighteenth-century editions of the English scientist's work, though they emerge less frequently and are less obvious.[7] These co-incidences are intriguing but not particularly surprising, as certainly, by the time both artists reached maturity, copies of Newton's works had been circulating, if at first somewhat furtively, among the great cities and centers of learning in Italy, including Naples and especially Venice, where they found serious supporters long before Algarotti published his commentary.[8] Strong parallels between any artist's compositional tendencies and the illustrations of the arguments in Newton's scientific works would of course remain superficial and at best mere curiosities, if not for the fact that, in Tiepolo's case, they reinforce other indications of a commitment to Newtonian and even more modern ideas, a commitment to which the work of De Mura does not testify.

This difference is doubtless relevant to the artists' longer-term reputations; it is also, above all, verified by their disparate treatments of the sky. It is in the very air that they paint that De Mura and Tiepolo declare themselves in what was certainly the most intensive and enduring scientific debate of the eighteenth century, that between the Cartesians and the Newtonians. Central to this debate was the already-old controversy concerning the existence of true nothingness—the void. Briefly, Descartes, backing up Aristotle, goes to some pains to undermine the notion of true nothingness in the fourth book of his *The World, or Treatise on Light* (1632),[9] while Newton, in the opening pages of the *Principia* (first published in 1687), champions the equally ancient position in favor of the existence and even the logical necessity of true emptiness. Furthermore, with nothing comes true freedom of movement, as later in the same work Newton explains:

> Bodies projected in our air suffer no resistance but from the air. ... And the parity of reason must take place in the celestial spaces above the Earth's atmosphere, in which spaces, where there is no air to resist their motions, all bodies will move with the greatest freedom.[10]

In Newton, then, there is something—actually, nothing—that nevertheless exists as the heavens, and this "element," this airless air,[11] is in fact what Tiepolo strives to give us when he paints the sky over our heads. As already noted, Tiepolo presents more air, and, significantly in a Newtonian sense, more space between comparatively diminished figures than we typically find in De Mura. Moreover, even a cursory comparison of

their ceiling projects—both the preparatory studies as well as the finished works—confirms that De Mura is fonder of the sculptured frieze or stele as artistic model, and usually gives us a stable, if not necessarily horizontal, axis or ground. The greater speed implied by the steeper perspectives typical of Tiepolo's vault decorations, on the other hand, captures well the Newtonian idea of the greater freedom of movement available to entities (planets and comets in Newton, divine and mythological figures in Tiepolo) unfettered by matter, including air. Similarly, Tiepolo is far more likely than De Mura to present a void in the center of his larger compositions, or at least, to keep that area free of figures; whereas both De Mura and Tiepolo often represent clouds as solid matter, leaving them to do much of the heavy lifting in a divine apparition or celestial reunion, De Mura invariably layers them with solid figures in the centers of his scenes.

It is important to avoid sharp dichotomies here, and not to lose sight of the many qualities shared by the Venetian and the Neapolitan. For example, both De Mura and Tiepolo are masters of dynamism—artists whose arrangements of human figures brilliantly exploit the potential of contrapuntal movement to engage and excite the eye. But overall, De Mura's dynamism is inward-bound, whereas Tiepolo's, comparatively but almost invariably, tends away from the center. Architectural forms, and even accessories and details, often reiterate this tendency among portable paintings as well as ceilings. In De Mura's best-known work, the Louvre's *Allegory of the Arts* (fig. 23), a sculpturally solid woman, swathed in cloth like the tangible cloud beyond, circumscribes the air with her compass, while behind her an armillary sphere compacts the solar system into an attribute and before her another attribute, the bust of a woman, tips into the picture plane.[12] Similarly, in one of De Mura's last great masterpieces, the *Annunciation* on the high altar of the church of the Annunziata in the

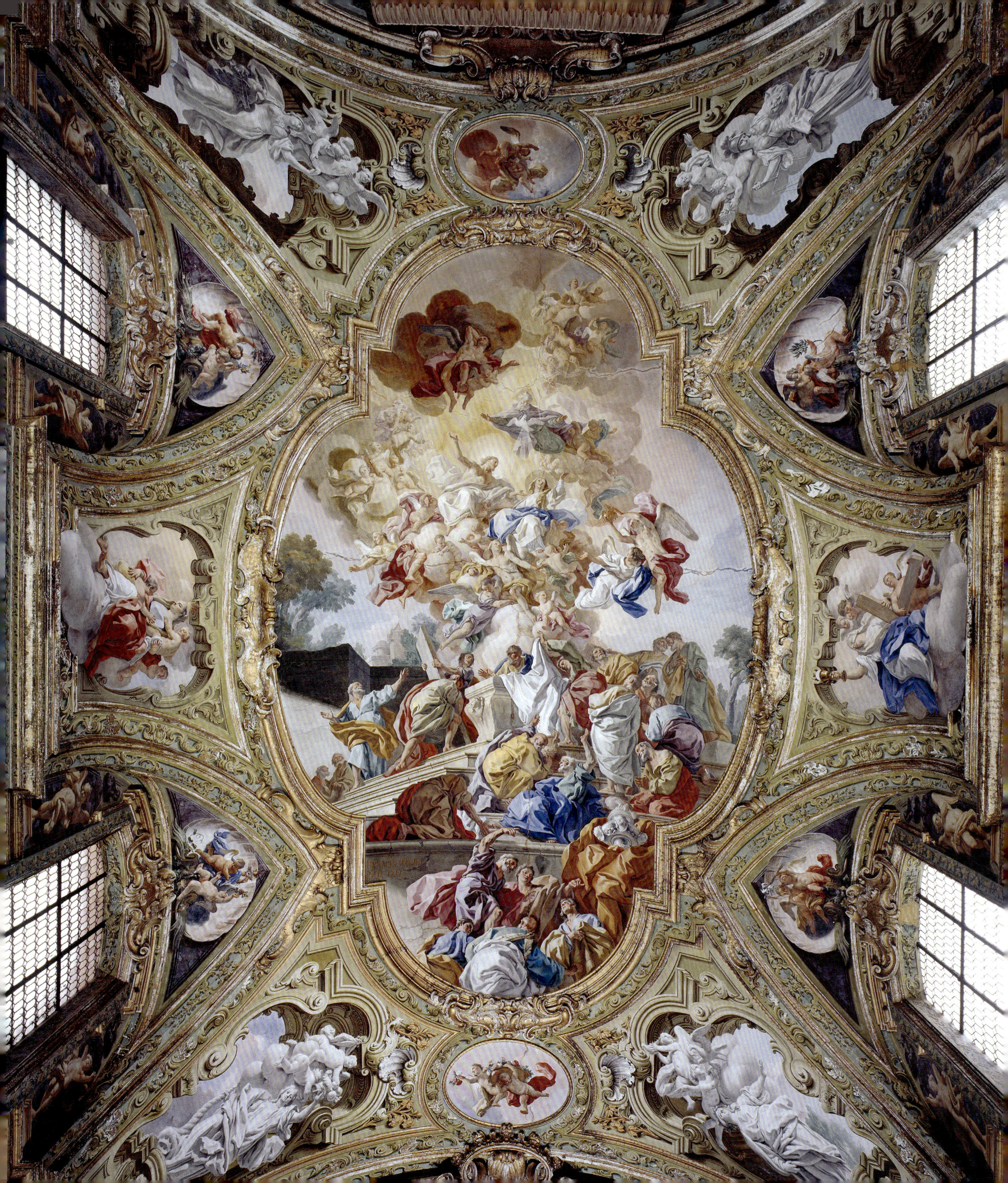

Fig. 21
Francesco de Mura, *The Assumption of the Virgin*, 1751, fresco, church of Nunziatella, Naples

Fig. 22
Tracing of the straight edges and trajectories of De Mura's *The Assumption of the Virgin*, fresco, the church of Nunziatella, Naples

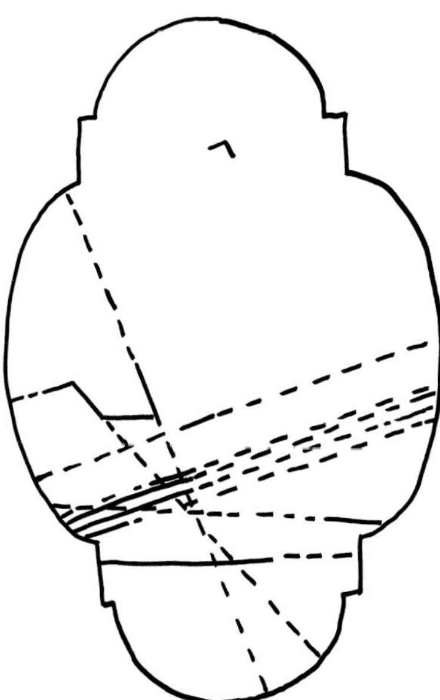

Forcella district of Naples (1761), the Virgin is shown entertaining the angel Gabriel in the aftermath of that most Mediterranean of calamities, an earthquake; again, the column in the foreground has fallen *into* the painted space, and like it, we are brought closer to the mortal woman's world and story.

From an artist's perspective, is more air—*is emptier space*—better? Not necessarily. But it is undeniably more in keeping with the course of modern science to conceive of the universe as larger and more expansive than De Mura's heavens suggest. One might argue that De Mura, with his solid grounding of figures and his tendency to bring those figures closer together, is in fact reflecting the most famous of Newton's discoveries, the force of gravity. There is more reason to believe than to doubt this, especially given the artist's popularity among educated patrons who had recourse to and documented interest in the latest scientific ideas; in Naples, for example, De Mura was clearly the favorite artist of the Jesuits, who employed him repeatedly on major commissions over at least three decades.[13] But again, in their proportions and in their solidity, which they maintain even as they descend from or are assumed into the

infinite, De Mura's figures betray a traditional artistic, rather than a progressive, observational approach. The greater clarity of De Mura's sky-borne forms, only partly attributable to their greater closeness, contrasts sharply with what we find in Tiepolo.

Tiepolo at his best, which is most of the time, treats form as ephemeral and, in retrospect, that, like his "handling" of air, is modern. Though on a large scale, and often also on a small one, he is operatic in his approach to narrative, composition, etc., his actual approach to human form is comparable to—even the grandiloquent equivalent of—Gainsborough's or Watteau's. What his Venetian compatriot Canaletto implies with scale—the smallness of Canaletto's famously calligraphic creatures set against vast, usually urban, spaces, locates them in a quintessentially Northern European and modern tradition of coming to terms with the true scale of the individual human being in the universe—Tiepolo communicates with time: that is, with his instinct for suggesting infinite space and motion. Tiepolo's figures flash, and they often appear caught mid-movement; it is perhaps when they indulge but do not pause in their gestures that they are most arresting for the viewer. Complementary to this, they are most often painted lightly or suggestively, and at least part of their appeal surely derives from the fleetingness of their presence, their sketchiness, even in finished oil paintings, and especially as they hover in and disappear into the frescoed sky. In their ephemerality, we understand they are like us, the modern version of us: fast moving, mutable, and temporary.

De Mura, especially when we consider the evolution of his large-scale projects, instead invariably emphasizes three-dimensional solidity, the actuality and the centrality of the physical human presence. If modern scientific ideas can be traced in both De Mura and Tiepolo, Tiepolo proves to be *more* modern than his

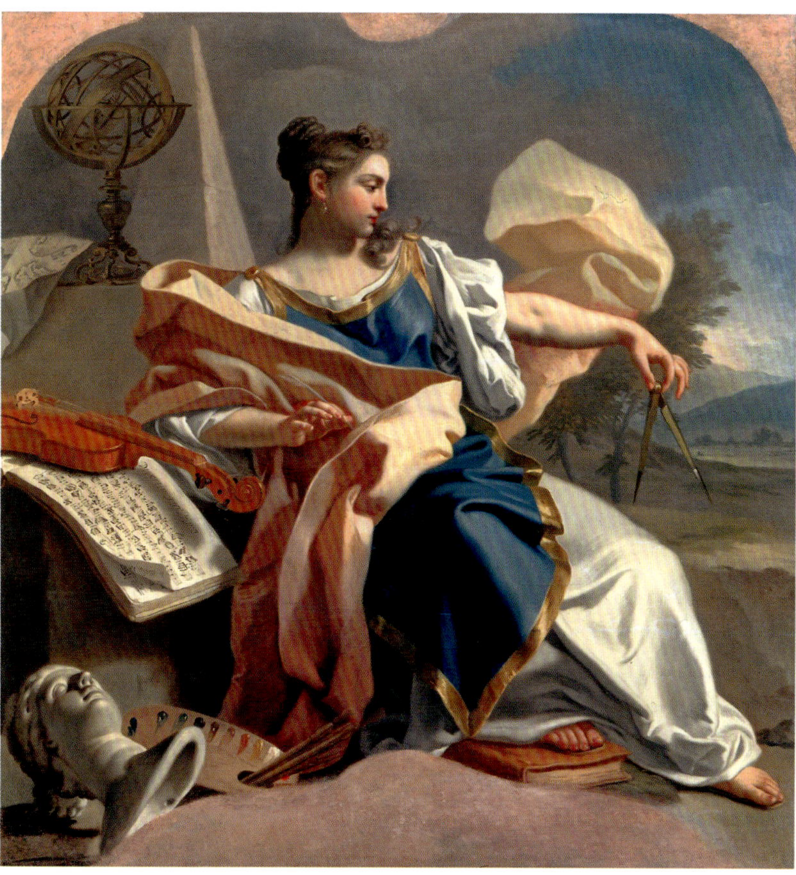

Fig. 23
Francesco de Mura, *Allegory of the Arts*,
ca. 1758–62, oil on canvas, 56 × 52 in.
(142 × 132 cm), Musée du Louvre, Paris

Neapolitan peer, and consequently more accessible to a post-Enlightenment, scientific understanding of all—including human—matter.

Tiepolo was, of course, even more modern than he knew. In his airy, decentered vault compositions, he also adumbrated another major modernist scientific idea, that of the expanding universe. Tiepolo's recurring conception of his ceiling figures as existing around and even hurtling outward from the central zones of his compositions corresponds as well to his method of working from sketch to finished painting, a process which Alpers and Baxandall rightly identify as "decompacting."[14] Along the same lines, and at least as fascinating, is to follow the development of Tiepolo's skies over his entire career; in short, from the earlier to the later, they expand, they become emptier. Anyone who walks into the throne room at the Palacio Real in Madrid cannot help but be struck by the immense, empty intervals of blue sky. With or without knowledge of Immanuel Kant's *Universal*

History of Nature and Theory of Heaven (1755),[15] Tiepolo has had the good fortune to illustrate a truly modern version of the universe.

Which leaves us back in the world of solid forms with the less modern De Mura. If Tiepolo's enduring appeal derives partly from his science, the subjectivity of his vision, and the luck of his instincts, what is De Mura's legacy? De Mura's greatest strengths—his draftsmanship, ardently and justifiably praised by his teacher, Solimena; his unique, extraordinary, extraordinarily broad palette; his range and variability; his charm— appeal less to a world which prioritizes conceptualism and an interdisciplinary redefinition of medium, one in which photography and cinema have become the primary artistic vehicles of illusionism and narrative. Like—and because of—his great predecessor, Luca Giordano, with his repertory of modes, De Mura was a master of many styles, and indulged in a greater range of approaches to form and color than Tiepolo throughout his career. He is consequently—and paradoxically, given his general preference for solid forms moving gracefully in a heaven that is close to home—hard to pin down.

But he is consistent in one thing—he is *human centered*, and looks not to an infinite universe as his subject, but to the solid human form, which is invariably the focus of his artistic eye. And in this he is to some extent at odds with Tiepolo and a modernist, scientifically derived understanding of the human scale in the cosmos. He is in this, instead, a lot like Raphael.

Notes

1. For respective examples: De Mura was the favorite of the many pupils of his teacher, Francesco Solimena; he was patronized by the courts of Naples, Turin, and Spain; he was the favorite painter in Naples of Vanvitelli, and he received generally favorable notices from traveling French artist-diarists Charles-Nicolas Cochin and the Abbé de St. Non.

2. Both studies are reproduced in Michael Levey, *Giambattista Tiepolo: His Life and Art* (London: Yale University Press, 1994), 113.

3. Which of course, Tiepolo also uses, as, for instance, in his Gesuati *St. Dominic Instituting the Rosary*, ca. 1737–39.

4. Svetlana Alpers and Michael Baxandall draw our attention to these accessories, without following up, in their fascinating book, *Tiepolo and the Pictorial Intelligence* (New Haven: Yale University Press, 1994).

5. Most famously via his bestseller, *Il newtonianismo per le dame, ovvero Dialoghi sopra la luce e i Colori* (Milan, 1737), though, interestingly, the first edition made the false claim of having been printed in Naples. See Luigi Cerruti, "Dante's Bones," in *The Sciences in the European Periphery During the Enlightenment*, ed. Kostas Gavroglu (Dordrecht: Kluwer Academic Publishers, 1999), 107.

6. Something is due to be made of the recurring resemblance between the illustrations in Newton and the underlying geometries of Tiepolo. For instance, the artist's Palazzo Labia ceiling, representing *Bellerophon and Pegasus* (1740s), and plate 12, figure 2, in Newton's *Principia*, bk. 1, 136. Isaac Newton, *The Mathematical Principles of Natural Philosophy*, trans. Andrew Motte (London, 1729). The illustrations in Newton's work were made to accompany and clarify the geometric exercises and *lemmata* of his larger arguments about the physical properties of nature. As far as I can see, there is no deeper or ulterior connection between the figures in Newton and the substructures in Tiepolo—in other words, there is no reason to suggest that the latter represent evidence of Tiepolo actually undertaking to reconstruct Newton's mathematical tests, or that their similar designs evince any intention on the artist's part to convey mathematical, much less philosophical, meaning. It is, at the same time, worth noting that the prominent, upward-pointing perpendicular underpinning so many of Tiepolo's vault decorations (and rarely found in the work of De Mura) is a standard tool in more than one traditional method used to draw an ellipse.

7. The connections are indeed few, and very tenuous. For example, *The Vision of St. Benedict* (fig. 19) and Newton, *Mathematical Principles*, bk. 1, 298, pl. 33, fig. 1. In De Mura's armature, the sole, central perpendicular points downward, unlike a majority of the explicit vertices in Tiepolo, which point up. That all of these *are* coincidences is clear, but that they highlight the simple fact that Tiepolo's geometrical patterns have less in common with those in the work of De Mura, and more in common with the plates in Newton, seems worthy of note.

8. A succinct and helpful summary of the early dissemination of Newton's ideas in Italy is Paolo Casini, "Les débuts du newtonianisme en Italie: 1700–40," *Dix-huitième siècle* 10 (1978): 85–100.

9. René Descartes, *The World, or Treatise on Light*, trans. Michael S. Mahoney (New York, 1979), http://www.princeton.edu/~hos/mike/texts/descartes/world/worldfr.htm.

10. Newton, *Mathematical Principles*, bk. 3, 388. See also p. 369, where the speed of celestial bodies is advanced as another proof of the absence of resistance.

11. Not to be mistaken for Aristotle's aether, which is not, by any means, nothing.

12. Here it would be impossible not to mention that, in precisely the same period in which De Mura executed the *Allegory of the Arts* (ca. 1758–62), he painted a series of four allegories of the elements. The *Allegory of Air* from that series, now in a private collection in Turin, is as solid and statuesque and every bit as compact an allegory as the great image in the Louvre (cat. no. 38). For a reproduction of the *Air*, and the other elements, see the online catalogue of La Fondazione Federico Zeri: http://catalogo.fondazionezeri.unibo.it.

13. At the Nunziatella, beginning in the early 1730s, at the Gesù Vecchio in the late 1750s. The relationship is covered in David Nolta, "Francesco de Mura: Lives and Works" (Ph.D. diss., Yale University, New Haven, Conn., 1989), [vol. 1.]:106ff. Generally speaking, the Jesuits were deeply involved in the dissemination of Newtonian ideas, though the so-called Jesuit Edition (1739–42) of Newton's *Principia* was not in fact the work of Jesuits but of two French Minim Friars, Thomas Le Seur (1703–70) and François Jacquier (1711–88). See Paolo Bussotti and Raffaele Pisano, "On the Jesuit Edition of Newton's *Principia*: Science and Advanced Researches in the Western Civilization," *Advances in Historical Studies* 3, no. 1 (2014): 37.

14. See Alpers and Baxandall, *Tiepolo and the Pictorial Intelligence*, 90, where, regarding the evolution from drawing to finished ceiling at the Gesuati, the authors remark, "the bud has burst"; see also p. 66.

15. Surely without. Kant is tricky on the notion of the void, and advocates a new version of the old aether. For his prophetic physical theory, see "The Evolution of the Sphere. Kant's Theory of Matter and the Expanding Universe," in *The Harmony of the Sphere: Kant and Herschel on the Universe and the Astronomical Phenomena*," ed. Silvia De Bianchi (Newcastle upon Tyne: Cambridge Scholars Publishing, 2013), 17–45.

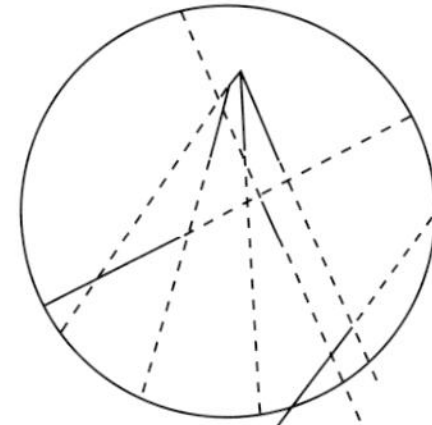

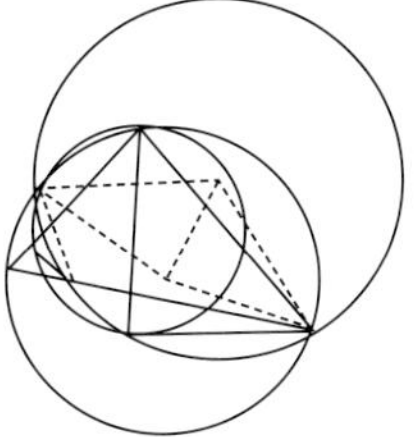

A
Diagram of the straight edges and trajectories underlying Tiepolo's *Bellerophon and Pegasus*, Palazzo Labia, Venice

B
Isaac Newton, *Principia*, book 1, pl. 22, fig. 2 (from 1729 London edition)

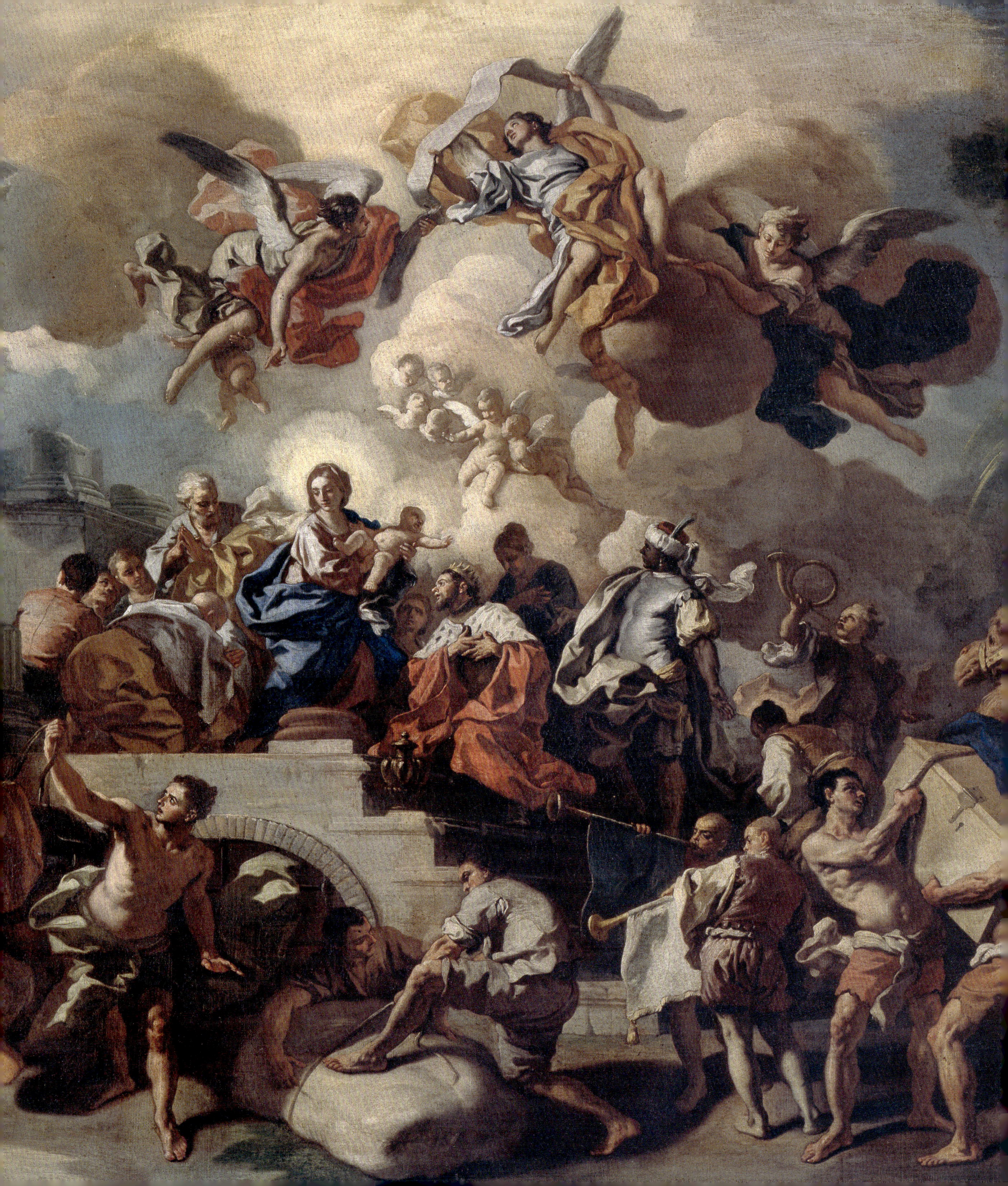

From Naples into the World: The Dispersal of Francesco de Mura's Works

Loredana Gazzara

Pio Monte della Misericordia in Naples

Pio Monte della Misericordia (literally, the "Pious Fund of Mercy") is one of the most important and among the oldest charitable institutions in Naples. It was founded in April 1602 as a benevolent brotherhood by seven young noblemen who, as the sources say, met every Friday at the Hospital for Incurables and ministered to the sick. They were aware of the poverty in Naples, of a population in need of help and community support at all levels, and they wanted to practice the seven Christian acts of corporal mercy, which, thanks to the generosity of Pio Monte Associates, continues uninterruptedly even today. The founding noblemen decided to donate part of their property to the rescue of the distressed, devoting their lives to good works. For nearly four centuries, Pio Monte della Misericordia, with its *Governatori* (trustees) and all its Associates, has continued its involvement in works of charity and assistance in many forms: through individual donations that help solve difficult issues, through the management and financial support of kindergartens, and donations to many associations and through various means that target the people most in need.

Its seat is in a historic palazzo, built by the noted royal architect Francesco Antonio Picchiatti (1619–94), that conceals in its interior an elegant Baroque church where Caravaggio's great canvas of *The Seven Acts of Mercy* (1607) is located (fig. 24), as well as other masterpieces of painting and sculpture in the Picture Gallery on the upper level (it is one of the greatest art collections in Italy open to the public). The palazzo, the church, and the Picture Gallery together create an inseparable whole and constitute a historic ensemble of the greatest charm, allowing visitors to go back in time to savour an earlier period of the charitable work of the Neapolitan nobility.

Public Auctions, Exhibitions, and Conservation Efforts

The art collection of Pio Monte della Misericordia was formed through bequests and donations of paintings and furnishings (in addition to real estate). Excluded from these bequests and donations were some commissions by the church of Pio Monte della Misericordia, according to the wishes of the trustees of the organization. Pio Monte was charged with the task of selling this inheritance to convert the assets into funds to advance the institution's charitable goals. Despite numerous dispersals of works from its art collection, Pio Monte still today holds the greatest number of large paintings and *bozzetti* by Francesco de Mura, critical for reconstructing his corpus of works.

The first monographic study of Pio Monte's collections, and therefore of its important group of paintings by De Mura, was Raffaello Causa's *Opere d'arte nel Pio Monte della Misericordia a Napoli* (1970), published in time for the public opening of Pio Monte's *Quadreria* (Picture Gallery) in 1972. The book still stands as the most important study of the art collections. In his book, Causa identified the two principal donations to the collection: the bequest of Francesco de Mura himself in 1782, and that of Corelli-Capece Galeota in 1933. A third important bequest was that of Giuseppe Marciano in 1802. There are other gifts still to be identified and studied whose provenances are yet unknown to scholars.

At the beginning of the nineteenth century, after the bequests of De Mura and Marciano, Pio Monte found itself housing at least 292 paintings, intended by the donors to be sold "to benefit poor gentlemen and poor ladies." De Mura's generosity of spirit informs Pio Monte's mission to this day.

Of the 192 works bequeathed by De Mura to Pio Monte, thirty-nine (thirty *bozzetti* and nine paintings) remain today. By analyzing these works—the technique and the *modus operandi* of the artist, the *palmi* (measuring canvas size: one *palmo* is 10½ in. or 26.7 cm), descriptions of paintings in Pio Monte inventories, numbers, and sealing-wax stamps affixed to the paintings be-

fore sale by Pio Monte—some fifty paintings of De Mura's bequest have been traced to the current collections of various museums in Italy and other countries.

Though some of De Mura's most magnificent works are lost forever—the decorative cycles in the abbey at Monte Cassino, part of the ceiling frescoes for the Palazzo Reale in Naples, and the great canvases for the church of Santa Chiara in Naples—with *In the Light of Naples: The Art of Francesco de Mura*, we have the first exhibition devoted entirely to this painter, one that brings together important surviving examples of his prolific output. De Mura's paintings contain a disconcerting and mysteriously deep quality. Formerly, De Mura was the subject of miscellaneous essays and studies by only a handful of scholars, but now, at last, he is presented to the world, the focus of an exhibition and a monographic work.

A full examination by Loredona Gazzara of the archives of Pio Monte della Misericordia that includes public auctions and sales, the history of conservation of Francesco de Mura's works, and the efforts to restore and reconstruct Francesco de Mura's bequest is available online at rollins. edu/cfam/exhibitions/2016/demura.com. A summary appears on the following pages.

Fig. 24
Main altar of the church of Pio Monte della Misericordia, with the painting by Caravaggio of *The Seven Acts of Mercy* (1607), viewed from the upstairs Sala del Coretto in the Picture Gallery

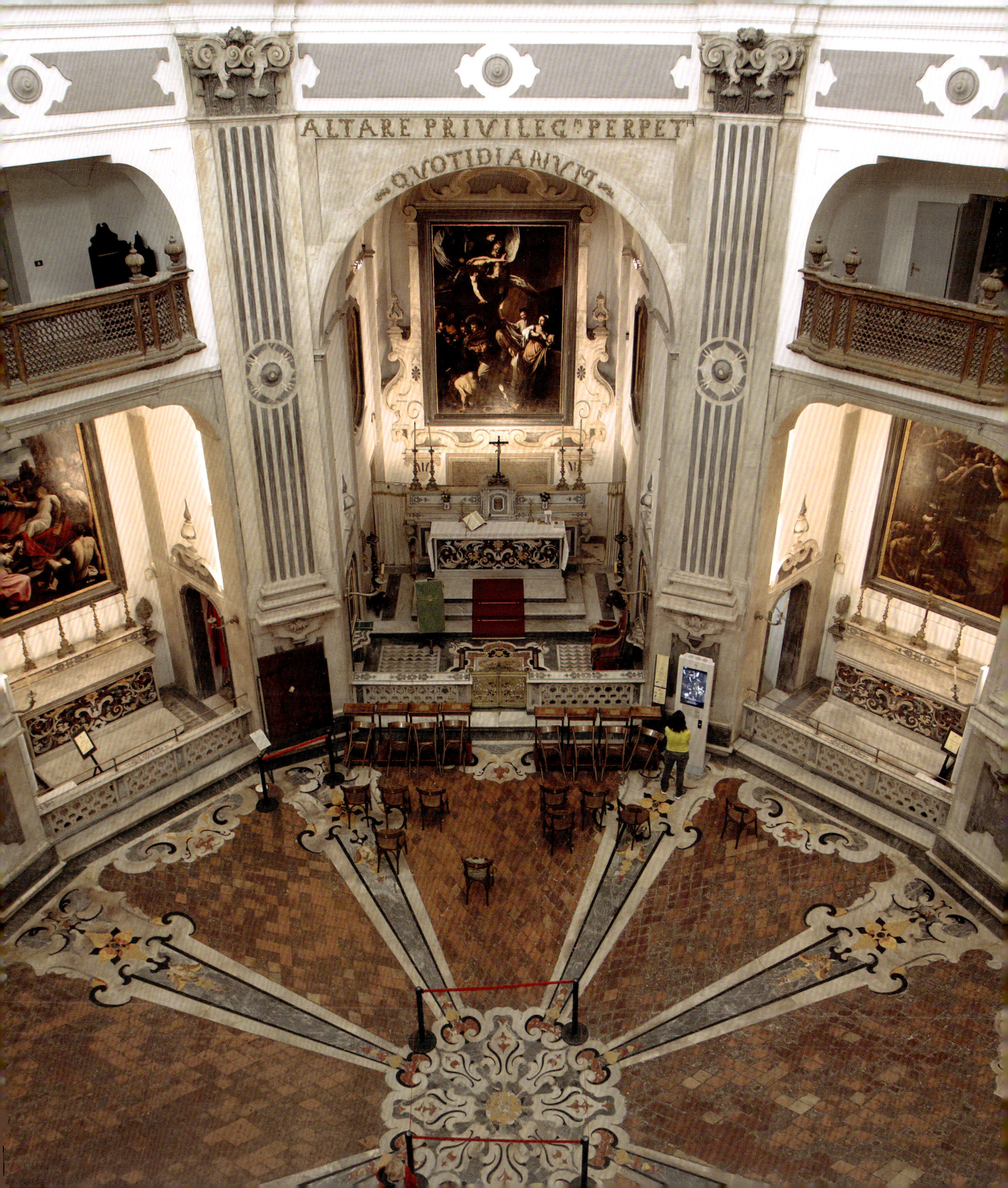

ALTARE PRIVILEGᵗᵐ PERPETᵗᵐ
QVOTIDIANVM

Francesco de Mura and Pio Monte della Misericordia

Loredana Gazzara

Early 1800s
Pio Monte della Misericordia held within its walls at least 292 paintings that were to be sold, as donors stipulated, to raise funds for charitable causes: to sell "things … to benefit poor gentlemen and poor ladies."

1838
Professor and painter Aniello D'Aloisio (1775–1855) organized a list of numbered works and affixed canvases with red stamps and sealing wax to prepare them for sale. Before the 1845 auctions, a second inventory was drawn up by Nicola la Volpe and Camillo Guerra.

1845
Auctions of 78 paintings from Pio Monte, including 37 works by De Mura, were held between March 31 and November 17 with the intent of converting artistic inheritance to cash.

1851
Giuseppe Simonetta submitted a report on the states of conservation of the collection, recommending Pio Monte's paintings no longer be sold to avoid the danger of underselling them.

1906–7
The Gattini Commission singled out 23 De Mura paintings from Pio Monte to be acquired in preparation for the late-eighteenth-century halls of the Galleria at the Museo Nazionale of Naples. In a private transaction, this block of works sold for only 10,000 lire (around $30,000 today). As a result, the canvases are today separated from the original De Mura nucleus of paintings and are held in different government museums in Naples, Florence, and Bari.

1914
Pio Monte ended the history of selling its precious art inheritance.

1925
Pio Monte had 79 works of art described and catalogued, including all of the De Mura paintings in the current collection. For the first time, the cultural and monetary value of Pio Monte's collection was fully realized by specialists and governing officials.

1936
Work began on a critical catalogue of the Pio Monte collection by Sergio Ortolani, director of the Real Pinacoteca di Napoli, but was interrupted, most likely due to the outbreak of World War II.

1938
Pio Monte lent many paintings to a large exhibition at Castelnuovo in Naples (*La Pittura napoletana dei secoli XVII, XVIII, XIX*), the first great survey and civic event to promote local art. Inside this vast pantheon of Neapolitan painting was an anthology of eighteen paintings from the Pio Monte collection, including ten De Mura paintings.

1941
The outbreak of World War II. In order to protect Naples' cultural heritage from aerial bombing, the state evacuated works from Palazzo Reale, the Museo Nazionale, and the Neapolitan churches. Spurred by heavy aerial attacks and with the assistance of the Italian government, Pio Monte transferred 74 canvases by De Mura, Caravaggio, Battistello, and others to the abbey of Mercogiano, near Avellino, for safekeeping.

1950s
The wisdom of Pio Monte administrators during the war years saved a great number of paintings we enjoy today. In the post-war years, restoration efforts were necessary only on the canvases that remained at Pio Monte and were not transferred to the abbey of Mercogliano. Numerous bomb-damaged paintings left at Pio Monte underwent restoration, thus the excellent state of conservation today.

1960
Pio Monte lent De Mura's *The Visitation* (cat. no. 23) and *Scene of Terror* to a Paris exhibition of eighteenth-century art. This decade is characterized by Pio Monte's participation in loans to great Italian exhibitions sent abroad.

1969
A new superintendent, Tommaso Leonetti di Santo Janni, arrived at Pio Monte and expressed a desire for Pio Monte, for the first time in history, to open its doors to share its art collection with the public. He had a precise idea in mind: to put the paintings in order and place them in suitable locations in the halls for public enjoyment. Francesco de Mura's paintings were given privileged placement in the exhibition areas.

1972
With a solemn ceremony, Pio Monte opened its Picture Gallery (see figs. 25, 26, and 29), making its beautiful De Mura paintings and the rest of the collection open to everyone—not just to a small, privileged circle of associates and art specialists.

1975
In an important step forward, the Italian Ministry for Cultural and Environmental Heritage declared Pio Monte's art collection as being "of exceptional artistic interest." From this moment on, Italian law defined the nucleus of Francesco de Mura's paintings as an inseparable *unicum* (a unique collection of his art).

1979
Forty-one years after the first 1938 Neapolitan exhibition, fifteen magnificent De Mura paintings were included in the exhibition *Civiltà del '700 a Napoli* (Neapolitan Civilization of the Eighteenth Century) in Naples and Florence, curated by Nicola Spinosa—the first great survey of eighteenth-century Naples. De Mura distinctly emerged from the panorama of eighteenth-century Neapolitan painters that included his own students and his master, Francesco Solimena.

2003

The most recent restoration work on the palazzo rooms of Pio Monte was completed. This work permitted the inauguration of a new setting that maintained the same criteria for exhibitions at the first public opening. The remodeling left unaltered the privileged space where De Mura's canvases hang to this day.

2004

In preparation for conservation efforts, restorers examined Francesco de Mura paintings and noted with amazement the *prima tela* (unlined canvas) conditions of his works. It was evident that the original cloth of the canvases, though not stretched like modern canvas cloths (missing the central traverses to support excessive tautness), were, however, still crafted in a such a way as to guarantee the tension in the canvas.

2005–6

In recent times, Pio Monte has restored 99 paintings, including 38 by De Mura. Because the De Muras are well framed, the main degradation was in the flattened tones of the oxidized varnishes. The cleaning of the paintings eliminated the time-yellowed varnish and has restored the paintings' full transparency, allowing us to appreciate the diverse, brilliant colors used by De Mura in his signature palette.

2016–17

Three paintings by De Mura—*Adoration of the Magi*; *Christ Receiving St. Joseph into Heaven with the Madonna and Saints*; and *Glory of the Princes* (cat. nos. 12, 13, and 35)—travel to the first-ever Francesco de Mura exhibition, organized by the Cornell Fine Arts Museum, and traveling to the Chazen Museum of Art, University of Wisconsin, and the Frances Loeb Art Center, Vassar College.

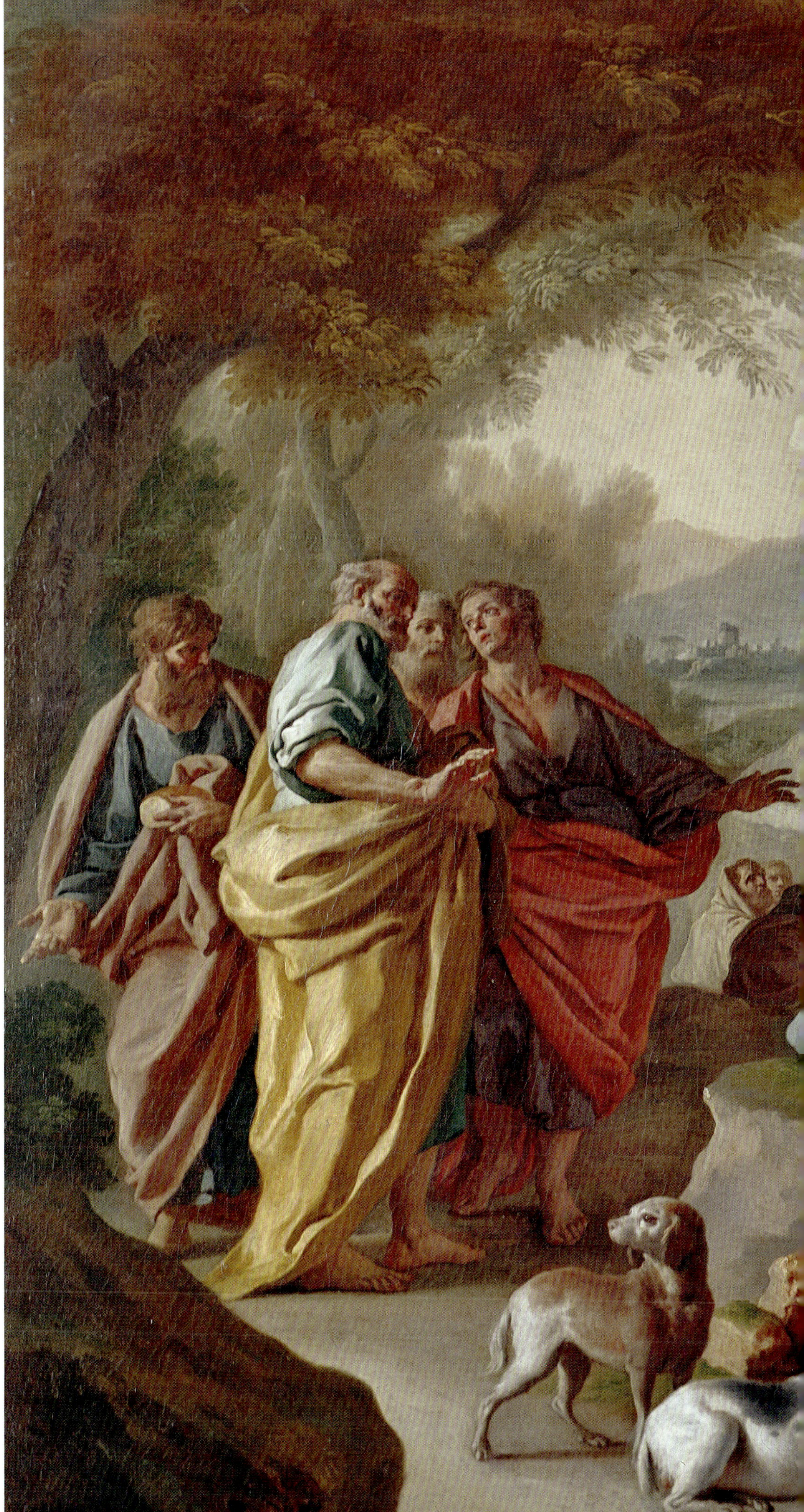

Cat. 24 (detail)

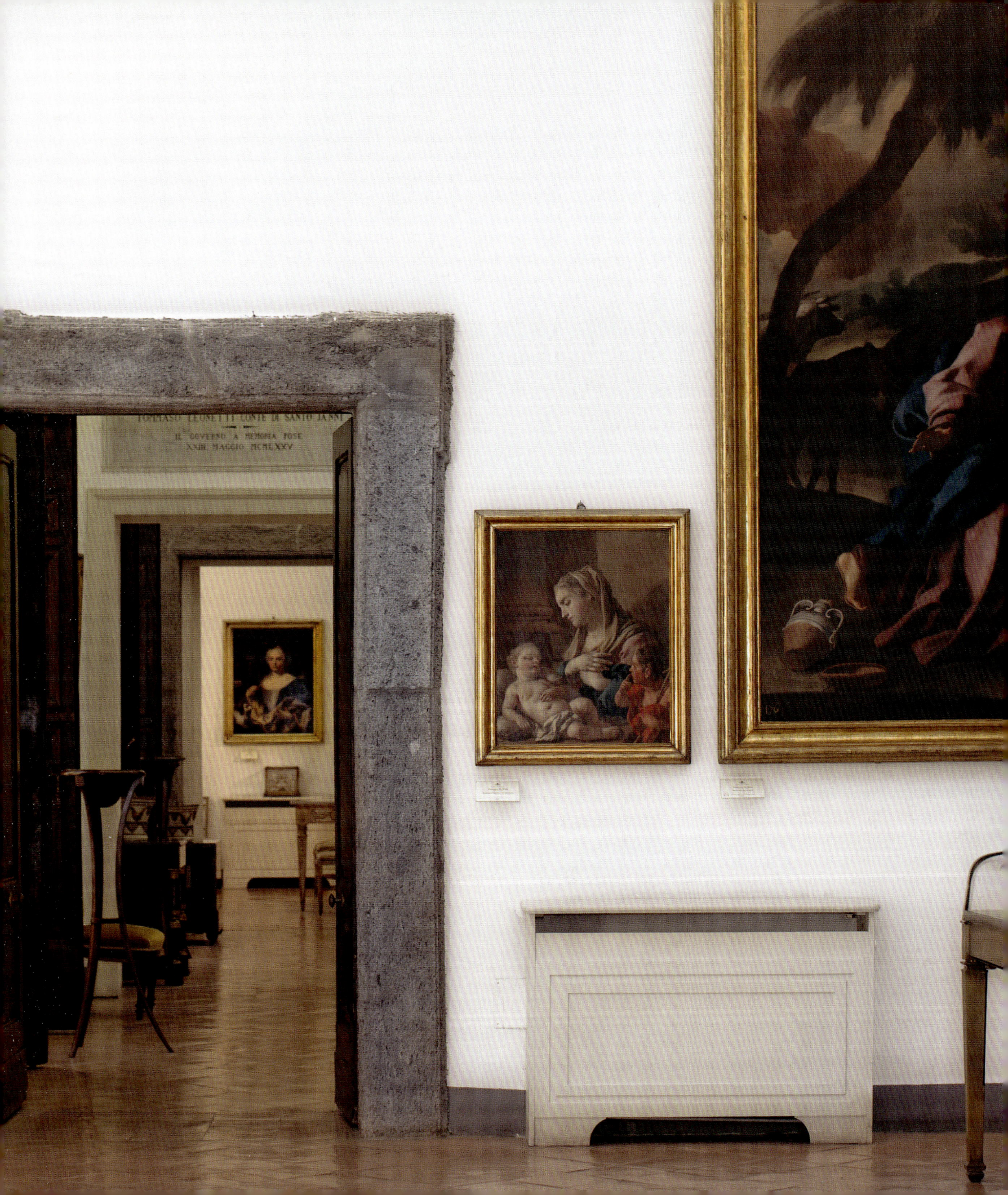

Francesco de Mura's Gift to Pio Monte della Misericordia and Its Rediscovery in the U.S.

Maria Grazia Leonetti Rodinò

To understand the connection between Francesco de Mura and Pio Monte della Misericordia, one first needs to examine the historical background. During the eighteenth century, Naples was a beautiful and extraordinary city that had been part of the Crown of Aragon since 1503, when the Catholic King Ferdinand (1452–1556) conquered the Kingdom of Naples in battle against France. As a result, the city had become the capital of the Spanish viceroyalty, and in the following century, one of the largest cities in Europe. Huge public resources were invested to embellish Naples, providing it with the aura of a Baroque city, which is still admired today, especially in religious art: everywhere, called from other cities, were famous architects, engineers, artists, artisans, marble workers, potters, and masons, all working together. They constructed about 300 churches and 120 convents, and hundreds of archconfraternities.

The Birth of Pio Monte della Misericordia

A prevailing belief in the seventeenth century was that, in order to be deserving of paradise and earthly glory, people needed to work on behalf of their less fortunate neighbors. At the beginning of 1601, in order to try to fill the wide social gap that existed between the nobility and the population they were accountable to, seven young aristocrats began to meet every Friday at the Ospedale di Santa Maria del Popolo degli Incurabili (Hospital of Saint Mary of the People for the Incurable, meaning those who lacked the money to pay for their care). The young gentlemen who defined themselves as *Governatori* (trustees) were Cesare Sersale, Giovan Andrea Gambacorta, Girolamo Lagni, Astorgio Agnese, Giovan Battista d'Alessandro, Giovan Vincenzo Piscicelli, and Giovan Battista Manso—almost all second-born sons of ancient noble families. Each in turn would assume the role of superintendent, *primus inter pares* (first among equals). They instituted a *Monte*—a repository of property, funds, alms, and contributions for charitable purposes.

Fig. 25
Picture Gallery, a view toward the Salone delle Assemblee, the room where the *Portrait of the Artist's Wife* is hung, Pio Monte della Misericordia, Naples

After a few years, the Monte attracted exponents from prestigious families—those belonging to the ranks of Spanish power or related to the viceroy and to the most important clergymen, magistrates, military officers, and noble citizens—who were all convinced that this charitable institution was the best way "to gain Glory with God and with the world." In 1604, through the efforts of the Viceroy Juan Alonso Pimentel de Herrera, Count of Benavente (viceroy from 1603 to 1610), a *regio assenso* (royal assent) came from King Phillip III (1578–1621) in the form of a sealed *privilegium*, an important legal deed. Pope Paul V (Camillo Borghese, 1552–1621, elected pope in 1603) encouraged the initiative in 1605 with a *breve* (brief) in which he approved the statute establishing that Pio Monte della Misericordia

> was not to be subject to the Bishopric and that the works of the aforementioned Pio Monte be free and exempt from the jurisdiction of said Bishopric, even though they be immediately subject to the Apostolic See ... so that in no way may the Bishopric impose itself upon the vision of their affairs, nor in any other functions of the aforementioned Pio Monte.[1]

By 1605, Pio Monte had bought, for 2,900 ducats, in the area of the Decumano Maggiore (which is today Via dei Tribunali), Via del Sole, Via della Luna, and all of the area between the narrow streets of Via Zuroli and Via Carbonari, with the buildings and property of Maria and Francesco Caracciolo della Gioiosa and of Orazio Tomacelli. A small church had been built there—the work of Giovanni Giacomo di Conforto. In 1606, the association commissioned Caravaggio to paint for the main altar *The Seven Acts of Mercy* (see fig. 24). In an official resolution by the *Governatori* on August 27, 1613, it was declared that the painting was never to be sold or removed, and it remains today the manifesto of Pio

Monte della Misericordia and serves as a reminder of the tasks for which the *Governatori* are elected.

At the end of the first half of the seventeenth century, having overcome many difficulties, which had absorbed a great deal of resources, Pio Monte saw a significant increase in subscribers and followers, thanks to the widespread sense of solidarity of the surviving association members. At last, the *Governatori* were able to expand their undertaking. They decided to construct a bigger church and headquarters that would be more suitable to the fame and prestige their association had acquired and which would be a bit more sheltered from the street noise of the Via dei Tribunali. They turned to the well-known and much-admired royal engineer Francesco Antonio Picchiatti (1617–94) to restructure and enlarge Conforto's small church to accommodate the association's new requirements. Construction was completed at the end of the 1650s, and the portico of the church and the entrance to the headquarters were joined in front. *Piperno*, a sturdy lava rock from Mount Vesuvius, was used throughout the building, even for the impressive staircase that leads to the historical quarters, as well as for the frames around interior windows and doors. From the street, one can still get a complete view of the façade. Coming down the staircase that was the main entrance to the cathedral, one can see how impressive the structure is, with the lightness of its white and gray façade and its five majestic arches. On the architrave is the motto that the founders adopted from the beginning, FLUENT AD EUM OMNES GENTES, from Isaiah 2:2: "At day's end, the Mount of the Temple of the Lord will be elevated above the hilltops and be higher than mountain peaks ... *and all the nations will flow into it.*"

Fig. 26
Picture Gallery, Salone delle Assemblee, Pio Monte della Misericordia, Naples

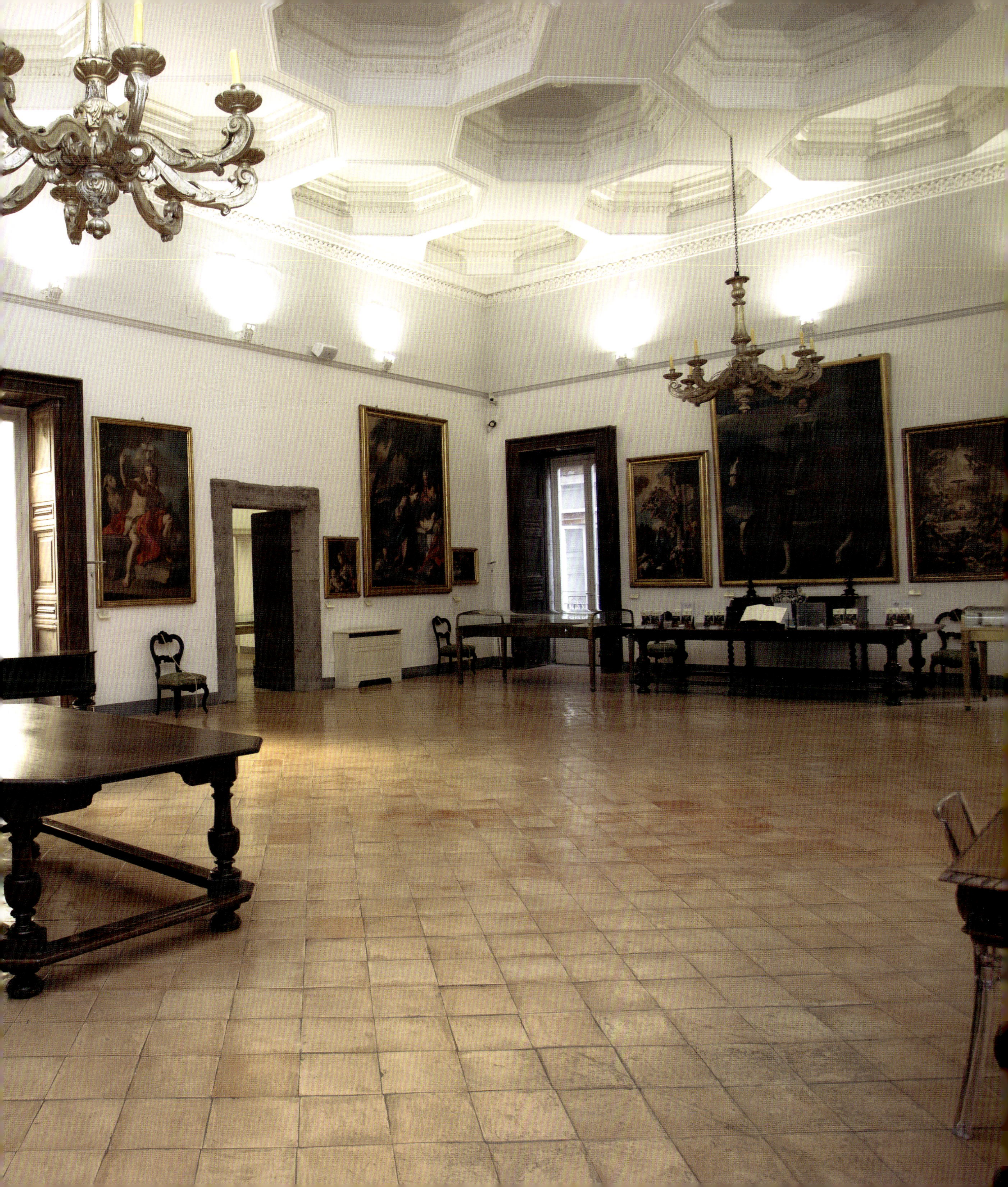

The Birth of an Exhibition

By 2005, I had just been elected *Governatore* of Pio Monte della Misericordia. For the first time a woman was a member of the governing council and, since I was an instructor and art historian, I soon faced the issue of introducing and spreading the great artistic patrimony of the institution, of which it was the much-envied custodian. Only since 1972 has the institution been open to the public, and then only by appointment. This policy was important to Pio Monte, underscored by the words of Superintendent Tommaso Leonetti di Santo Janni:

> We have, in fact, maintained, that to open the massive doorway and to admit the general public into our facilities so that it might admire so many art treasures represented a specific obligation for our administration. This was for three considerations: 1) To open to the public our Picture Gallery, a significant resource for the most in-depth study of Neapolitan art. 2) To make Pio Monte more productive, in the sense that the proceeds from entrance fees would logically be earmarked for institutional goals, so that a nonprofit patrimony of enormous value might become profitable and contribute to the purposes of the entity. 3) To expose to many Neapolitans, who perhaps might even have been unaware of its existence, their own Pio Monte della Misericordia, so that, by becoming familiar with it, they might support it.[2]

I had the same feeling that came over my father when—with the Superintendent of Fine Arts and Galleries, Raffaello Causa—he decided to open the doors of Pio Monte della Misericordia. Deep within me was the sense of obligation to always make known the wonderful reality that, after more than four centuries, it was being used for the benefit of the weakest and need-iest in our society. My original intent then passed from publicizing the church—where *The Seven Acts of Mercy* by Caravaggio had rightfully monopolized the attention of scholars and tourists—to, above all, promoting the Picture Gallery, which at that moment was less studied and certainly less appreciated. The interior was restored and reopened to the public in 2003, after years of being closed because of damage caused by the devastating earthquake of 1980. It is an art collection of great value, focusing on the seventeenth and eighteenth centuries. A new thought began to take root and my attention was turning to Francesco de Mura.

The Bequest of Francesco de Mura

Today, 39 of Francesco de Mura's canvases have been preserved at Pio Monte. These bear witness to his great productivity, from his early years to those of his late maturity. De Mura decided that, upon his death, he would bequeath to Pio Monte whatever remained in his studio. Between *bozzetti* (oil sketches) and finished works, this comprised 192 canvases of varying sizes. Of course, as was his character, he decreed that, if needed, all could be sold at auction in order to obtain funds for Pio Monte's charitable purposes. And thus it was done, with monthly sales that continued until 1845. At that point, it was decided to handle the exigencies of the charity through other means available and, thanks to this decision, the Picture Gallery, known as the *Quadreria*, was formed. Other donations soon began coming in, and today the patrimony consists of more than 150 paintings by many artists (including contemporary works).

From an artistic point of view, one of the most important events for Pio Monte was De Mura's decision to name Pio Monte as the sole heir of his huge estate; this was a determining factor in the founding of the

Picture Gallery. The official act of donation by Francesco de Mura was drawn up by the notary Michele Valenzia, and the executors were two of his friends, the Marquis Angelo Granito di Belmonte, president of the Tribunal of the Royal Chambers of Sommaria, to whom he bequeathed two canes with golden knobs and two weapons called *doppie di Spagna* (Spanish doubloons), and Salvatore Gallotti, his *comparello* (buddy) who was almost a nephew, to whom he gave six paintings chosen by his father—the lawyer Giambattista, his dear friend—and a gold box. In light of the fact that his wife, Anna Ebreù (see figs. 5 and 57), had died in 1767, the painter totally excluded from the inheritance his adopted daughter, his niece Grazia, and his great-niece Giovanna. He affirms in writing that he wanted "to be free of their troublesomeness ... because of which I had suffered many anxieties." Moreover, he had abundantly provided for them "by way of expenses of many thousands of ducats." Then, except for some bequests made *ex frate* (for his family), to his nephews, he resolves: "the fruits of my own efforts as a professional artist ... I, the undersigned, establish, effect, declare, name and believe [an emphatic use of five verbs to be exceedingly explicit and clear in order to avoid having his testimony impugned] my sole and particular heir to be to the Pio Monte della Misericordia... to aid poor gentlemen and ladies" (figs. 30–31).[3]

Besides his house in the Chiaja area of Naples, he left an estate of about 57,000 ducats, without counting the fruits of his labor, the paintings. There were 192 paintings in his studio when his last will and testament was first declared (the notaries Michele Valenzia and Giuseppe Ventrella had made a precise inventory). These works were mostly *bozzetti*; the painter was very conscientious about pleasing his clients and was capable of making two or even three versions of the same subject, slightly different only in small details (see cat. no. 39 and fig. 88; cat. no. 40 and fig. 91).

Soon after that, the *Governatori* of Pio Monte asked two artists to take charge of the inventory: Pietro Bardellino and Fedele Fischetti, young painters who had studied with De Mura and closely followed his Rococo style, and were, thus, well qualified to certify authenticity. The documents that describe the arrival of De Mura's paintings, preserved in the historical archives of Pio Monte della Misericordia, are extremely detailed and clarify much information. (Managing the dealings relative to the bequest of the painter was long and elaborate and got to such a point that the Secretary of Pio Monte, Antonio Venuto, was awarded, in addition to his normal salary, another 100 ducats, "for his labors undertaken.") De Mura's bequest is recorded in the minutes of the *Governatori* meeting of February 29, 1783:

The Honorable Professor of Painting Don [Francesco] Di Muro [*sic*], reaching an advanced age, and not having close relatives, wishes that his possessions, personally acquired, be used for pious works. Therefore, in testimony and under three uniform codicils, which will ratify his disposition, has established that his inheritance shall go to Pio Monte della Misericordia of this city...[4]

However, the Real Santa Casa dell'Annunziata also claimed the painter's bequest, on the grounds that De Mura had been an orphan and was educated and brought up by the orphanage, which was thus due the inheritance. Documents detail Pio Monte's efforts to retain De Mura's bequest: *On Behalf of Pio Monte della Misericordia on the Occasion of the Preamble of Don Francesco Di Muro* [sic], and the more extensive *On Behalf of Pio Monte della Misericordia against the Regal Casa Santa of A. G. P. on the occasion of the Preamble of Don Francesco di Muro* (Naples, February 19, 1783). The succeeding document *On Behalf of Pio Monte della*

In virtù dell'ordine dell'EE. loro: Noi sotti Pittori ci
siamo conferiti nel Monte della Misericordia
per ivi considerare tutti li Quadri pervenuti
frà l'Eredità del fù Celebre Pittore D. Fran.co dé
Muro, ed alli med.i dar prezzo con la mag.r accura
ta perizia, che perciò ci damo l'onore dé seg.ti
prezzi ultimativi, e decisivi

Numeraz.ne   Prezzi

1. Un Quadro di Paesi pal. 2. e n 1/2 con cornice abbozzato — 3.
2. Un Quadro di Paesi pal. 3. e d.a con cornice finito — fr 4.
3. Altro dell'istessa misura bizaro — 50
4. Macchia dell'Ascunta di pal. 4 1/2 e d 6. Dipinta nell'Annunziatella sopra di Pirofalcone — 125.
5. Sopraporta di pal. 4. e d 2. La favola dell'Aurora e Titone — 60.
6. Sopraporta di pal. 3 1/2 e d 2. La favola dell'Aurora e Titone — 80.
7. Un quadro di palmi 6. e d 8. Diana, ed Endimione con cornice — 75.
8. Macchia dell'Annunziata pal. 3 1/4 e d 5 1/2 — 50.
9. Macchia di pal. 4. e d 6. La Vergine S. Luigi, e Scolari — 70.
10. Quadro 5. e d 2. Coriolano con la Madre, Moglie, e figli nell'assedio di Roma con cornice — 100.
11. Macchia di pal. 6. e d 5. 3/4 La Storia dei Principi dipinta nel Palazzo Reale — 60.
12. Altra Macchia di pal. 3. e d 4. di simil'soggetto — 30.
13. Macchia del Tempio di Salomone di pal. 4. e d 5. fatto in Foggia — 70.

Fig. 27
*Inventory of 1783 of the Paintings of
Francesco de Mura,* signed by the painters
Pietro Bardellino and Fedele Fischetti,
Historical Archive of Pio Monte della
Misericordia (photo by Paola Tufo)

Fig. 28
*Inventory of 1783 of the Paintings of
Francesco de Mura,* signed by the painters
Pietro Bardellino and Fedele Fischetti,
Historical Archive, Pio Monte della
Misericordia (photo by Paola Tufo)

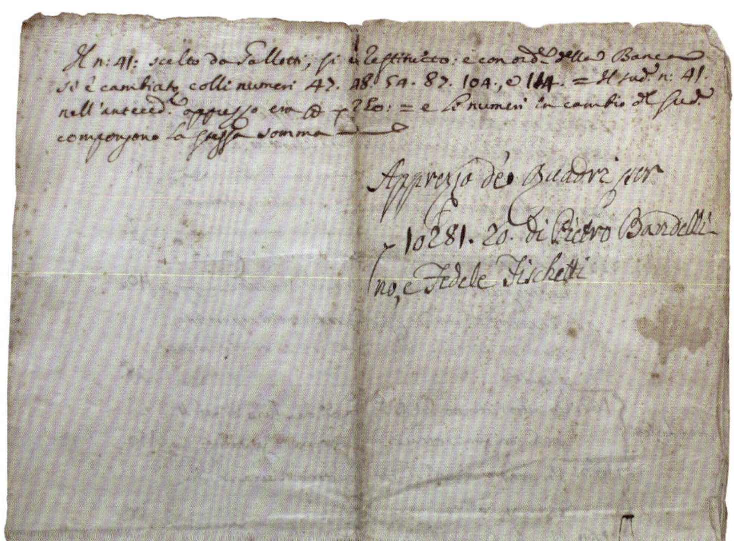

*Misericordia against the Royal Family Santa di A.G.P. on
the Occasion of the Preamble of Don Francesco de Mura*
(Naples, February 1783) insists, on the evidence, in favor
of Pio Monte della Misericordia: the painter was not,
as the legal representatives of the Annunziata family
wished to demonstrate, "one of their born-out-of-
wedlock projects" but the legitimate son of Giuseppe
de Mura and Anna Linguito.[5]

The inventories were edited by Fischetti and
Bardellino, with the purpose of establishing a value for
the paintings. Both were working without much data, but
came up with two drafts. One, signed first by Fischetti
and then by Bardellino, indicates a total "fair" appraisal
of 15,631.20 ducats (fig. 27). The other contains the
signature of Bardellino, followed by that of Fischetti,
and shows a "decidedly" inferior value of 10,281 (fig. 28).
Of the 192 paintings left to Pio Monte by the artist, 39
of them remain in the collection today. According to the
will of the donor, the paintings, at best, were to be sold
through regular auctions with the purpose of acquiring
funds for charitable works.

From De Mura's early period, we have preserved
in Pio Monte della Misericordia *Madonna delle Grazie
with Sts. Rosa and John* and *St. Anthony of Padua.* These
are two youthful works, especially with the theme of the
Madonna and Child, which will often be depicted in his
compositions during the long course of his artistic life.
Also from his early years are *bozzetti* for the church of
San Nicola alla Carità: *The Glory of St. Nicholas, Saints
in Glory* (which, however, was stolen in 1983), and *The
Visitation.* The *bozzetto* of *The Visitation* in the Cornell

Fine Arts Museum (see cat. no. 23; fig. 67) certainly
comes from the nucleus of De Mura paintings at Pio
Monte della Misericordia. *The Adoration of the Shepherds*
in the collection of the Gaetano Filangieri Museum of
Naples is a study of the painting done on the right wall of
the church of San Nicola alla Carità.

In 1727, the Benedictine abbey of Monte Cassino
invited De Mura to work on the chapel there, where
the relics of St. Benedict were stored. In the monastery,
he finished over 30 paintings and frescoes. Of those
frescoes, only a few *bozzetti* remain (see cat. nos. 8 and
11). Unfortunately, during World War II, this great body
of art was destroyed in the American bombardments in
1944—one of the greatest artistic disasters ever.

In 1740, De Mura dated and signed the decorations
in the vault of the nave in the Benedictine church of
Santi Severino e Sossio in Naples (see cat. nos. 14, 15, and
16). During this period, the painter jealously stored all
of his *bozzetti* in his studio. Perhaps he was well aware
of his personal success, now finally free of the cumber-
some presence of his master Francesco Solimena. In
the Picture Gallery, of the originally inherited fourteen
bozzetti, there remain only seven: *St. Benedict Orders
the Crow to Remove the Poisoned Bread, St. Benedict
Extinguishes the Fire in the Convent Kitchen*, and *St.
Benedict Miraculously Provides His Monks with Wheat,*
together with two *grisailles* of the *Angels with Incense
Burners*, and another two of the *Angels with Staff, Miter,
and Book.* This period corresponds with the "full maturity of the artist," one of the most revealing moments
of his central production and his greatest success, as

affirmed by Nicola Spinosa.[6] The other seven *bozzetti* that completed the series were removed in 1907 and bought by the government to be entrusted to the Museo di Capodimonte. Two are there now: *The Vision of St. Benedict* and *St. Benedict Welcomes Totila.* (cat. nos. 15 and 16). The former was a preparatory study to be used for the central fresco in the vault of Santi Severino e Sossio. Another four, from the same period, wound up being housed in other museums. A pen-and-ink study of the central fresco is in The Metropolitan Museum of Art (cat. no. 14).

Signed and dated in 1751 are works done for Jesuits in the church of the Nunziatella, dedicated to St. Francis Saverio and connected with its Jesuit school (see cat. nos. 20 and 21). After the expulsion of the Jesuit Order by the Kingdom of Naples in 1767, with the royal decree issued by Ferdinand IV, the Order was dissolved by Pope Clement XIV in 1773. After all of its property, convents, and schools were confiscated, in 1787, the school became—through the desires of King Ferdinand IV himself—the headquarters of the Military Academy and the church assumed the name of the Nunziatella. There are some pieces from this period that can be found in Pio Monte della Misericordia's collection. The first of these is *The Adoration of the Magi*, a *bozzetto* prepared for the fresco in the curve of the apse (cat. no. 12). The *bozzetti*, made for the vault, of *The Assumption of the Virgin* and *The Rest on the Flight into Egypt*, were purchased by the Italian government in 1907. Together with the four *Allegorical Figures*, they were first kept in storage at the Museo del Sannio di Benevento and are now, along with eight *putti nudi* (naked cherubs), in the Museo Duca di Martina in the Villa Floridiana in Naples, where an important collection of decorative arts can be admired.

In 1735, De Mura signed the *Portrait of the Artist's Wife, Anna Ebreù* (see figs. 5 and 57), the woman whom he had married in 1727. In 1970, Raffaello Causa referred

to the subject of this portrait as displaying "the exalted ostentation of youthful beauty."[7] The luminous folds of the clothing and the portrayal of an enriched commoner posing and dressed as a grand lady was the topic of wide discussion in a lecture organized by the Friends of the Museo di Capodimonte, and given by Laura Giusti, an official of the Soprintendenza Speciale per il Polo Napoletano, which has always been professionally tied to Pio Monte. From 1741, there are two very similar canvases that represent *Christ Receiving St. Joseph into Heaven* (cat. no. 13) and which form part of the same preparatory sequence for the fresco of *The Triumph of St. Joseph in Paradise* from the cupola of the church of San Giuseppe dei Ruffi in Naples. From 1750 are *The Last Supper* and *The Visitation*, *bozzetti* for the side altars of the transept in the church of Santissima Annunziata di Capua.

Two preparatory *bozzetti* for De Mura's *Scenes of Terror* are datable to around 1755–57. These were done for the little cupola of the noble Sedile di Porto, which existed during the Bourbon era, and which was next to the church of San Giuseppe Maggiore, destroyed in 1845. The *Sedile* or *Seggio* (seat), a kind of district parliament begun in the period of the Spanish viceroyalty, would meet in the Capital Hall of the San Lorenzo convent and outline a program for the administration of the district. Altogether there were seven officials, six of whom had their position by right of being members of historical families of the noble class: Capuana, Portanova, Nilo, Porto, Montagna, and Forcella. The sixth seat was held and exclusively represented from the general population and, in fact, was called the *Sedile del Popolo* (Seat of the People). These were important and prestigious positions, and for that reason the offices were decorated by talented artists, though in the following century the offices were no longer used.

In the Picture Gallery of Pio Monte, there are four *bozzetti* for the Palazzo Reale in Naples (fig. 29). Two

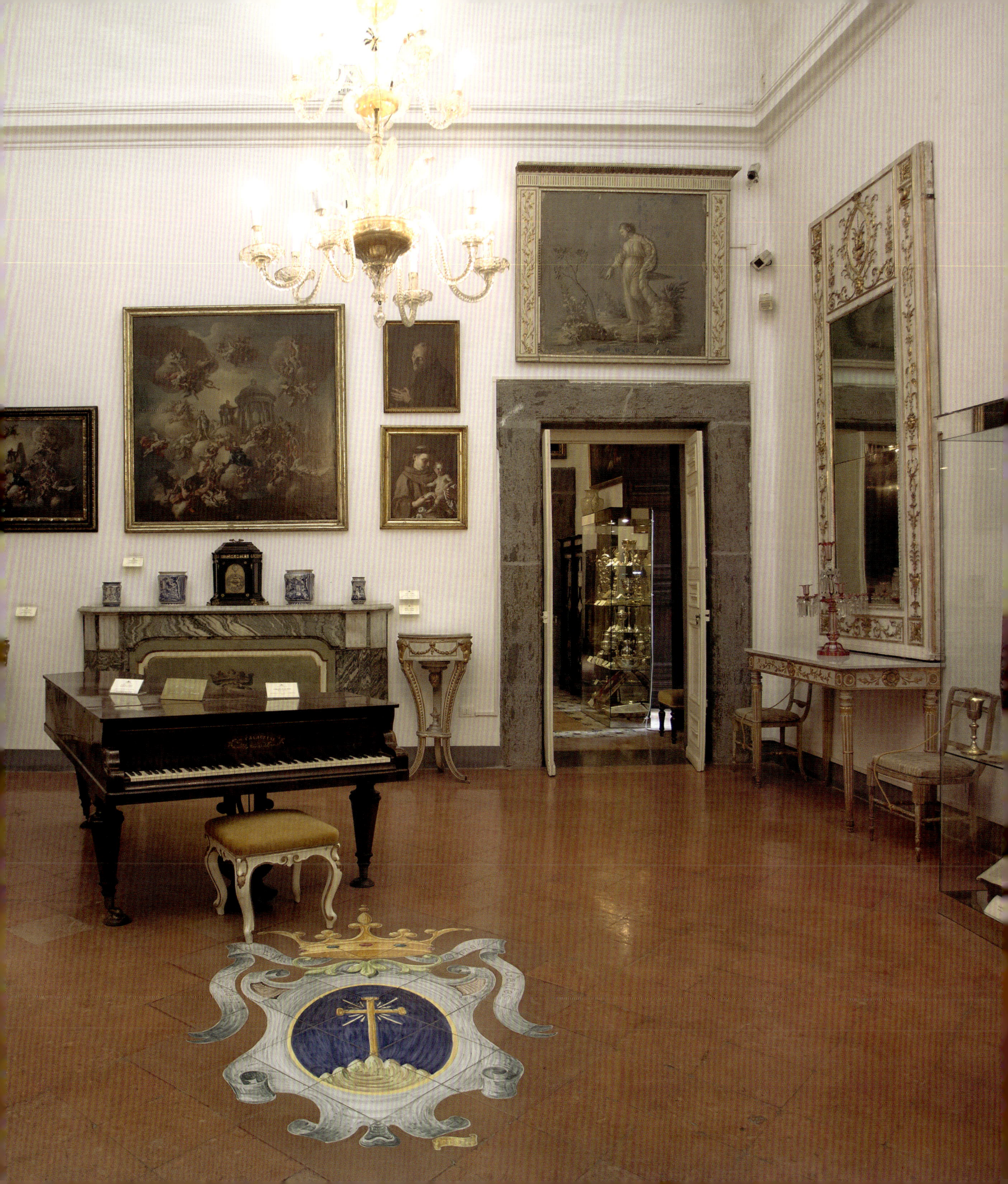

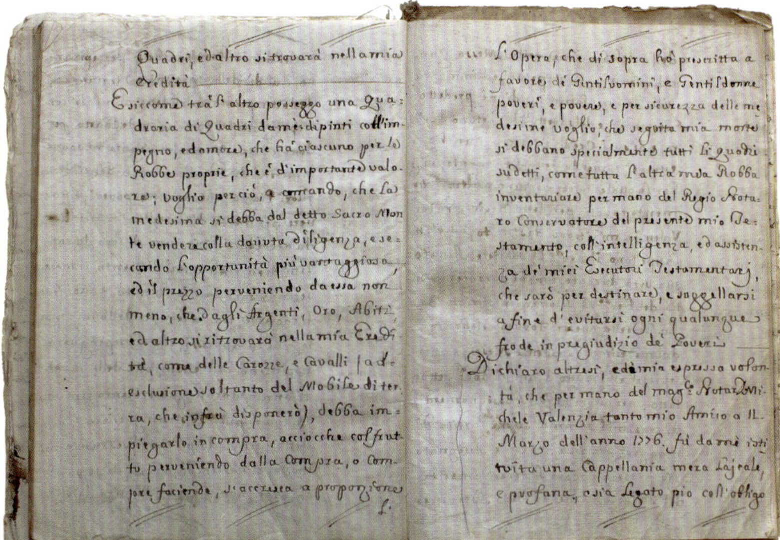

Fig. 30
*Last Will and Testament of
Francesco de Mura*, 1782,
Historical Archive of Pio
Monte della Misericordia

Fig. 31
*Last Will and Testament of
Francesco de Mura*, 1782,
Historical Archive of Pio
Monte della Misericordia

of them are very similar to *The Glory of the Princes* and one of them is included in this exhibition (cat. no. 35). From the same period, and also for the Palazzo Reale, are another two *bozzetti* of *Aurora and Tithonus* (see fig. 82), which again have some slight differences. The large canvases exhibited in the entrance hall to the Picture Gallery show *St. John the Baptist, The Penitent Magdalene, The Rest on the Flight into Egypt, Christ at the Column*, and *St. Paul the Hermit Adores the Crucifix*. At the time of his death, De Mura had these great canvases in his house in the so-called "gallery"—which was almost a personal museum. Perhaps he kept them because they were commissioned works that had not yet been paid for, or maybe because he was already quite old and very attached to his final works. He undertook them with great precision and paid special attention to even the tiniest details. Each work amply demonstrates De Mura's long experience, fastidiously employing all the elements that characterized his painting: a broken column, a small jar, a cushion, the skull, and the open book, but above all, the theatrical poses of the figures that make them seem like actors treading the planks of a stage, the folds and flutters of their clothing created with shades of color.

In 1907, there occurred an event that today would be unheard of: the sale of the artworks to the government. After more than sixty years had passed since the last public auction in 1845, the Secretary for Public Instruction, Luigi Rava (1860–1938)—to whom is credited the law of 1907 that created the Superintendents—asked for and received 23 paintings from the De Mura bequest that had remained at Pio

Monte della Misericordia. In a document signed by Superintendent Camilo Giudice Caracciolo, Duke of Sciavi, we read the following:

> on the occasion of the reorganization of the Art Gallery of the Museo Nazionale of Naples, it was evident that there was a lack of art representing the school of Neapolitan painting. Therefore, these initiatives began with the aim of obtaining a transfer of 23 paintings to be housed in a suitable venue … and with the condition that the hall in which they would be placed would maintain the presence of the name of Pio Monte della Misericordia.[8]

Then, selecting with "a not very crafty hand" (as Raffaello Causa, himself Superintendent, wrote in his publication *Opere d'arte nel Pio Monte della Misericordia a Napoli* [*Works of Art in Pio Monte della Misericordia*] in 1972), the government bought for a mere 10,000 lire 23 selected paintings from an auction presided over by Giovanni Gattini, who was then the director of the Museo Nazionale of Naples. The price paid by the government for all 23 paintings was certainly not a price that corresponded to the value of Francesco de Mura's works. The Picture Gallery was impoverished by losing one-third of its De Mura collection. Of the 63 paintings listed in 1905 by Giuseppe Ceci for Antonio Natale's selections, 23 were sold, leaving 40 with Pio Monte—though this became 41 due to another inheritance, *St. Clare Adores the Crucifix*, which had not been part of the artist's bequest. From this number, however, must be subtracted the *bozzetto The*

Stip: 50 = Scanz: 1 = Fasc: 1 = Num: 1 =

Testamento in iscritto per gli atti del N.° Michele Valenzia di Napoli, con cui il celebre
Dipintore D. Francesco de Mura dopo aver
dichiarato di non aver Figli, nè Flli, a Sll.
nè Congionti infino, e 6.° grado, nè Per-
sone da legitimamente succederli, e che
sebbene le Femine allevate in Casa
da sua Moglie; per inerire a qta, avesse
considerate con Stt.° di Adozione, ed
Dotazioni, e perciò naoltissimo siesi in-
teressato, nullameno, dando per roti,
e cassi tali Sttti per essere la robba, che
possiede, tutta opera di suo laborioso fa-
tiche, chiama a se suo Erede Utile e
particolare il S. M.° delle Sette opere d.
la Mis.a per impiegarne li frutti

Emperor Ludovico II Arrives at Monte Cassino; Raffaello Causa had many doubts about its being attributed to De Mura, and recently Nicola Spinosa has decisively concluded that it should be attributed to Pietro Bardellino. In addition, *St. Michael the Archangel* was stolen in 1983, leaving a total of 39 paintings in the Pio Monte collection today. The loss sustained by Pio Monte after the government sale—almost tantamount to expropriation—is not easily quantifiable. This kind of mistake would not have been made today: the officials of the Superintendence, with their modern cultural sensibilities, would not have consented to it. Another sticking point, which I hope will soon be settled, concerns the clause specifying that the paintings are to be placed "in a suitable venue" with a recognition of their provenance, the condition with which the Italian government had bought the paintings for such a low price.

The alarming dispersal of De Mura's works in Italy, Europe, and North America, due to their sale, should not be entirely blamed on the administration of Pio Monte della Misericordia, as some past studies have claimed.[9] The fact that they were sold, in some sense, permitted their becoming better known. Otherwise, they would have been confined to the Picture Gallery and perhaps neglected for quite some time. In addition, the auction sales had to be undertaken since the works had been donated to Pio Monte with an expressed purpose that could not be ignored. In reality, until 1845, every bequest assumed a following obligatory sale of the inherited assets, and all of the evidentiary documentation of how the auction sales were organized has been preserved. Paintings were considered, as is stated in an archived document, "*inactively* hanging on the white walls" ("inactively" being synonymous with "uselessly"), since they were not being sold to gain income for charitable works.[10] Then times changed, and the inherited works were finally conserved and exhibited in the Picture Gallery, to adorn the beautiful seventeenth-century site

of Pio Monte della Misericordia. The last auctions had been held in November 1845. From that point, no other paintings or other works of art left the collection until the regrettable sale of August 22, 1907. Mario Morelli, in the *Bollettino d'Arte* of 1910, recalls the events and admits that "the government has reaped the best of what remained of that talented artist that was conserved in Pio Monte della Misericordia."[11] (He never speaks of the paltry sum that was paid!)

The De Mura works lost to Pio Monte della Misericordia in the government sale took different paths. Soon after the sale, a beautiful self-portrait—which had been a signature work in the Pio Monte collection—with the painter sitting in an armchair, wearing sumptuous Baroque attire, in front of one of his paintings, was sent to Florence (see fig. 59). It is now in the rarely opened Vasari Corridor in the Galleria degli Uffizi, along with other self-portraits by great artists. As for the remaining 22 De Mura paintings at Pio Monte, instead of being in "an appropriate venue," as was written in the bill of sale, a different fate befell them. After 1907, they were placed in the Museo Nazionale for about fifty years. Then, in 1957, they were transferred to the renovated Museo di Capodimonte by Superintendent Bruno Molaji. After shifting from site to site, they are now distributed between Capodimonte and the Museo Duca di Martina (Villa Floridiana). In 1929, De Mura's *Allegory of Modesty* was sent to Rome to decorate the Palazzo Madama; after many years it was returned and is now housed in the Capodimonte (see fig. 76).

A more serious offense—almost an insult to the collection—was the dispersal of the series of pictorial cycles still present in the Picture Gallery, as in the case of the *bozzetto* undertaken for the large canvas at Monte Manso, founded in 1608 by Gianbattista Manso di Scala, one of the seven founders of Pio Monte della Misericordia (see fig. 74). The only thing that remains from that is the *Portrait of St. Francis di Girolamo*.

Fourteen *bozzetti* for the cycle of frescoes in the vault of Santi Severino e Sossio, with the *Vision of St. Benedict* (cat. nos. 14–15), a masterpiece from the artistic maturity of De Mura (seven of the small side panels are still in Pio Monte della Misericordia), together with *The Virgin Receiving St. Luigi Gonzaga* (cat. no. 28), are all now in the Museo Duca di Martina (Villa Floridiana). Worse was the fate of the *bozzetti* made for the extensive decorations of the Nunziatella in Pizzofalcone, the complete series of which had been conserved. Pio Monte's holding was reduced to three; now in the Museo Duca di Martina are *The Adoration of the Magi* (compare cat. no. 12), *St. Joseph's Workshop*, and *The Assumption of the Virgin* (compare cat. nos. 20–21), as well as *The Death of St. Joseph*, *The Rest on the Flight into Egypt*, and *The Assumption*, together with eight *bozzetti* of *Angels* in monochrome and *Strength, Meekness, Abundance*, and *Charity*, allegorical works for Monte di Pietà. Two *bozzetti* are under subconsignment in the Provincial Picture Gallery, directed by Lilia Rocco; *The Visitation*, undertaken, as Causa says, for the chapel of the Assumption of the church of the Certosa di San Martino (see fig. 68), and *The Assumption*, for the church of the Annunziata, have, since 1967, have been in Bari.

After seven years, aware of the results of the last sale and certainly embittered by the dividing up of the substantial De Mura painting cycles that Pio Monte della Misericordia possessed, Superintendent Vincenzo Caracciolo di Pettoranello and the other *Governatori* decreed on October 9, 1914, that "anything that might contain a historical artistic interest was inalienable," thus terminating sales of any kind and the transfer of artistic assets, a resolution that was dated more than a century ago. Just twenty-five years later, the Italian government considered legislation regarding the protection and safeguarding of artistic and cultural patrimony, and Fundamental Law 1089 was issued in 1939.

Recently, we thought it would be fitting to reorganize the Francesco de Mura paintings in the Picture Gallery and rearrange the halls dedicated to him by hanging his decorative cycle works in order by date and patron, assisting scholars in reconstructing De Mura's artistic process. Our desire was to give our artist, who had been set aside and forgotten, the prominence he deserved. We began a series of events to further this aim. The first, in 2010, was Dr. Arthur Blumenthal's lecture at the Istituto Italiano di Cultura in New York. In 2012, his first lecture spawned another, very scholarly one, well supplied with images, on the same theme, this time in Naples at Pio Monte della Misericordia. It featured the works of De Mura that are found abroad.

We long wanted to find the funds for the first monographic exhibition of the great De Mura and, to accompany the show, a scholarly catalogue, until now non-existent. At last, the time that we have been waiting for has arrived. I am happy to admire the paintings from the collection of Pio Monte della Misericordia that are in this prestigious exhibition: *The Glory of the Princes* (cat. no. 35), a *bozzetto* for the fresco in the Palazzo Reale in Naples; *The Adoration of the Magi* (cat. no. 12), a study for the fresco in the apse of the church of the Nunziatella; and *Christ Receiving St. Joseph into Heaven* (cat. no. 13), a *bozzetto* for the cupola of the church of San Giuseppe dei Ruffi. We admire and salute the success of this exhibition, the fruit of tenacity, of great commitment, and of great love for Francesco de Mura.

Translation by Edward Borsoi, Professor Emeritus, Rollins College

Notes

1. Archivio Storico del Pio Monte della Misericordia (ASPMM), *La Fondo Antico*, transcribed apostolic brief.
2. Bobina Magnetica Registrata, ASPMM, *Carteggio*, Fa/6, 1972, fasc. 1.
3. Testament and codicils of Francesco de Mura; notaries: Michele Valenzia and Giuseppe Ventrella, Aug. 19, 1782, Collocation: ASPMM, Patrimonio [Patrimony], *Eredità*, Bib LXII, vol. 114, fasc. 2, folios 1r–44v.
4. ASPMM, *Libro delle Conclusioni*, 1772–1784, Deliberation of June 30, 1783, folio 327v.
5. Published in Naples, Dec. 9, 1782: ASPMM, Patrimonio, *Eredità*, Bib LXII, vol. 114, p. iii.
6. Nicola Spinosa, "Francesco de Mura al Pio Monte," in *Il Pio Monte della Misericordia di Napoli nel Quarto Centenario*, ed. Mario Pisani Massamormile (Naples: Electa Napoli, 2003), 193–211.
7. Raffaello Causa, *Opere d'Arte nel Pio Monte della Misericordia* (Cava dei Tirreni: Mauro, 1970), 128.
8. ASPMM, Deliberations from July to Dec. 1906, vol. 118, art. 2, p. 1; ASPMM, Deliberations from July to Dec. 1907, vol. 119, art. 31, p. 199.
9. Loredana Gazzara, "Note e documenti inediti per lo studio delle collezioni della Quadreria del Pio Monte della Misericordia (I)," *Napoli Nobilissima* (5th ser.), 9 (May–Aug. 2008): 160–79; Loredana Gazzara, "Note e documenti inediti per lo studio delle collezioni della Quadreria del Pio Monte della Misericordia (II)," *Napoli Nobilissima* (5th ser.), 9 (Sept.–Dec. 2008): 213–38.
10. ASPMM, Volume delle Deliberazioni, Jan. 8, 1838, fol. 151v.
11. Mario Morelli, "I dipinti di Francesco de Mura acquistati per la Galleria del Museo Nazionale di Napoli," *Bollettino d'Arte* (1910): 293–302.

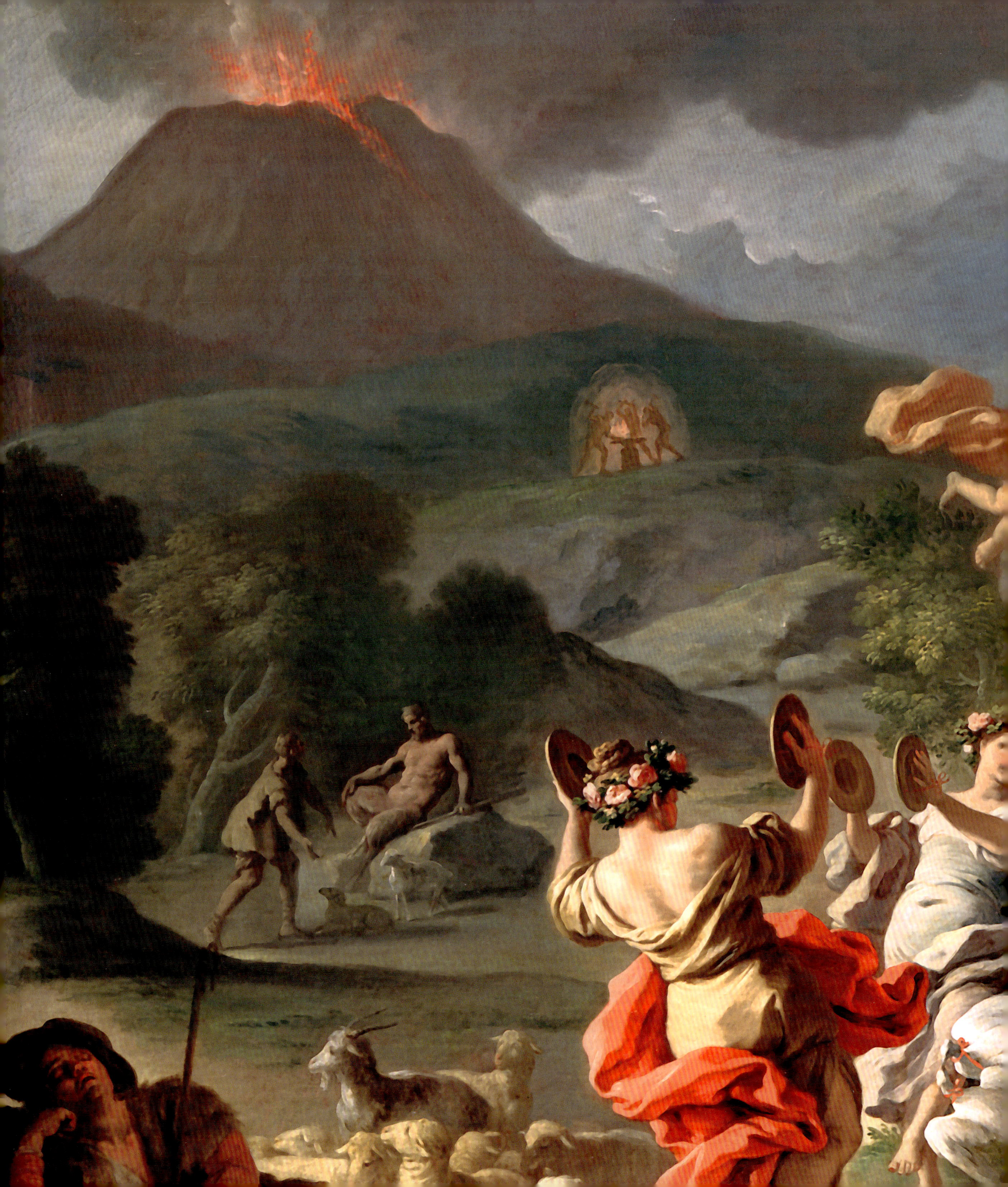

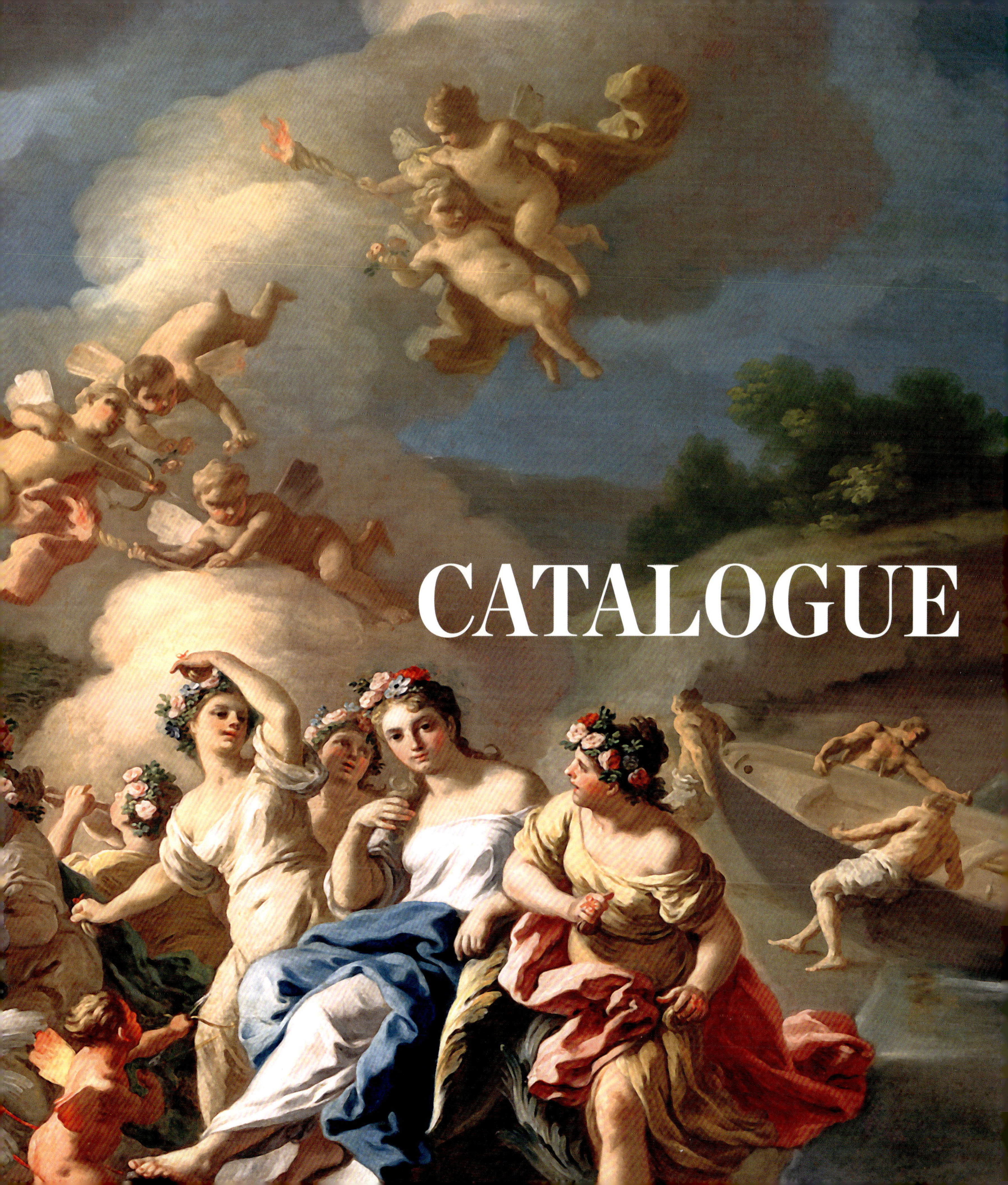

CATALOGUE

1

Francesco de Mura
Charity, ca. 1718–20?
Oil on canvas, 29 × 24 in. (73.7 × 60.9 cm)
Stamped on reverse: *Francis Leedham* [He lived from 1794 to 1870, and was the leading conservator/picture-liner in London in the 1830s; his studio was at 83 Berwick St., in Soho.]
Collection of Federico Castelluccio

Of the virtues, charity is considered the greatest of all. The word "charity" is often used interchangeably with "love," as in the translation of the Greek word *agape* (in Latin, *caritas*) in Paul's letter to the Christian congregation in Corinth: "When I was a child, I talked like a child, I thought like a child, I reasoned like a child … And now these three [virtues] remain: Faith, Hope, and Love. But the greatest of these is Love [Charity]."[1] By extension, the allegorical personification of Charity is often depicted as Maternal Love, with a mother nursing a baby while tending to two other children.[2] Cesare Ripa, in his *Iconologia* of 1611, illustrated and described how one should depict the virtue of Charity (fig. 32); De Mura uses these iconographical elements in an original way. The mother in this work nurses an infant who sits on her lap, as a second child leans on her lap and holds a small loaf of bread; at her feet is the eldest child eating from a bowl with a spoon. The figures form part of a right-angle triangle composition. The mother wears a flowing cape of bright red-orange—the symbolic color of Charity—that flies upwards behind her. The fire over her head is a symbol of "the fire of charity."[3]

Until recently, this painting had been thought to be by Francesco Solimena. In 2015, Nicola Spinosa identified it rather as an early work of Francesco de Mura, possibly a *bozzetto* (oil sketch) for a lost composition. Comparisons to the *Madonna Presenting St. Dominic with the Rosary*, a *bozzetto* done by De Mura in about 1718–20 (fig. 33; a study for the larger work in Monte Manso di Scala in Naples),[4] reveals striking similarities—in the drapery, the rock bases, the infants, and the light and shadows—that allow us to date this work also to around 1718–20, when De Mura was in his early twenties. What Spinosa wrote about that work can be applied here as well: "Compared to Solimenesque examples, the young De Mura used lighter, almost precious, materials, as well as evidently drawing on a more intimate (almost sweetened) expressive rendering by way of a sumptuous and refined manner."[5] Thus, *Charity* distinguishes De Mura from his master even at this early stage. Twenty-three years later, De Mura painted another, very different *Allegory of Charity* (cat. no. 19), which, nevertheless, featured some of the same elements: pyramidal composition, flying red cape, nursing child, etc.

1. 1 Corinthians 13:11–13.
2. Perhaps this was to differentiate the depiction of Maternal Love from images of the Madonna and Child.
3. The Renaissance humanist Pico della Mirandola, in his *Oration on the Dignity of Man* (1487), wrote that the highest point of being human is like the angels that "burn with charity."
4. See Vincenzo Rizzo, "L'Opera giovanile di Francesco de Mura," *Napoli Nobilissima* 17 (1978): 95, fig. 2.
5. Nicola Spinosa, *Museo e Gallerie Nazionali di Capodimonte: Dipinti del XVIII secolo; La scuola napoletana* (Naples: Electa Napoli, 2010), 52. See also Vincenzo Rizzo, "Francesco de Mura," *Dizionario biografico degli italiani*, vol. 38 (Rome: Istituto della Enciclopedia italiana, 1990), 238.

Provenance:
Private collection, England, 1780s–1840s?; Auction Gallery of the Palm Beaches, Inc., July 13, 2015, auction, LiveAuction.com, lot 144 (Italian School, 19th Century, "Madonna and Child")

Fig. 32
"Charity," in Cesare Ripa, *Iconologia* (Padua, 1611), p. 72

Fig. 33
Francesco de Mura, *Madonna Presenting St. Dominic with the Rosary,* ca. 1718–20, oil on canvas, 29⅞ × 20 in. (75.5 × 51 cm), Cobbe Hatchlands Park

Fig. 32

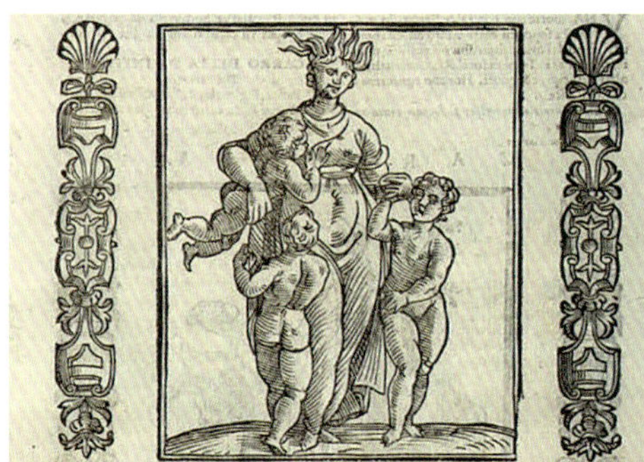

Fig. 33

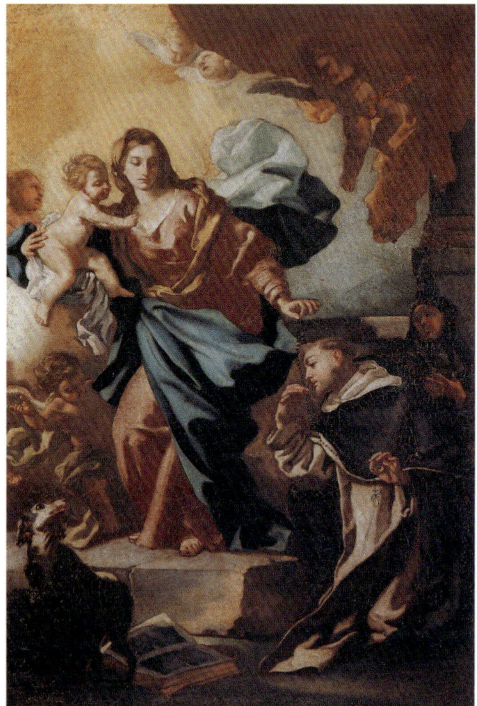

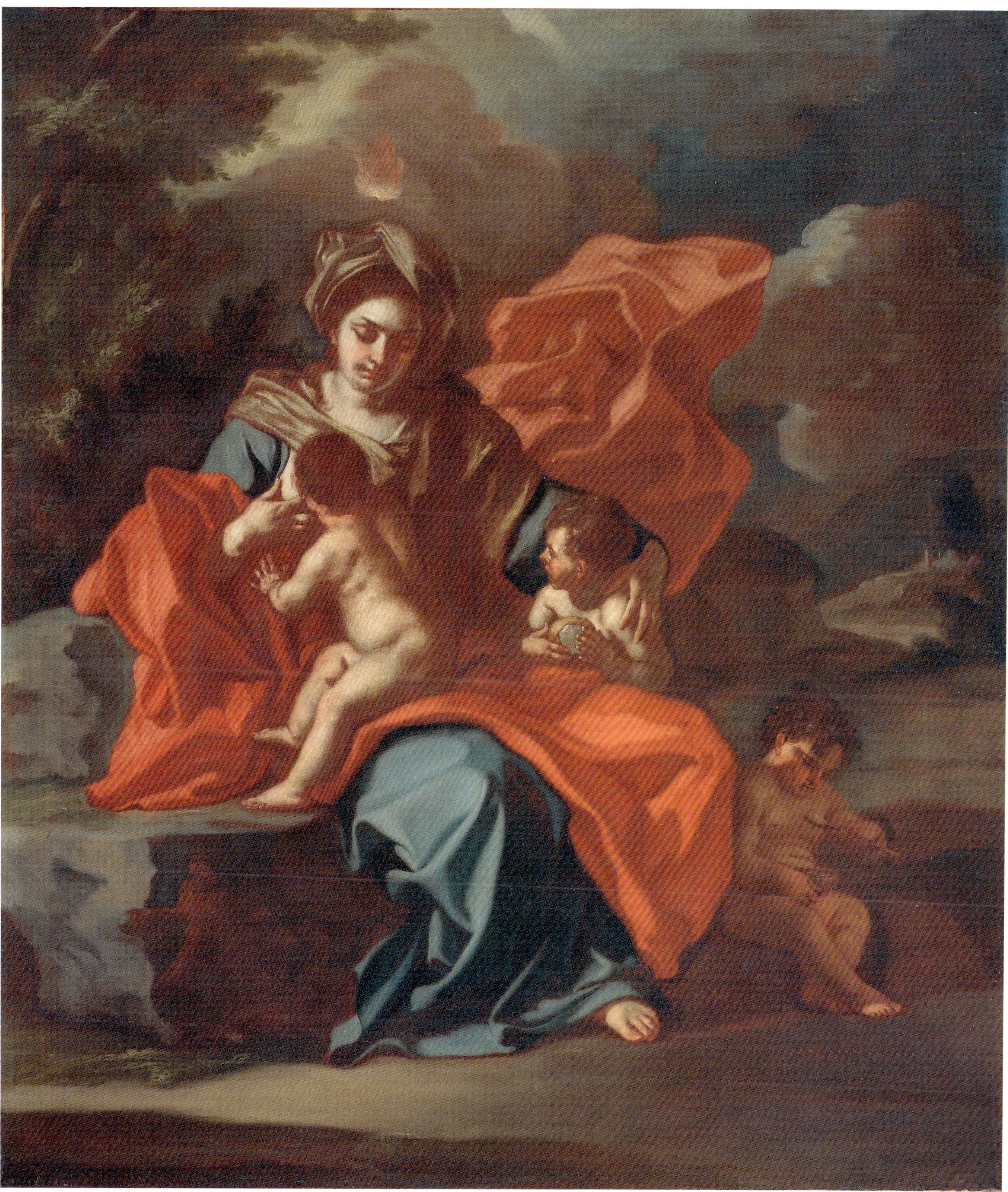

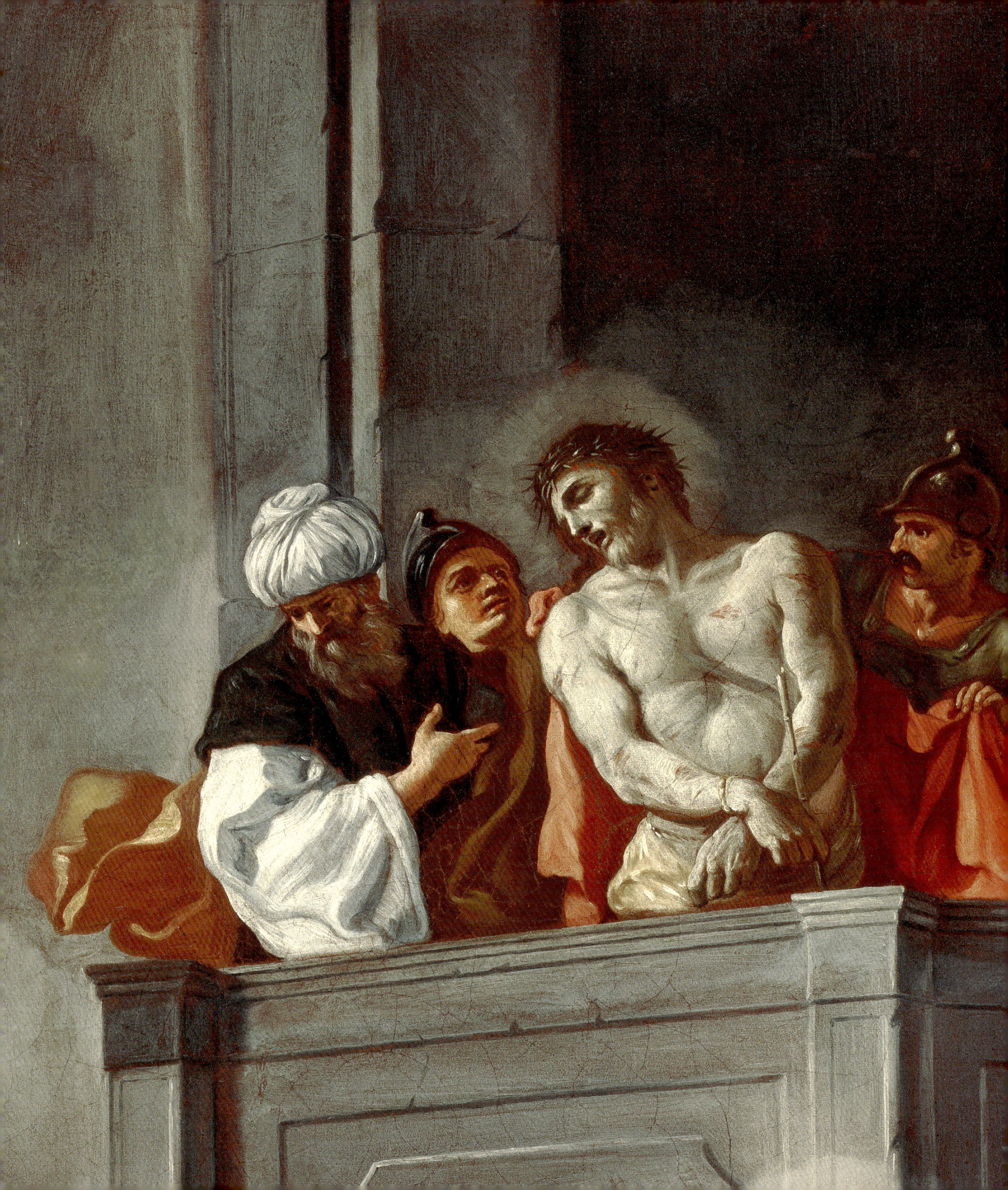

2

Francesco de Mura
Ecce Homo, ca. 1726
Oil on canvas, 25⅜ × 30¼ in. (62.2 × 74.9 cm)
Bob Jones University Collection, acc. no. P.51.15

Ecce homo ("Behold, the man!" or "Here is the man!") are the words shouted by Procurator Pontius Pilate in the Latin translation of the Gospel of John 19:5, when he presents a scourged Jesus, bound and crowned with thorns, to a hostile crowd shortly before Jesus' crucifixion: "Then Jesus came out, wearing the wreath of thorns and the crimson robe, and Pilate said to them, 'Behold, the man!' When the high priests and their supporters saw Jesus, they cried, 'Crucify him! Crucify him!'" The scene of the *Ecce Homo* is a standard element of cycles illustrating the Passion of Christ (Ecce Homo follows the Flagellation of Christ, the Crowning with Thorns, and the Mocking of Christ). This depiction shows the haloed Jesus bare-chested, with bloody stripes from his recent flagellation. His wrists are tied together, and in his right hand he holds a stick scepter, as he turns his head to his right and looks downward. Pilate, wearing a white turban, speaks the words, "Behold, the man!" pointing to Jesus, whose robe is held by two soldiers. They stand on a balcony overlooking an open square filled with thirteen men, women, and children in various states of agitation, some pointing to Jesus, others scowling. Here, too, we see several turbans, and the bearded man looking to the right has his head covered in a prayer shawl. This early in De Mura's career (he was still in his twenties), it is remarkable to see the smaller size of the figures, the theatrically composed narrative, and the brilliant colors—especially the turquoise, rose, and fiery yellow-orange. These elements forecast the break with the monumental style of Solimena, De Mura's master.

Nicola Spinosa identified this work as a *bozzetto* for a larger painting of *Ecce Homo* (see fig. 35), one of two pictures at the basilica of Santa Maria dell'Assunta at Castel di Sangro in Isernia (Abruzzo), in the province of L'Aquila.[1] The pendant is a *Christ Carrying the Cross with St. Veronica*, for which there is a *bozzetto* in the Molinari Pradelli collection (fig. 34).[2] The works were commissioned about 1725–26 for the consecration of the church of the Collegiata dell'Assunta, and, since the final painting was executed about 1725–27, this oil sketch must also date from about the same time. There is an almost identical version of this painting, also in Greenville, S.C., in the Bob and Teresa Wilson collection (cat. no. 3).

1. Spinosa, *Pittura napoletana del Settecento*, 1:334. Roger Ward, in his review of the exhibition *Botticelli to Tiepolo* in *The Burlington Magazine* 137, no. 1106 (May 1995): 347, doubted that this *bozzetto* of *Ecce Homo* is by De Mura; he suggested calling it "after Francesco de Mura."
2. Chiara Naldi, essay in *Baroque Art from the Holy Sepulchre: The Image of Jerusalem in the Pre-Alps*, ed. Manuela Kahn-Rossi and Chiara Naldi, exhib. cat. (Lugano: Galleria Canesso, 2014), 96.

Provenance:
John Levy Galleries, New York, until 1951, when purchased by Bob Jones.

Exhibitions:
Columbus Gallery of Fine Arts, Ohio, before 1954 (1952 or 1953); Palazzo Reale, Naples, July 1980–Jan. 1981, *Pittura Sacra a Napoli nell '700*; North Carolina Museum of Art, Raleigh, June 7–Sept. 2, 1984, *Baroque Paintings from the Bob Jones University Collection*; Yale University Art Gallery, New Haven, Conn., John and Mable Ringling Museum of Art, Sarasota, Fla., Nelson-Atkins Museum of Art, Kansas City, Mo., Sept. 9–June 12, 1988, *A Taste for Angels: Neapolitan Painting in North America, 1650–1750*; Philbrook Museum of Art, Tulsa, Okla., Joslyn Art Museum, Omaha, Neb., New Orleans Museum of Art, La., Birmingham Museum of Art, Ala., Dayton Art Institute, Ohio, Sept. 11, 1994–Sept. 17, 1995, *Botticelli to Tiepolo: Three Centuries of Italian Painting from Bob Jones University*.

Bibliography:
Hans Tietze and E. Tietze-Conrat, *The Bob Jones University Collection of Religious Paintings* (Greenville: BJU Press, 1954), 84–85 (as Solimena); "Religious Art on the Campus," *Arts* 32, no. 7 (April 1958): 39; Alfred Scharf, ed., *Bob Jones University Catalogue of the Art Collection: Italian and French Paintings* (Greenville: BJU Press, 1962), 1:161 (as Solimena); Burton B. Fredricksen and Federico Zeri, *Census of Pre-Nineteenth Century Italian Paintings in North American Public Collections* (Cambridge: Harvard University Press, 1972),

Fig. 34
Francesco de Mura, *Christ Carrying the Cross with St. Veronica*, ca. 1725–27, oil *bozzetto*, 24 × 29 in. (61 × 73.5 cm), Molinari Pradelli collection

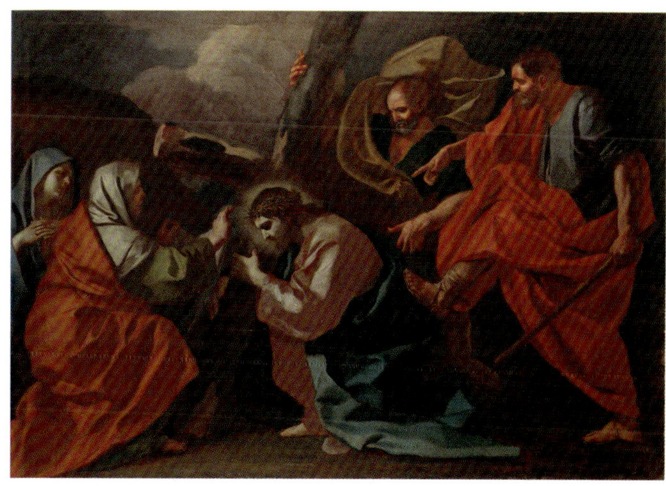

2 — continued

284; Nicola Spinosa, *Pittura sacra a Napoli nel '700*, exhib. cat. (Naples: Società Editrice Napolentana, 1980), 102, 334, no. 53, pl. 284; D. Stephen Pepper, *Bob Jones University Collection of Religious Art, Italian Paintings* (Greenville: BJU Press, 1984), 80, 234 (ill.), Raleigh 1984, no. 26; David Steel, *Baroque Paintings from the Bob Jones University Collection* (Raleigh: North Carolina Museum of Art, 1984), 80, 91–93, no. 81.1; Nicola Spinosa, *Pittura napoletana del Settecento*, vol. 1, *Dal barocco al rococò* (Naples: Electa Napoli, 1993), 156, 334 (ill.), no. 239, fig. 284; *A Taste for Angels: Neapolitan Painting in North America, 1650–1750*, exhib. cat. (New Haven: Yale University Art Gallery, 1987), 271–72, no. 33; Christopher Wright, *The World's Master Paintings: From the Early Renaissance to the Present Day* (London: Routledge, 1992), 1:417; Richard Townsend, *Botticelli to Tiepolo: Three Centuries of Italian Painting from Bob Jones University* (Tulsa: Philbrook Museum of Art, 1994), 186–87; Roger Ward, "Tulsa: Botticelli to Tiepolo: Three Centuries of Italian Painting from Bob Jones University," exhibition review, *The Burlington Magazine* 137, no. 1106 (May 1995): 347; Christie's, *Old Master Pictures* (London: Christie's, Dec. 15, 2000), 29.

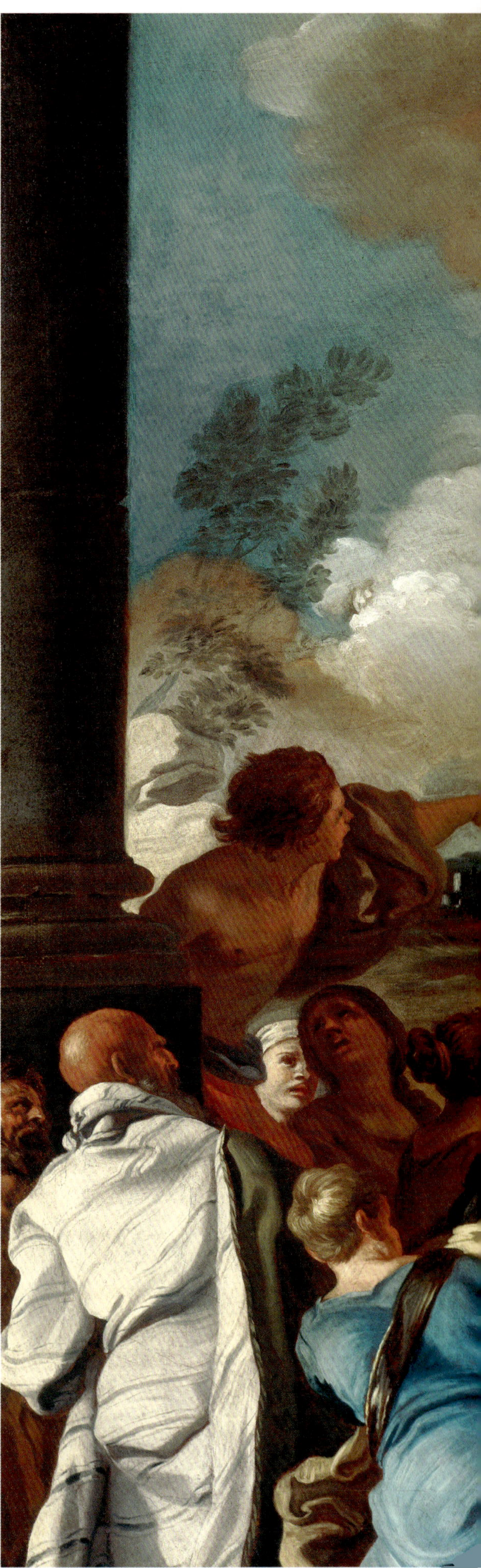

Cat. 2

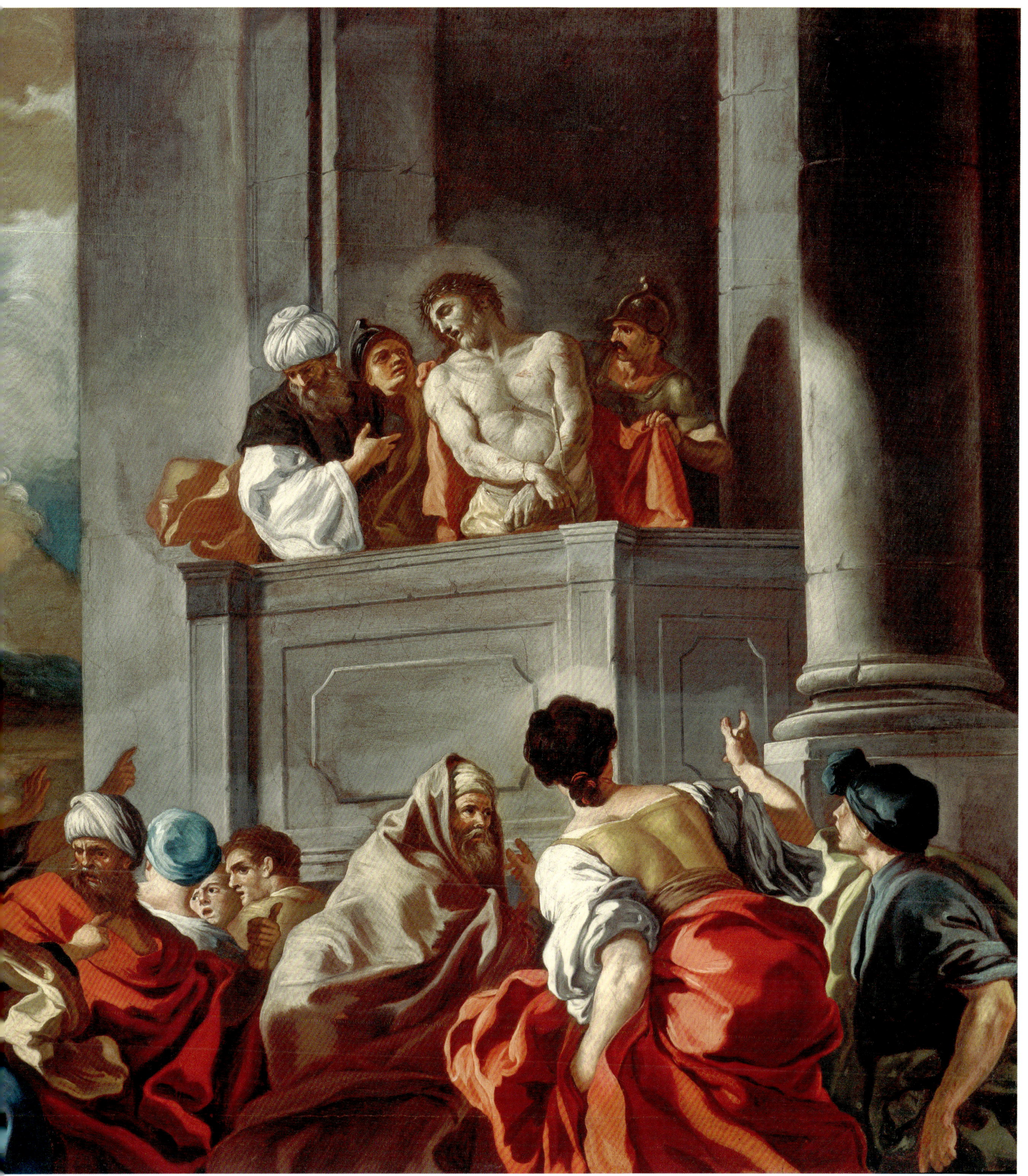

3

Francesco de Mura
Ecce Homo, ca. 1726
Oil on canvas, 24½ × 31⅛ in. (62.2 × 79.1 cm)
Collection of Bob and Teresa Wilson

This painting could be a replica done by De Mura of his *bozzetto* for the large *Ecce Homo* in the basilica of Santa Maria dell'Assunta at Castel di Sangro, Isernia, L'Aquila (fig. 35). But arguments can also be made for this *Ecce Homo*, owned by Bob and Teresa Wilson, being the earlier of the two *bozzetti*. This wider version (by 1⅝ in., or 4 cm) has somewhat more muted, warmer colors; a softer, suppler light throughout; less rigid outlines of the figures; and, generally, more convincing, less flat, and less distorted anatomies. The more sculptural and pleasing forms seen here seem to exist in a real, three-dimensional space, and the overall coloring is closer to the *Veronica bozzetto* (see fig. 34), the pendant for the *Ecce Homo* in the Molinari Pradelli collection. The final, much larger painting in Castel di Sangro differs from both of these *bozzetti* in the landscape background and the more elaborate balcony decoration, as well as in a slight variation in the pose of Jesus (he looks down over his left shoulder, not his right) and the more prominent lighting of his figure.

Provenance:
Christie's, London, December 15, 2000, sale no. 8986, lot 38 (published in the catalogue).

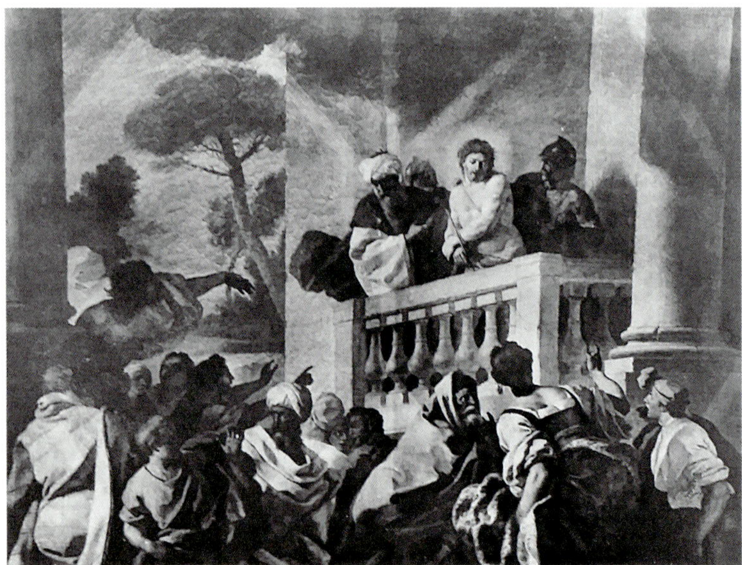

Fig. 35
Francesco de Mura, *Ecce Homo*, ca. 1727, oil on canvas, basilica of Santa Maria dell'Assunta, Castel di Sangro, Isernia, L'Aquila

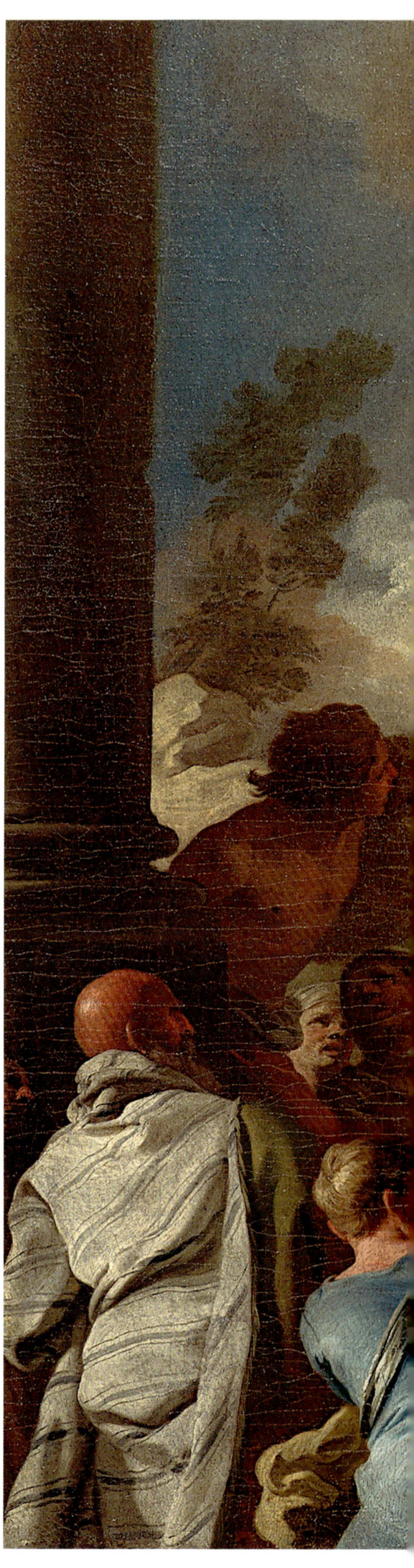

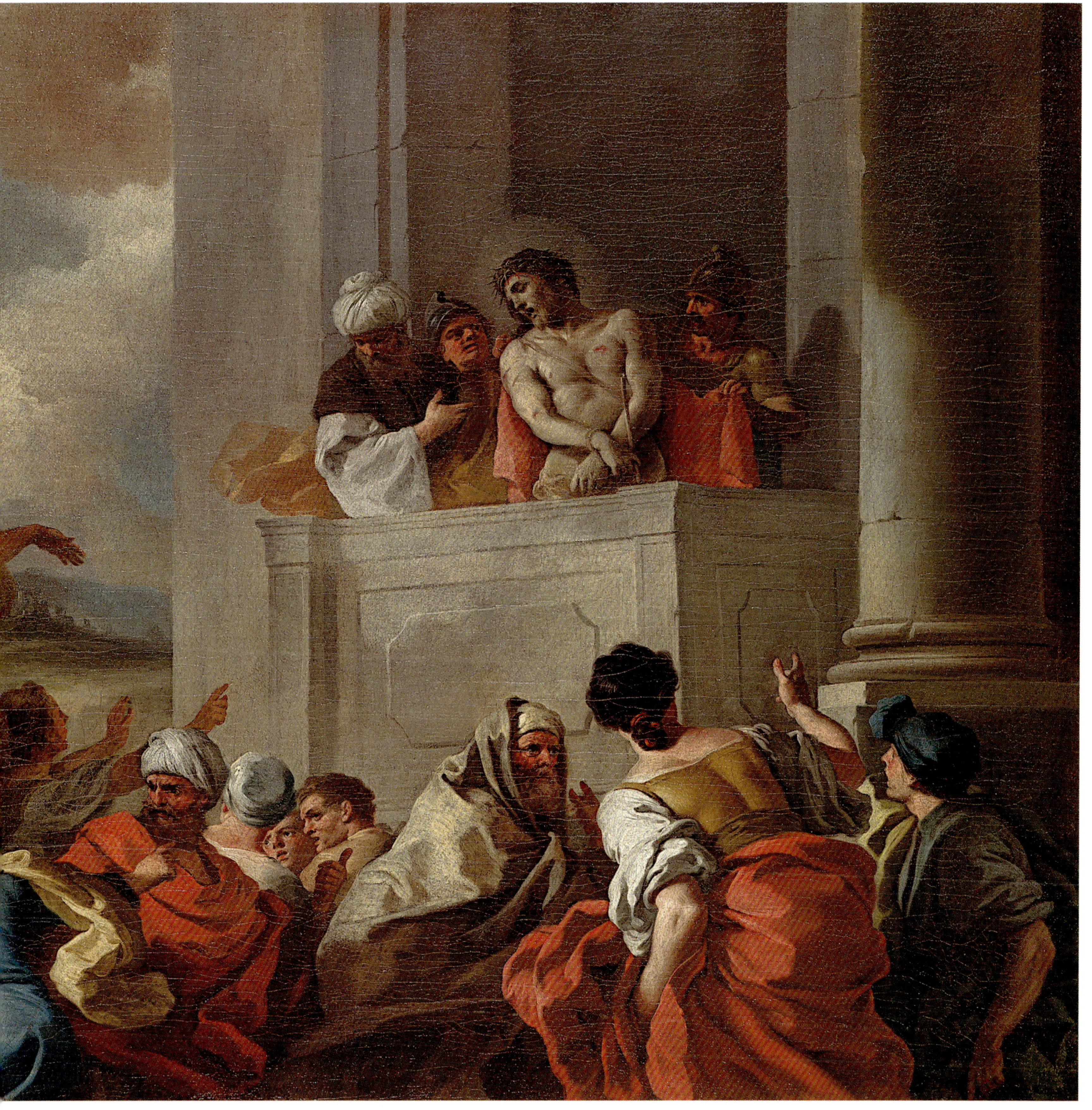

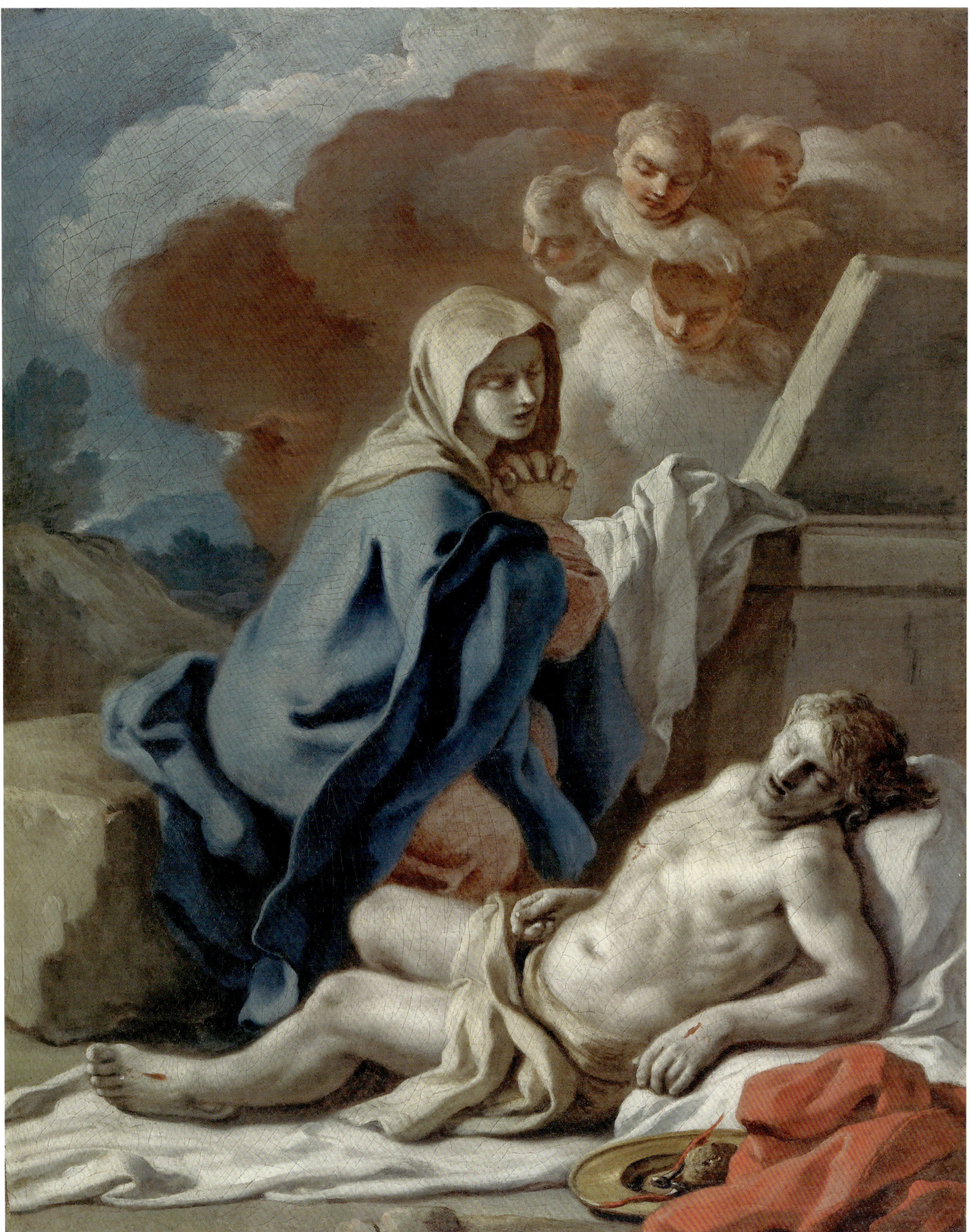

4

Francesco de Mura
Pietà, ca. 1725–30
Oil on canvas, 24⅞ × 19⅜ in. (63.2 × 49.3 cm)
The Walters Art Museum, acc. no. 37.1125

The Italian word *pietà* means "pity" or "compassion." The subject of this work is common in Christian art, although mentioned only indirectly in the gospels.[1] It refers to the moment, after Jesus has been removed from the cross, when his mother Mary weeps over his dead body. The scene here shows Mary, covered in her blue robe, sitting on a stone block near the tomb of Joseph of Arimathea (who had offered his rock tomb for Jesus' burial). Her hands are clasped tightly under her chin as she gazes sorrowfully down at Jesus, who lies against a shroud-covered boulder, seemingly propping up his body with his bent left arm. His crimson robe lies in the lower-right corner next to a salver containing a thorn wreath and two bloodied nails from the cross. Mary's body creates a diagonal (from upper right to lower left) with the stone slab leaning against a sarcophagus behind Jesus. Four winged cherubs float in the clouds above, and the hills of Jerusalem are seen in the distance. The cherubs, Mary, and the dead Christ form a triangle close to the picture plane.

The subject was meant for the contemplation of Christ's sacrifice. This painting is De Mura's oil *bozzetto* for the *Pietà* on the altar of the church of the Santissima Annunziata in Airola, near Benevento in the Campania; the painting is now in the Museo Civico in Airola (fig. 36). This 1730 commission was among De Mura's first after leaving Solimena's studio, and he seems to have considered several ideas for the work. The final result in Airola appears to have been executed very much under Solimena's influence. This oil sketch, however, has a translucent quality, as if it were painted in watercolors. This may reflect the artist's working quickly to get his idea on the canvas, without spending too much time on a fully realized composition.

De Mura's newly cleaned series of paintings in the Holy Sepulcher in Jerusalem also feature a large *Lamentation* depicting the Madonna and the Magdalene at the foot of the cross, of about 1730 (fig. 37).[3] The overall darkness and heavy figures of all of these works point to De Mura's continued closeness to his master.

1. Matthew 27:55–67; Mark 15:40–47; Luke 23:49–56; John 19:38–42.
2. Nicola Spinosa, "Neapolitan Painting in the Holy Land," in *Baroque Art from the Holy Sepulchre: The Image of Jerusalem in the Pre-Alps*, ed. Manuela Kahn-Rossi and Chiara Naldi (Lugano: Galleria Canesso, 2014), 90ff.
3. *Ibid.*

Provenance:
Don Marcello Massarenti collection, Rome (1897 catalogue, no. 165, as Guido Reni); purchased by Henry Walters, Baltimore, 1902; by bequest to the Walters Art Museum, 1931.

Exhibition:
Washington County Museum of Fine Arts, Hagerstown, Md., 1951, "The Life of Christ," no. 25 (as Italian, 17th century).

Bibliography:
Edouard van Esbroeck, *Catalogue du musée de peinture, sculpture et archéologie au Palais Accoramboni* (Rome, 1897), 1:31, no. 165; *Walters Catalogue* (1909), no. 527 (as Guido Reni); Federico Zeri, *Italian Paintings in the Walters Art Gallery* (Baltimore: Walters Art Gallery, 1976), 2:548–549, no. 437, pl. 286 (as De Mura, tentatively dated to the 1720s); David Nolta, "Francesco de Mura: Lives and Works" (Ph.D. diss., Yale University, 1989), 1: 300, 311.

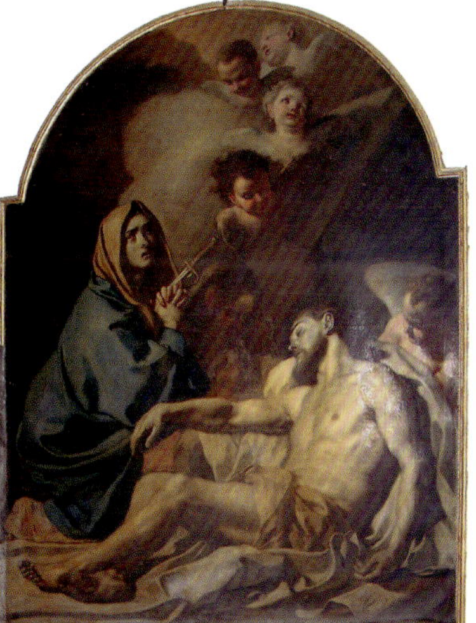

Fig. 36
Francesco de Mura, *Pietà*, 1727, oil on canvas, 70½ × 50 in. (180 × 127 cm), Museo Civico, Airola

Fig. 37
Francesco de Mura and assistants, *Lamentation*, ca. 1730, oil on canvas, 50 × 70⅞ in. (127 × 180 cm), Holy Sepulcher, Jerusalem

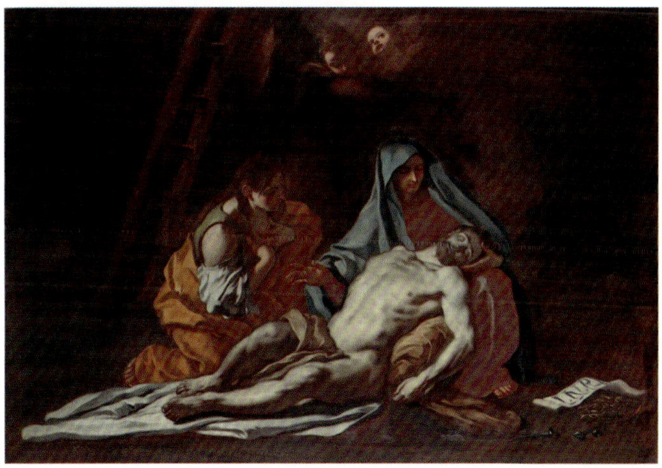

5

Francesco de Mura
St. Didacus of Alcalá (*San Diego de Alcalá*), ca. 1727
Oil on canvas, 39½ × 29⅜ in. (100.5 × 74.5 cm)
Inscription on verso: *Orga/di Francesco di Muro/del Pri[nci]pe di Scilla /n.o/No. 85*
Collection of Frank and Demi Rogozienski

In this painting, the Franciscan saint sits on a boulder and holds a crucifix in his left hand. He pulls the crucifix towards his heart as he gazes towards heaven; two cherubs watch him from the upper right. The saint is garbed in the brown habit of his order and tilts to the left, opening his left hand in a gesture of prayer. Light pours into the dark painting from the upper left, spotlighting his head, which is framed with a transparent halo. The tilt of his body and the open left hand create a strong diagonal from upper left to lower right.

The monk is San Diego de Alcalá (in English, St. Didacus of Alcalá; 1400–63), a Spanish lay brother of the Order of Friars Minor.[1] Originally, he was a wandering hermit. He died at Alcalá de Henares in 1463 and was canonized by Pope Sixtus V in 1588. Didacus is the saint after whom the Franciscan mission of San Diego (in San Diego, California) was named and thus is the patron saint of the city of San Diego. Founded on July 16, 1769, by Spanish friar (now saint) Junípero Serra, the mission of San Diego was the first Franciscan mission in the province of Las Californias of the Viceroyalty of New Spain.

Don Guglielmo Ruffo, prince of Scilla and duke of Guardia Lombardi (a town near Naples) probably commissioned this work from De Mura in about 1730 as part of a group of other images of saints (fig. 38). Vincenzo Pugliese has noted the similarity of these images to compositional models of Solimena, whose studio De Mura had recently left.[2] The name of Prince Ruffo, a great promoter of De Mura, is found in an inscription on the reverse of the unrelined *St. Didacus*, along with the number 85, inscribed probably during an inventory of his collection at Ruffo's death in 1747. (De Mura executed a portrait of Prince Ruffo in 1738, now in the Palazzo Reale, Caserta.) The figure of San Diego in the Rogozienski collection closely follows that of St. Bertharius in De Mura's *Martyrdom of St. Bertharius* in the Molinari Pradelli collection (fig. 39), a work done in 1731 for the monastery of Monte Cassino (it survives only in this *bozzetto*).

1. "Diego" is a corruption of "Santiago" (St. James).
2. Christie's, *Dipinti e disegni antichi* (Rome: Christie's, 2004), lot 604, cat. no. 2462; Vincenzo Pugliese, "A proposito di alcuni dipinti del De Mura in Puglia," *Per la storia dell'arte in Italia e in Europa* (Rome: Università degli Studi di Bari Aldo Moro, 2004), 53ff.

Provenance:
Guglielmo Ruffo, prince of Scilla and duke of Guardialombarda (inventory of March 27, 1747); Im Kinsky auction house, Frankfurt, Germany, Old Master Sale, Nov. 27, 2014, lot 851.

Fig. 38
Francesco de Mura, *San Pasquale (St. Paschal)*, ca. 1730, oil on canvas, 32 × 27⅛ in. (81.5 × 69 cm), private collection

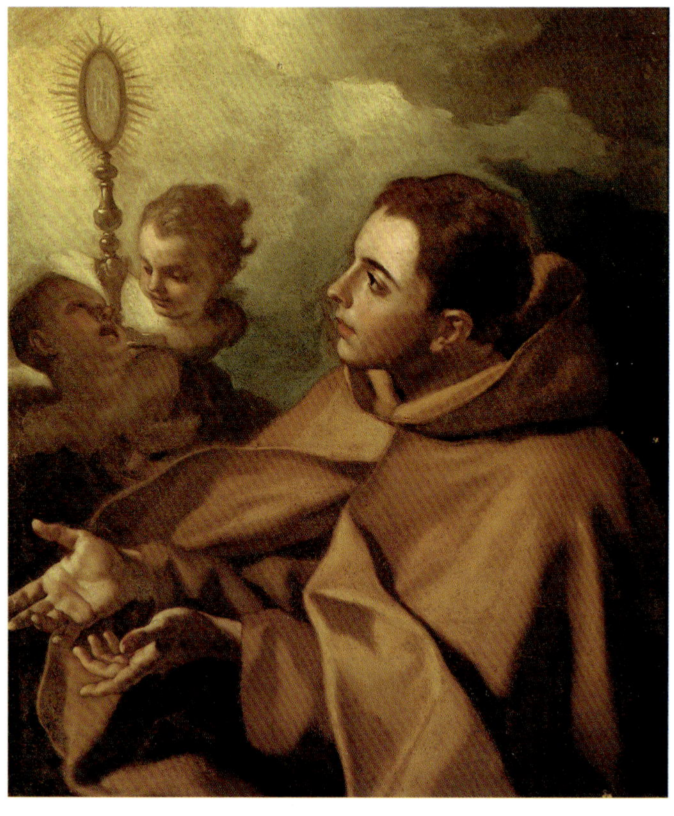

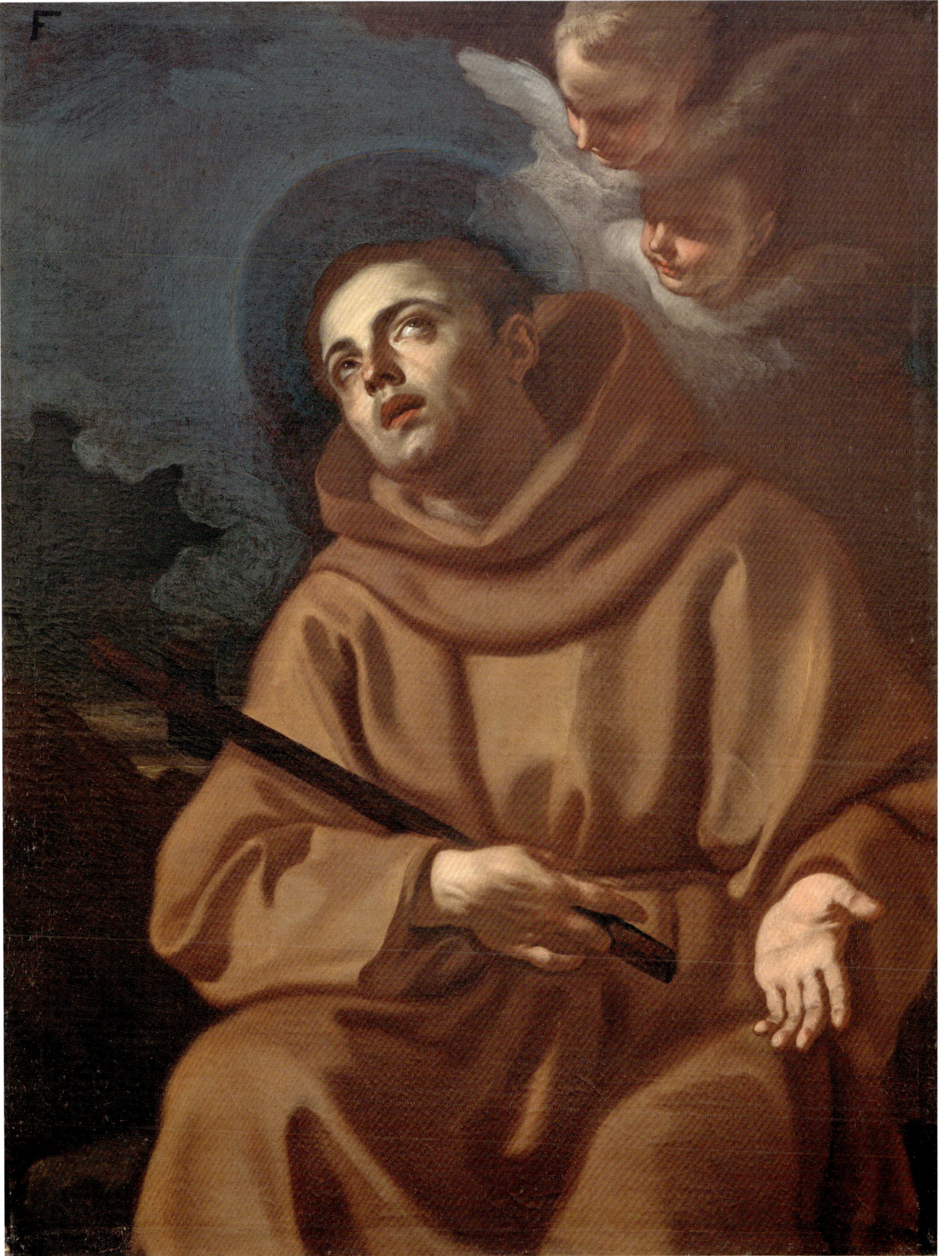
F

5 — continued

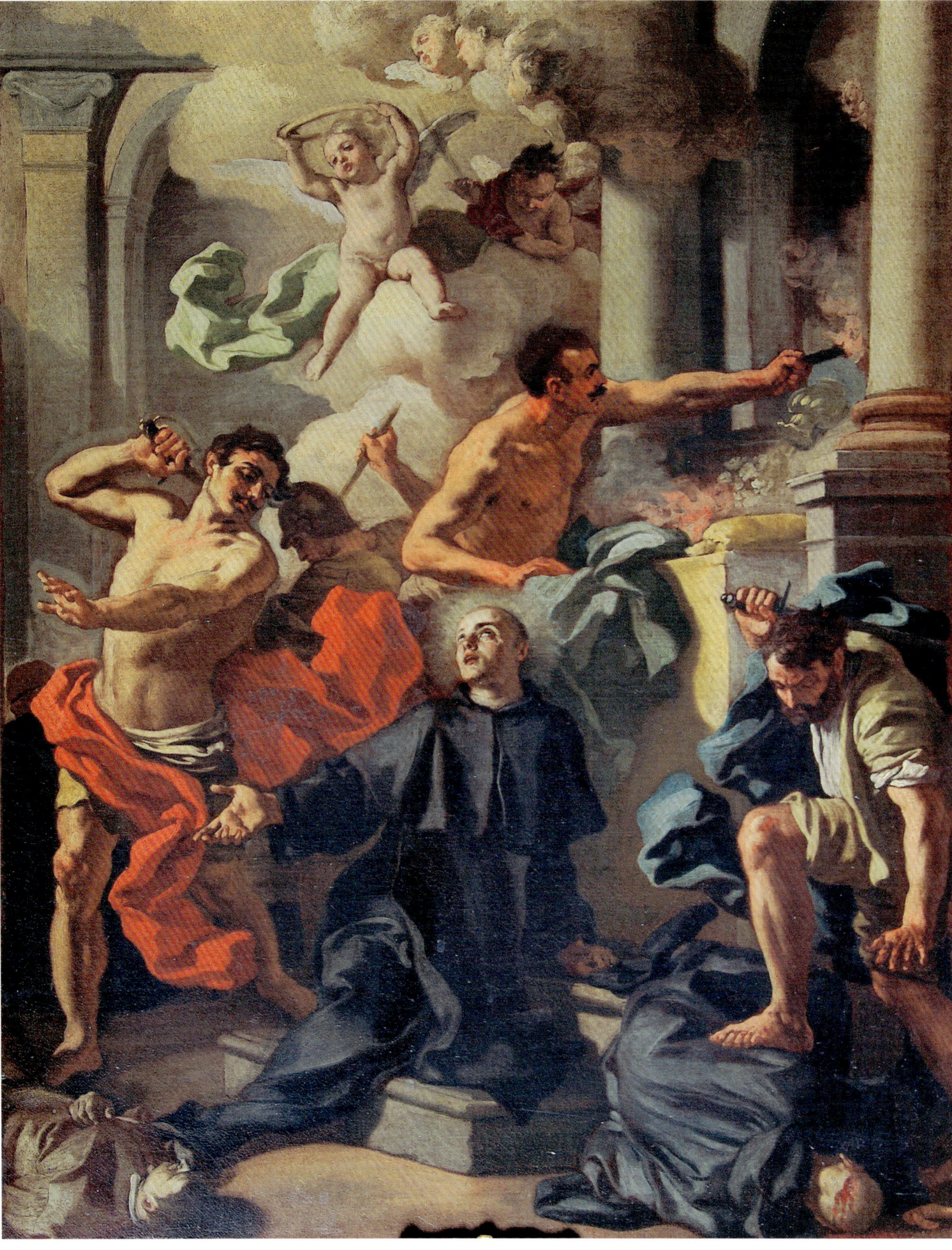

Fig. 39
Francesco de Mura,
*Martyrdom of St.
Bertharius*, 1731, oil on
canvas, 24⅜ × 19⅛ in.
(62 × 48.7 cm), Molinari
Pradelli collection

6

Francesco de Mura
Noli Me Tangere, ca. 1727–30
Oil on copper, 15⅜ × 20¹¹⁄₁₆ in. (39.1 × 52.5 cm)
Davis Museum at Wellesley College, anonymous gift in 1956, acc. no. 1956.12

Noli me tangere means "touch me not" and is the Latin translation of the words spoken, according to the Gospel of John 20:17, by Jesus to an astonished Mary Magdalene when she recognized him after his resurrection:

> Jesus said to her, "Mary!" She turned and replied in Aramaic, *"Rabboni*!" (which means my teacher). Jesus admonishes her, "Stop clinging to me, for I have not yet ascended to the Father; but go to my brethren and say to them that I am ascending to my Father and your Father, and my God and your God." Mary Magdalene came, announcing to the disciples, "I have seen the lord," and that he had said these things to her.

The original Koine Greek phrase may be better translated as "cease holding on to me" or "stop clinging to me."

This small work and the following *Supper at Emmaus* (cat. no. 7) are painted on copper and were likely meant for private devotions. The haloed Jesus, in the center of the composition, holds a long hoe over his left shoulder (appearing to Mary in the guise of a gardener) as he walks to the right, his head turned toward Mary as his white shroud billows behind him. His outstretched right arm warns the Magdalene not to touch him. She kneels behind him on the left half of the composition, both hands reaching to embrace him. Her salmon-colored robe encircles her, exposing her right shoulder and her long auburn curls. De Mura depicts the garden, near where Jesus was entombed, as if it were a theatrical stage, with Jesus and Mary spotlit from the upper left, with a palm tree stage left, the hills of Jerusalem in the center distance, and wooden planting beds and earthen pots stage right. The walking Jesus and the kneeling Magdalene form a right-angle triangle.

De Mura probably executed this painting and its pendant in the late 1720s, just before he left Solimena's studio. Indeed, the influence of his master is still apparent in the dark shadows obscuring the face of the Magdalene and the generally formal and stiff figures. Solimena did a small *bozzetto* of a *Noli Me Tangere* (fig. 40) for an unidentified altarpiece, probably around 1720.[1] Solimena was clearly the inspiration for De Mura's small work; the brilliance and sense of movement of Solimena's figures far outshine his student's version. De Mura's large and graceful *Noli Me Tangere* (really *The Vision of Christ before the Virgin Mary*, fig. 41) in the Holy Sepulcher in Jerusalem, however, is a far more successful composition of a very similar subject, although it, too, is closely tied to Solimena's art.[2]

1. On sale at Sotheby's, London, Old Master and British Paintings Sale, December 5, 2012, lot 23.
2. De Mura's commission for eight paintings for the Holy Sepulcher in Jerusalem, only recently "rediscovered," was extremely important and probably the first major one after his departure from Solimena's studio. See Nicola Spinosa's essay "Neapolitan Painting in the Holy Land" and entries in *Baroque Art from the Holy Sepulchre: The Image of Jerusalem in the Pre-Alps*, ed. Manuela Kahn-Rossi and Chiara Naldi, exhib. cat. (Lugano: Galleria Canesso, 2014), 58–73, 90–97.

Provenance:
Professor and Mrs. John McAndrew, Wellesley, Mass., to 1956.

Fig. 40
Francesco Solimena, *Noli Me Tangere*, ca. 1720, oil on canvas, 26⅛ × 20⅞ in. (66.5 × 53 cm), private collection

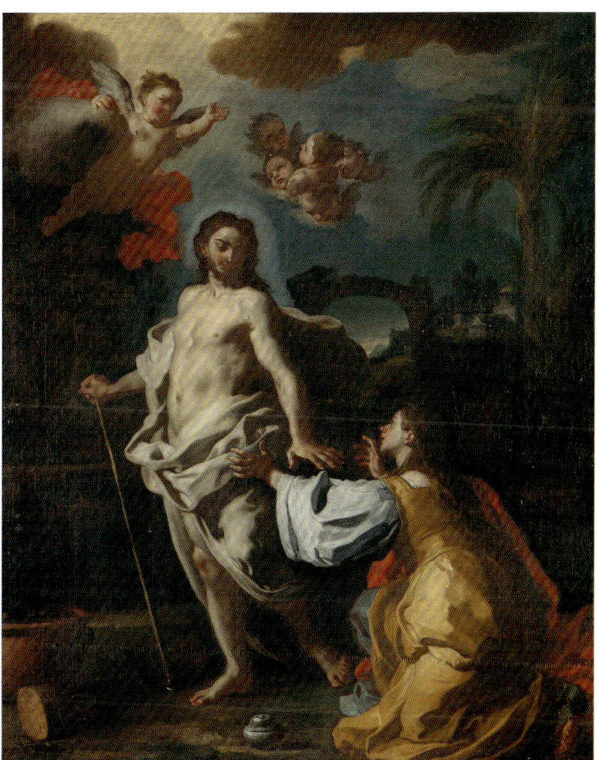

6 — continued

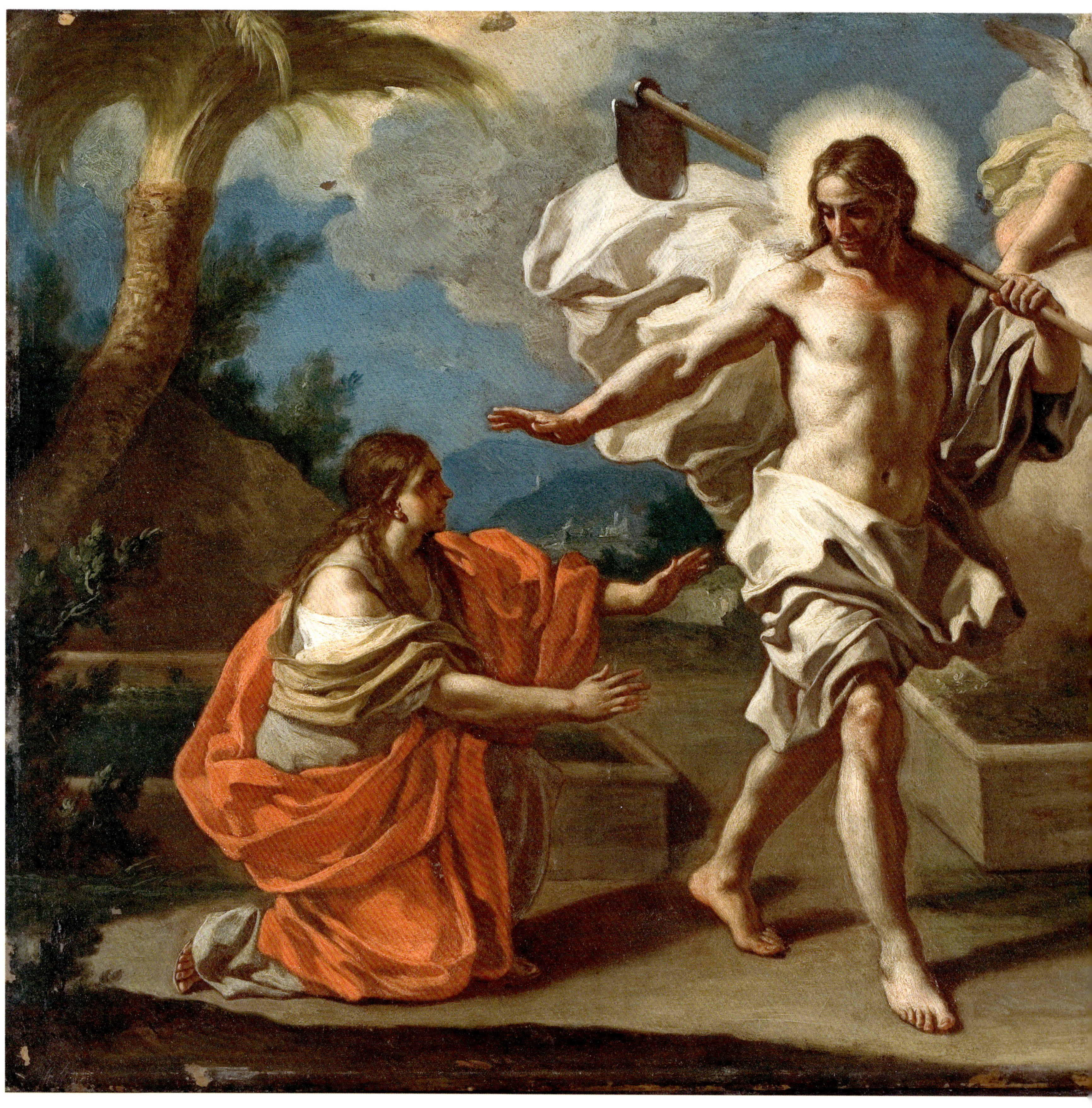

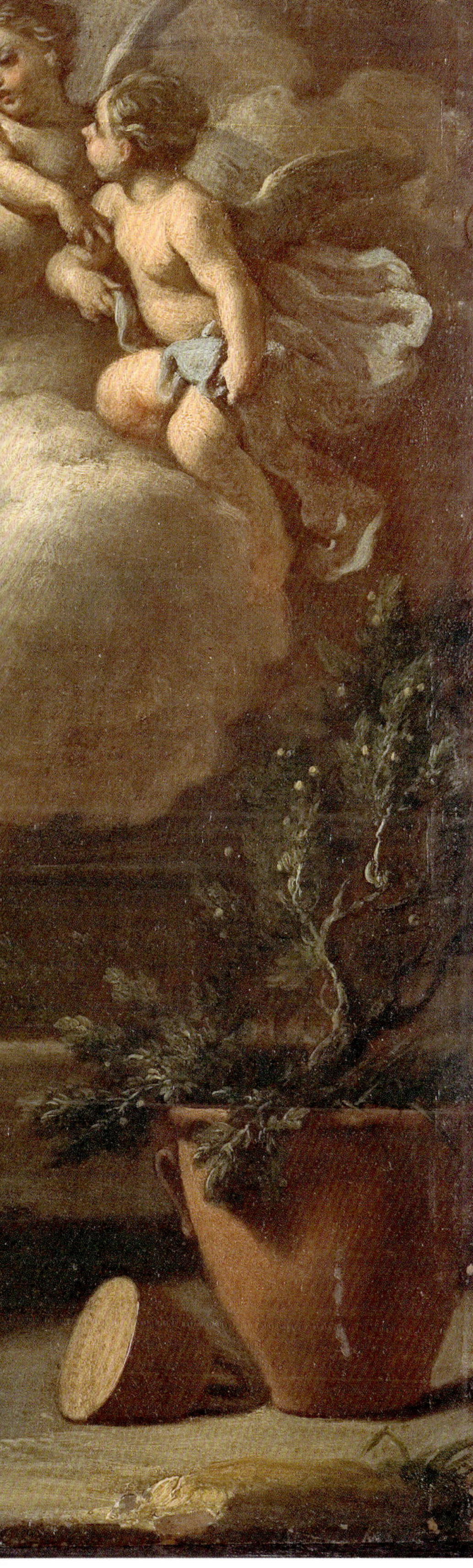

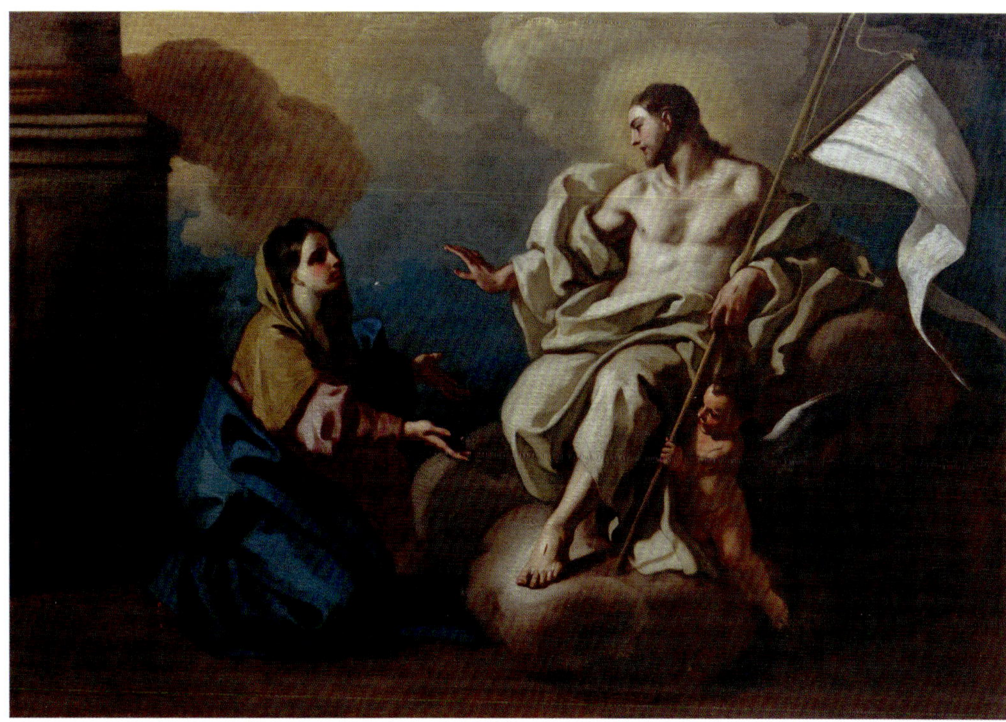

Fig. 41
Francesco de Mura, *Noli Me Tangere* (or *The Vision of Jesus before Virgin Mary*), ca. 1730, oil on canvas, 50 × 70⅞ in. (127 × 180 cm), Holy Sepulcher, Jerusalem

7

Francesco de Mura
Supper at Emmaus, ca. 1727–30
Oil on copper, 15⁷⁄₁₆ × 20¹³⁄₁₆ in. (39.2 × 52.9 cm)
Davis Museum at Wellesley College, anonymous gift in 1956, acc. no. 1956.13

The subject of this work is inspired by the Gospel of Luke 24:13–32, which describes the encounter, on the Sunday after the crucifixion, between Jesus and two disciples walking on the road from Jerusalem to the town of Emmaus (about 7 miles, or 11 kilometers). The two disciples (one named Cleopas) have heard the tomb of Jesus was found empty earlier that day. They talk about the events of the past few days as they walk, when a stranger asks them what they are discussing. The stranger on the road is Jesus, unrecognized by the disciples. He soon rebukes them for their unbelief and gives them a Bible study on prophecies about the Messiah. They ask the stranger to join them for the evening meal. When he blesses the bread and breaks it to begin the meal, the disciples suddenly recognize the stranger as Jesus, whereupon he disappears.

De Mura's small oil on copper sets the story at the moment when the disciples suddenly recognize Jesus. As if on a stage set, the scene shows three figures sitting around a small table outside a simple country home; the city of Jerusalem can be seen on a "backdrop" in the distance at "stage left," as a curious small dog looks in on the scene. Light from the upper left bathes the figures, who are joined by cherubs and an angel on the upper right. Jesus, between the two disciples, faces us and looks up to heaven, having just divided the loaf in two after blessing it. He holds one half in each hand, as a pilgrim's staff leans against his right arm, parallel with the staff leaning on Cleopas' arm to the left. Cleopas, his back to us and his water flask securely tied to his leather belt, holds both hands together in prayer. His fellow disciple on the right looks at Jesus, as if seeing him for the first time, his left hand open in a gesture of surprise. All three figures form an off-center oval. On the ground by the disciple's bare feet lie his hat and staff. The light-infused clouds behind Jesus expand his halo, which acts as the focus of the composition; the spotlight on Jesus reminds the viewer of God's presence.

The *Noli Me Tangere* (cat. no. 6) and this *Supper at Emmaus* depict scenes from two of the appearances of Jesus after his Resurrection. Contemplation of such subjects was an aid to prayer and a reminder of the truth of the gospels, and the hope of the eventual return of Jesus.

The carefully painted figures in the Wellesley works recall De Mura's *Noli Me Tangere* in the Holy Sepulcher in Jerusalem, dated about 1730 (see fig. 41). There are other versions of the *Supper at Emmaus*, attributed to the studio of De Mura and painted several decades later, one of which was in a recent auction.[1]

1. In Patrizia DeMaggio, "Aggiunte e precisazioni su Francesco de Mura," *Antologia di belle arti* 9, nos. 35–38 (1990): 101–2, another *Supper at Emmaus* by De Mura, dated to ca. 1755, is discussed and illustrated (fig. 8, p. 102). In addition, the author illustrates and discusses yet another *Supper at Emmaus* by De Mura in the church of San Ferdinando in San Leucio (figs. 6–7, pp. 101–2).

Provenance:
Professor and Mrs. John McAndrew, Wellesley, Mass.

Bibliography:
Curtis Shell and John McAndrew, *Catalogue of European and American Sculpture, Paintings and Drawings at Wellesley College*, 2nd ed. (Wellesley, Mass.: Wellesley College, 1964), 82.

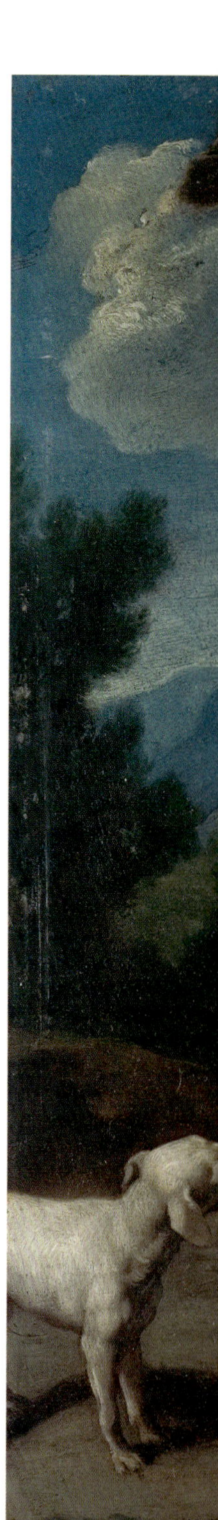

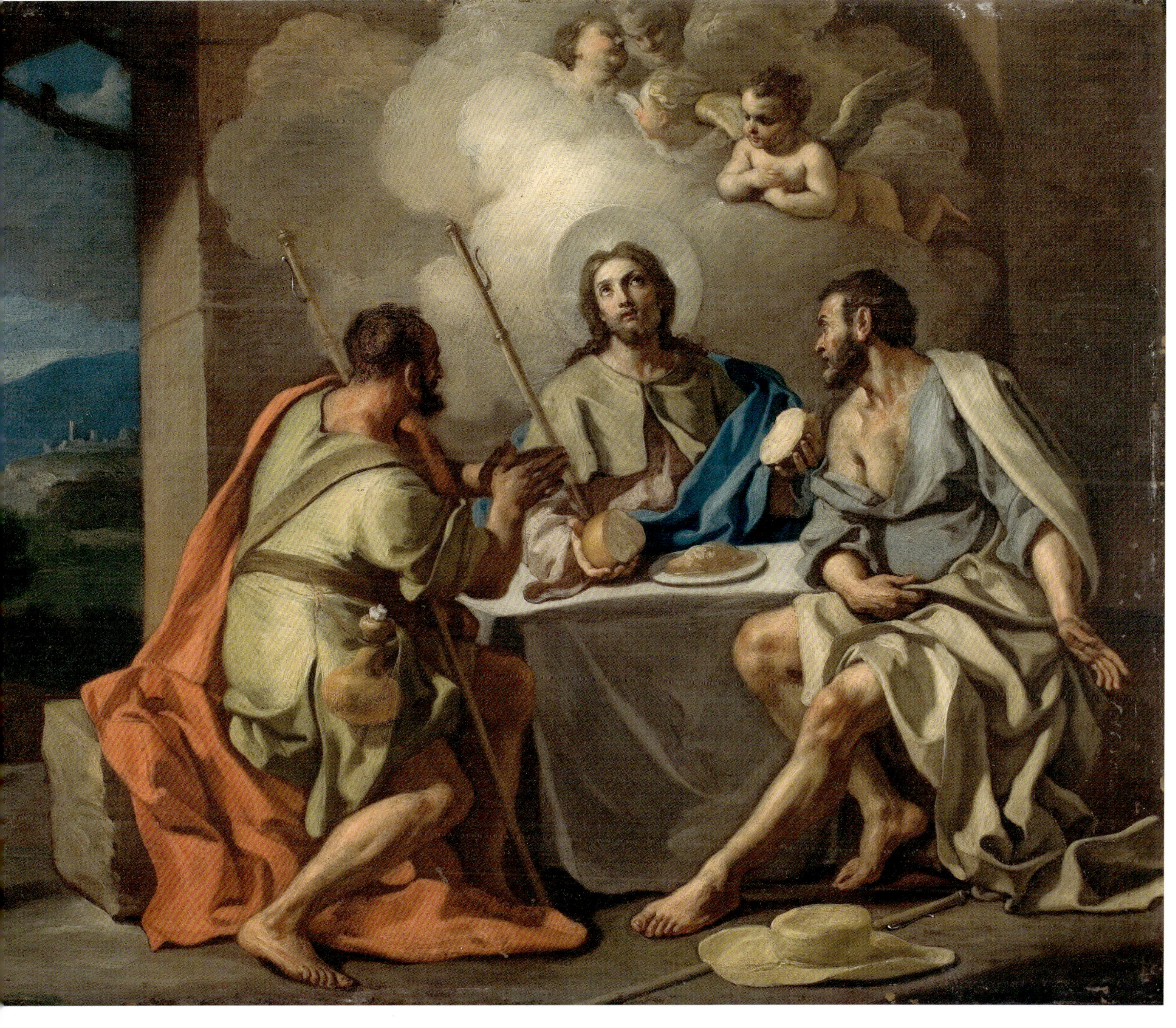

8

Francesco de Mura
St. Carloman Dons Benedictine Habit Given to Him by Pope St. Zacharias, ca. 1730
Oil on canvas, 23⅞ × 18¼ in. (60.4 × 46.3 cm)
Private collection

Carloman (707–755) was the eldest son of Charles Martel, king of the Franks (737–741). In 741, he became king of Austrasia, the northeastern section of the Merovingian Kingdom of the Franks. He supported the founding of monasteries in Germany and Belgium, and the missionary work of St. Boniface. On August 15, 747, on the advice of Boniface, Carloman abdicated the throne in favor of his brother, and became a monk, being tonsured in Rome by Pope St. Zacharias. He entered the abbey of Monte Cassino, halfway between Rome and Naples, where he toiled as a shepherd and spent hours in prayer and meditation. He died on August 17, 755, and was buried in Monte Cassino.

This work is a *bozzetto* for a larger work that De Mura executed in March 1731 for the chapel of San Carlomano in Monte Cassino, when the relics of St. Carloman were transferred to the main altar of the chapel; the final, larger painting was destroyed in the Allied bombing of 1944 during World War II. In a crowded scene filled with light from above and a dozen figures, Pope St. Zacharias sits on a red-velvet papal chair as he places the black monastic habit of the Benedictines over the head of the youthful Carloman (he was actually 40 years old in 747). Carloman kneels on a red cushion, head and eyes lowered in a pose of humility, his arms crossed over his chest. The colors of the pope's red hat and golden-yellow cape are repeated in the red caps and yellow surplices of the two assistants on either side of him. A golden baptismal vessel sits on a golden salver near Carloman's right foot, at center bottom. Four additional servants stand or kneel around the two central figures and drapery winds around a column on the left, creating a dynamic swirl around Carloman. The clouds and brilliant light behind and above add to the golden shimmer of the scene.

We see here De Mura's masterful storytelling, which gracefully compresses much in a small amount of space. His brilliant color sense already separates him from the heavier and darker style of Solimena. In addition, De Mura demonstrates his superlative drawing of the human figure, completely convincing in its energetic depiction of implied movement.

With this work, De Mura begins more than a decade of commissions for the monks of Monte Cassino. In one of the great artistic tragedies of World War II, all of De Mura's many magnificent frescoes and large canvases created for this monastery (and for Santa Chiara in Naples)—accounting for nearly one-third of his *œuvre*—were destroyed in a misguided bombing raid. Thus, this small surviving oil sketch—and other *bozzetti* of this period, such as *The Preaching of St. Bertharius* in the Molinari Pradelli collection, of almost the same size and date (fig. 42; cat. nos. 10 and 11)—becomes most precious in helping us imagine what the impact of De Mura's final version must have been.

There is a *bozzetto* by De Mura for an unidentified work of about 1731 (or about 1743) that has been thought to depict *St. Carloman Renouncing His Secular Life*; it is in the Molinari Pradelli collection..[1]

1. Nicola Spinosa, *Pittura sacra a Napoli nel '700*, exhib. cat. (Naples: Società Editrice Napoletana, 1980), 104, no. 56; Spinosa, *Pittura napoletana del Settecento*, 1:164, 165, 354, no. 269, fig. 322, pl. 65.

Provenance:
New York dealer, until ca. 1970.

Exhibitions:
M. Knoedler & Co., New York, N.Y., April 4–29, 1967, *Masters of the Loaded Brush: Oil Sketches from Rubens to Tiepolo*; Yale University Art Gallery, New Haven, Conn., John and Mable Ringling Museum of Art, Sarasota, Fla., Nelson-Atkins Museum of Art, Kansas City, Mo., Sept. 9–June 12, 1988, *A Taste for Angels: Neapolitan Painting in North America, 1650–1750*.

Bibliography:
Masters of the Loaded Brush: Oil Sketches from Rubens to Tiepolo, exhib. cat. (New York: Columbia University, Department of Art History and Archaeology, 1967), 34–35, fig. 25; Nicola Spinosa, *Pittura napolentana del Settecento*, vol. 1, *Dal barocco al rococò* (Naples: Electa Napoli, 1986), 157, no. 248, fig. 294; *A Taste for Angels: Neapolitan Painting in North America, 1650–1750*, exhib. cat. (New Haven: Yale University Art Gallery, 1987), 272–73, no. 34.

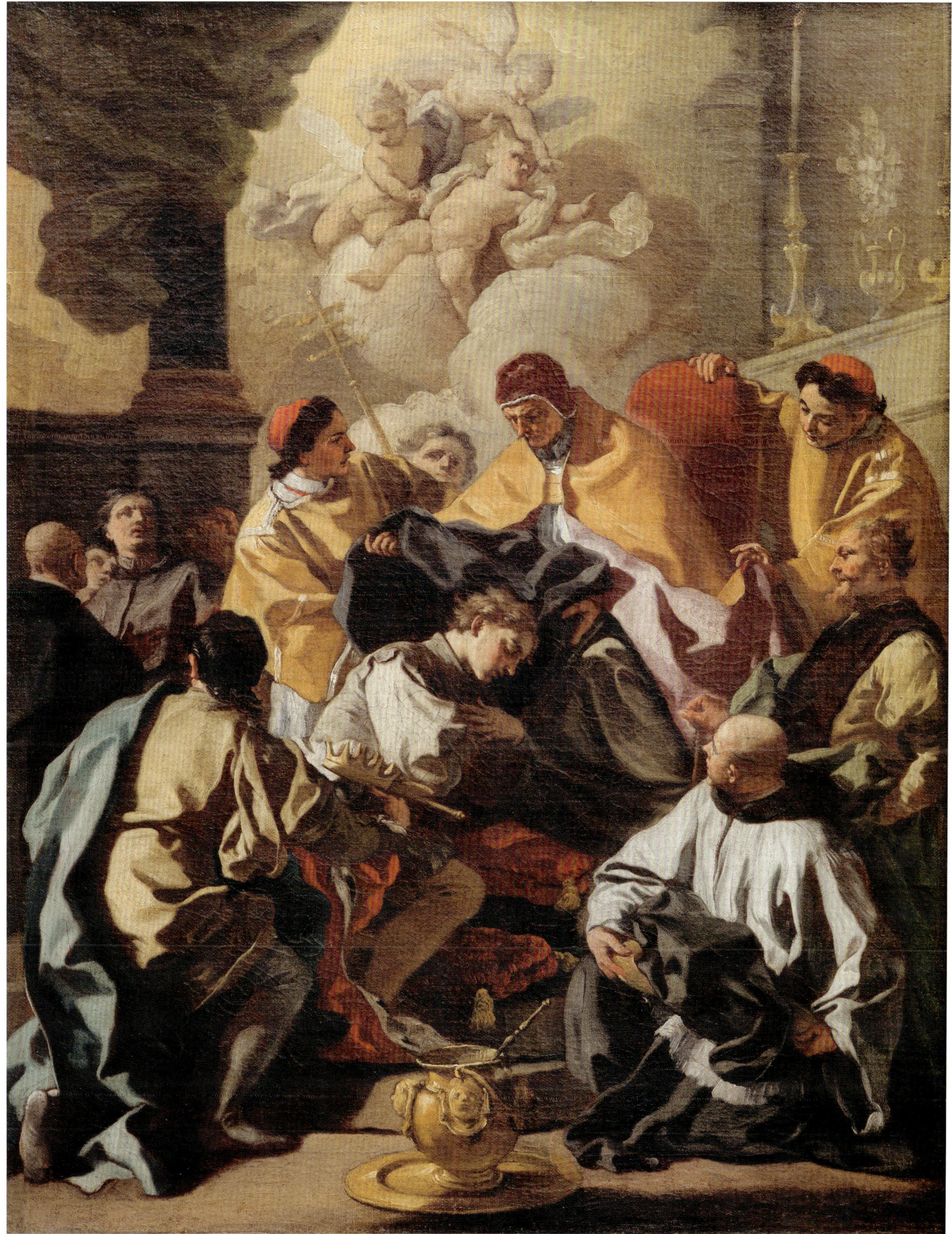

8 — continued

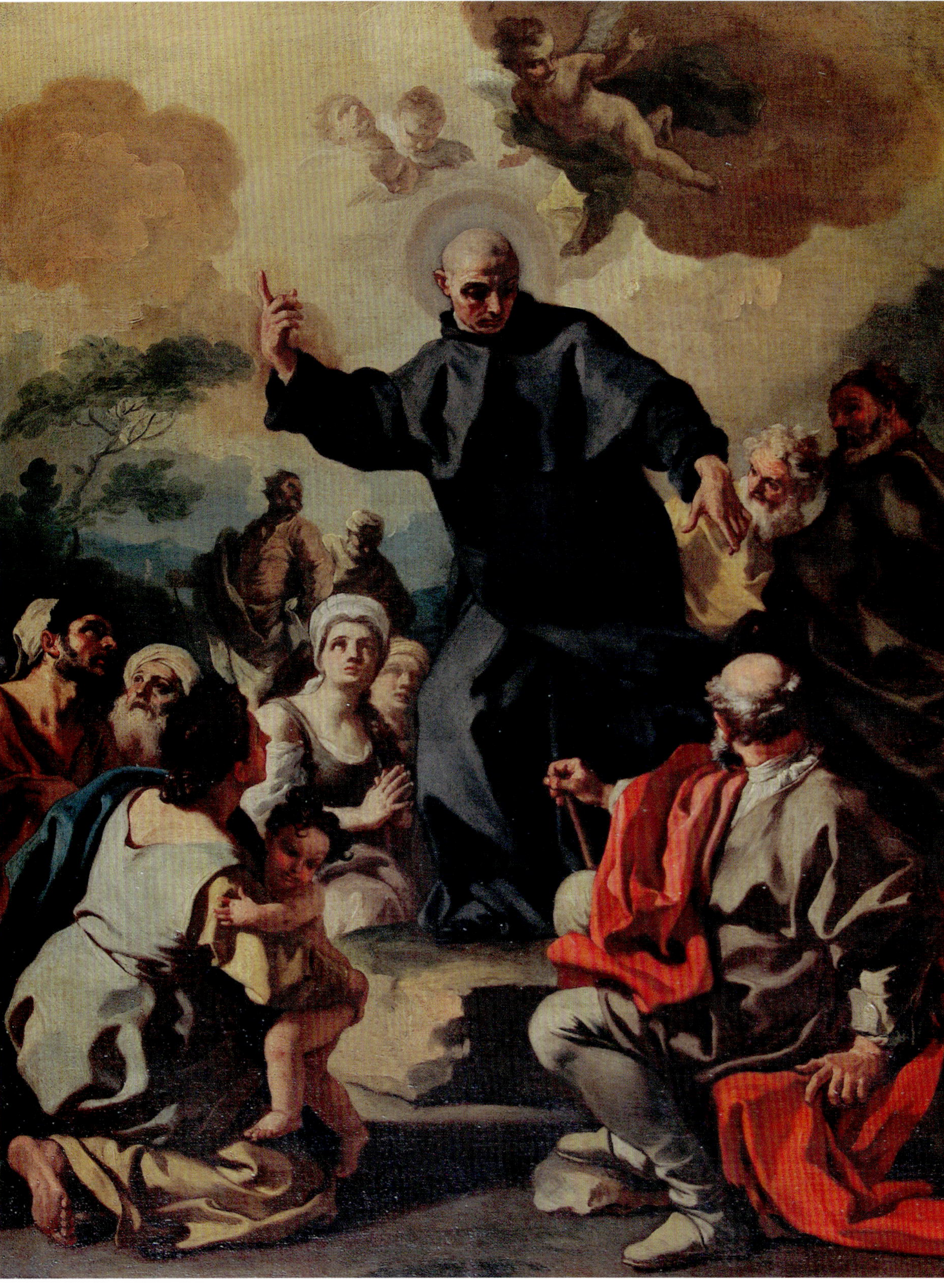

Fig. 42
Francesco de Mura, *Preaching of St. Bertharius*, ca. 1731, oil on cavas, 24⅜ × 19⅛ in. (62 × 48.7 cm), Molinari Pradelli collection

9

Francesco de Mura
An Ecclesiastic Blessing a Kneeling Woman, ca. 1740–50?
Pen and brown ink, gray wash, over black chalk, on paper, squared for transposition,
12⁵⁄₁₆ × 7³⁄₁₆ in. (31.3 × 18.3 cm)
The Morgan Library & Museum, gift of János Scholz, acc. no. 1993.264

This interesting drawing, which bears affinities to other drawings by
Francesco de Mura (cat. nos. 14, 20, and 26), depicts an unknown histori-
cal-religious subject. On the right, an ecclesiastic—possibly a pope—holds up
his right hand in an act of blessing over the head of a kneeling woman, on our
left. He sits in an elaborate chair reminiscent of the chair of De Mura's *Pope
Gregory the Great* (see fig. 45), and like the figure of Gregory, our ecclesiastic
also wears a similar papal *mozzetta* (hooded cape) over his shoulders and
raises his right hand in an analogous gesture. Angels fly over clouds in the
upper left, and a dove, representing the Holy Spirit, flies at the highest and
brightest point above. At the right, more angels hold back a curtain; columns
appear in the background, and two male figures stand in shadow, in the
background behind the woman. She kneels on the top step of a stairway
leading up to the ecclesiastic; just below her knee, on the second rung, is a
crown, below which the lowest portion becomes a semicircular archway.
Light pours in from the upper left. The drawing has a grid drawn over it,
indicating its preparation for a transfer to a bigger format, either another
(larger) drawing or a painting.

The subject of this drawing, which may have been a study for a painting
in Monte Cassino, remains a mystery. The ecclesiastic who is blessing could
be Pope St. Silvester (d. 335), and the kneeling woman Queen St. Helena
(ca. 250–ca. 330), the mother of Emperor Constantine and the traditional
"discoverer" of the so-called true cross. Pope Silvester accompanied Helena
to Jerusalem in her search for the actual cross of Jesus' crucifixion, and he
remained close to her for many years. He may not only be blessing her in the
drawing, but also affirming her recent conversion to Christianity, after an
earlier conversion from paganism to Judaism.

Nicola Spinosa has suggested that the drawing, although close in style
to De Mura, "presents, particularly in the depiction of the figure types,
results similar to those found in paintings by Jacopo Cestaro [1718–78], a
pupil of Solimena, but also very influenced by De Mura, with whom he is
sometimes confused."[1] Comparisons to Cestaro's *Circumcision of Jesus* of
about 1757 in the Staatsgalerie in Stuttgart (fig. 43) reveal clear parallels
with the Morgan Library drawing. The composition uses a similar architectural setting with a curved top, a comparable angel grouping, a stairway
from the lower left to the center, and a very similar kneeling figure of Mary.
Cestaro was one of many artists in Naples (including Giacinto Diano,
Pietro Bardellino, and others; see cat. no. 43) who were greatly influenced
by De Mura. A drawing (also gridded) by Cestaro for this painting is in the
Philadelphia Museum of Art (fig. 44).

1. Nicola Spinosa, personal correspondence, June 2015.

Provenance:
János Scholz, New York (no
mark; see Lugt S. 2933b).

Bibliography:
Robert Manning, *In the
Shadow of Vesuvius: Neapolitan
Drawings from the Collection of
János Scholz*, exhib. cat. (New
York: Finch College Museum
of Art, 1969), 31, no. 46 (as
Francesco de Mura); Nicola
Spinosa, *Civiltà del '700 a
Napoli, 1734–1799*, exhib. cat.
(Florence: Centro Di, 1979),
1:384–85, no. 212.

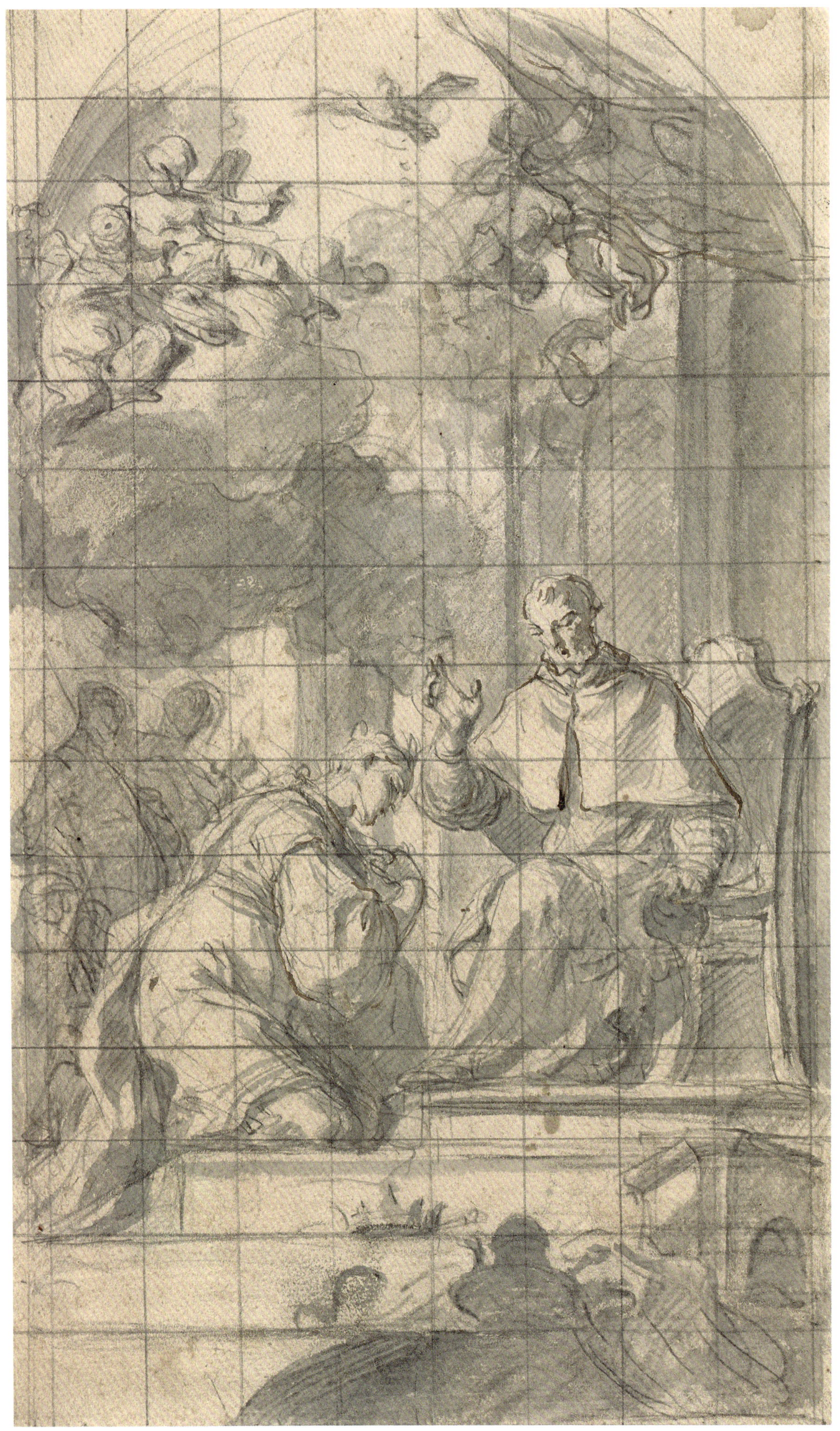

Cat. 9

9 — continued

Fig. 43
Jacopo Cestaro, *The Circumcision of Christ*, ca. 1757, oil on linen, 52³⁄₁₆ × 30¹⁵⁄₁₆ in. (132.5 × 78.5 cm), Staatsgalerie, Stuttgart

Fig. 44
Jacopo Cestaro, *The Circumcision of Christ*, ca. 1757, pen and black ink with brush and brown and gray washes, black chalk, heightened with white opaque watercolor, squared in black chalk, on cream laid paper, mounted down, 14¹³⁄₁₆ × 9¹⁄₂ in. (37.6 × 24.1 cm), Philadelphia Museum of Art

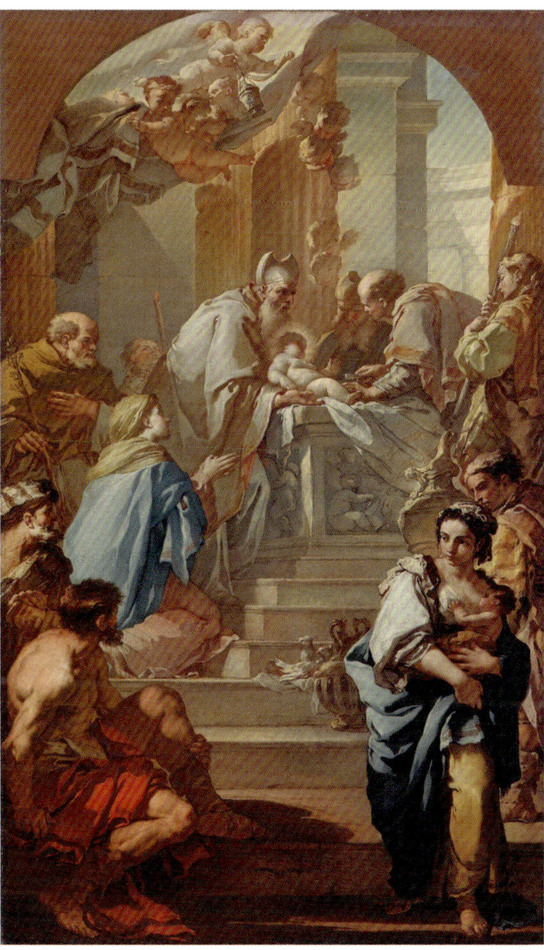

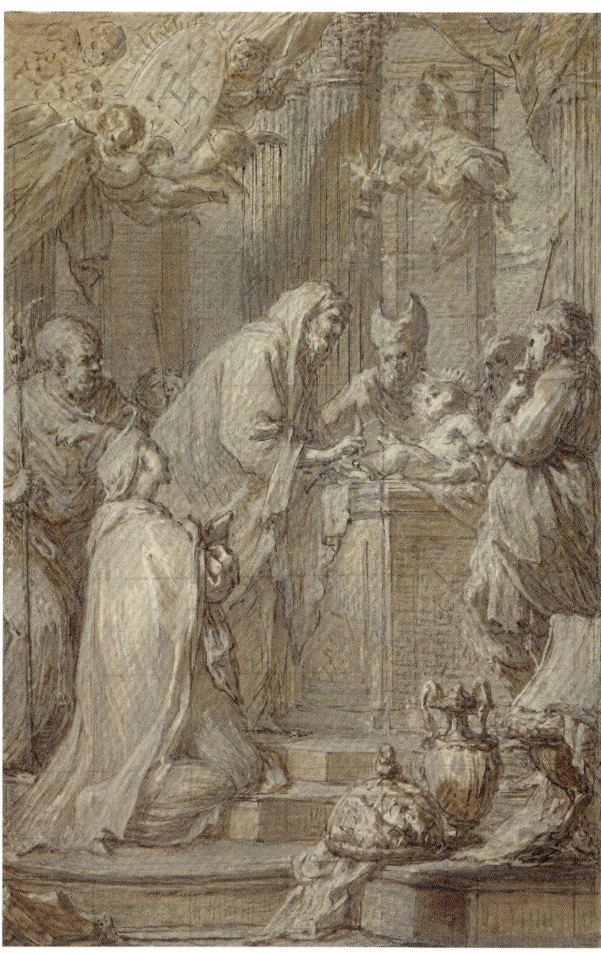

10

Francesco de Mura
Pope Gregory Ends the Plague, ca. 1730–35?
Oil on canvas, 22 × 34¹⁄₂ in. (55.9 × 87.6 cm)
W.L.M. King collection, Library and Archives of Canada, Ottawa, e011154406

Catalogue only.

The abbey of Monte Cassino, founded by St. Benedict (480–547; see cat. nos. 15 and 16), had a special relationship with Pope St. Gregory (ca. 540–604), who helped rebuild the monastery after the Arian Goths pillaged and burned it in the late 590s. This lunette and another one in the W.L.M. King collection—*Pope Gregory the Great Approving the Benedictine Rule* (fig. 45)—are *bozzetti* of paintings that were destroyed in the Allied bombing of 1944. The lost paintings probably fit in two semicircular panels in a chapel dedicated to and telling the story of St. Gregory, an admired Benedictine monk who became pope in 590. (A similar series of lunettes concerning the life of St. Bertharius was also created by De Mura for Monte Cassino about this time.)

The scene shows the commanding figure of Gregory standing to the right, attired in the golden yellow papal mantel and *camauro* (red velvet cap) trimmed in ermine. Two assistants stand behind him, as he raises his right hand and two fingers in a sign of blessing over a group of deacons, priests, and ordinary believers. Gregory had organized a grand procession through the streets of Rome, according to tradition, on April 25, 591, a year after he became pope. The procession's purpose was to end the plague that had ravaged Rome after a series of natural disasters, which were thought to be a chastisement from God (note the corpses at lower left; eighty people died in the march). As the groups advanced toward the church of Santa Maria Maggiore, Gregory joined them, and together they marched towards the Vatican. As the procession neared the Vatican, the participants all saw St. Michael the archangel appear on top of the mausoleum of the Roman emperor Hadrian as he unsheathed his flaming sword.[1] (Thereafter, the mausoleum/castle was called Castello Sant'Angelo, the Castle of the Holy Angel.) They took it as a sign that the plague's punishment had ended. In this lunette, the archangel flies to the top of Hadrian's mausoleum on the far left, as the clouds depart on the upper right.

De Mura no doubt knew of Solimena's *Meeting of Pope Leo and Attila*, now in the Pinacoteca di Brera, Milan, which was also commissioned by the abbey of Monte Cassino.[2] Both compositions use a long horizontal with figures carefully placed as if actors on a stage. The somewhat more dynamic figures of De Mura are in a compressed layout, and the naturalistic style of De Mura contrasts with his master's. Still, De Mura's stylistic relationship to Solimena remains strong in these works.

1. Hadrian died in AD 138 and his tomb (or mausoleum) was completed in 139.
2. Solimena's work has also been titled *The Meeting of Ratchis and Pope Zachary*; Solimena's pendant, also in the Brera, is titled *St. Wilibald Asks the Blessing of Pope Gregory*.

Provenance:
W.L.M. King collection (William Lyon Mackenzie King [1874–1950] was prime minister of Canada).

Exhibitions:
Laurier House National Historic Site, Parks Canada, Ottawa; National Gallery of Canada, Ottawa, on long-term loan.

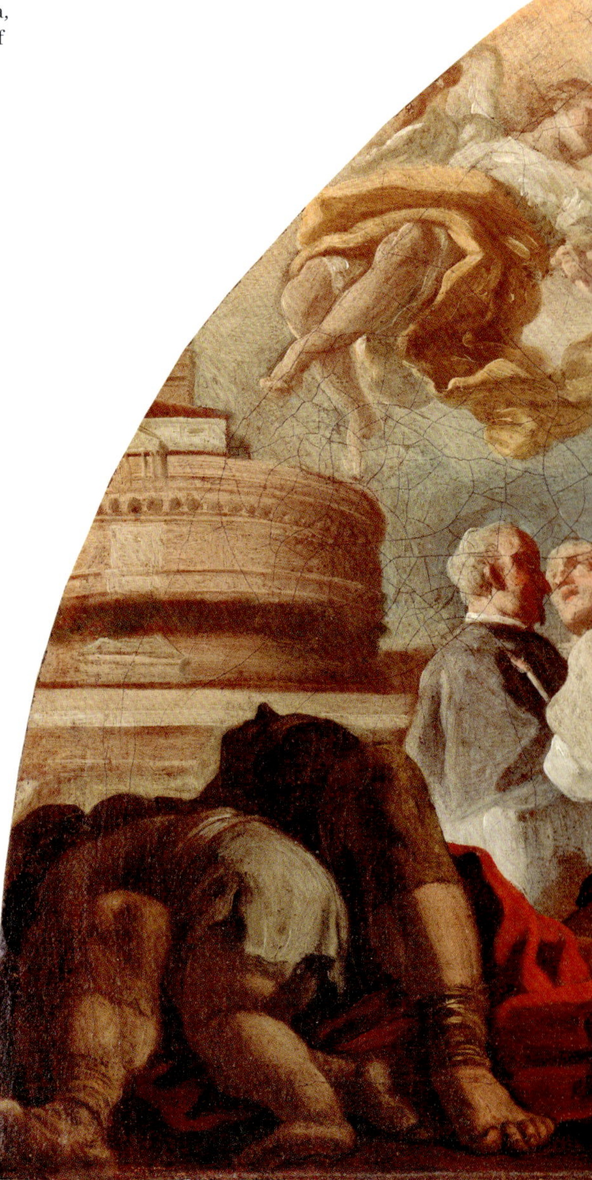

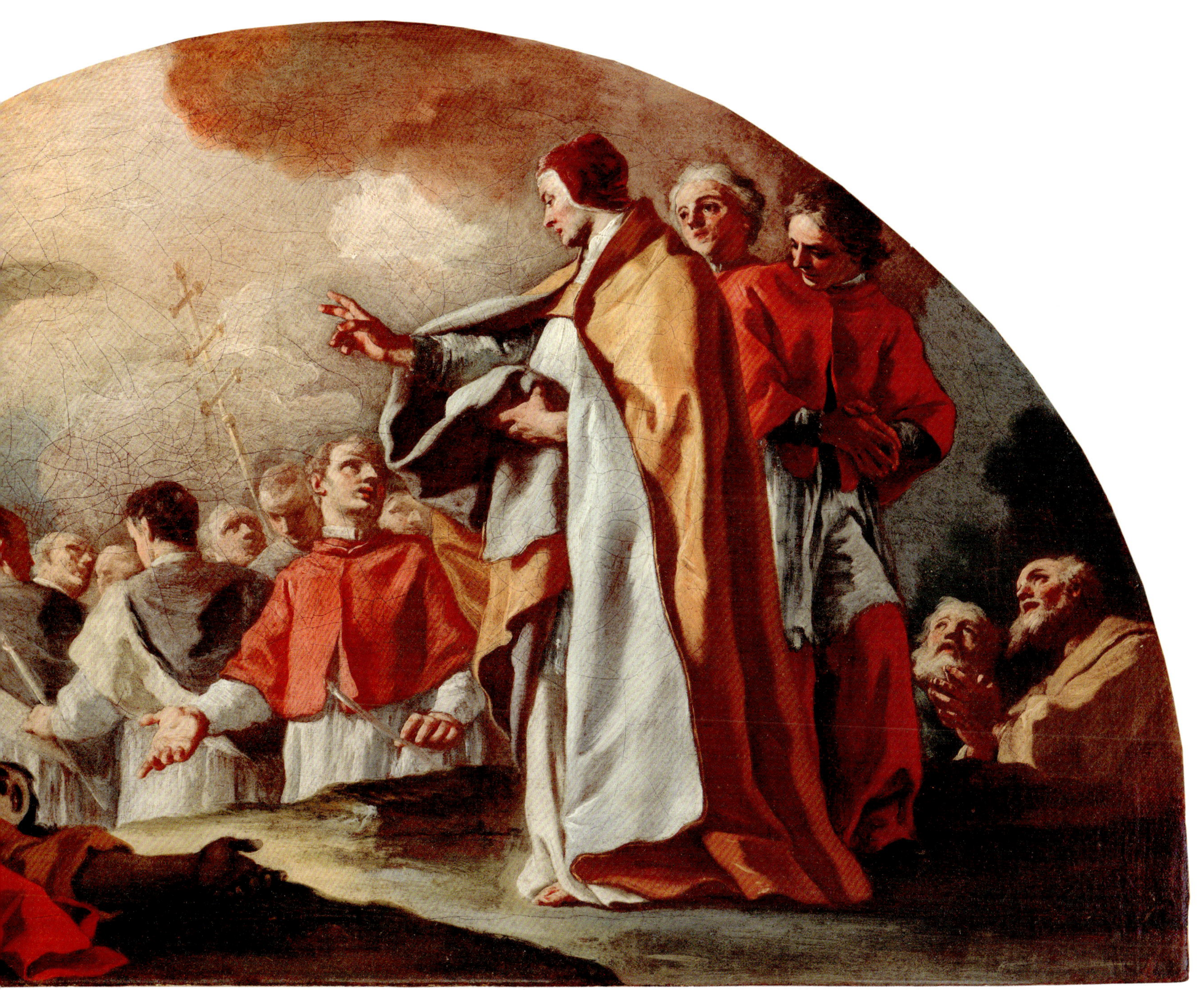

10 — continued

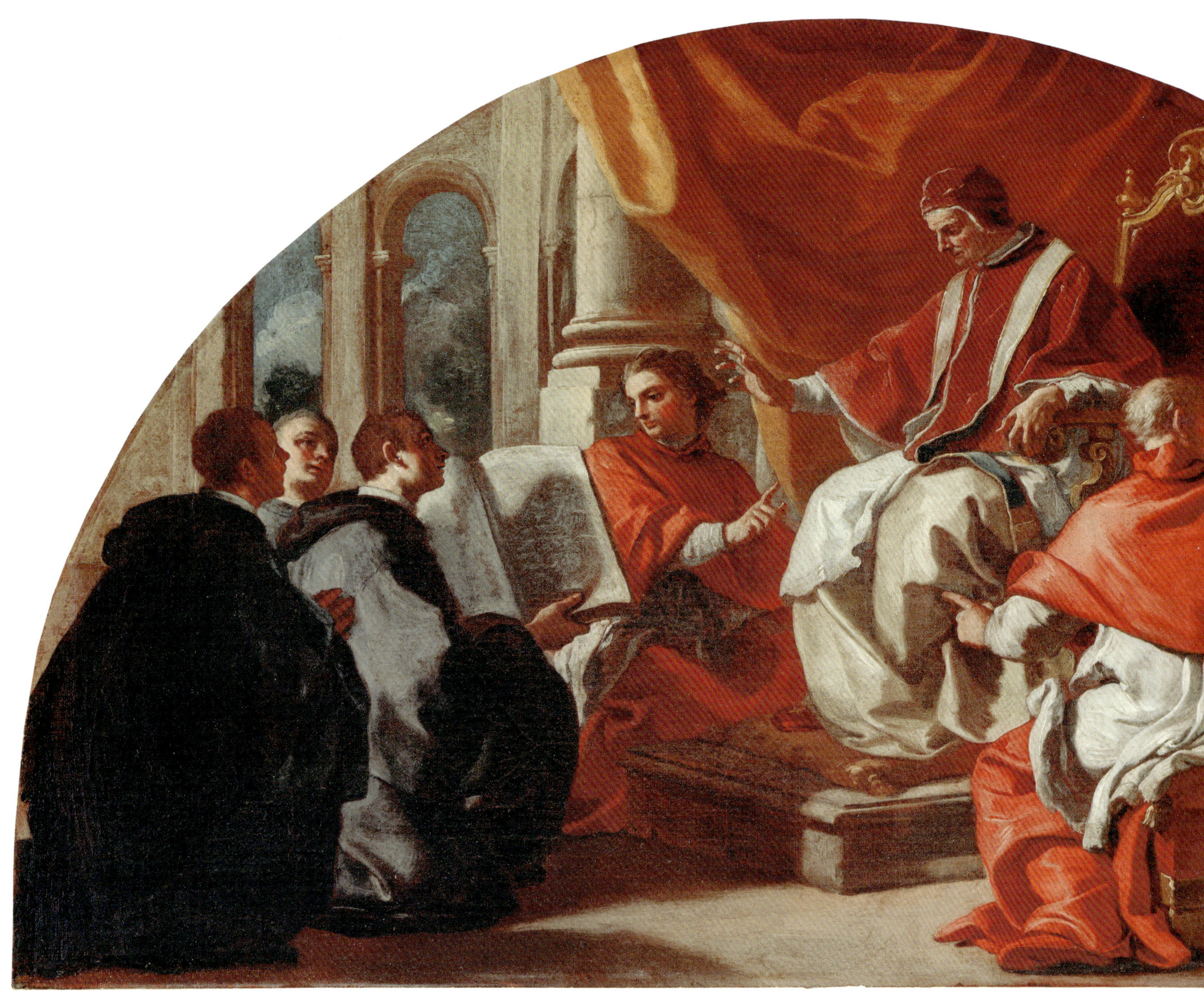

Fig. 45
Francesco de Mura, *Pope Gregory the Great Approving the Benedictine Rule*, ca. 1730, oil on canvas, 22 × 34½ in. (55.9 × 87.6 cm), W.L.M. King Collection, Library and Archives of Canada, Ottawa, ref. no. e011154407

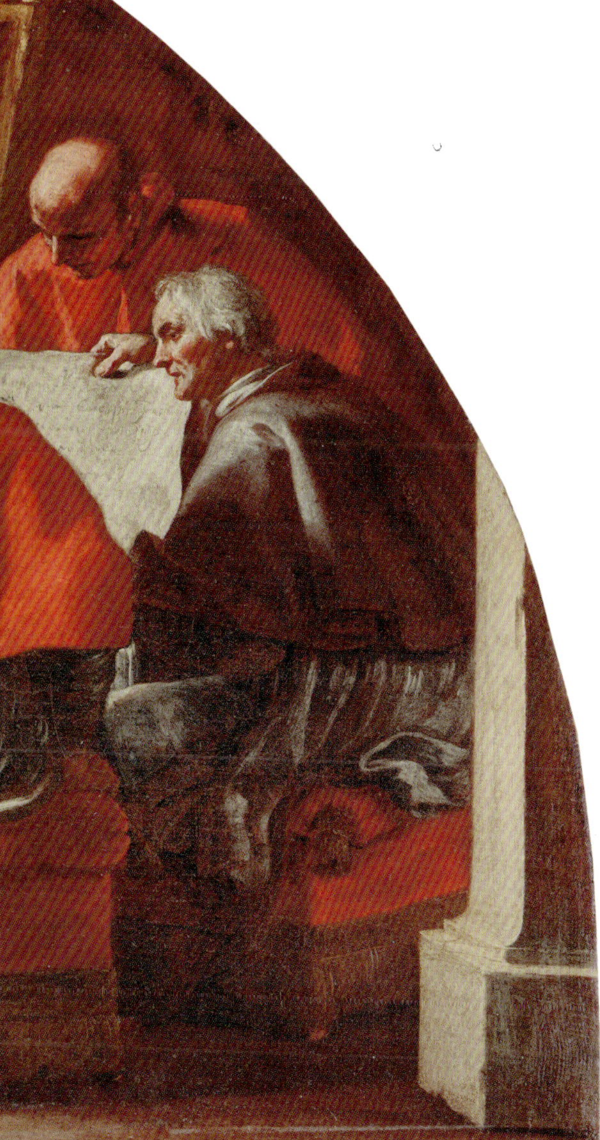

11

Francesco de Mura
St. Thomas Aquinas Inspired by Angels, ca. 1730–35
Oil on canvas, 29½ × 19¼ in. (74.9 × 48.9 cm)
Philbrook Museum of Art, museum purchase and gift of Rosemary Titus
Reynolds and Robert Dance, acc. no. 1995.23

Tommaso d'Aquino (known in English as Thomas Aquinas; 1225–74) was an Italian Dominican friar and a hugely influential Scholastic philosopher and theologian. When he was just five years old, Thomas was sent to the abbey of Monte Cassino to be educated by the Benedictine monks and remained there until he was thirteen, when he returned to Naples to complete his education. In September 1261, he was called to Orvieto, where he produced for Pope Urban IV the liturgy for the newly created Feast of Corpus Christi ("body of Christ"), which celebrates the belief that the body and blood of Jesus Christ are actually present in the Eucharist.

Around 1730–35, De Mura painted this oil *bozzetto* for a chapel altar in Monte Cassino. It shows Thomas, dressed in monastic habit with an image of the sun (his symbol) blazing on his chest. He is about to kneel as he slips off his stool, where he was composing the liturgy for Corpus Christi (he holds a pen in his right hand). Leaning to the left and twisting his head to the right, he rests his elbow on a desk with an open book. Above his left arm floats an angel and a cherub lifting up the Host in a golden monstrance. The winged, blond angel shows the Host to Thomas as another angel and cherub fly above in clouds filled with more bodiless cherubs. The abbey was undoubtedly proud of its association with Thomas, this most important philosopher-saint, and probably commissioned from De Mura the larger painting (perhaps destroyed in 1944), possibly for an expanded or newly built chapel.[1]

The dark, somber style of this *bozzetto* reminds us of the other De Muras of this early period, such as his *Noli Me Tangere* (cat. no. 6) of about 1727–30, and the angel in De Mura's *Christ in the Garden of Gethsemane* of about 1730 in the Holy Sepulcher of Jerusalem (fig. 46). Although we can see De Mura's closeness to Solimena, De Mura's personal style is evident in his more naturalistic approach to the human figure.

Thomas Aquinas was a subject depicted a number of times by De Mura (fig. 47).[2] In 1758, De Mura painted a superb example of another *St. Thomas Aquinas* for the church of San Domenico in Salerno, where the arm of the saint is preserved and where a new chapel in his name was dedicated in 1765.[3]

1. There are no records indicating precisely when or for what reason this work was commissioned.
2. Solimena's *St. Thomas* in San Domenico Maggiore, Naples, was clearly the source for this *St. Thomas* attributed to De Mura.
3. This painting is illustrated in David Nolta's "Francesco de Mura: Lives and Works", 2 vols. (Ph.D. diss., Yale University, 1989), 2:fig. 77; see also 1:168.

Provenance:
Kurt Rossacher; Joseph Matzker; Sotheby's, London, Collection of Paintings and Drawings by Carlo Carlone and Contemporaries, Dec. 7, 1988, lot 25 (as Solimena); purchased with gifts of Rosemary Titus Reynolds and Robert Dance on November 3, 1995.

Exhibitions:
Hessisches Landesmuseum, Darmstadt, Salzburger Residenzgalerie, Salzburg, 1965–66, *Visionen des Barock, Entwürfe aus der Sammlung Kurt Rossacher*; Los Angeles County Museum of Art, Nelson-Atkins Museum, Kansas City, Mo., Toledo Museum of Art, Rhode Island School of Design Museum of Art, Minneapolis Institute of Arts, Oct. 1, 1968–June 8, 1969, *Image and Imagination: Oil Sketches of the Baroque*.

Bibliography:
Visionen des Barock, Entwürfe aus der Sammlung Kurt Rossacher, exhib. cat. (Darmstadt: Hessisches Landesmuseum, 1965), 152, 153, no. 73 (ill.).

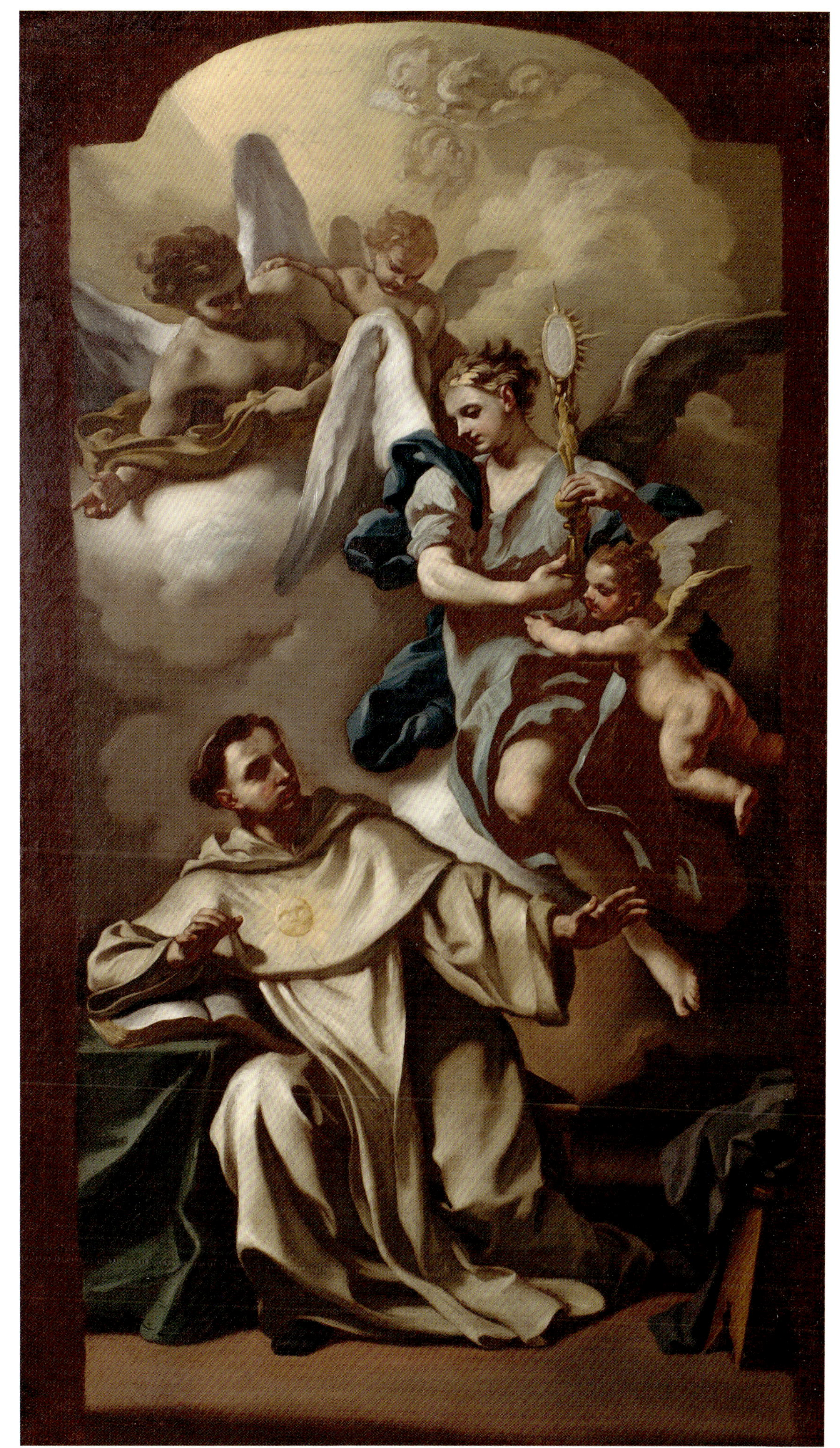

11 — continued

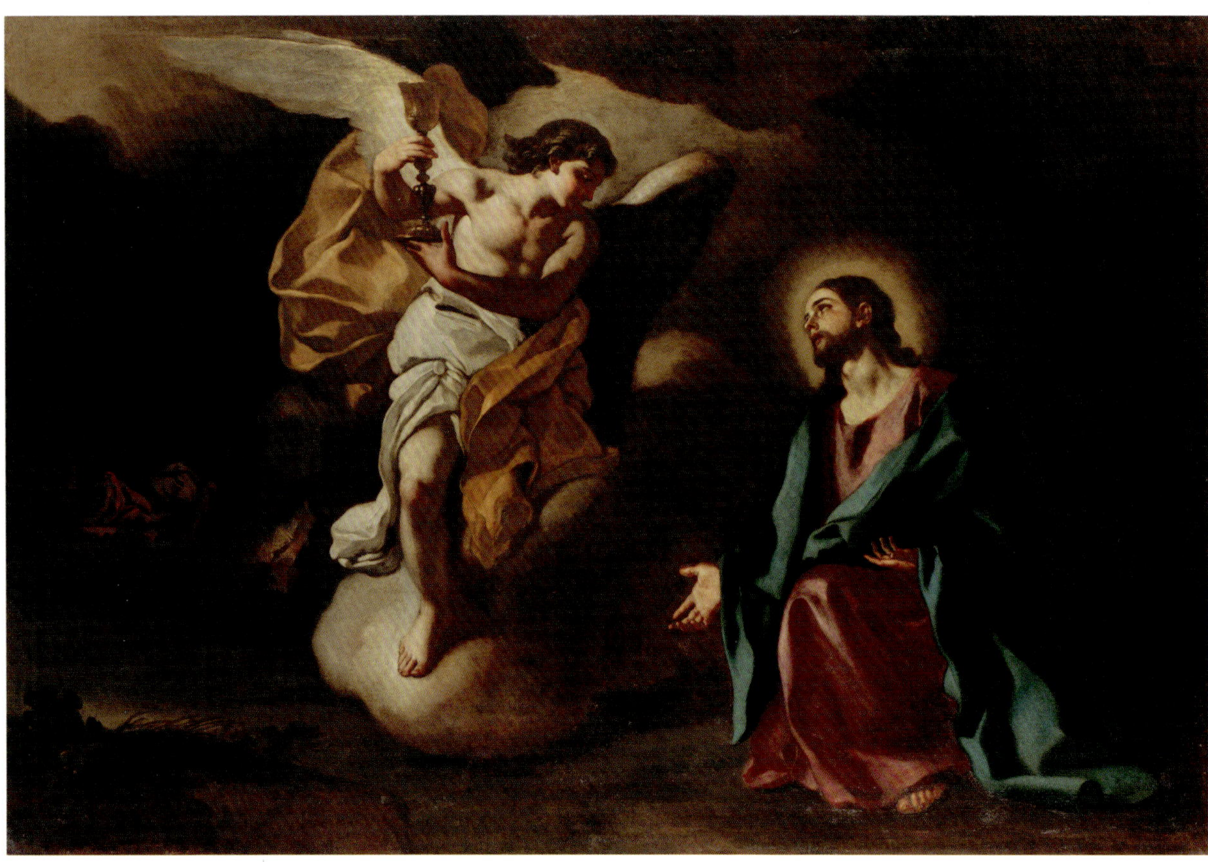

Fig. 46
Francesco de Mura, *Christ in Garden of Gethsemane,* ca. 1730, oil on canvas, 50 × 70 in. (127 × 180 cm), Holy Sepulcher, Jerusalem

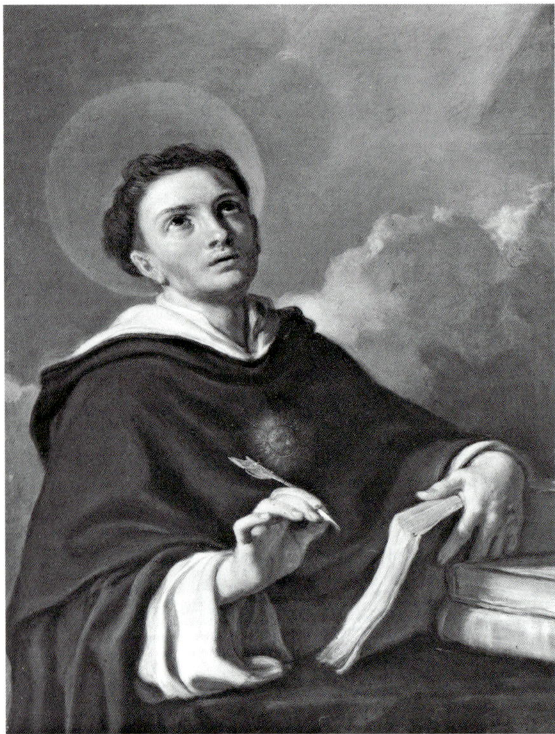

Fig. 47
Attributed to Francesco de Mura, *St. Thomas Aquinas,* oil on canvas, 10⅞ × 8 in. (27.5 × 20.5 cm), location unknown

12

Francesco de Mura
Adoration of the Magi (Epiphany), before 1732
Oil on canvas, 42⅛ × 83 in. (107 × 211 cm)
Pio Monte della Misericordia, bequest of the artist, inv. no. 101

In art, "The Adoration of the Magi" refers to the story in the gospel of Matthew (2:1–12) in which Magi—plural of *magus*, an astrologer or priest of the ancient Medes and Persians, called by Matthew "wise men from the East"—arrived at the house where the infant Jesus lay and paid homage to him with gifts of gold, frankincense, and myrrh (rare aromatic resins used in incense).

Our viewpoint in this large *bozzetto* is from below, looking up. De Mura places Mary and the infant Jesus outdoors, among ancient ruins. Both sit at the top of the remains of steps over an archway as the Magi (interpreted later as three kings) bow before the Child. Mary turns her head to the left (with cloudlike haloes behind her and Jesus' heads) to recognize a bowing king in a yellow robe, while the infant in her arms raises his left arm in blessing over the head of another king robed in ermine and red. Behind him on the right is a third king, black, in a silver cuirass. Joseph, robed in blue and yellow, stands behind Mary with hands clasped, looking at a kneeling king. In the lower right foreground, two muscular servants unload from the back of a camel a gift-filled chest. Trumpeters blow horns to announce the arrival of royalty; next to them, two other servants unwrap an enormous bundle, and another struggles to control a rearing horse. Six or more courtiers are supernumeraries in this grand opera. Three angels rejoice above; the center angel holds a scroll with quotes from the prophet Micah about the messiah's birth.

This is a study for the fresco in the curved portion of the apse, above the altar, in the church of the Nunziatella in Naples (fig. 49). The church belonged to the Jesuits, who renovated it in 1730 and shortly thereafter commissioned De Mura for this work. Jesus is worshipped at the altar below, and paid homage to in the Eucharist, just as the Magi are seen worshipping the infant Jesus, above.

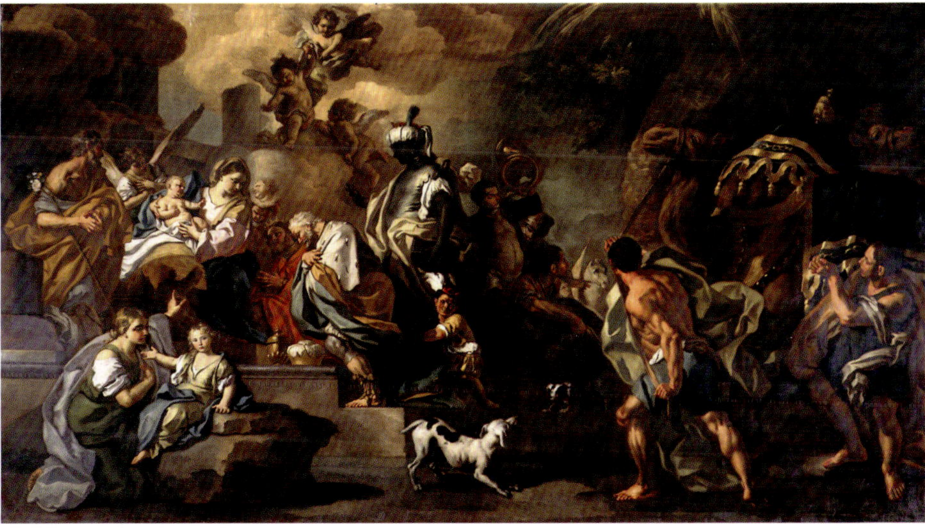

Provenance:
Studio of the artist, to 1782; bequest of Francesco de Mura in 1782.

Exhibitions:
Palazzo Reale, Naples, July 1980–Jan. 1981, *Civiltà del '700 a Napoli: Pittura sacra a Napoli nel '700*; Kunstforum der Bank Austria, Vienna, Castel Sant'Elmo, Naples, Dec. 10, 1993–July 24, 1994, *Settecento napoletano: Sulle ali dell'aquila imperiale, 1707–1734*.

Bibliography:
Giuseppe Ceci, "Lo 'Studio' di Francesco de Mura," *Rassegna storica napoletana*, nos. 2–3 (1933): 15; Costanza Lorenzetti "La pittura napoletana dei secoli XVIII," in *La mostra della pittura napoletana dei secoli XVII, XVIII, XIX*, ed. Sergio Ortolani and Maria Biancale, exhib. cat. (Naples: F. Giannini, 1938), 192; Raffaello Causa, entry 20 in *Mostra di bozzetti napoletani del Seicento e del Settecento*, exhib. cat. (Naples: Museo della Certosa di San Martino, 1947), 54–55, no. 51; Robert Engass, "Francesco de Mura alla Nunziatella," *Bollettino d'arte* 49 (1964): 133–35, fig. 3; Raffaello Causa, *Opere d'arte nel Pio Monte della Misericordia a Napoli* (Cava dei Tirreni: Mauro, 1970), 110, no. 101, pl. 31; Nicola Spinosa, *Pittura sacra a Napoli nel '700*, exhib. cat. (Naples: Società Editrice Napolentana, 1980), 104, no. 55; Nicola Spinosa, *Pittura napoletana del Settecento*, vol. 2, *Dal rococò al classicismo* (Naples: Electa Napoli, 1988), 167; Gino D'Alessio, "Nuove osservazioni sulle committenze reali per Francesco de Mura tra Napoli, Torino e Madrid," *Prospettiva*, no. 69 (1993): 80–81; Gino D'Alessio, entry 22 in *Capolavori in Festa*, exhib. cat. (Naples: Electa Napoli, 1997), 204–5; Nicola Spinosa, "Francesco de Mura al Pio Monte," in *Il Pio Monte della Misericordia di Napoli nel Quarto Centenario*, ed. Mario Pisani Massamormile (Naples: Electa Napoli, 2003), 194–95; Nicola Spinosa, "Francesco de Mura al Pio Monte della Misericordia," *FMR*, no. 29 (Jan.–Feb. 2009): 24–48; Nicola Spinosa, "Napoli e il viceregno austriaco," in *Settecento napoletano: Sulle ali dell'aquila imperiale, 1707–1734*, exhib. cat. (Naples: Electa Napoli, 1994), 166–67, no. 17; *Viaggio nel presepe napoletano del Settecento* (Moscow: Electa Napoli, 2011), 112–13.

Fig. 48
Francesco de Mura, *The Adoration of the Magi*, 1727–28, oil on canvas, 86⅝ × 165⅜ in. (220 × 420 cm), church of Santa Maria Donnarómita, Naples

12 — continued

This commission was a breakthrough for De Mura, first, because of the prominence of the Nunziatella on Pizzofalcone (Falcon's Peak), Naples' most fashionable hill. This was among the earliest of the many major commissions the artist received, raising his reputation greatly.[1] Second, this painting demonstrates a liberation from Solimena's style in the originality of the composition, and—possibly because of the darkness at the top of the apse—De Mura's lightened palette. De Mura also demonstrates here his theatrical bent.[2] The lighter colors are most apparent when we compare this *bozzetto* in Pio Monte della Misericordia with the actual Nunziatella fresco,[3] which is even lighter. Earlier, De Mura painted another large *Adoration of the Magi* about 1727 for the church of Santa Maria Donnarómita in Naples (fig. 48).[4] The transformation of his style from 1727–28 to 1730–32 is quite remarkable: gone is the dark and heavy Caravaggesque chiaroscuro of Solimena, where the setting always seems to be at night; present is an almost French Rococo palette, rich in pastels and filled with bright daylight.

1. He was already becoming almost as famous as Solimena: in 1731, De Mura appeared in the *Abecedario pittorico* (Painters' Listings) published by P. A. Orlandi and Antonio Roviglione, who, on their title page, "dedicated [the book] to Signor Francesco [de] Mura, excellent and magnificent Neapolitan painter..." This dedication greatly irritated Solimena and was removed in the next printing.
2. Nicola Spinosa, "Mura, Francesco de," *Dizionario enciclopedico Bolaffi dei pittori e degli incisori italiani dall'11° al 20° secolo*, vol. 28 (Turin: G. Bolaffi, 1976), 51–54: "In 1732, he painted the large fresco of the Nunziatella, where, despite the evident dependence on Solimenesque purism, the lucidity of the characters is quite original in the narrative's intense fervor. De Mura became agile and fast without losing his compositional harmony. And from this moment on, with ever greater clarity and always with results of the highest quality, De Mura's creative imagination emerges increasingly dependent, in particular, on *the imaginative inspiration from contemporary theater and opera*. The 'heroic' conception of Solimena is transformed into a vision of reality and into a concept of 'history' essentially resting on a delicate sentiment of humanity, inclined towards the depiction of a world of refined compositional harmony and precious formal elegance."
3. The fresco in the Nunziatella is signed and dated in the lower left corner: "Fran.ᶜᵒ de Mura F./A.D. 1732." See Patrizia di Maggio, "Aggiunte e precisazioni su Francesco de Mura," *Antologia di belle arti* 9, nos. 35–38 (1990): 99, fig. 1.
4. Nicola Spinosa, "Neapolitan Painting in the Holy Land," in *Baroque Art from the Holy Sepulchre: The Image of Jerusalem in the Pre-Alps*, ed. Manuela Kahn-Rossi and Chiara Naldi, exhib. cat. (Lugano: Galleria Canesso, 2014), 70–71, fig. 12. De Mura's *Adoration of the Magi* in Santa Maria Donnarómita was recently cleaned by Giulia Zorzetti in Naples.

Cat. 12

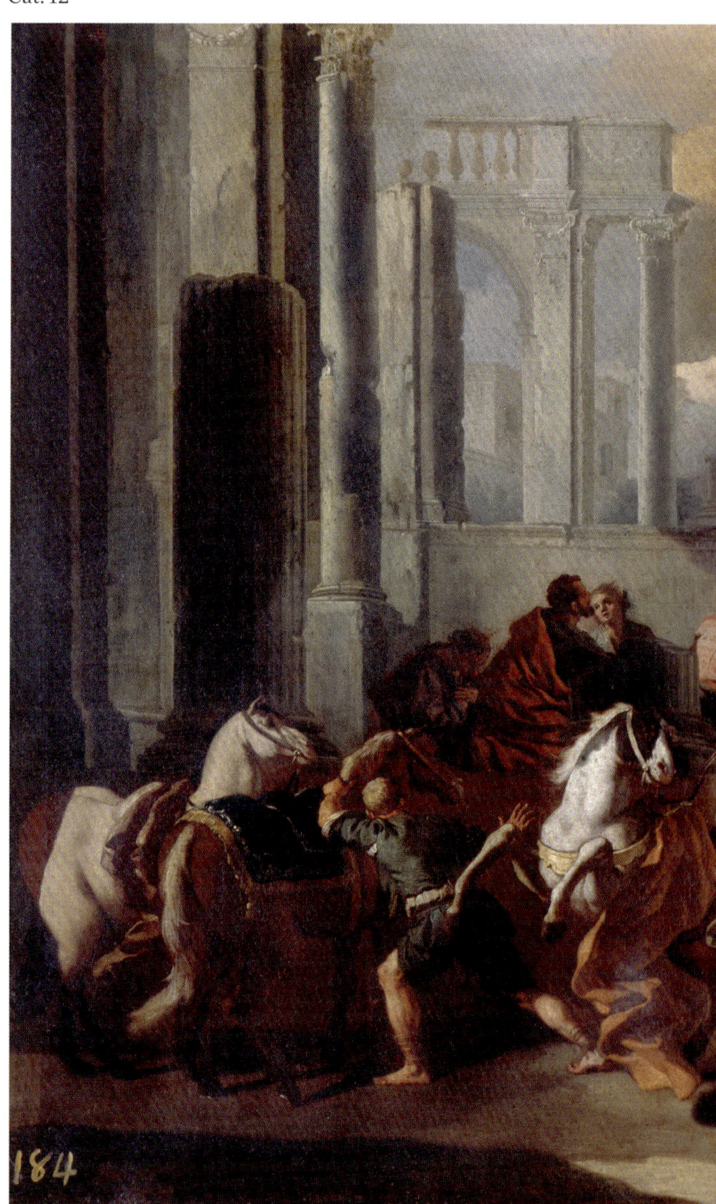

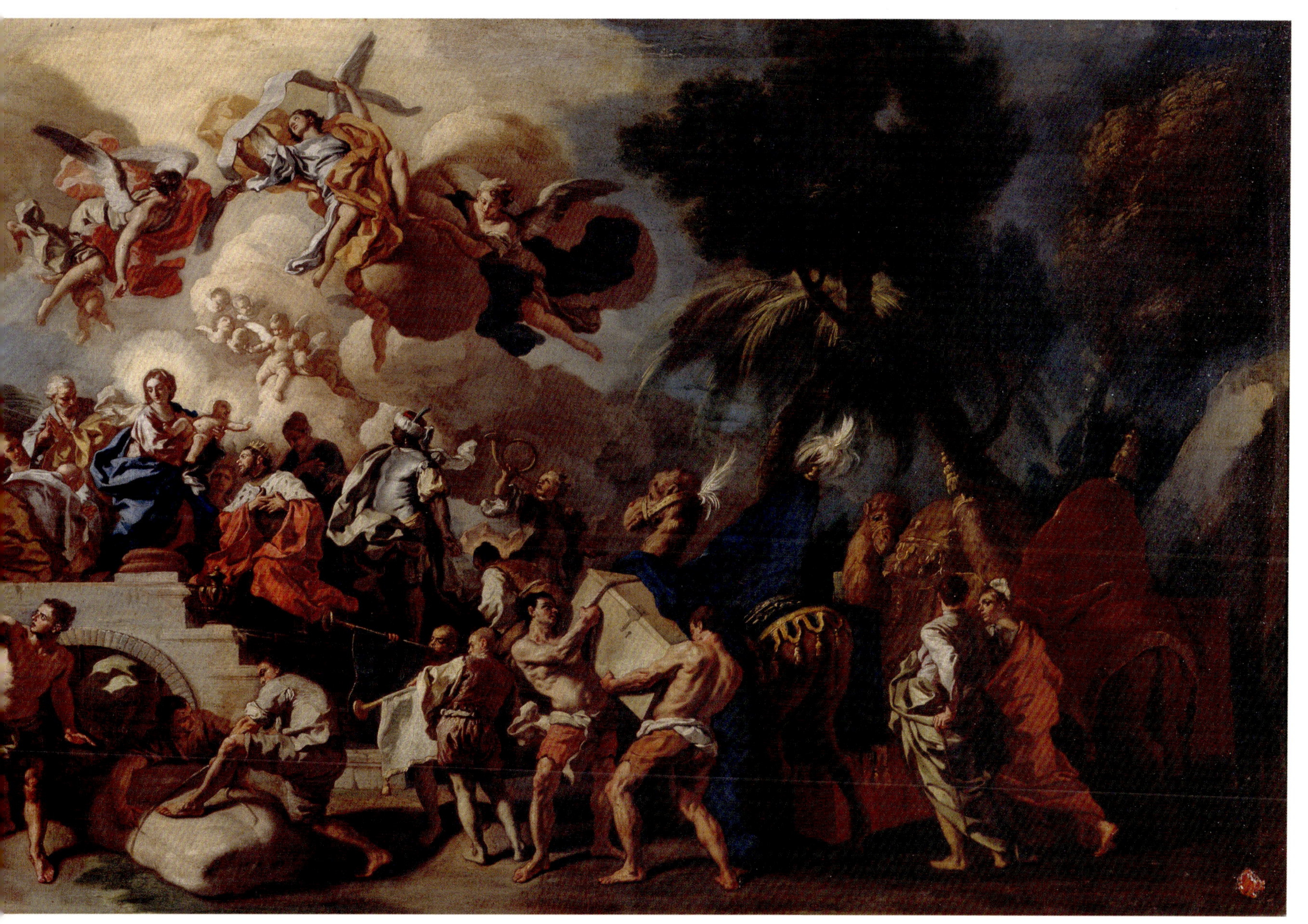

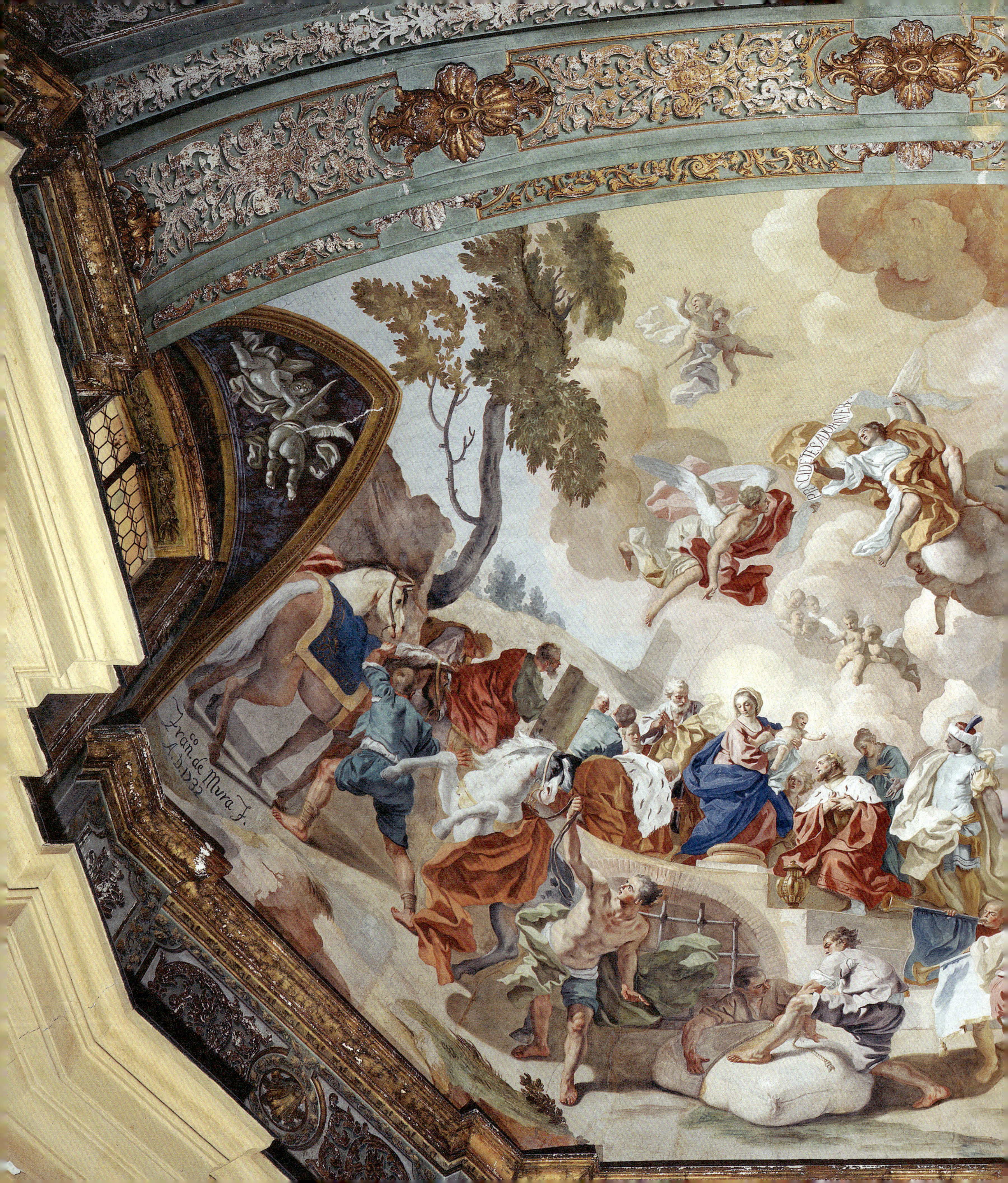

Franco de Mura F.
A. D. 1732
PROCIDĒTES ADORAV[ERVNT]

12 — continued

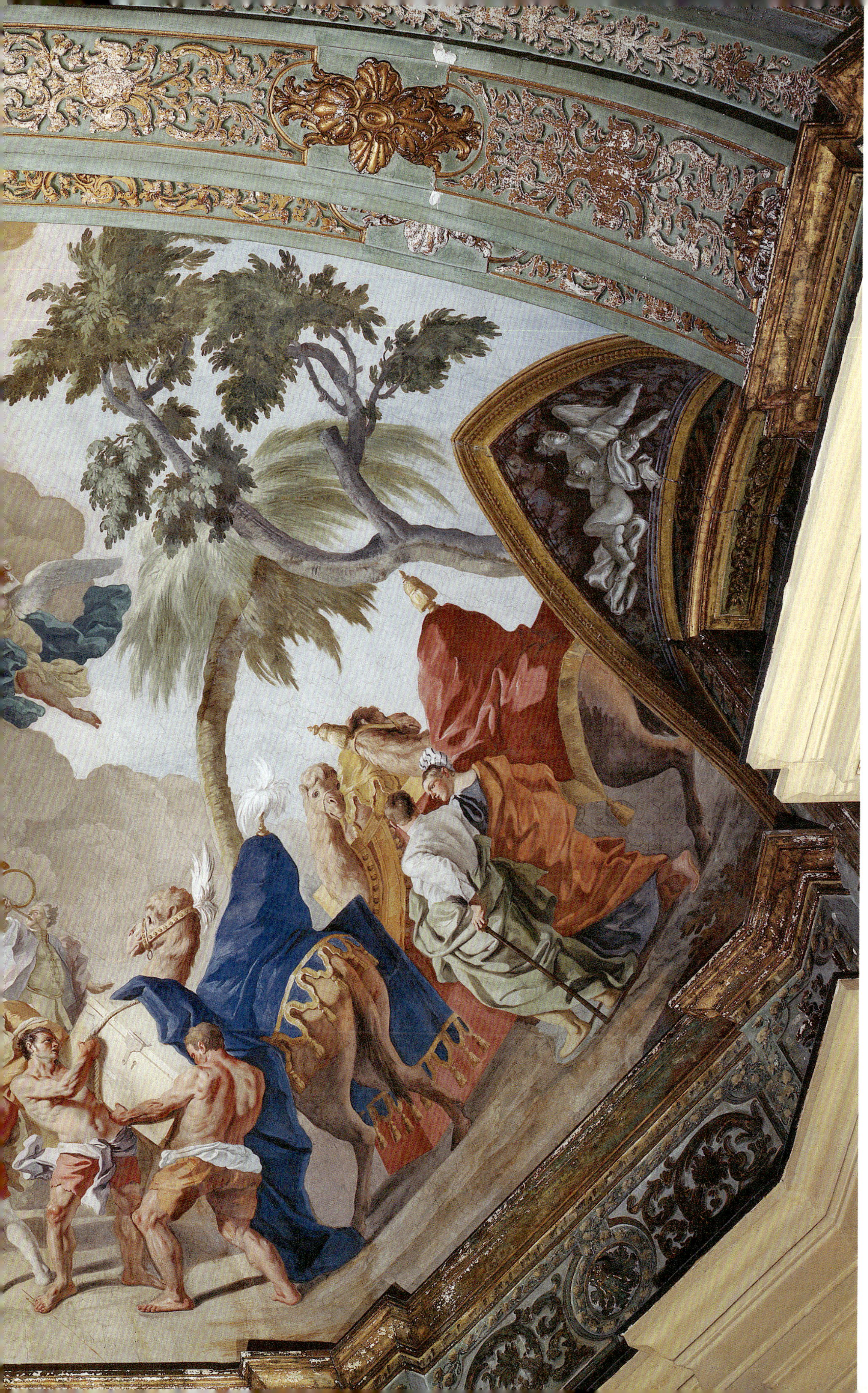

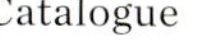

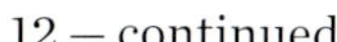

Fig. 49
Francesco de Mura, *The Adoration of the Magi*, 1732, fresco, ceiling of the apse, church of the Nunziatella, Naples

13

Francesco de Mura
Christ Receiving St. Joseph into Heaven with the Madonna and Saints, ca. 1741
Oil on canvas, 53½ × 87⅞ in. (136 × 223 cm)
Pio Monte della Misericordia, inv. no. 115

In 1734, the newly restored cupola of the Neapolitan church of San Giuseppe dei Ruffi was completed. De Mura was commissioned to fresco the ceiling of the cupola some time after 1740, completing it in the following years. The church requested that the cupola ceiling, which is directly above the main altar, be decorated with an Apotheosis of St. Joseph, after whom the church had been rededicated in 1611. The cult of St. Joseph enjoyed a resurgence in the mid-1700s in Naples, reflecting the Counter-Reformation's new emphasis on the humanity of Jesus and his earthly father.

This *bozzetto* is a study for the semispherical dome of the San Giuseppe dei Ruffi cupola, and not for a flat representation. The scene, set in a sunlit heaven, depicts at its highest point, the Trinity, with the bright-white Holy Spirit as a flying dove. To the right is God the Father with a triangular halo on his head. His robe is unfurled behind him, his right hand raised in blessing and his left holding a scepter, which he rests on the orb of the universe that is supported by two angels. Jesus is the most prominent of the three, floating above a cloud, seeming to fall backward as he raises his left arm, his chest bared, and a glowing halo around his head; two angels assist him in carrying the cross, conceived as two wooden poles and tilted to the right, as is Jesus' body. On either side of Jesus are Mary, on the left, and Joseph, on the right. In his raised right hand, Joseph holds his flowering cane, his symbol, as he sits sideways on a cloud below Jesus' arm. His head is turned to the right to acknowledge St. Augustine, who stands below, facing him, and offers him the flaming heart of Jesus. Below Augustine are St. Andrew with his cross, St. Paul with his sword, and St. Peter with his keys; Naples' own St. Januarius (San Gennaro) sits on the left, near Mary's foot. Dozens of additional saints are arranged in a large oval around Jesus. More than a dozen angels add to the crowded tableau.

Raffaello Causa wrote in 1970 that this composition is highly significant in understanding De Mura's mature period, since here he moves away from Solimena's style and revisits the 1600s and the work of Giovanni Lanfranco and Mattia Preti.[1] There is a similarly composed heavenly scene in another *bozzetto* by De Mura of *St. Nicholas of Bari Received into Heaven* in Compton Verney Art Gallery in Warwickshire, England, which he painted ca. 1735 for the cupola of the church of San Nicola alla Carità in Naples (fig. 50).[2] In addition, a drawing attributed to De Mura of *The Crowning of a Female Saint in Heaven*, sold at Sotheby's, London, in 2014 (fig. 51), may relate to Pio Monte's *bozzetto* for the *St. Joseph* fresco. The *St. Joseph* fresco and the *Adoration* fresco of the Nunziatella confirmed De Mura as one of the outstanding Neapolitan painters to come out of the studio of Solimena,[3] and led to De Mura's being invited to work on the frescoes for the Palazzo Reale in Turin in 1741 (see cat. nos. 18 and 19).

1. Causa, *Opere d'arte*, 113.
2. Spinosa, "Napoli e il viceregno austriaco," 168.
3. Bernardo de Dominici, *Vite dei pittori, scultori ed architetti napoletani* (Naples, 1743), 4:579–96.

Provenance:
Studio of the artist, to 1782; bequest of Francesco de Mura in 1782; Bardellino-Fischetti Inventory, no. 153.

Bibliography:
Giuseppe Ceci, "Lo 'Studio' di Francesco de Mura," *Rassegna storica napoletana*, nos. 2–3 (1933): 3–23; Raffaello Causa, *Opere d'arte nel Pio Monte della Misericordia a Napoli* (Cava dei Tirreni: Mauro, 1970), 113, no. 115, fig. 38; Nicola Spinosa, "Napoli e il viceregno austriaco," in *Settecento napoletano: Sulle ali dell'aquila imperiale, 1707–1734*, exhib. cat. (Naples: Electa Napoli, 1994), 168–69, no. 18; Nicola Spinosa, "Francesco de Mura al Pio Monte," in *Il Pio Monte della Misericordia di Napoli nel Quarto Centenario*, ed. Mario Pisani Massamormile (Naples: Electa Napoli, 2003), 191–211; Nicola Spinosa, "Francesco de Mura al Pio Monte della Misericordia," *FMR*, no. 29 (Jan.–Feb. 2009): 24–48; Loredana Gazzara, "Note e documenti inediti per lo studio delle collezioni della Quadreria del Pio Monte della Misericordia (I)," *Napoli Nobilissima*, 5th ser., 9 (May–Aug. 2008): 160–79; Franco di Spirito, *San Giuseppe dei Ruffi a Napoli: Il restauro degli affreschi* (Naples: Arte'm, 2011).

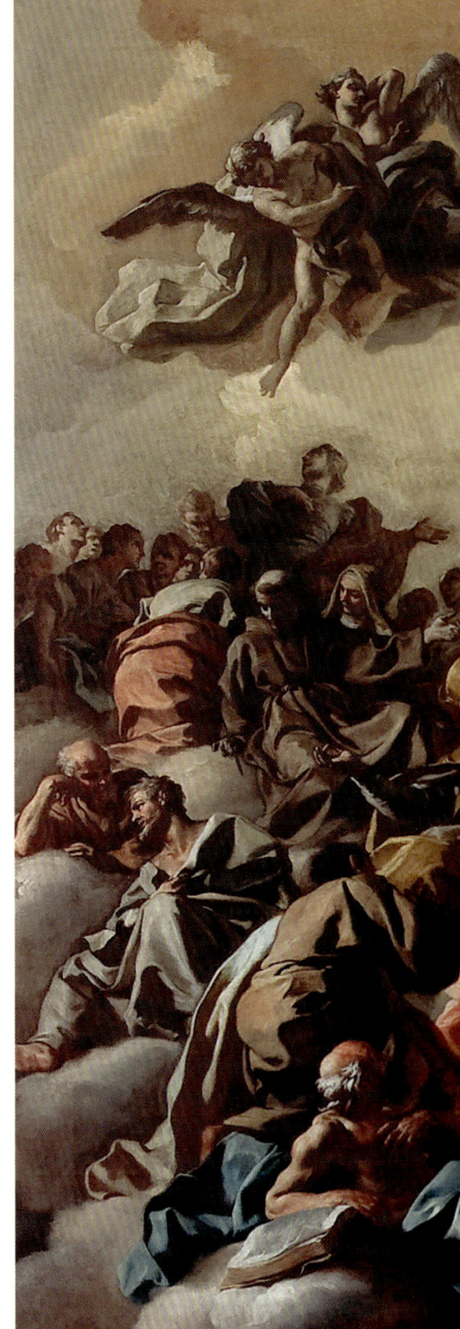

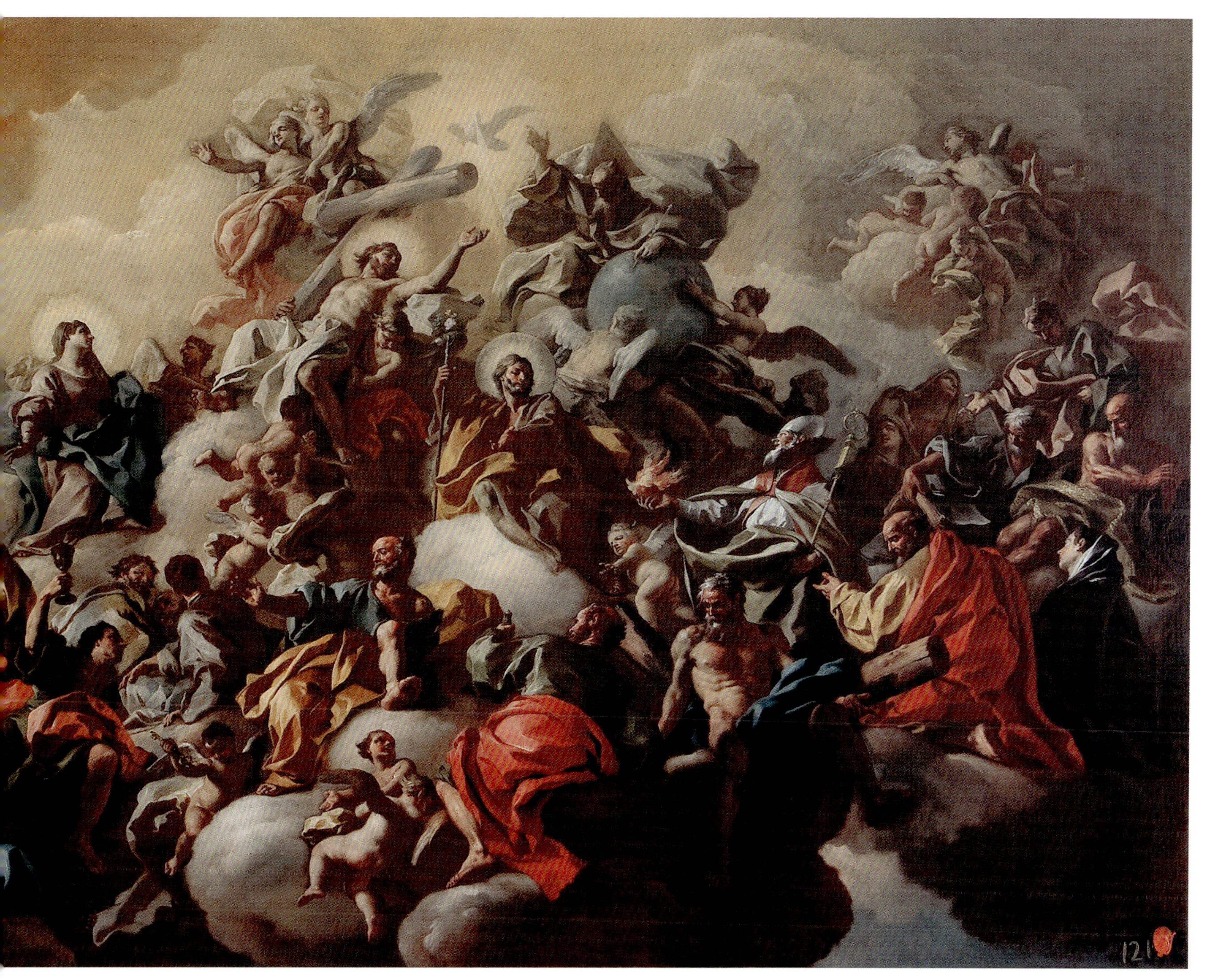

13 — continued

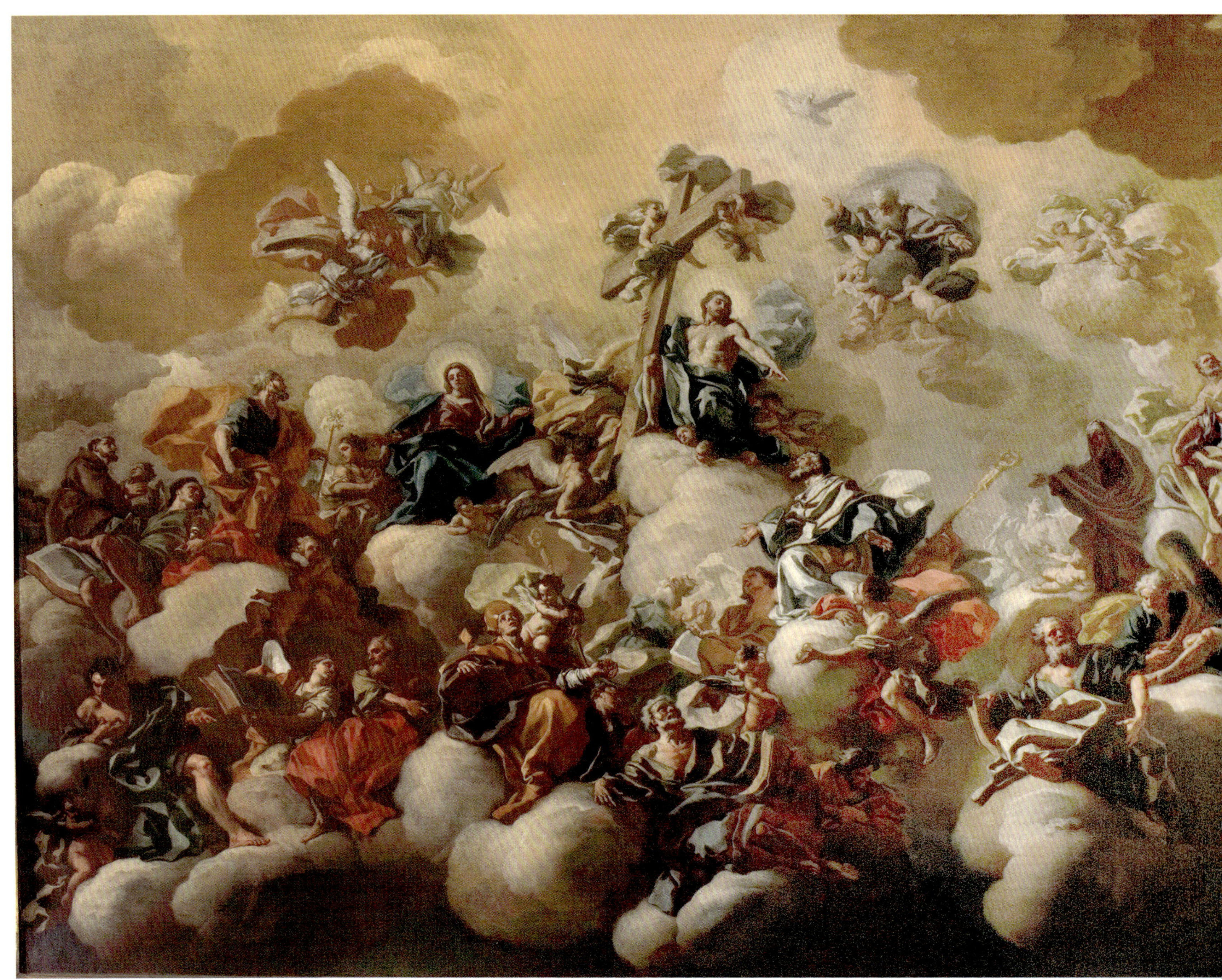

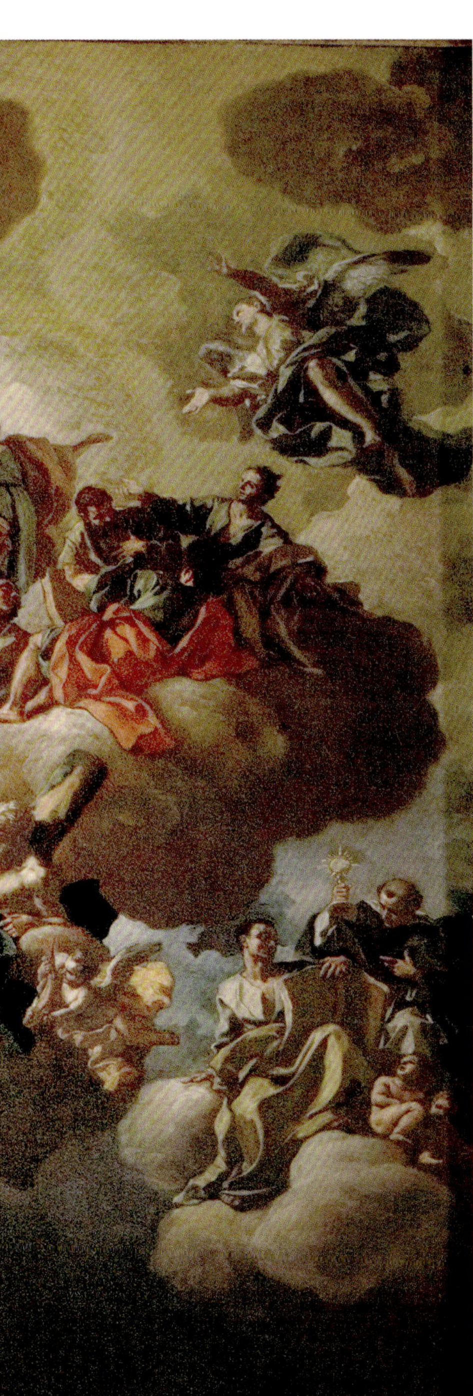

Fig. 50
Francesco de Mura, *St. Nicholas of Bari Received into Heaven,* ca. 1735, oil on canvas, 59¾ × 88¼ in. (139 × 224 cm), Compton Verney Art Gallery, U.K.

Fig. 51
Attributed to Francesco de Mura, *The Crowning of a Female Saint in Heaven*, ca. 1735–40, pen and gray ink and wash over chalk, 10⅜ × 16½ in. (26.5 × 42 cm), Sotheby's, London, April 29, 2014, lot 642

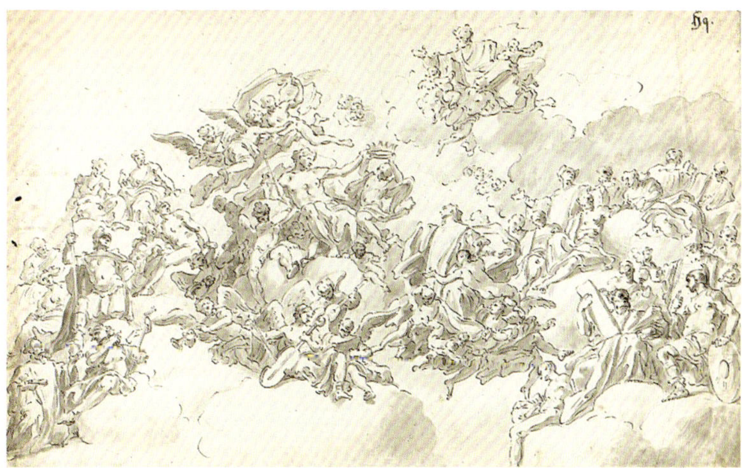

14

Francesco de Mura
The Vision of St. Benedict, ca. 1740
Pen and brown and gray ink, brush and gray wash, over graphite,
22¼ × 15 in. (56.5 × 38.2 cm)
The Metropolitan Museum of Art, purchased from Harry G. Sperling
Fund, acc. no. 1987.191

Around 905, the monks of the Benedictine order founded the Neapolitan church of Santi Severino e Sossio, naming it after two early saints— Severinus of Noricum (ca. 410–482) and Sossius (275–305)—whose relics they held. A decade after the roof of the church collapsed in the earthquake of 1731, De Mura was commissioned to re-fresco the ceiling of the nave and the counter-façade, where he completed the *Banquet in the House of Levi, the Pharisee* in 1746 (fig. 52).[1]

St. Benedict of Nursia (ca. 480–547), who is considered the founder of Western monasticism (he is also the patron saint of Europe), established the abbey of Monte Cassino around 529. He wrote a book of precepts or "rules" (still used today) for self-governing monks living as a community under an abbot. This drawing by De Mura from the Metropolitan Museum is an early idea of around 1740 for the ceiling fresco in the nave of Santi Severino e Sossio (see fig. 53), and represents the vision of St. Benedict.

In the pen and ink drawing, which differs in key elements from the final painted version of the ceiling, Benedict, in monastic garb, stands with open arms on the steps of a multicolumned building looking upward towards the heavens, where God the Father appears on the orb of the universe with more than fifteen angels flying under and around him. Surrounding God are dozens of figures—on the steps in front of him, behind him, and to his sides—who appear to be monks, nuns, and lay people involved with Benedict's rule. Directly below Benedict, a small dog (perhaps representing fidelity) is perched on the lowest step and looks up. The beauty of the composition, with its flickering, delicate lines, creates a powerful and clear image of the narrative.

1. See Spinosa, *Pittura napoletana dei Settecento*, vol. 1, *Dal barocco al rococò* (Naples: Electa Napoli, 1986), 159–60, no. 252.

Provenance:
[Colnaghi]; purchased by The Metropolitan Museum of Art, New York, in 1987.

Bibliography:
Jean-Luc Baroni, *Old Master Drawings Presented by Jean-Luc Baroni: Colnaghi Drawings*, exhib. cat. (New York: Colnaghi, 1987), no. 26 (ill.); Lawrence Turcic, "New York: Four Exhibitions of Drawings," *The Burlington Magazine* 129, no. 1014 (Sept. 1987): 622; Metroplitan Museum of Art, *Annual Report* (New York: Metropolitan Museum of Art, 1987–88), 3; Jacob Bean and William Griswold, *18th Century Italian Drawings in The Metropolitan Museum of Art* (New York: Metropolitan Museum of Art, 1990), 150–51, no. 139 (ill.).

Fig. 52
Francesco de Mura, *Banquet in the House of Levi, the Pharisee,* 1746, fresco, counter-façade, Santi Severino e Sossio, Naples

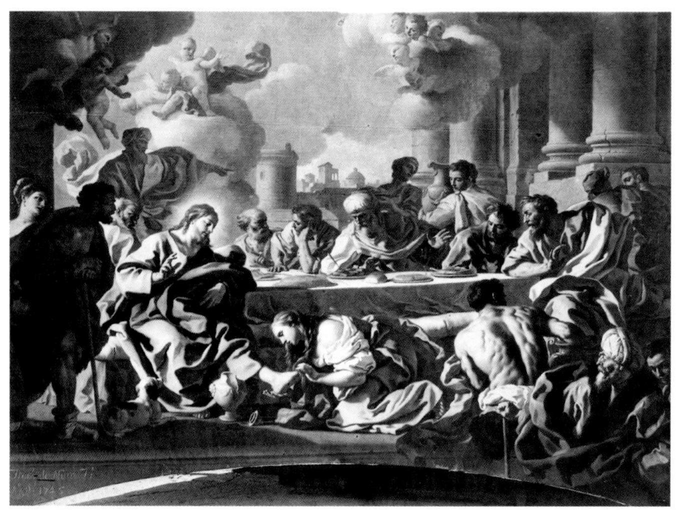

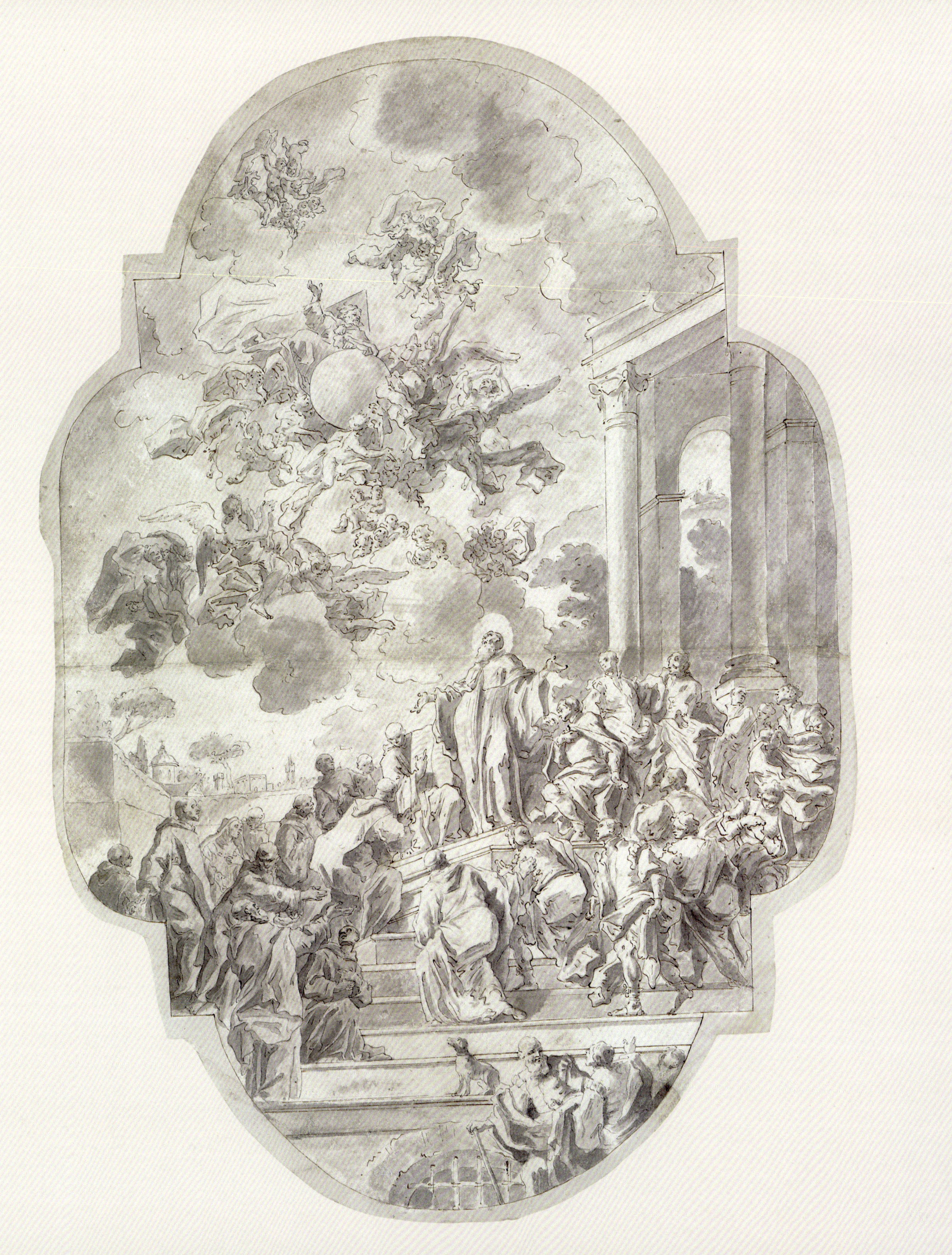

15

Francesco de Mura
The Vision of St. Benedict, 1738–40
Oil on canvas, 80 × 49⅝ in. (203.2 × 126 cm)
Museo e Gallerie Nazionali di Capodimonte, inv. no. Q 222

This large *bozzetto* is for *The Vision of St. Benedict*, the ceiling fresco in the nave of the Benedictine church of Santi Severino e Sossio in Naples. A study for the central panel, this *bozzetto* is one of thirteen that De Mura painted between 1738 and 1746. (The *bozzetto* for the panel above this central episode, *St. Benedict Welcomes Totila*, is cat. no. 16.) Nicola Spinosa has pointed out that—because De Mura worked on this key painting between his frescoes for the Palazzo Reale in Naples, begun in 1738, until the end of his work in the Palazzo Reale in Turin, completed in 1746—the *St. Benedict* paintings exemplify his gradual maturation from the Solimenesque to the full-blown Rococo.[1] This *bozzetto* for the central panel is the earliest of the *Benedict* paintings, begun in the middle of 1738 and completed in 1740, when it was signed and dated. Giacinto Diano, a former student of De Mura's, painted a very similarly composed *bozzetto* of *The Madonna and Child Appearing to St. Dominic* (fig. 54).

St. Benedict, the founder of Western monasticism and the abbey of Monte Cassino, stands at the entrance to a columned archway, dressed in a black habit with arms spread wide and palms up, as he tilts his head backward and gazes above at God the Father surrounded by flying angels. God leans against the orb of the universe, wearing his triangular halo and holding a scepter in his left hand, as he gazes down at Benedict. St. Scholastica, the twin sister of Benedict and founder of the first Benedictine-like convent near Monte Cassino, stands to his right, looking upward; behind her is a group of nuns. Below sits a monk holding a plaque with the Rule of St. Benedict. King Totila kneels in homage on Benedict's left; a queen stands behind the saint, who is surrounded by dozens of monks and lay people.

The fresco (fig. 53) follows this *bozzetto* in most regards, except in additional details and clarifications that enhance its energy. Although it has a more subdued color scheme, the fresco, according to Tiziana Scarpa, has "a brilliant and luminous colorism that … can be compared to the style of the Venetian artist Giovanni Battista Tiepolo."[2] The church and its frescoes became a "must-see" for all cultivated travelers on the Grand Tour, including the great French Rococo painter Jean-Honoré Fragonard, who toured Naples in 1760.

1. Spinosa, *Civiltà del '700 a Napoli*, 194.
2. Scarpa, entry in *Fierce Reality*, 101.

Provenance:
Bequest of Francesco de Mura to Pio Monte della Misericordia, Naples, 1789 (Bardellino-Fischetti inventory), inv. no. 64; acquired by the Italian state for the Museo e Gallerie Nazionali di Capodimonte, Naples, 1907.

Exhibitions:
Florence, 1922, *Mostra della pittura italiana del Seicento e del Settecento*, no. 377; Naples, 1938, *La pittura napoletana dei secoli XVII, XVIII, XIX*, no. 25 (Cappella di Santa Barbara); Various venues, Naples, Dec. 1979–Oct. 1980, *Civiltà del '700 a Napoli, 1734–1799*, no. 89; Dortmund, Milan, 1981, *Pittori e disegnatori del '700 a Napoli*, no. 17; Athens, 1984, *Il secolo d'oro della pittura napoletana*; Budapest, 1985, *A Napolyi festészet aranykora XVII–XVIII szàzad*; Museo Arqueológico Nacional, Madrid, Mar. 7–May 6, 1990, *El arte de la corte de Napoles en el siglo XVIII*, no. 11; Museo e Gallerie Nazionali di Capodimonte, Naples, 1994, *I capolavori di Capodimonte da Masaccio a Andy Warhol*, no. 7.2; Phoenix Art Museum, Ariz., Dec. 10, 2006–Mar. 4, 2007, *Fierce Reality: Italian Masters from Seventeenth-Century Naples*; Museo e Gallerie Nazionali di Capodimonte, Certosa e Museo di San Martino, Castel Sant'Elmo, Museo Pignatelli, Museo Duca di Martina, Palazzo Reale, Naples, Dec. 12, 2009–Apr. 11, 2010, *Ritorno al Barocco: da Caravaggio a Vanvitelli*.

Bibliography:
Mario Morelli, "I dipinti di Francesco de Mura acquistati per la Galleria del Museo Nazionale di Napoli," *Bollettino d'Arte* (1910): 293–302; Aldo de Rinaldis, *Guida illustrata del Museo Nazionale di Napoli, parte II: Pinacoteca* (Naples: Richter, 1911), 467; Emmanuel Bénézit, *Dictionnaire critique et documentaire des peintures…*, vol. 10 (Paris, 1924): 31; Aldo de Rinaldis, *La Pinacoteca del Museo Nazionale di Napoli* (Naples: Richter, 1928), 201–2; Giuseppe Ceci, "Lo 'Studio' di Francesco de Mura," *Rassegna storica napoletana*, nos. 2–3 (1933): 18; Costanza Lorenzetti, "La pittura napoletana dei secoli XVIII," in *La mostra della pittura napoletana dei secoli XVII, XVIII, XIX*, ed. Sergio Ortolani and Maria Biancale, exhib. cat. (Naples: F. Giannini, 1938), 191; Raffaello Causa, *Opere d'arte nel Pio Monte della Misericordia* (Cava dei Tirreni: Mauro, 1970), 112–13; Nicola Spinosa, *L'Arazzeria napoletana* (Naples: Libreria scientifica editrice, 1971), 459, 470; Nicola Spinosa, *Civiltà del '700 a Napoli, 1734–1799* (Florence: Centro Di, 1979), 1:194, no. 89; Nicola Spinosa, *Pittura napoletana del Settecento*, vol. 1, *Dal barocco al rococò*, 2nd ed. (Naples: Electa Napoli, 1993), 157, 160, no. 252, fig. 299; Tiziana Scarpa, article in *Utili*, 2002, 370; Tiziana Scarpa, entry in *Fierce Reality: Italian Masters from Seventeenth-Century Naples*, ed. Thomas J. Loughman, exhib. cat. (Milan: Skira, 2006), 100–101; Nicola Spinosa, entry 50a in *Museo e Gallerie Nazionali di Capodimonte: Dipinti del XVIII secolo; La scuola napoletana* (Naples: Electa Napoli, 2010), 66.

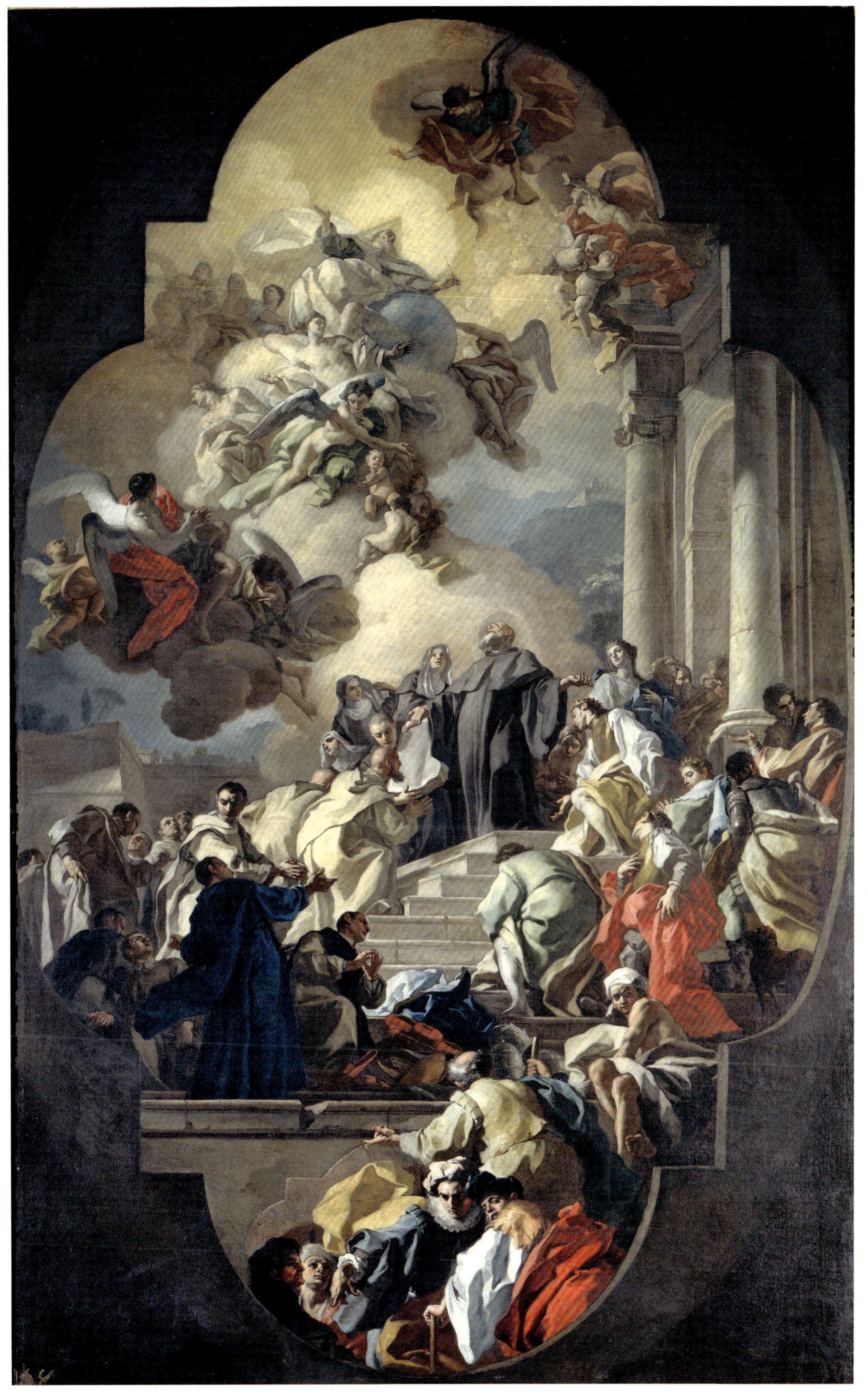

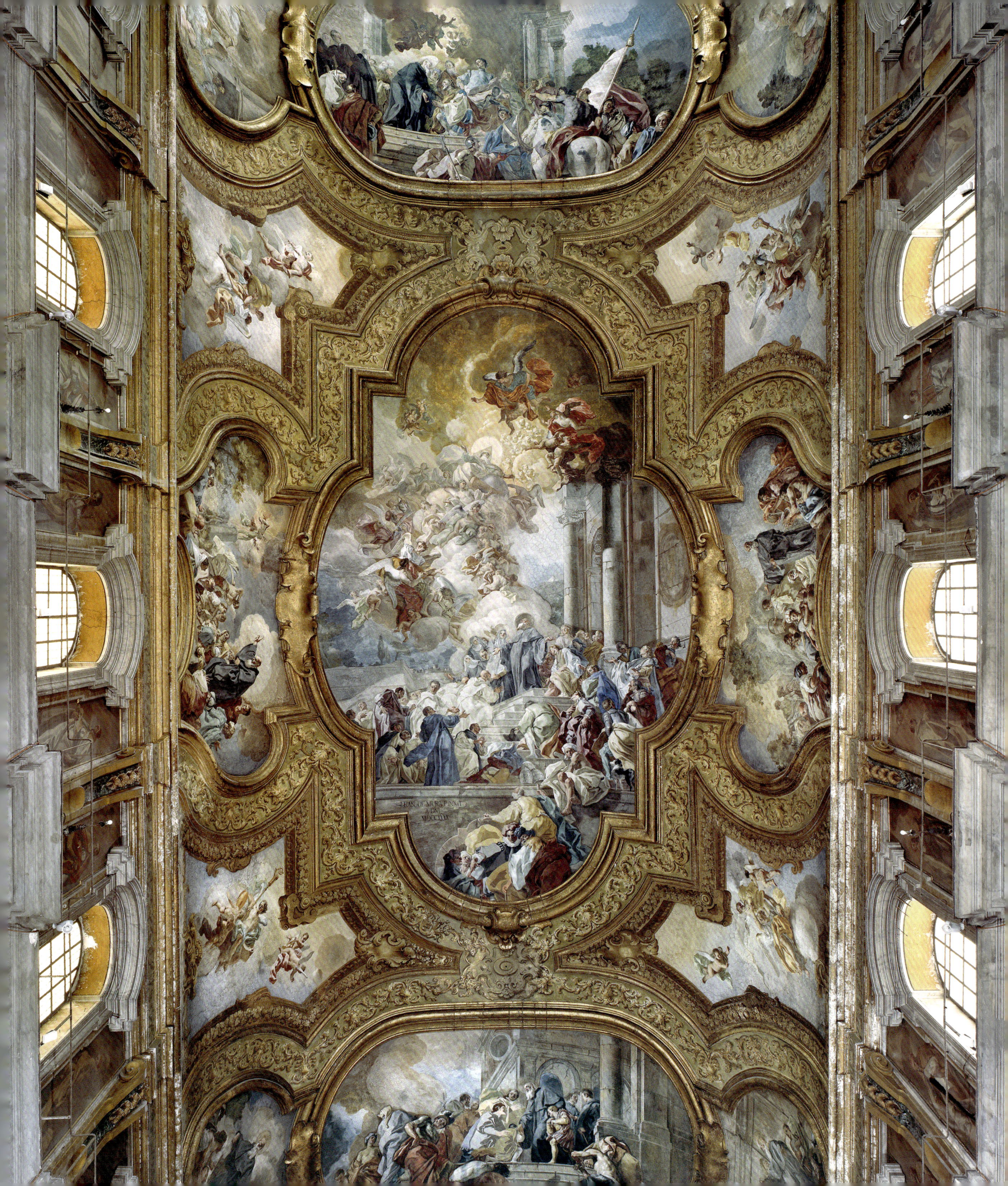

15 — continued

Fig. 53
Francesco de Mura, *The Vision of
St. Benedict*, 1738–40, fresco (with
oil panels on the side), ceiling of
church of Santi Severino e Sossio,
Naples

Fig. 54
Giacinto Diano, *The Madonna and
Child Appearing to St. Dominic
with Rosary*, ca. 1760?, *bozzetto* for
a ceiling painting, oil on canvas,
49¼ × 33 in. (125 × 84 cm),
Museum of Western and Eastern
Art Odessa, Ukraine

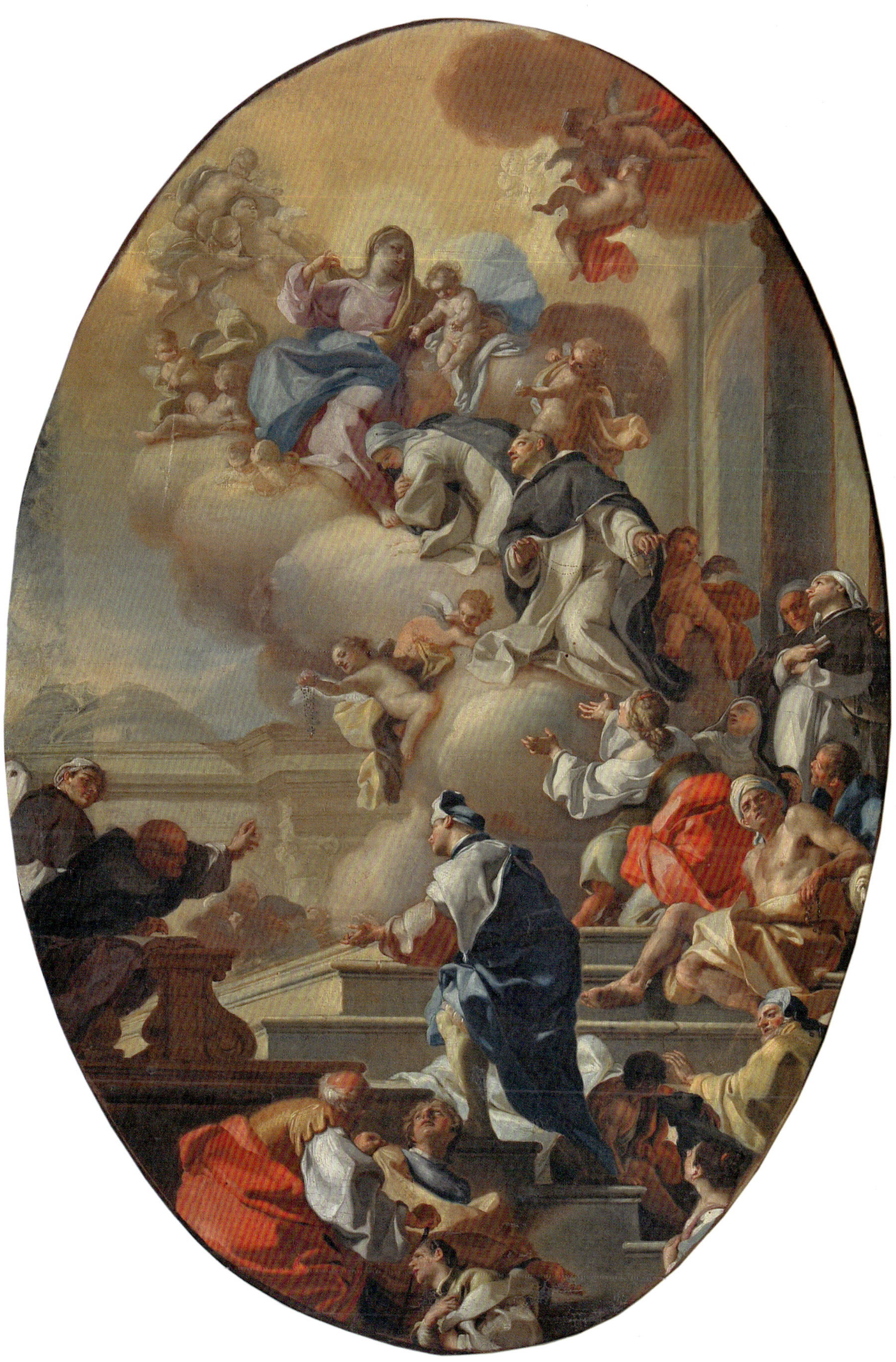

16

Francesco de Mura
St. Benedict Welcomes Totila, ca. 1738–40
Oil on canvas, 49⅞ × 80¾ in. (126.5 × 205 cm)
Museo e Gallerie Nazionali di Capodimonte, inv. no. Q 218

This is a *bozzetto* for the oil painting panel situated at the top of the central scene of *The Vision of St. Benedict* in Santi Severino e Sossio (see fig. 53), one of thirteen panels depicting various scenes from the life of Benedict. The scene places the viewer below, looking up, as Benedict greets Totila, king of the Visigoths, who bows before the saint with both hands clasped together. Armored soldiers and servants surround the central figures, who are at the top of the steps before a columned temple, with angels flying above. Brilliant sunlight appears behind clouds, illuminating the scene from the left. A sword-bearer named Riggio, in a pale blue-green jacket, stands in a contrapuntal pose behind the king and holds his robe, while a small African boy servant lifts the king's cape. On the right, a soldier on a horse (his back to us) points to the central figures with his left hand while holding a large banner with his right. Benedict's monks stand, like sentinels, watching on the left.

King Totila's meeting with St. Benedict at the abbey of Monte Cassino, described in Pope St. Gregory's *Dialogues* (2.14–15, "Life of St. Benedict"), occurred either before or soon after the siege of Naples; the Benedictines' traditional date of the meeting is March 21, 543. Gregory includes a story about the saint's discernment: Benedict identified Totila's aide—his sword-bearer Riggio, whom Totila dressed in his own royal robes—as an impostor. Totila, the *nom de guerre* of Baduila (d. 552), wanted to see if Benedict would discover the truth. Immediately, the saint detected the impersonation, and Totila was induced by this to pay Benedict homage. The pointing figures underscore the "miraculousness" of the story.

The final painting (fig. 55) differs in small details from this oil sketch: the king has transformed into an old man, the horse is now dappled, and the shape of the composition has changed from a horizontal oval to a hippodrome shape—straight at the top and bottom, and curved at the sides. The brilliant colors and the lively gestures of the elegant figures in this composition create one of De Mura's most powerful narratives.

Provenance:
Bequest of Francesco de Mura to Pio Monte della Misericordia, Naples, 1789 (Bardellino-Fischetti inventory), inv. no. 63; acquired by the Italian state for the Museo e Gallerie Nazionali di Capodimonte, Naples, 1907.

Bibliography:
Mario Morelli, "I dipinti di Francesco de Mura acquistati per la Galleria del Museo Nazionale di Napoli," *Bollettino d'Arte* (1910): 293–302; Giuseppe Ceci, "Lo 'Studio' di Francesco de Mura, *Rassegna storica napoletana*, nos. 2–3 (1933): 18; Costanza Lorenzetti, "La pittura napoletana dei secoli XVIII," in *La mostra della pittura napoletana dei secoli XVII, XVIII, XIX*, ed. Sergio Ortolani and Maria Biancale, exhib. cat. (Naples: F. Giannini, 1938), 191; Raffaelo Causa, *Opere d'arte nel Pio Monte della Misericordia* (Cava dei Tirreni: Mauro, 1970), 112–13; Nicola Spinosa, *L'Arazzeria napoletana* (Naples: Libreria scientifica editrice, 1971), 459, 470; Nicola Spinosa, *Civiltà del '700 a Napoli, 1734–1799*, exhib. cat. (Florence: Centro Di, 1979), 1:194, no. 89; Nicola Spinosa, ed., *The National Museum of Capodimonte* (Naples: Electa Napoli, 1996), 142 (ill.); F. Capobianco, *Il Pio Monte della Misericordia: La chiesa e la quadreria* (Castellammare di Stabia, 1997), 45–46, 64; Nicola Spinosa, *Museo di Capodimonte: La "Galleria napoletana": Le Arti a Napoli dal Duecento all'Ottocento* (Naples, 1999), 55; Nicola Spinosa, *Pittura napoletana del Settecento*, vol. 1, *Dal barocco al rococò*, 2nd ed. (Naples: Electa Napoli, 1999), 157, 160, no. 252, fig. 299; Tiziana Scarpa, entry in Mariella Utili (ed.), *Museo di Capodimonte,* Milan: Skira, 2002, 370; Nicola Spinosa, "Francesco de Mura al Pio Monte," in Mario Pisani Massamormile (ed.), *Il Pio Monte della Misericordia di Napoli nel quarto centenario*, Naples, Electa, 209; Tiziana Scarpa, entry 47, in *Fierce Reality: Italian Masters from Seventeenth-Century Naples*, ed. Thomas J. Loughman, exhib. cat. for Phoenix Art Museum (Milan: Skira, 2006), 142; Nicola Spinosa, entry 50a in *Museo e Gallerie Nazionali di Capodimonte: Dipinti del XVIII secolo; La scuola napoletana* (Naples: Electa Napoli, 2010), 53, 54.

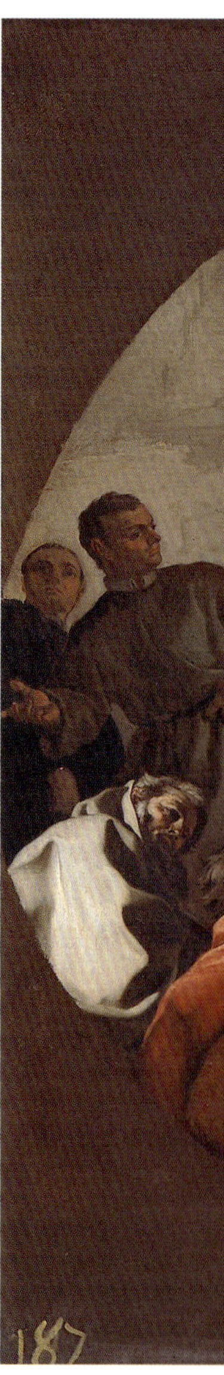

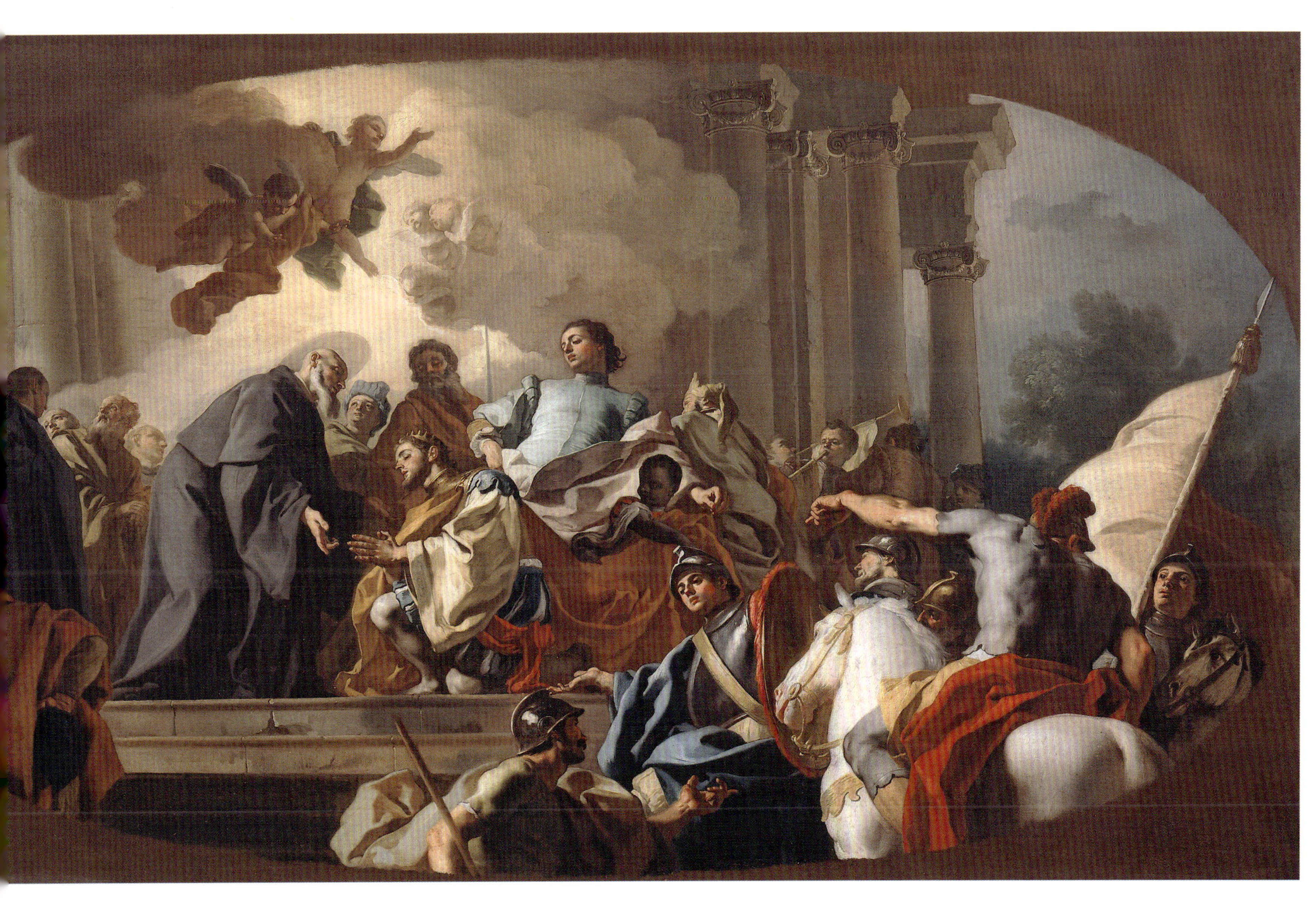

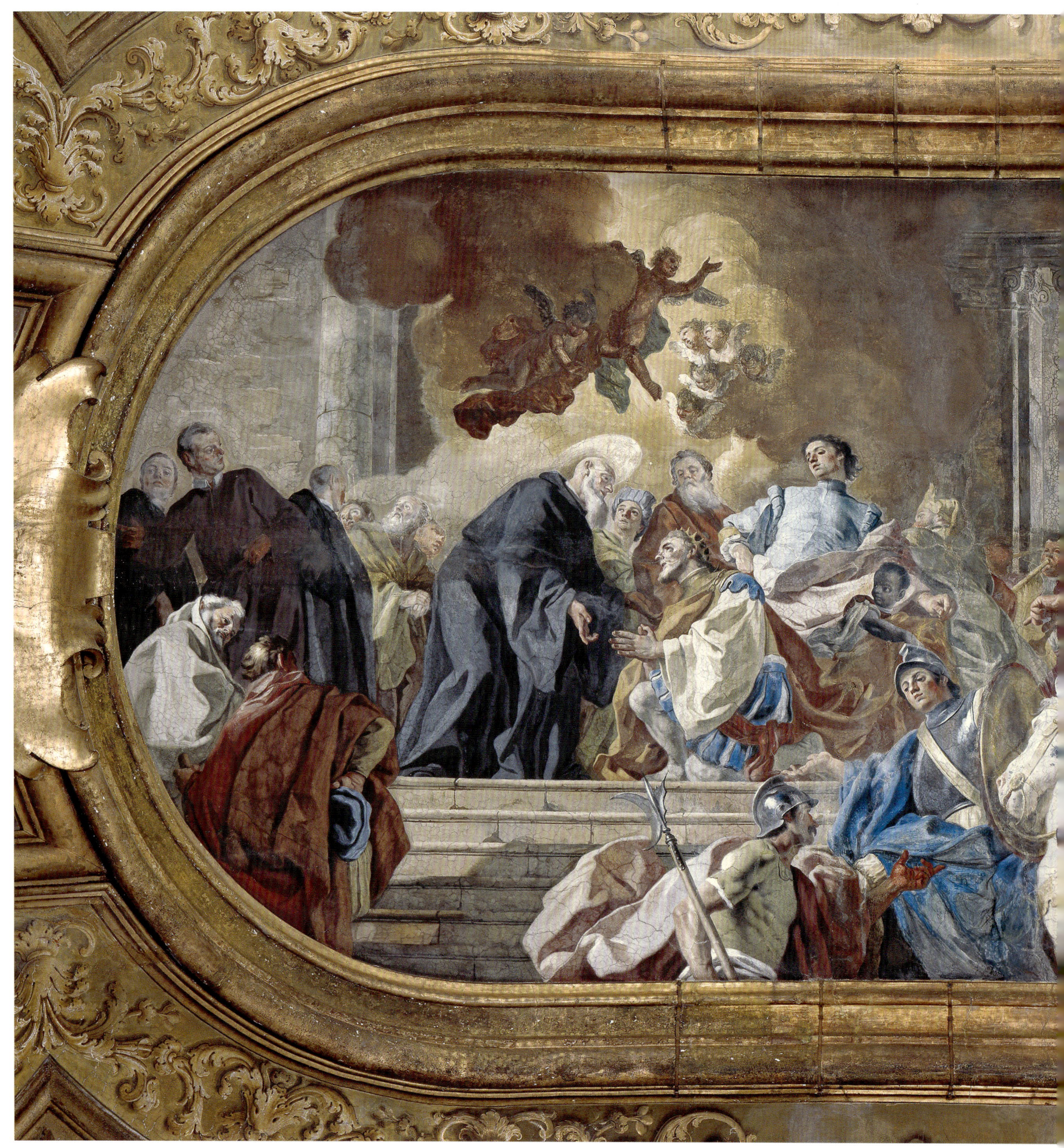

16 — continued

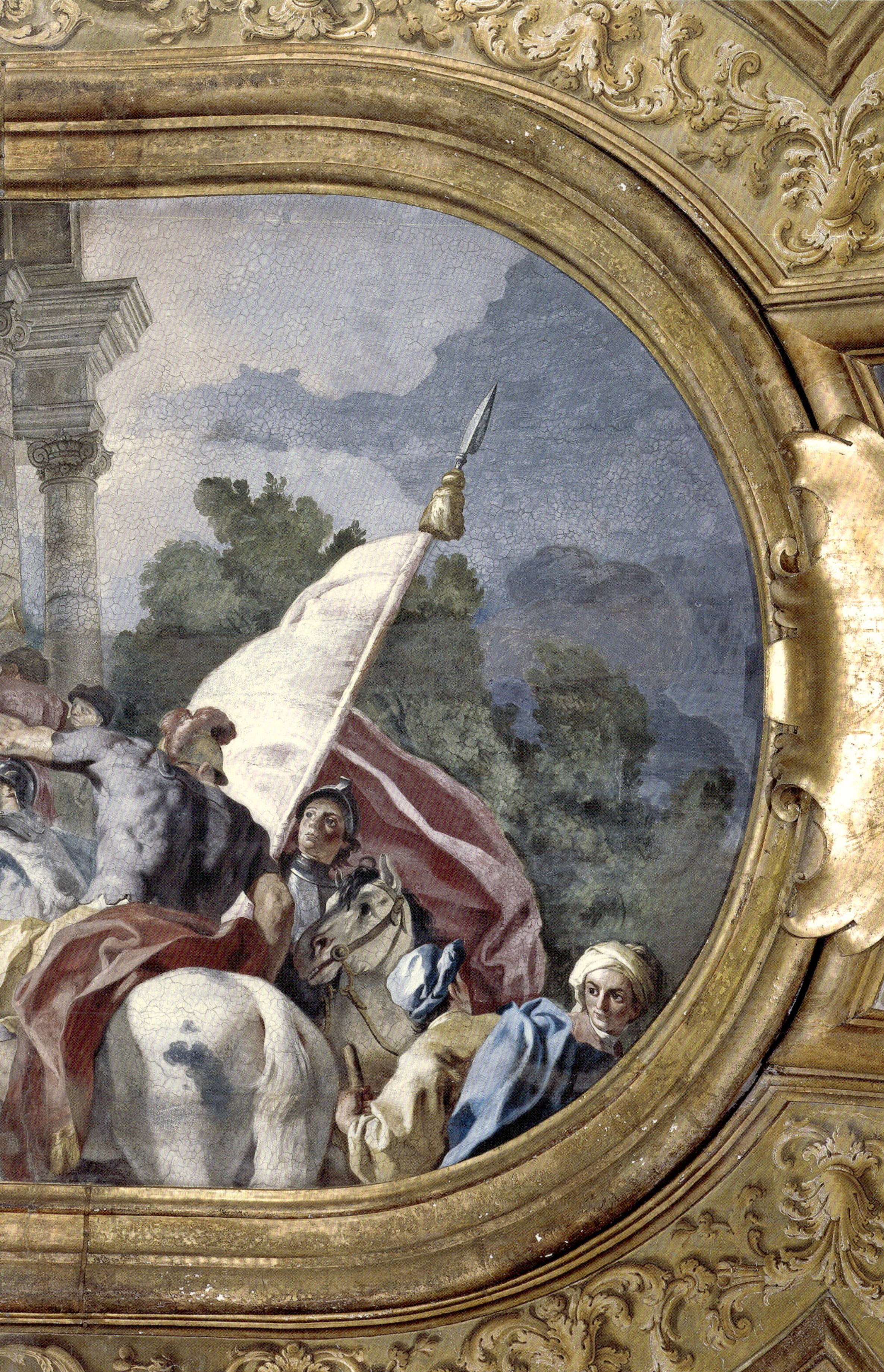

Fig. 55
Francesco de Mura, *The Vision of St. Benedict: St. Benedict Welcomes Totila*, 1741–42, oil, ceiling of church of Santi Severino e Sossio, Naples

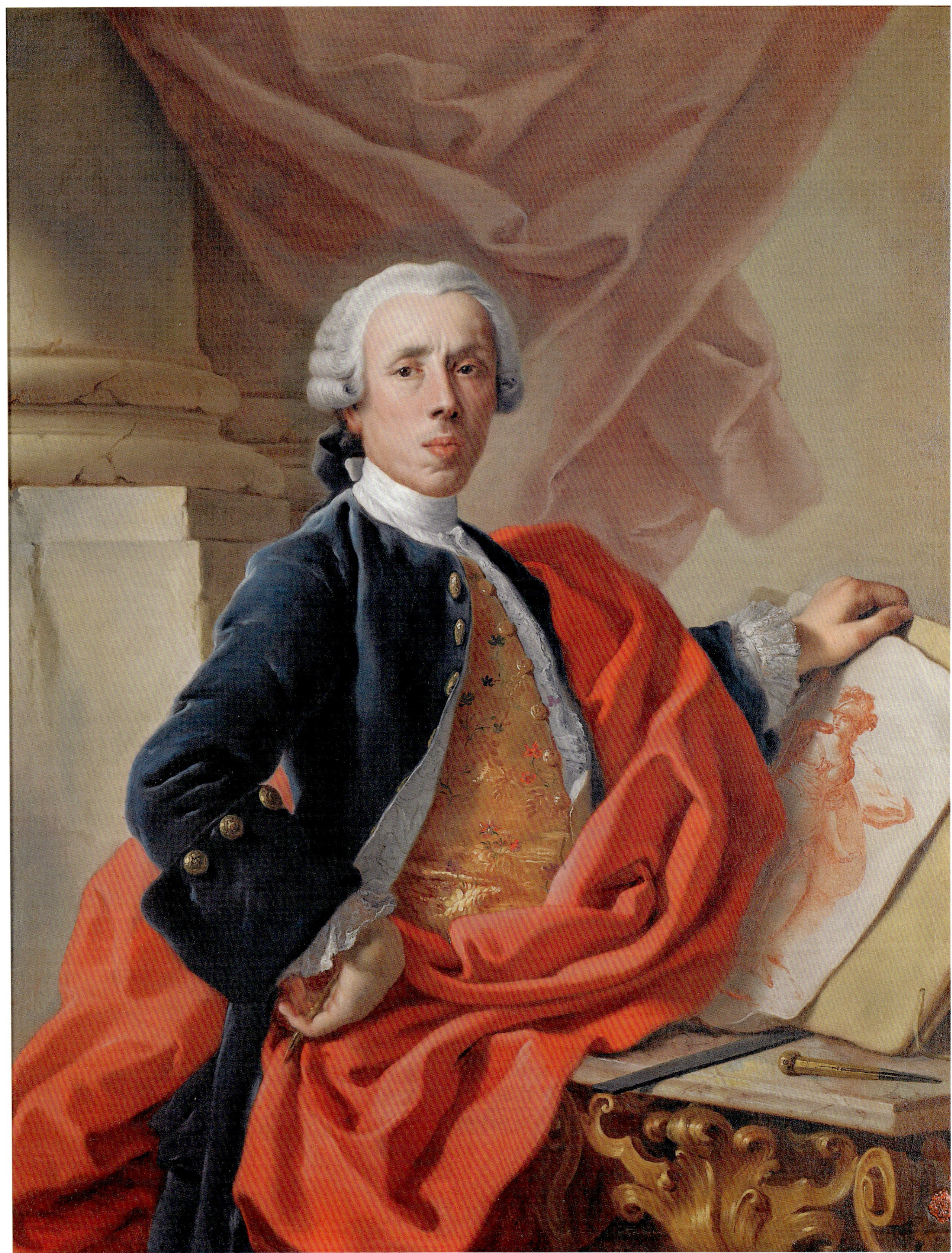

17
Francesco de Mura
Self-Portrait, ca. 1745–47
Oil on canvas, 51 × 40 in. (129.54 × 101.6 cm)
Crushed wax armorial seal on the l.r (probably from the Pio Monte della Misericordia bequest)
The Minneapolis Institute of Art, purchased with funds from the John R. Van Derlip Fund, acc. no. 62.48

De Mura completed this elegant self-portrait at the age of almost forty-nine, during one of the most successful periods of his career.[1] He enjoyed written acclaim from Bernardo de' Dominici in *Vite dei pittori, scultori, ed architetti* (1742–43), the great Lives of the Artists of his day; he had been commissioned to fresco the ceilings of the royal palaces in both Turin and Naples; he had begun and partially completed the glorious cycle from the *Life of St. Benedict* in the church of Santi Severino e Sossio; the king of Spain had requested his work be sent to Madrid; and he was inundated with commissions. It is no wonder, then, that he presents himself as a serious and imposing aristocrat.

His expression of concentration seems to derive from staring into a mirror, studying his face and trying to get it right. He wears a fashionably powdered wig of the mid-1700s, and a dark blue-green velvet jacket lined in white silk brocade with gold buttons. His golden vest is partially opened to reveal his laced shirt; and over his left shoulder he bears a crimson cape that flows behind him and is held in place with his right hand, folded in and resting on his right hip. De Mura stands before a marble and gilded table where a portfolio is open to a red chalk sketch of an armored Minerva, the goddess of wisdom and benefactress of the arts. (There is a De Mura chalk drawing of a *Standing Roman Soldier* [fig. 56] that reminds us of this painted "drawing.") He holds the drawing in his left hand, with a chalk holder with black chalk below it. Behind him, to the left, the base of a column is partially covered with

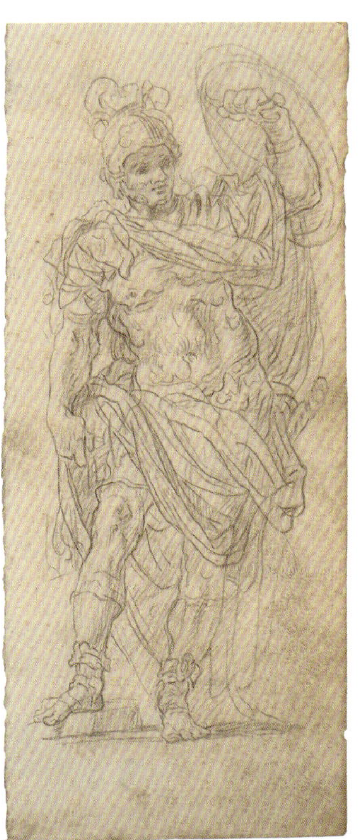

Fig. 56
Francesco de Mura, *Standing Roman Soldier*, black chalk on paper, 10⅝ × 4¼ in. (27 × 11 cm), Collection Mattia Jona, Milan

Provenance:
Studio of the artist; bequest to Pio Monte della Misericordia by the artist, 1782; purchased by Giovan Battista Gallotti, a friend of De Mura, in Naples, 1784; private collection, Rome; private collection (Rossi?), Florence; P. & D. Colnaghi, London, art market, by 1962; Marco & Carlo Sestieri, Piazza di Spagna, Rome, in 1962; purchased by Minneapolis Institute of Arts in 1962 with funds from the John R. Van Derlip Fund.

Exhibitions:
Detroit Institute of Arts, Art Institute of Chicago, Aug. 11, 1981–Mar. 8, 1982, *The Golden Age of Naples: Art and Civilization under the Bourbons, 1734–1805*, no. 36.

Bibliography:
Gino Doria, Ferdinando Bologna, and Guido Pannani, *Settecento napoletano* (Turin: ERI, 1962), 77, pl. 21 (as private collection, London); *The Art Quarterly* 25 (Winter 1962): 409; Selvig Forrest, ed., *European Paintings in The Minneapolis Institute of Arts* (Minneapolis: Minneapolis Institute of Arts, 1963); "La Chronique des Arts," supplement, *Gazette des Beaux-Arts* 61, no. 1129 (Feb. 1963): 33, no. 132 (ill.); *The Connoisseur Year Book 1964* (London: Connoisseur, 1964), 102; *Catalogue of European Paintings in The Minneapolis Institute of Arts* (Minneapolis: Minneapolis Institute of Arts, 1970), 467, no. 248 (ill. p. 466); *A Guide to the Galleries of the Minneapolis Institute of Arts* (Minneapolis: Minneapolis Institute of Arts, 1970), 108, no. 26 (repr. p. 109); Burton B. Fredericksen and Federico Zeri, *Census of Pre-Nineteenth Century Italian Paintings in North American Public Collections* (Cambridge: Harvard University Press, 1972), 146; Nicola Spinosa, "Neapolitan Painting under Charles and Ferdinand Bourbon: Continuity and Crisis within a Tradition," in *The Golden Age of Naples: Art and Civilization Under the Bourbons, 1734–1805*, exhib. cat. (Detroit: Detroit Institute of Arts, 1981), 1:131–32, no. 36 (repr.); Eleanor Tufts and Luis Melendez, Eighteenth-*Century Master of the Spanish Still Life* (Columbia: University of Missouri Press, 1985), 11, fig. 11.

17 — continued

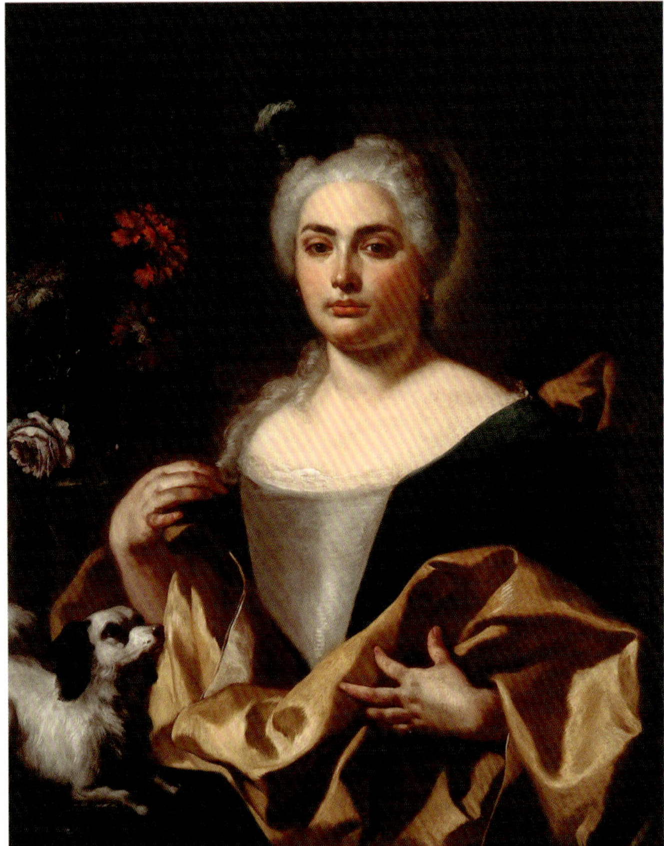

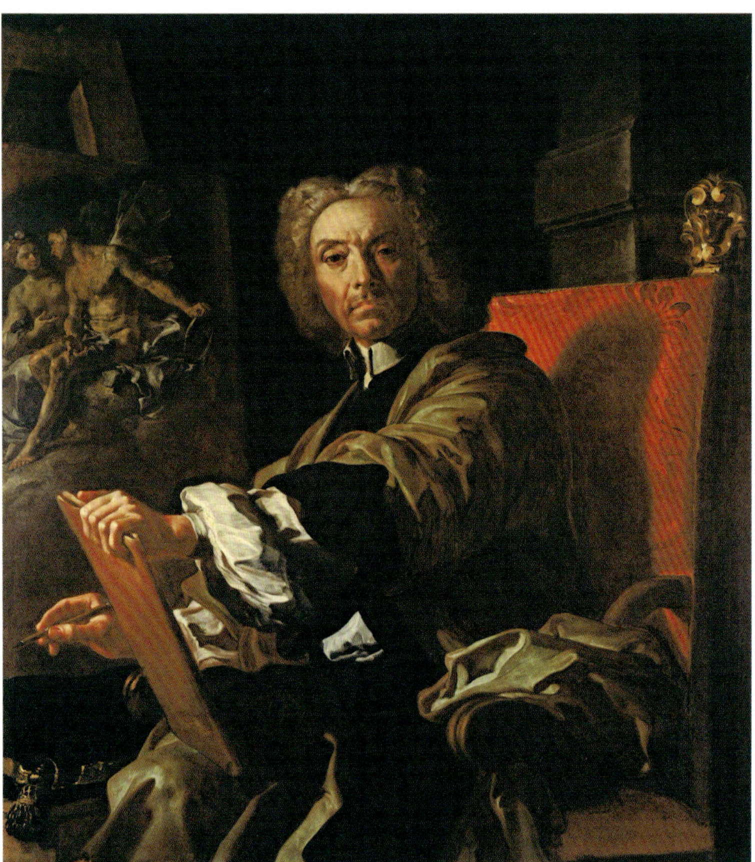

a large golden drapery. The light streams from the upper left, but a breeze from the right seems to be spreading his red cape to the lower left, creating a strong diagonal from lower left to upper right. This powerful and impressive portrait captures us and holds us—by means of the pose, the intense gaze, and the brilliant colors—and tells us who De Mura was and who he aspired to be.

A comparison to a 1715 *Self-Portrait* by his master Solimena (fig. 58), who was nearly ninety when De Mura's *Self-Portrait* was done (he died in 1747), reveals De Mura's more contemporary approach to light, color, and pose.[2] Indeed, De Mura's own style had been transformed in just a decade, as seen in the darker *Portrait of the Artist's Wife, Anna d'Ebreù* (fig. 57) of around 1733.[3] Another, later (and different) *Self-Portrait* by De Mura (with the same dimensions) hangs in the Uffizi in Florence (fig. 59), and is also originally from the Pio Monte bequest. A nearly identical replica by De Mura of the Uffizi *Self-Portrait* was in a sale at Christie's in 2010. These two self-portraits derive from De Mura's *Self-Portrait* in Minneapolis. De Mura painted some of the greatest portraits in eighteenth-century Naples (see cat. nos. 25 and 27).

1. Spinosa, "Neapolitan Painting," 131, no. 36: "The style of the [*Self-portrait*] painting is close to the *Allegories of the Virtues* [see *Allegory of Charity*, cat. no. 19 in this volume] executed around 1743/44."
2. *Ibid.*
3. Loredana Gazzara, in her essay for this catalogue, confirms that this portrait is, indeed, an image of Anna d'Ebreù, wife of Francesco de Mura.

Fig. 57
Francesco de Mura, *Portrait of Anna d'Ebreù, the Artist's Wife*, ca. 1733, oil on canvas, 38½ × 29½ in. (98 × 75 cm), Pio Monte della Misericordia, Naples

Fig. 58
Francesco Solimena, *Self-Portrait*, ca. 1715, oil on canvas, 50⅜ × 44 in. (128 × 112 cm), Museo e Gallerie Nazionali di Capodimonte, Naples

Fig. 59
Francesco de Mura, *Self-Portrait*, ca. 1745, oil on canvas, 50½ × 40 in. (128.3 × 101.6 cm), Vasari Corridor, Galleria degli Uffizi, Florence

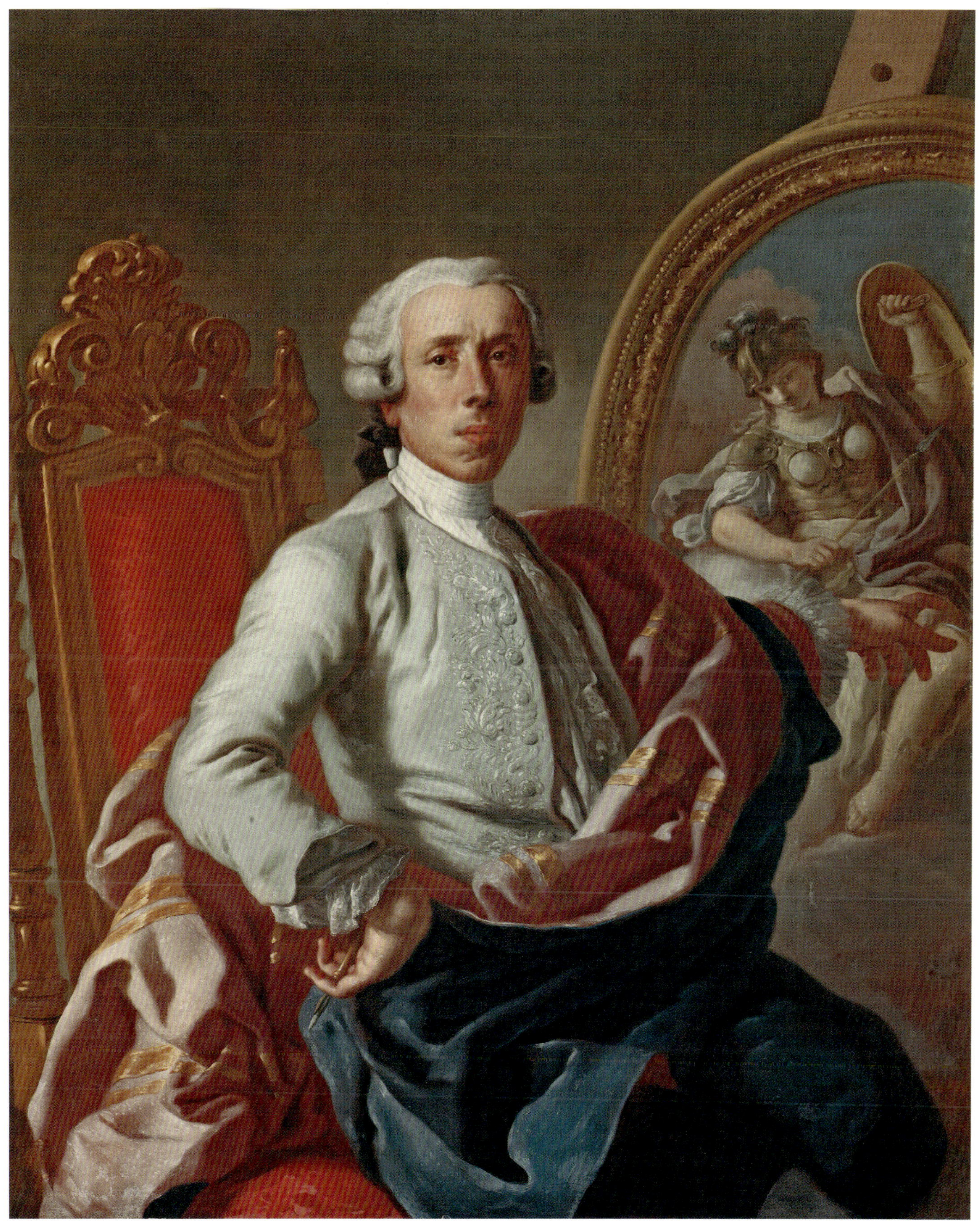

18

Francesco de Mura
Achilles Learning to Hunt, ca. 1741–43
Oil on canvas, 19⅜ × 27½ in. (49.2 × 69.8 cm)
Chazen Museum of Art, University of Wisconsin–Madison, bequest of
Joseph F. McCrindle, acc. no. 2010.14.7

One of the most important commissions in De Mura's career—sometimes considered his chief work—came from Benedetto Alfieri (1699–1767), the royal architect of the kingdom of Sardinia. In 1741, Alfieri, in charge of completing the new rooms of the sumptuous Palazzo Reale in Turin, summoned De Mura to fresco the ceilings and decorate the overdoors (see cat. no. 19). This palace was the home of Charles Emmanuel III, King of Sardinia and Duke of Savoy. *Achilles Learning to Hunt* is a preliminary study for a small section of the ceiling of the Gabinetto delle Miniature in the palace.[1] The theme of that ceiling was "Episodes from the Stories of Achilles"; a *bozzetto* in a private collection in Milan (fig. 60)[2] depicts a scene directly following the narrative in this work, as we see in the final, partially destroyed oil painting on the ceiling (fig. 61).

The classical subjects, which also included De Mura's paintings *Legend of Theseus* and *Scenes from the Olympic Games*, undoubtedly were chosen by the architect but must have reflected the heroic-military mindset of King Charles Emmanuel himself. This *bozzetto* depicts the prowess of Achilles, the Greek hero of the Trojan War and the central character in Homer's *Iliad*. Pindar, the ancient Greek lyric poet, wrote in the *Achilleid* that Achilles (at the age of six) brandished a hunting spear "as swift as the wind, killed lions in battle."[3] Chiron, a centaur and the teacher of Achilles, trained him in the hunt. However, in this work, Achilles, covered at the waist by a leopard skin, prepares to spear a lion with the aid of a servant, who holds the animal in place with his own spear sunk into the lion's back. A hunting dog is on the far left. On the right, as a second servant rushes into the scene, another dog, killed by the lion, lies on its back; this dead dog is alive in the fresco. The *bozzetto* in Milan appears to be an Achilles narrative that follows the hunt. De Mura completed a study for the Palazzo Reale in Naples of *The Glory of the Princes* (see cat. no. 35) that included a similar depiction of Hercules with the Nemean lion (see p. 173). De Mura's luscious colors and sunlit scenes reflect the Rococo setting of the palace rooms themselves. De Mura was also influenced by the Rococo style of the other artists painting at the same time, such as Corrado Giaquinto (see cat. nos. 44–45). The impact of De Mura's magnificent Turin frescoes on his own subsequent painting was profound.[4]

1. Bean and Stampfle, *Eighteenth Century in Italy*, 6, no. 20. The Chazen *bozzetto* was one of a pair by De Mura that the Robert Mannings owned in 1971; the other was titled *Achilles and the Centaur Chiron*, with the same measurements.
2. Nicola Spinosa, *Pittura napoletana del Settecento*, vol. 1, *Dal barocco al rococò* (Naples: Electa Napoli, 1986), 157, no. 250, fig. 295.
3. Elaine Fantham, *Roman Readings: Roman Response to Greek Literature* (Boston, 1989), 101, quoting Pindar, *Achilleid* 3.43–64.
4. Grisieri, "Francesco de Mura," 36. In the Museo Civico in Turin is yet another similar oil study on canvas by De Mura of the *Education of Achilles*, 19 × 27⅛ in. (48 × 69 cm).

Provenance:
Bertina Suida Manning (d. 1992) and Robert L. Manning (d. 1996), New York; Joseph F. McCrindle (1923–2008), New York, from 1996?; bequest of Joseph F. McCrindle to the Chazen Museum of Art, University of Wisconsin–Madison, 2010.

Bibliography:
Andreina Griseri, "Francesco de Mura tra le corti di Napoli, Madrid e Torino," *Paragone* 13, no. 155 (1962): 36, fig. 36; Andreina Griseri and Vittorio Viale, eds., *Mostra del barocco piemontese* (Turin: Città di Torino, 1963) 2:91; Andreina Griseri, *Le metamorfosi del barocco* (Turin: Einaudi, 1967), 341–42, 345–46, note 4; Jacob Bean and Felice Stampfle, *The Eighteenth Century in Italy*, Drawings from New York Collections 3, exhib. cat. (New York: Metropolitan Museum of Art and Pierpont Morgan Library, 1971), 6, no. 20.

Fig. 60
Francesco de Mura, *Episode from the Education of Achilles*, 1741, oil on canvas, 19⁵⁄₁₆ × 16¹⁵⁄₁₆ in. (49 × 43 cm), private collection, Milan

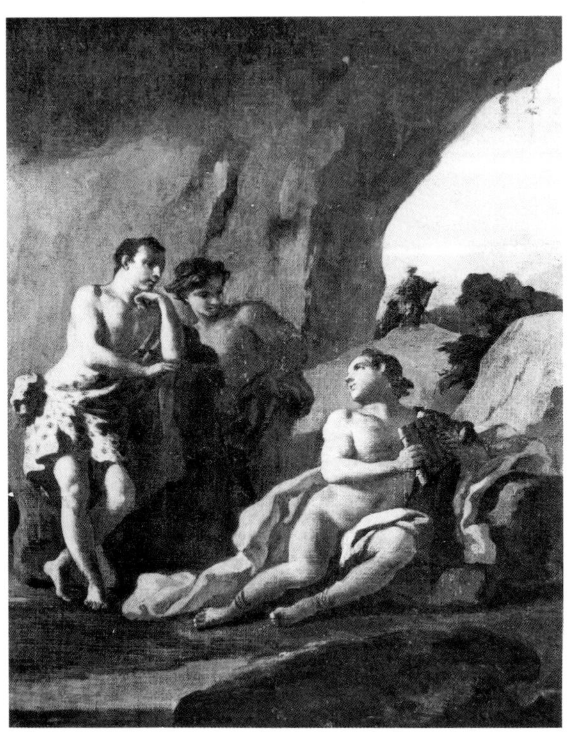

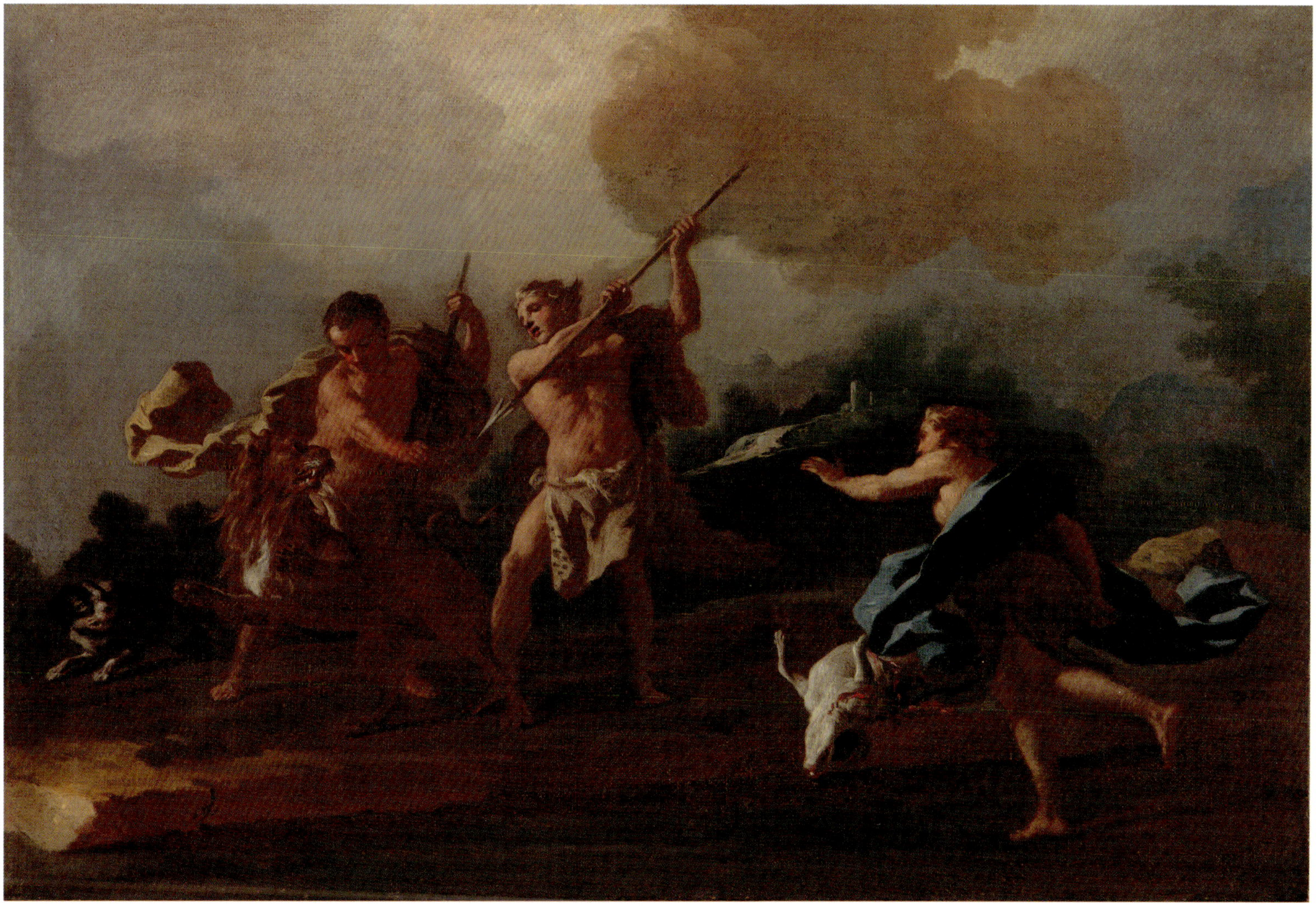

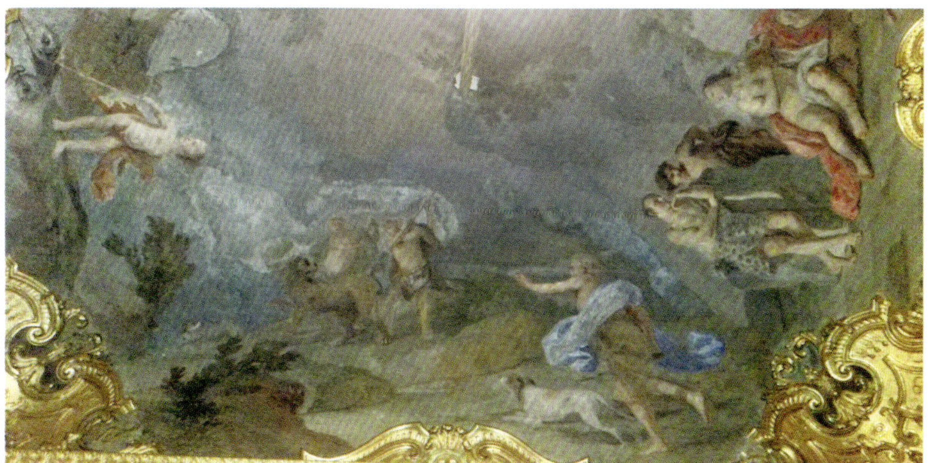

Fig. 61
Francesco de Mura, *Episodes from the
Education of Achilles*, 1741, partially
destroyed fresco, ceiling, Gabinetto
delle Miniature, Palazzo Reale, Turin

19

Francesco de Mura
Allegory of Charity or *Allegory of Maternal Love*, 1743–44
Oil on canvas, 54¹⁵/₁₆ × 53 in. (139.5 × 134.6 cm)
The Art Institute of Chicago, Preston O. Morton Memorial Fund, acc. no. 1971.429

In this lovely work, De Mura depicts a voluptuous woman nursing an infant in a crib, while turning to her right and uncovering the blanket of another sleeping child (a girl?) in a small bed. A third child, a nude dark-haired boy with his back to us, tries to gain his mother's attention. The child looks to the lower right at a small pelican picking at its bleeding breast in an attempt to feed its two chicks. The figures form part of a dramatic right-angle triangle composition, supported by the double columns in the right background. The mother wears a flowing cape of brilliant red-orange—the symbolic color of Charity—that the wind has lifted upwards behind her.

De Mura has used the traditional elements of the personification of Charity, but composed them in a most original way. De Mura added the pelican to underscore the symbolism for Charity. The pelican, illustrated in Christian art from the Renaissance on (fig. 62), was believed to pierce its own breast with its beak to feed its young with blood, becoming a symbol of self-sacrifice, as in motherhood.[1] (Most representations of Charity do not use the pelican symbol).

This work was likely meant for a *sovrapporta* (an overdoor painting) in the Palazzo Reale in Turin, where De Mura had worked on the frescoed ceiling in 1741–42.[2] The monumentality of the figures and the simplified composition would have aided one in viewing it from below. De Mura painted three other *Allegories* as overdoors in the Palazzo Reale in Turin—*Fortitude*, *Magnanimity*, and *Nobility*—where they remain today. Earlier in his career, about 1720, De Mura had painted a *Charity* (cat. no. 1) that also uses the billowing red cape and other features. A comparison with the earlier work shows us how far the artist had traveled from Solimena's darker, more ponderous style. De Mura repeated the subject of Charity in 1752 in the ceiling decoration of the nave of the church of the Nunziatella in Naples. Nicola Spinosa, among others, has praised the beautiful Chicago *Charity* for its striking composition, intense colors, and "figures of great elegance and reserve, and [a] profound sense of humanity."[3]

1. The belief may have originated in the pelican's red-tipped beak and very white feathers. Pelicans were also considered to be a reminder of Christ, who gave of his own blood from his chest to feed all sinners.
2. Griseri, "Francesco de Mura," 36: "In the same Hall of Machines [in the Palazzo Reale in Turin], on three *sovrapporte*, perhaps sent from Naples [since De Mura had already returned home], as a document of 1748 seems to attest; that could correspond to those recorded by De Dominici [*Vite dei pittori*, 3:701] as 'Education,' 'Maternal Love,' 'Fortitude,' 'Nobility,' 'Magnanimity'; ..." De Dominici saw these works in De Mura's studio in 1743 before they were sent to Turin.
3. Spinosa, *Pittura napoletana del Settecento*, 1:130. There is yet another *Allegory of Charity* in the Museo di Capodimonte (inv. no. Q 1930-..., n. 235), a second *bozzetto* for the Nunziatella ceiling, that also uses the pelican image. See Spinosa, *Museo e Gallerie Nazionali di Capodimonte: Dipinti del XVIII secolo; La scuola napoletana* (Naples: Electa Napoli, 2010), 56–57, fig. 53.

Provenance:
Probably commissioned by Charles Emmanuel III, Turin (see Pinto, *Arte di corte a Torino*, 21); collection of Francesco de Mura; Pio Monte della Misericordia?; Peretti, Rome, by 1971 (according to Heim Commission Book, Heim Gallery Records, 1965–1991, Getty Research Institute, Los Angeles); Heim Gallery, London, 1971; sold to the Art Institute of Chicago, 1971.

Exhibitions:
Naples, 1938, *La pittura napoletana dei secoli XVII, XVIII, XIX*; London, Heim Gallery, May 13–August 28, 1971, no. 14; Detroit Institute of Arts, Art Institute of Chicago, Aug. 11, 1981–Mar. 8, 1982, *The Golden Age of Naples: Art and Civilization under the Bourbons, 1734–1805*, no. 34; Worcester Art Museum, Mass., *Hope and Healing: Painting in Italy in a Time of Plague 1500–1800*, April 3–September 25, 2005, no. 9 (ill.).

Bibliography:
Bernardo de Dominici, *Vite dei pittori, scultori ed architetti napoletani* (Naples, 1742), 3:701; Andreina Griseri, "Francesco de Mura fra le corti di Napoli, Madrid e Torino," *Paragone* 13, no. 155 (1962), 36; Art Institute of Chicago, *Annual Report, 1970–71* (Chicago: Art Institute of Chicago, 1971), 26–27 (ill.); *Country Life*, June 3, 1971; Nicola Spinosa, *Civiltà del '700 a Napoli, 1734–1799*, exhib. cat. (Florence: Centro Di, 1979), 1:196, no. 90; *The Golden Age of Naples: Art and Civilization under the Bourbons, 1734–1805*, exhib. cat. (Detroit: Detroit Institute of Arts, 1981), vol. I:129–30, no. 34; Nicola Spinosa, *Pittura napoletana del Settecento*, vol. 1, *Dal barocco al rococò* (Naples: Electa Napoli, 1986), 160, no. 255, pl. 59; *A Taste for Angels: Neapolitan Painting in North America 1650–1750*, exhib. cat. (New Haven: Yale University Art Gallery, 1987), 262, fig. 114; Sandra Pinto, ed., *Arte di corte a Torino da Carlo Emanuele III a Carlo Felice* (Turin: Cassa di risparmio di Torino, 1987), 21; Mercedes Precerutti Garberi, ed., *Dal quattrocento al settecento*, vol. 2, *Arte antica e moderna nelle collezioni della Banca Commerciale Italiana* (Milan: Banca Commerciale Italiana, 1998), 262–63; Franco Mormando, "Introduction: Response to the Plague in Early Modern Italy: What Primary Sources, Printed and Painted, Reveal," in *Hope and Healing: Painting in Italy in a Time of Plague, 1500–1800*, ed. Gauvin Alexander Bailey et al., exhib. cat. (Worcester, Mass.: Worcester Art Museum, 2005), 27, 194–95, no. 9 (ill.).

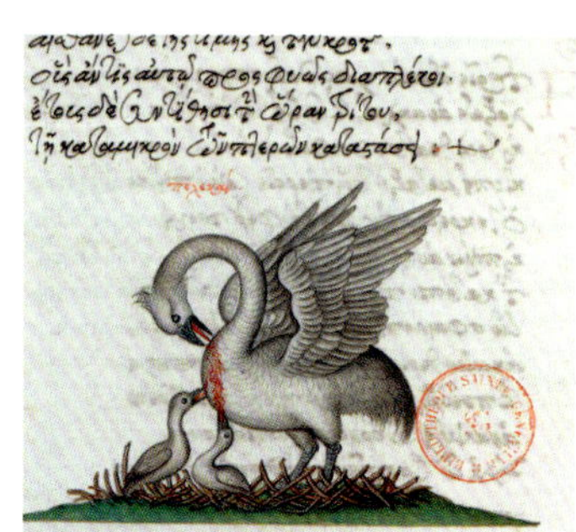

Fig. 62
Pelican Piercing Its Breast to Feed Its Young, from a Greek Bestiary by Manuel Philes, 1566, Bibliothèque Sainte-Geneviève, Paris

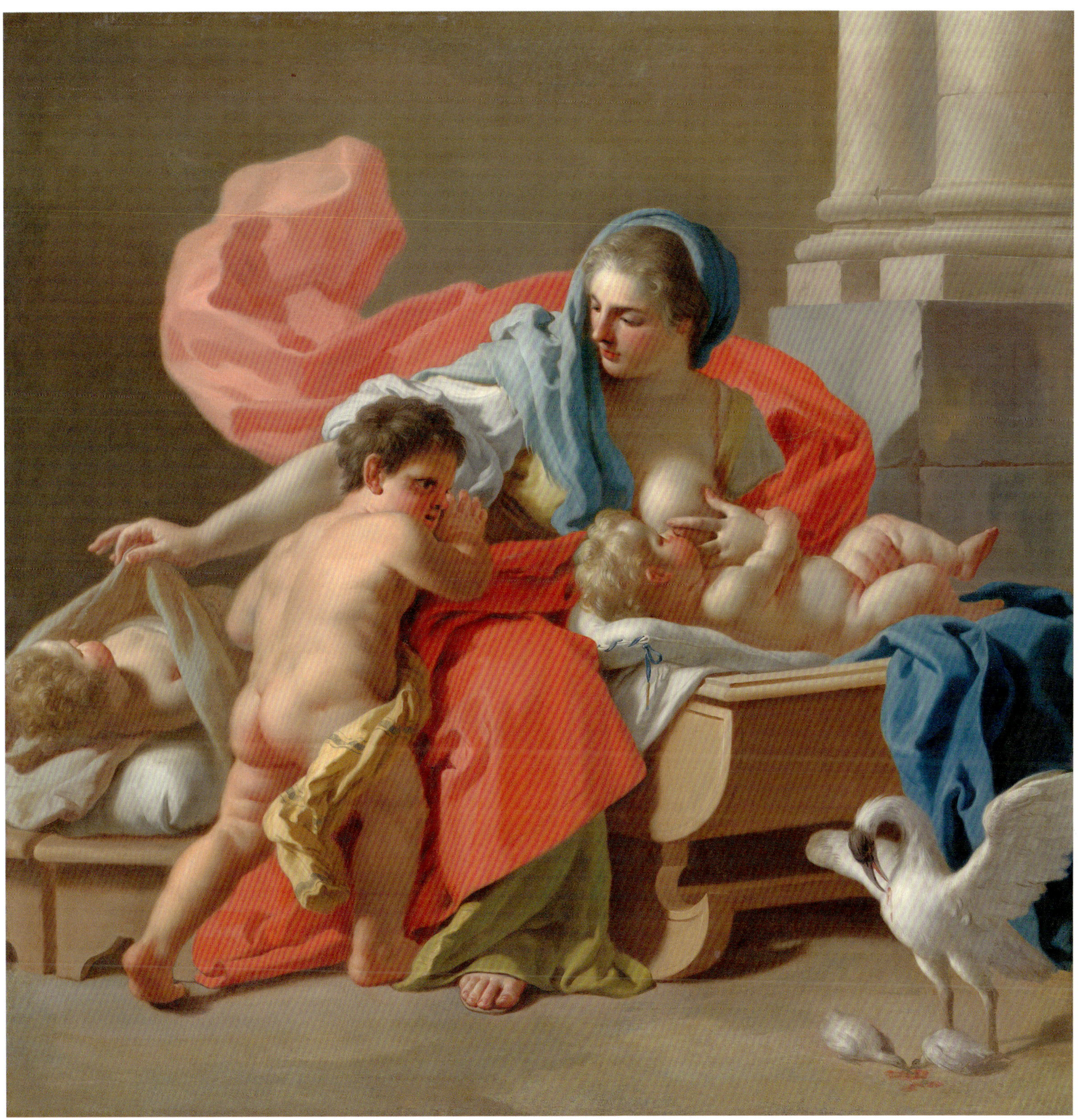

20

Francesco de Mura
The Assumption of the Virgin, ca. 1750
Pen and black ink, gray wash over black chalk, 17³⁄₁₆ × 10 in. (43.6 × 25.4 cm)
Inscription on reverse in graphite: *J. Jouvenet*
The Metropolitan Museum of Art, purchased with gifts from Mr. and Mrs.
Carl L. Selden and Mrs. Barbara K. Caturani, and Rogers Fund, acc. no. 1971.243

According to tradition, the bodily assumption (or "taking up") of the Virgin
Mary into heaven occurred on the third day after her dormition ("falling
asleep"; she was believed never to have died). This belief was influenced by
Revelation 12:1: "A great and wondrous sign appeared in heaven: a woman
clothed with the sun, with the moon under her feet, and a crown of twelve
stars on her head." In 1950, the Catholic Church adopted the belief and the
Feast of the Assumption is celebrated on August 15.

This drawing depicts a triumphant Mary on top of a cloud in the upper
portion of the composition. Her arms are spread wide, hands turned upward
expressively as she gazes up at an angel, who flies in from several darker
clouds. As angels and small putti pull Mary upward, she sits centered before
a large sun. The clouds beneath her float from an open sarcophagus, which
we view from below, looking up. On the left of the sarcophagus (from which
Mary has just been assumed), one of the apostles holds the heavy stone that
covered the tomb. The stone is set at the top of a series of steps that, in turn,
are placed over an archway. In the center, another apostle (Thomas?) pulls
up her shroud in search of the Virgin, whom he seems not to notice floating
above. Surrounding the sarcophagus, eight other apostles sit, stand, kneel,
and look up, pointing at Mary. In the distant right and left are columns and
arches. The black ink and chalk drawing is set in a cut-out rectangular field
that is straight on both sides but curved and pinched above and below.

This is a sketch for De Mura's *Assumption of the Virgin*, painted in
1751 on the ceiling of the Nunziatella, a church on the Pizzofalcone hill in
Naples (see fig. 65). An oil study of the ceiling painting is in the Museo di
Capodimonte (see fig. 64), and a workshop replica is in the Art Gallery of
Ontario (cat. no. 21). The Nunziatella ceiling was one of De Mura's most
important commissions since completing his ceiling paintings of the Palazzo
Reale in Turin (see cat. no. 18). Differences in the drawing from the fresco
include the lack of the Trinity with Christ welcoming his mother Mary into
Heaven, the depiction of far fewer figures (apostles and servants), and the
architectural setting in an open landscape. Also, the shape of the drawing is
wider, while the shape of the fresco reflects the shape of the nave ceiling. The
Metropolitan Museum drawing shows a strong similarity to an earlier composition of the *Assumption*, dated 1727, executed for the vault of the sacristy
in the church of the Annunziata in Airola (fig. 63), a *bozzetto* for which is in
the Pio Monte della Misericordia. (De Mura also painted a Pietà for the altar
of this church; see fig. 36.)

Provenance:
Adolphe Stein; Saretta Barnet;
purchased by The Metropolitan
Museum of Art in London, 1971.

Exhibition:
Katonah Museum of Art,
New York, *Divine Mirrors:
The Madonna Unveiled*,
Jan. 13–Apr. 7, 2002.

Bibliography:
*Old Master Drawings Presented
by Lorna Lowe and Adolphe
Stein*, exhib. cat. (London: 1971),
no. 80 (as "Neapolitan School
[18th Century]"); Metropolitan
Museum of Art, *Annual Report*
(New York: Metropolitan
Museum of Art: 1971–72),
40; Jacob Bean and William
Griswold, *18th Century Italian
Drawings in The Metropolitan
Museum of Art* (New York:
Metropolitan Museum of Art,
1990), 149–51, no. 138.

Fig. 63
Francesco de Mura, *The
Assumption of the Virgin*, ca.
1727, fresco, ceiling of vault
of the sacristy, church of the
Annunziata, Airola

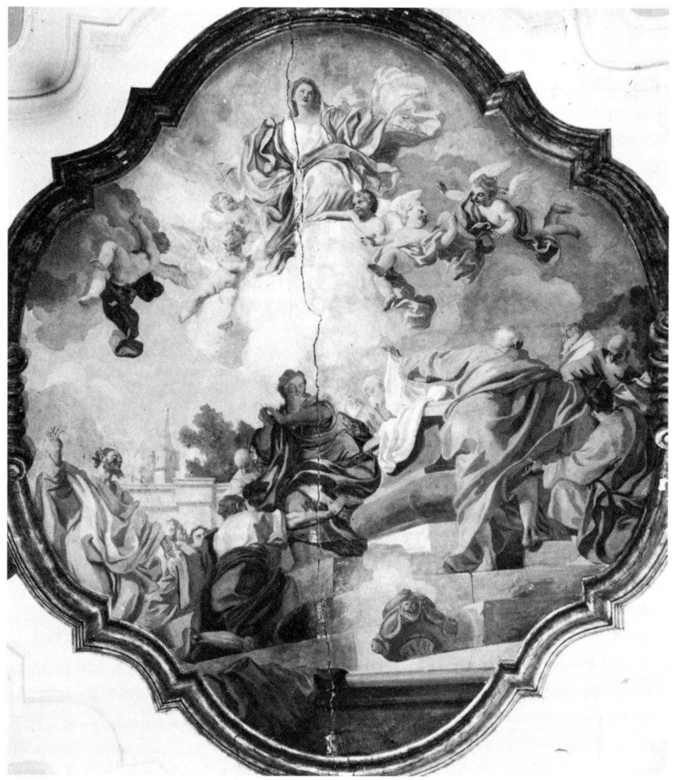

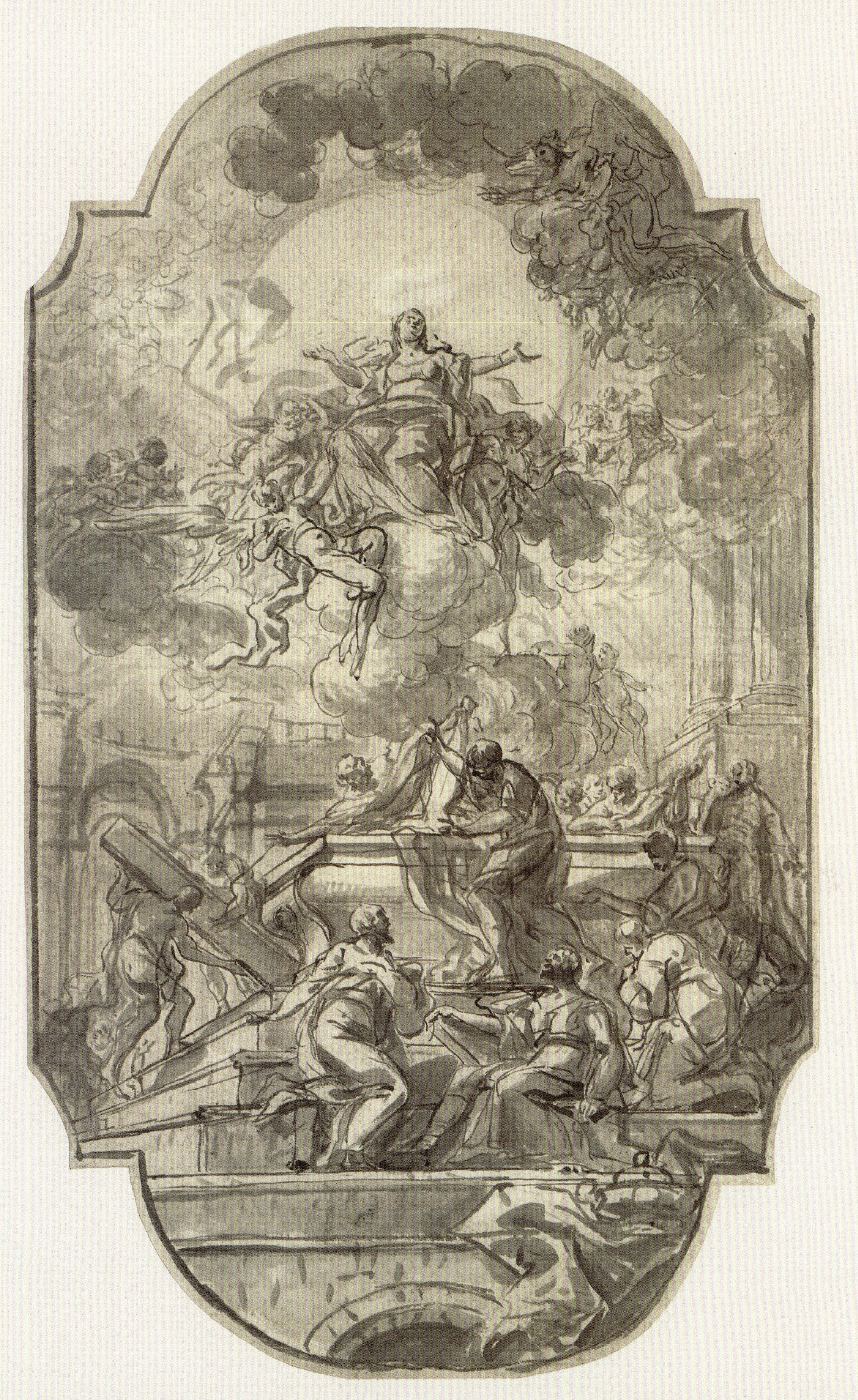

21

Workshop of **Francesco de Mura**
The Assumption of the Virgin, ca. 1751–52
Oil on canvas, 66⅜ × 48⅝ in. (168.6 × 123.5 cm)
Art Gallery of Ontario, purchased in 1951, acc. no. 1951/51/8

Catalogue only.

This imposing and energetic *Assumption of the Virgin* is a workshop copy of De Mura's oil *bozzetto*, now in the Museo di Capodimonte (fig. 64), which is a study for his vast frescoed ceiling of the *Assumption* for the church of the Nunziatella in Naples, executed in 1751 (fig. 65).[1] These frescoes, commissioned by the Jesuits, are perhaps De Mura's greatest achievement and certainly his best known. In contrast to the *Adoration of the Magi* fresco De Mura executed in the curved apse of the same church of the Nunziatella in 1732, almost two decades earlier (see fig. 49), the *Assumption* demonstrates the artist's full expression of the Rococo, while still depending on compositional elements of his master Solimena. As David Nolta writes in his essay in this volume (pp. 45–55), De Mura's Nunziatella frescoes of the *Assumption* are often compared favorably to the striking ceiling frescoes by the famous Venetian Giambattista Tiepolo, such as *The Coronation of the Virgin* of 1752 (see fig. 16). De Mura shows a remarkable transition from the more staid and formal *Vision of St. Benedict* ceiling in Santi Severino e Sossio of 1738–40 (see fig. 53), to the *Assumption* frescoes created ten years later, in which every figure vibrates in motion, the lighter colors shimmer, and the whole image flickers like a fire.

This painting depicts a version of the central panel on the ceiling of the church of the Nunziatella: we look upward at the scene from the nave below. In heaven, God the Father, Jesus, the Holy Spirit, and several dozen angels (with putti and cherubs) greet the Virgin Mary three days after her burial. Mary is lifted up (assumed) from her tomb, which is surrounded by apostles and servants. By the sarcophagus, one apostle lifts off the stone cover, while three others search for her body inside, one lifting the burial shroud. Mary's raised left arm mirrors the raised right arm of Jesus, and the arms of the angels and apostles skillfully direct our eyes to the climactic scene of Mary's reception in heaven. As they spin through the air, the flying angels, the floating Madonna, and the gesticulating apostles below create a literal deus ex machina, in a thoroughly theatrical and explosive setting.

This composition varies from the fresco, which is proportionately longer and wider, and the sides of which are curved, not straight. In addition, in the fresco, Mary tilts her head upward and to the right, not meeting the eyes of Jesus, as in the Toronto work. The fresco, which contains more figures, is considerably brighter and lighter in color and the compositional focal point of Mary and Jesus is clearer. Yet the Toronto work gives us a sense of the grandeur of the brilliant, unforgettable fresco.

1. This work is stored in the Museo Villa Floridiana (known also as the Museo Duca di Martina) in Naples. There was another version (variant) of De Mura's *Assumption* (oil on canvas within a shaped frame, 39½ × 24¼ in., 100.2 × 61.5 cm), possibly a copy after the *bozzetto* in Naples, at auction at Sotheby's, New York, on July 9, 1998, Old Master Paintings, lot 326. The composition of the Toronto version has been cut off at the top and bottom.

Provenance:
Mrs. A. Ashton by 1950, Sotheby's, London, Feb. 1950, lot 30 (as Mattia Preti); P. & D. Colnaghi Co., Ltd., London, to 1951.

Exhibitions:
Art Gallery of Toronto, Montreal Museum of Fine Arts, National Gallery of Canada, Jan.–Feb. 1954, *Paintings by European Masters from Public and Private Collections in Toronto, Montreal and Ottawa*, no. 23; *Art Gallery of Toronto, Painting and Sculpture*, 1959; Witchita Art Museum, Kansas, 1972; Toronto, Art Gallery of Ontario, 1981–82, *The Arts of Italy in Toronto Collections: 1300–1800*, no. 101; Yale University Art Gallery, New Haven, Conn., John and Mable Ringling Museum of Art, Sarasota, Fla., Nelson-Atkins Museum of Art, Kansas City, Mo., Sept. 9– June 12, 1988, *A Taste for Angels: Neapolitan Painting in North America, 1650–1750*, no. 36; Frist Center for the Visual Arts, Nashville, Tenn., Apr. 8–July 8, 2001, *European Masterworks: Paintings from the Art Gallery of Ontario, Frist Center for the Visual Arts*.

Bibliography:
Paintings by European Masters from Public and Private Collections in Toronto, Montreal and Ottawa, exhib. cat. (Toronto, Art Gallery of Ontario, 1954), no. 23; Art Gallery of Toronto, *Painting and Sculpture* (Toronto: Art Gallery of Toronto, 1959), no. 13 (ill.); Robert Enggass, "Francesco de Mura alla Nunziatella," *Bollettino d'arte* 49 (1964): 139, fig. 8; *Handbook* (Toronto: Art Gallery of Ontario, 1974), 54 (ill.); Nicola Spinosa, *Pittura sacra a Napoli nel '700*, exhib. cat. (Naples: Società Editrice Napoletana, 1980), 106, no. 58; David McTavish et al., *The Arts of Italy in Toronto Collections: 1300–1800*, exhib. cat. (Toronto: Art Gallery of Ontario, 1981), 85, no. 101; David Nolta, entry 36 in *A Taste for Angels: Neapolitan Painting in North America, 1650–1750*, exhib. cat. (New Haven: Yale University Art Gallery, 1987), 276–78 (ill.); Nicola Spinosa, entry 52 in *Museo e Gallerie Nazionali di Capodimonte: Dipinti del XVIII secolo; La scuola napoletana* (Naples: Electa Napoli, 2010), 56.

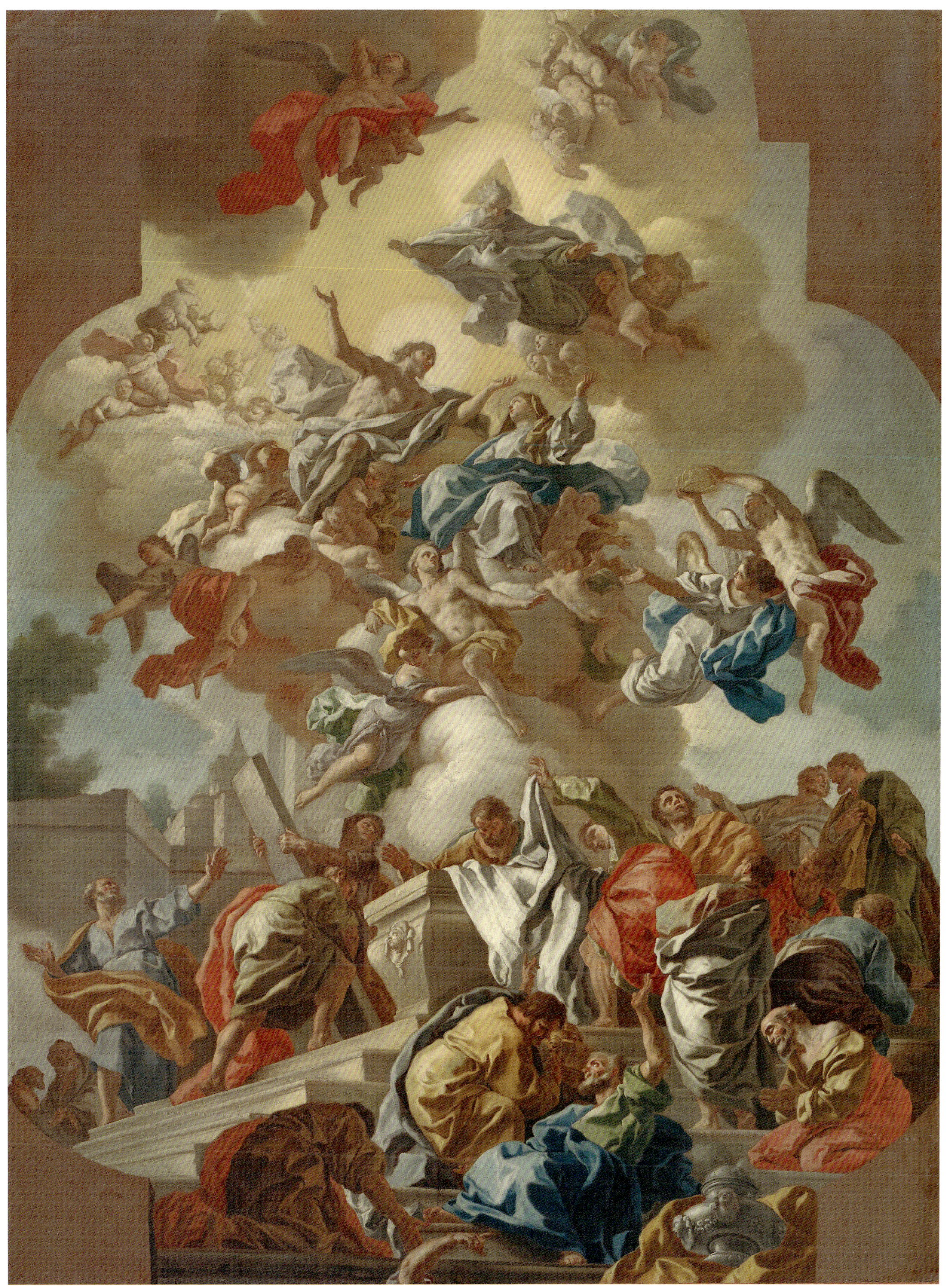

21 — continued

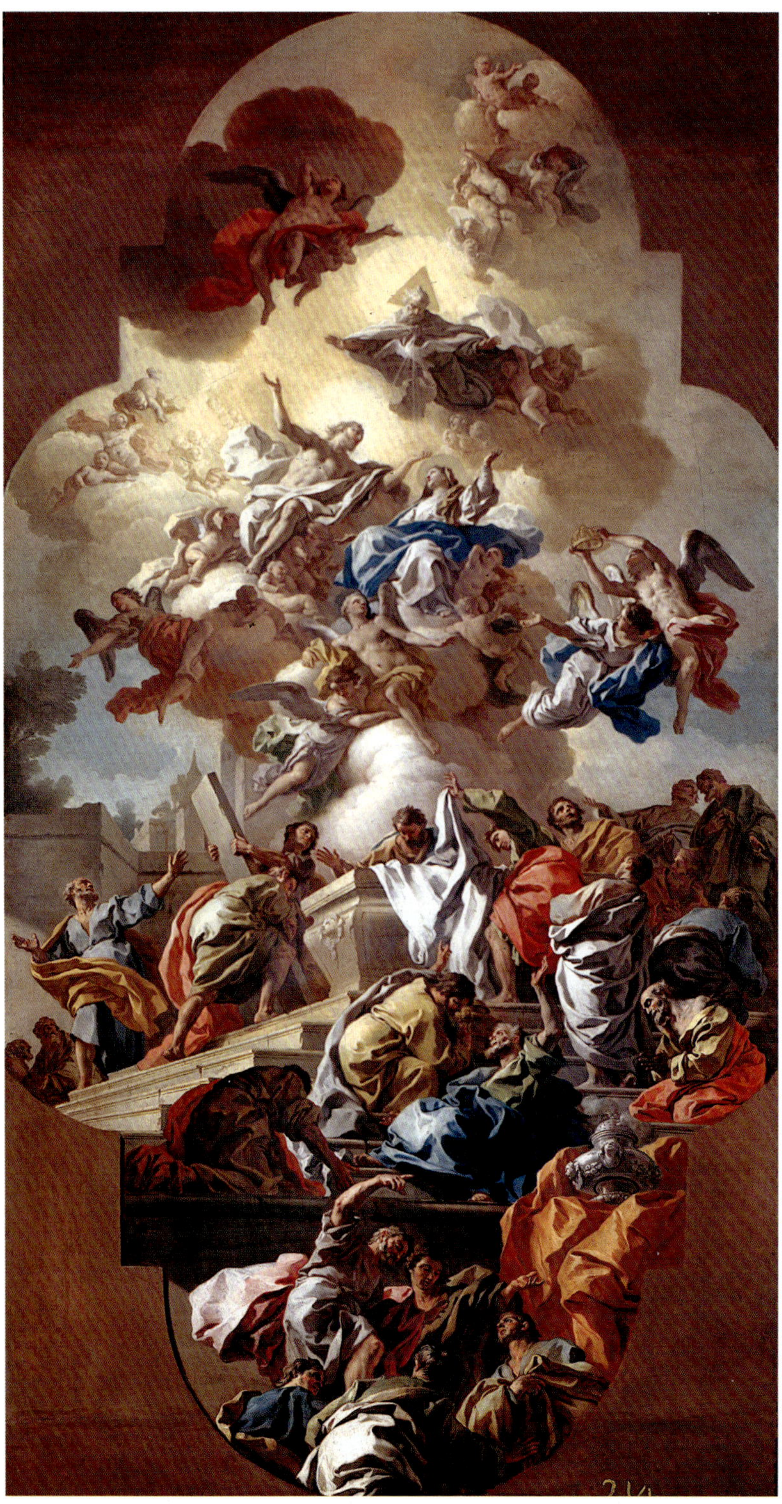

Fig. 64
Francesco de Mura, *The Assumption
of the Virgin*, 1751, oil on canvas,
92⅛ × 48⅜ in. (234 × 123 cm), Museo e
Gallerie Nazionali di Capodimonte (Villa
Floridiana), Naples

Fig. 65
Francesco de Mura, *The
Assumption of the Virgin*, 1751,
fresco, ceiling of the nave,
church of the Nunziatella,
Naples

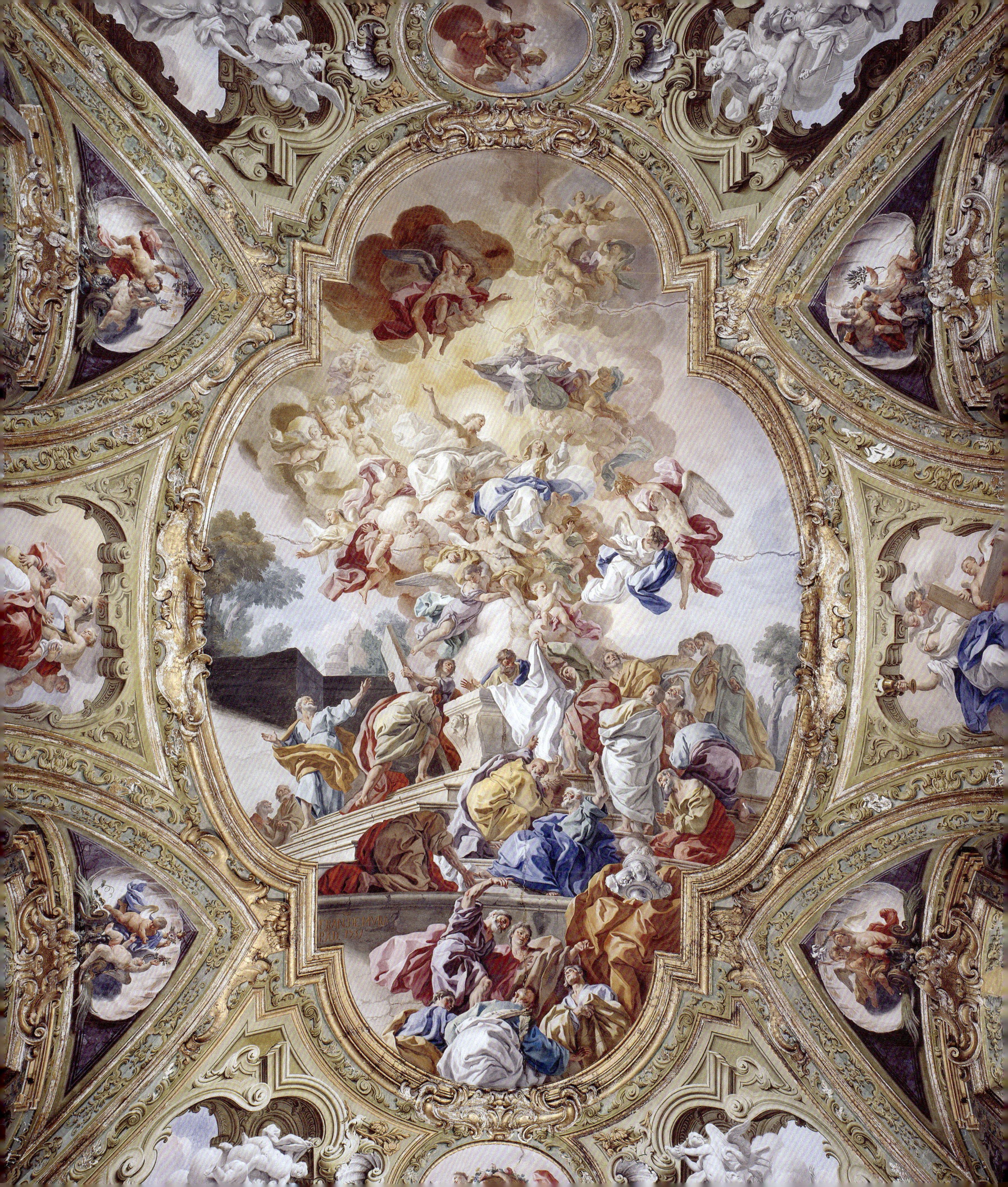

22

Francesco de Mura
The Annunciation, ca. 1757
Oil on canvas, 23¾ × 20¼ in. (60.3 × 51.4 cm)
Collection of Frank and Demi Rogozienski

This elegant painting depicts the Gospel of Luke 1:26–33, which describes the annunciation (or announcing) by the archangel Gabriel to the Virgin Mary that she would give birth to the messiah: "The angel [Gabriel] went to Mary and said: 'You will conceive and give birth to a son, and you are to give him the name Jesus … and he will be called the son of the Most High … the Holy Spirit will come upon you and the power of the Most High will overshadow you.'" In this study, Mary sits at a desk and turns to the *left*, as the winged Gabriel flies in on a cloud, grasping a white lily in his left hand, the symbol of modesty and virginity, as he points to heaven above. At the top of the composition, a white dove, representing the Holy Spirit, spreads its wings, sending rays of light to a graceful Mary, clad in a rose-colored garment, with a yellow head scarf and a deep blue robe tossed over her shoulders. The base of a column closes off the right side of the composition, while red drapery billows behind it.

This painting is a *bozzetto* or, more likely, a *prima idea* (first sketch), for the fresco of the *Annunciation* in the chapel of the Assumption, in the church of the Certosa (Carthusian monastery) of San Martino, in Naples. (The artist also painted an *Assumption* and a *Visitation* for this chapel; there is a variation of this *Annunciation bozzetto*, by or after De Mura, in the Barockmuseum in Mühlbach bei Oberaudorf in Germany.) De Mura has turned that much larger *Annunciation* painting (fig. 66) into a horizontal composition and added nine putti, a second column, and a cat (symbol of domestic goodness) on a chair to the scene. De Mura's image of the Virgin Mary has some of the same monumentality and simplicity of the mother figure in *Allegory of Charity* (cat. no. 19) of the previous decade, and the composition as a whole demonstrates the artist's classicizing tendencies.[1] A few years later, in 1760, the artist painted another *Annunciation*, this time for the apse of the church of the Annunziata in Naples, which owed much to this simpler composition.[2]

1. David Nolta, entry in *A Taste for Angels: Neapolitan Painting in North America, 1650–1750*, exhib. cat. (New Haven: Yale University Art Gallery, 1987), 267.
2. Nicola Spinosa, entry no. 57 in *Museo e Gallerie Nazionali di Capodimonte: Dipinti del XVIII secolo; La scuola napoletana* (Naples: Electa Napoli, 2010), 58–59.

Provenance:
Anonymous sale; Bonhams, London, Dec. 9, 1993, lot 94; unknown collector; Christie's, New York, Jan. 31, 2013, Old Master Paintings, Part II, sale no. 2676; Robert Simon Gallery, New York; Otto Naumann, Ltd., New York.

Fig. 66
Francesco de Mura, *The Annunciation*, ca. 1757, wall painting, 85⅜ × 124 in. (217 × 315 cm), left chapel, church of the Certosa di San Martino, Naples

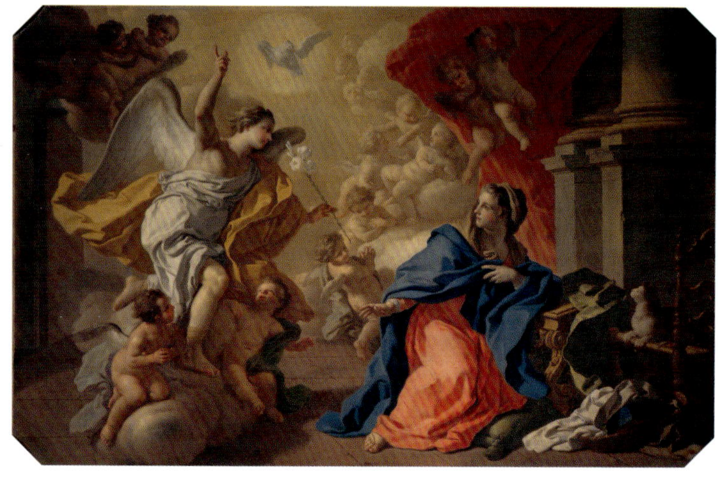

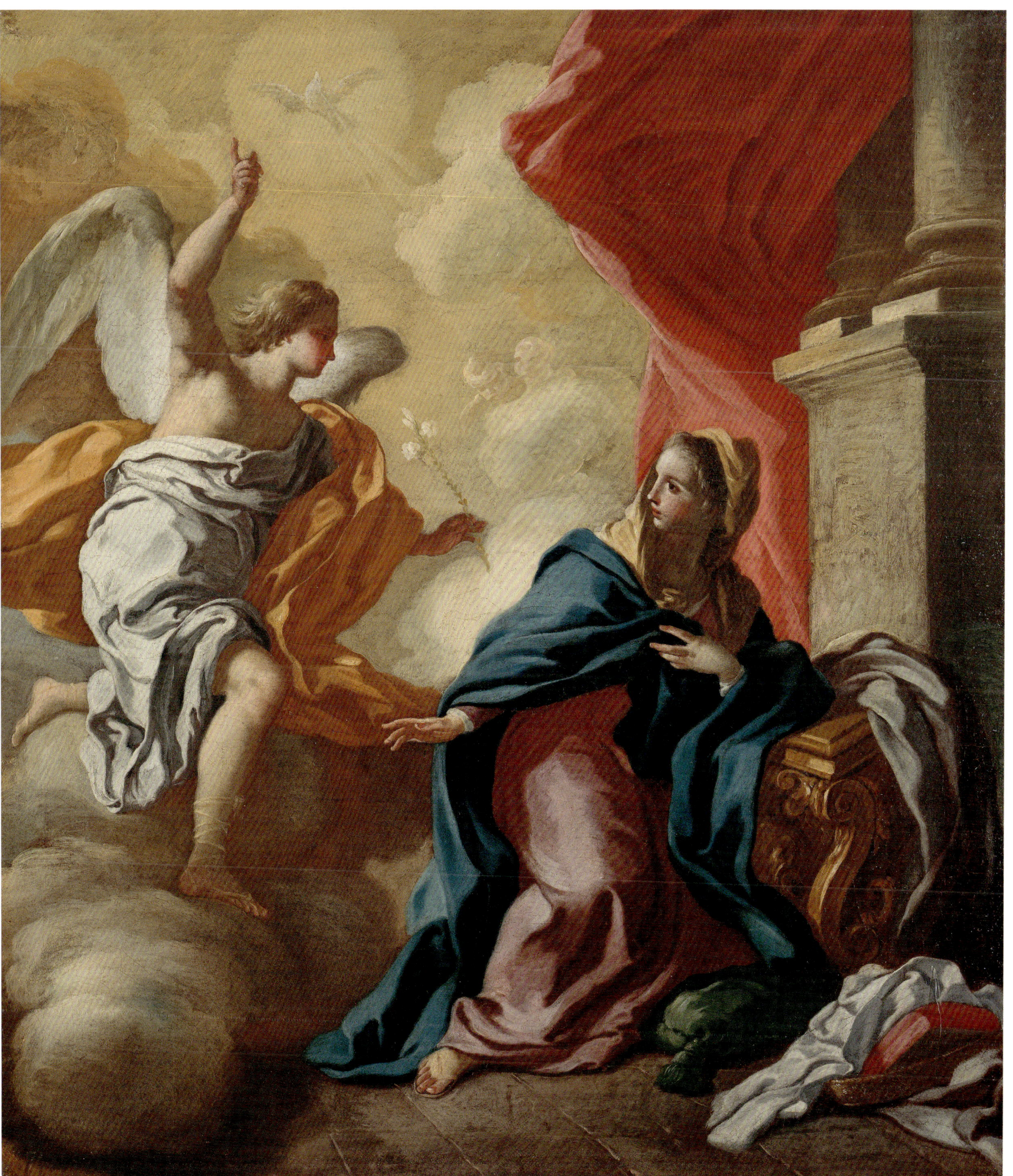

23

Francesco de Mura
The Visitation, ca. 1752
Oil on canvas, 37 × 46½ in. (94 × 118.1 cm)
Cornell Fine Arts Museum, gift of George H. Sullivan in memory of his
parents, acc. no. 1952.34

Luke (1:39–56) describes the visit Mary made to her cousin Elisabeth and
her husband Zechariah, some days after Gabriel announced to her that she
would give birth to the messiah (see cat. no. 22): "Mary entered their house
and greeted Elisabeth [who was pregnant with John the Baptist] and the
child leaped for joy in her womb, and Elisabeth was filled with the Holy
Spirit and exclaimed, 'Blessed are you among women, and blessed is the
child you will bear!'" This painting shows Mary and Elisabeth, like human
parentheses, in a dance, as they greet each other at the town gates. Mary
grasps her sapphire-blue mantle, folding it as if to demonstrate her conception. The elderly Elisabeth bends over to meet Mary's eyes and grasps her
hand; her shawl is golden yellow, symbolizing hospitality and compassion.
Aged Zechariah, clad in a yellow cape, stands at the archway, cane in hand,
gazing at the two women. Two townspeople to his right regard the women,
and a third sits on the lowest step, wearing a Neapolitan headdress and
watching her baby, who looks at us while pointing to Zechariah. Joseph,
carrying a bedroll, leads a donkey behind Mary; above her, putti frolic on a
cloud and wave a billowing pale gold cloth. De Mura has composed a theater
stage set, with an obelisk for stage left and sturdy columns for stage right; he
defines the stage edge with shadow. The landscape background could almost
be a backdrop, and the ground a stage floor. The sun pours in from the left,
spotlighting the central figures, perfectly joined in a theatrical focus.

This painting is a *bozzetto* for (or *ricordo* of) De Mura's powerful
painting of *The Visitation*, done about 1751–52 for the left lateral wall flanking
the altar in the Neapolitan church of San Nicola alla Carità (fig. 67). (On the
opposite right wall is De Mura's *Adoration of the Magi*; De Mura had painted
the *Glory of St. Nicholas* in San Nicola in 1734.). De Mura has transformed
the composition for the large *Visitation* (13¾ × 7½ ft., or 4.2 × 2.3 m) into
a vertical scene; he removed the donkey and a townsperson, as well as the
obelisk and parts of the sky (for the curved top). The columns on the right
echo the actual columns of the church. But the colors are the same, as are the
figures and the overall shimmering blond light. A much darker and smaller
version of the Cornell *Visitation* is in Pio Monte della Misericordia, where
the Cornell work may have been part of De Mura's bequest. De Mura used the
vertical version for his *Visitation* in the church of the Annunziata in Capua,
done about 1750 (Pio Monte has a *bozzetto* for this version also, inv. no. 123).

This composition, called by Federico Zeri "one of the most beautiful
paintings by De Mura in the U.S.,"[1] and undoubtedly inspired his much
grander and more powerful *Visitation* in the chapel of the Assumption in the
church of the Certosa di San Martino (fig. 68), and *The Visitation* of 1753 in
the monastery of the Visitación in Madrid.

1. Federico Zerri, Cornell Museum files.

Provenance:
Studio of the artist; possibly
in the bequest by De Mura to
Pio Monte della Misericordia
in Naples in 1782?; private col-
lection, Naples; Dr. Giuseppe
Manittoli collection, Naples;
M. Knoedler & Co., Inc., New
York, no. 50.066?; Algernon
Sydney Sullivan, New York,
ca. 1910–ca. 1920?; George H.
Sullivan, New York, to 1952.

Exhibiitons:
John and Mable Ringling
Museum of Art, Sarasota,
Fla., Mar.–Apr. 1962, *Special
Exhibition for Art Museum
Directors*; Museum of Fine Arts,
St. Petersburg, Fla., Feb. 1989,
Treasure of the Month; Cornell
Fine Arts Museum, Rollins
College, Winter Park, Fla.,
Mar. 14–May 5, 1991, *Italian
Renaissance and Baroque
Paintings in Florida Museums*,
no. 33.

Bibliography:
Burton B. Fredricksen and
Federico Zeri, *Census of
Pre-Nineteenth-Century
Italian Paintings in North
American Public Collections*
(Cambridge: Harvard
University Press, 1972), 146,
659 (as Francesco de Mura);
Arthur R. Blumenthal, *Italian
Renaissance and Baroque
Paintings in Florida Museums*,
exhib. cat. (Winter Park, Fla.:
Cornell Fine Arts Museum,
Rollins College, 1991), 66, no.
33 (ill.); Arthur R. Blumenthal
et al., *Treasures of the Cornell
Fine Arts Museum* (Winter
Park, Fla.: Cornell Fine Arts
Museum, Rollins College,
1993), 22–23, no. 11 (also used
as exhib. cat.).

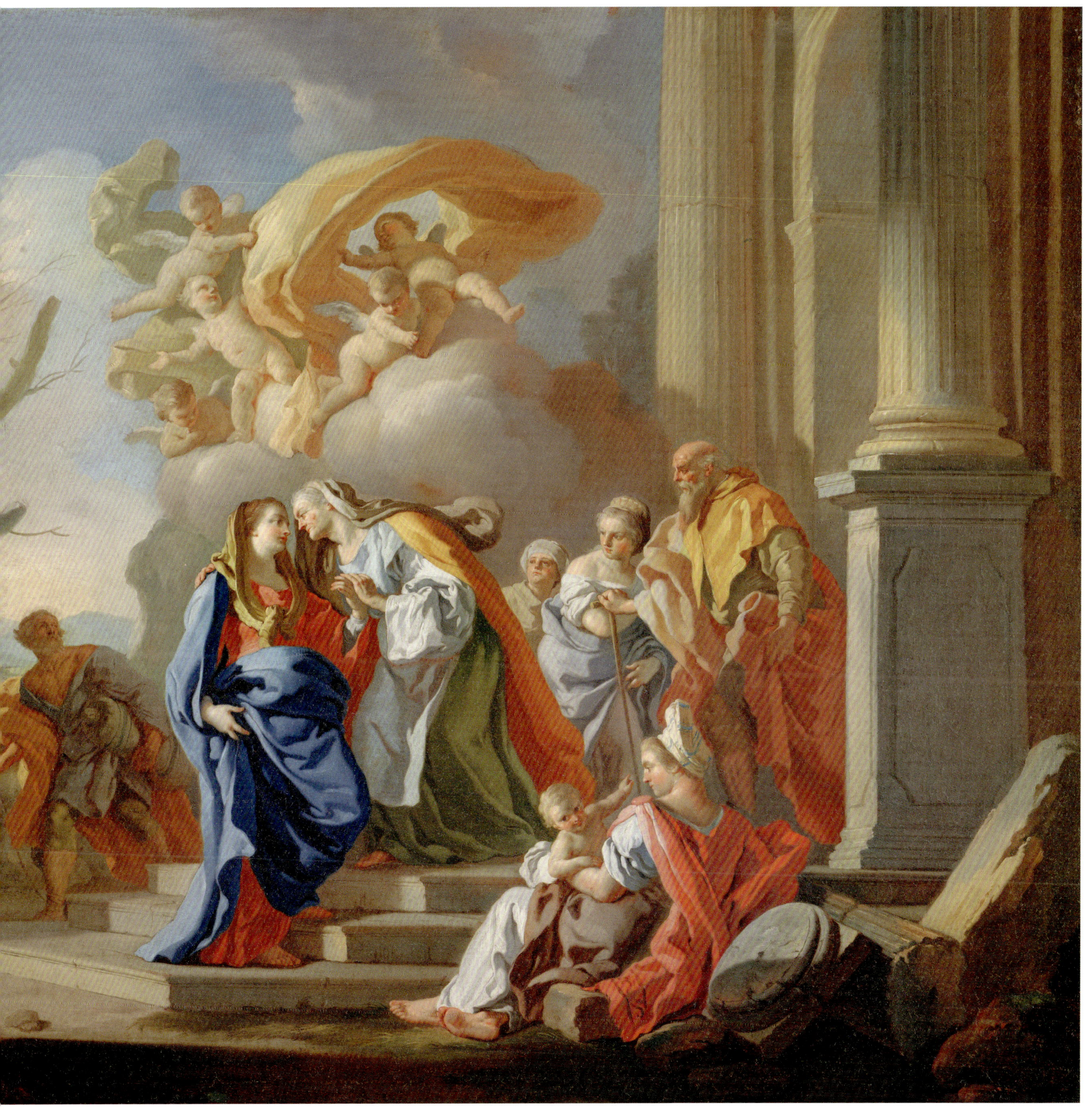

23 — continued

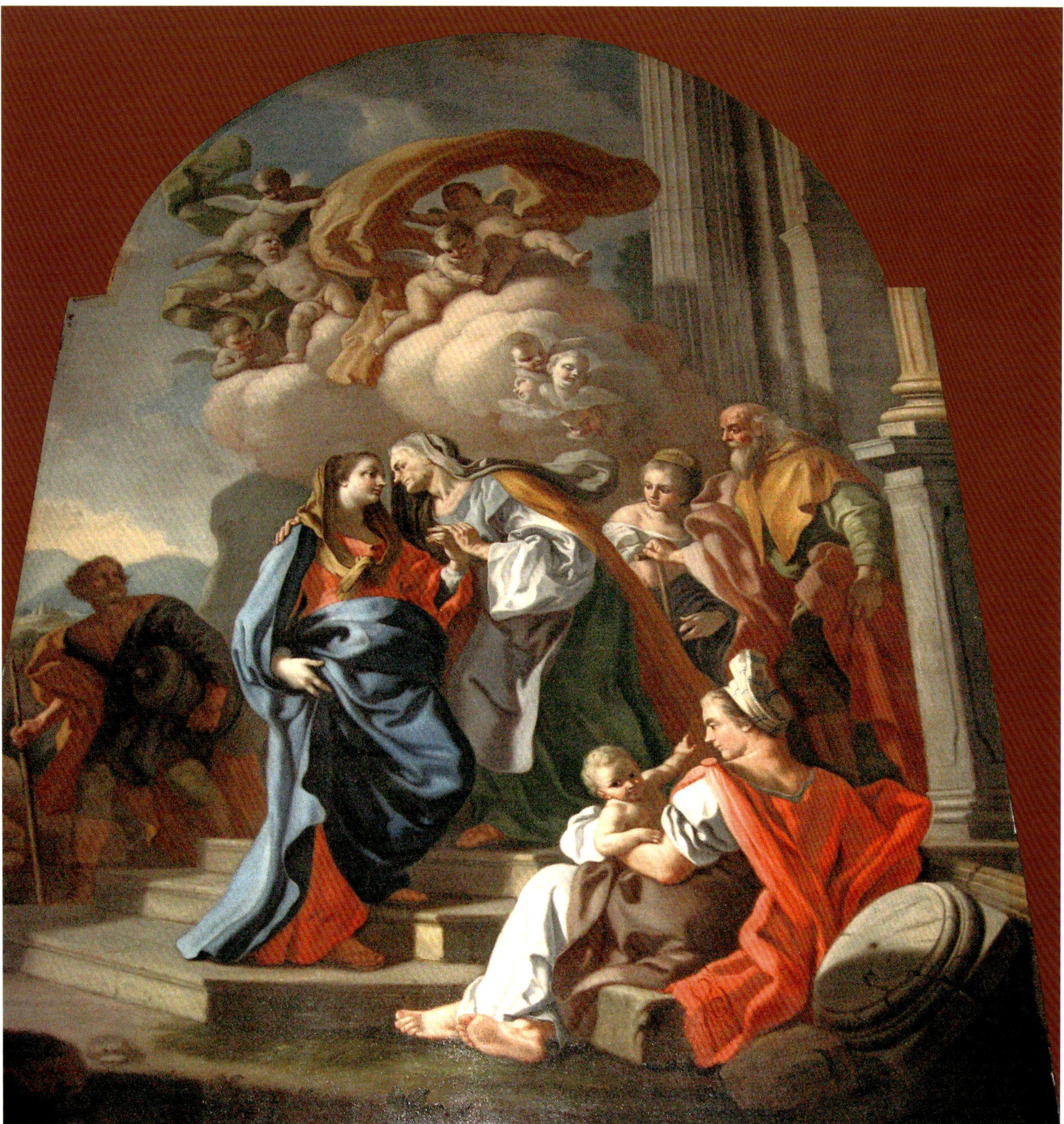

Fig. 67
Francesco de Mura, *The Visitation*, ca. 1752, oil on canvas, church of San Nicola alla Carità, Naples

Fig. 68
Francesco de Mura, *The Visitation*, ca. 1757, oil on canvas, chapel of the Assumption, church of the Certosa di San Martino, Naples

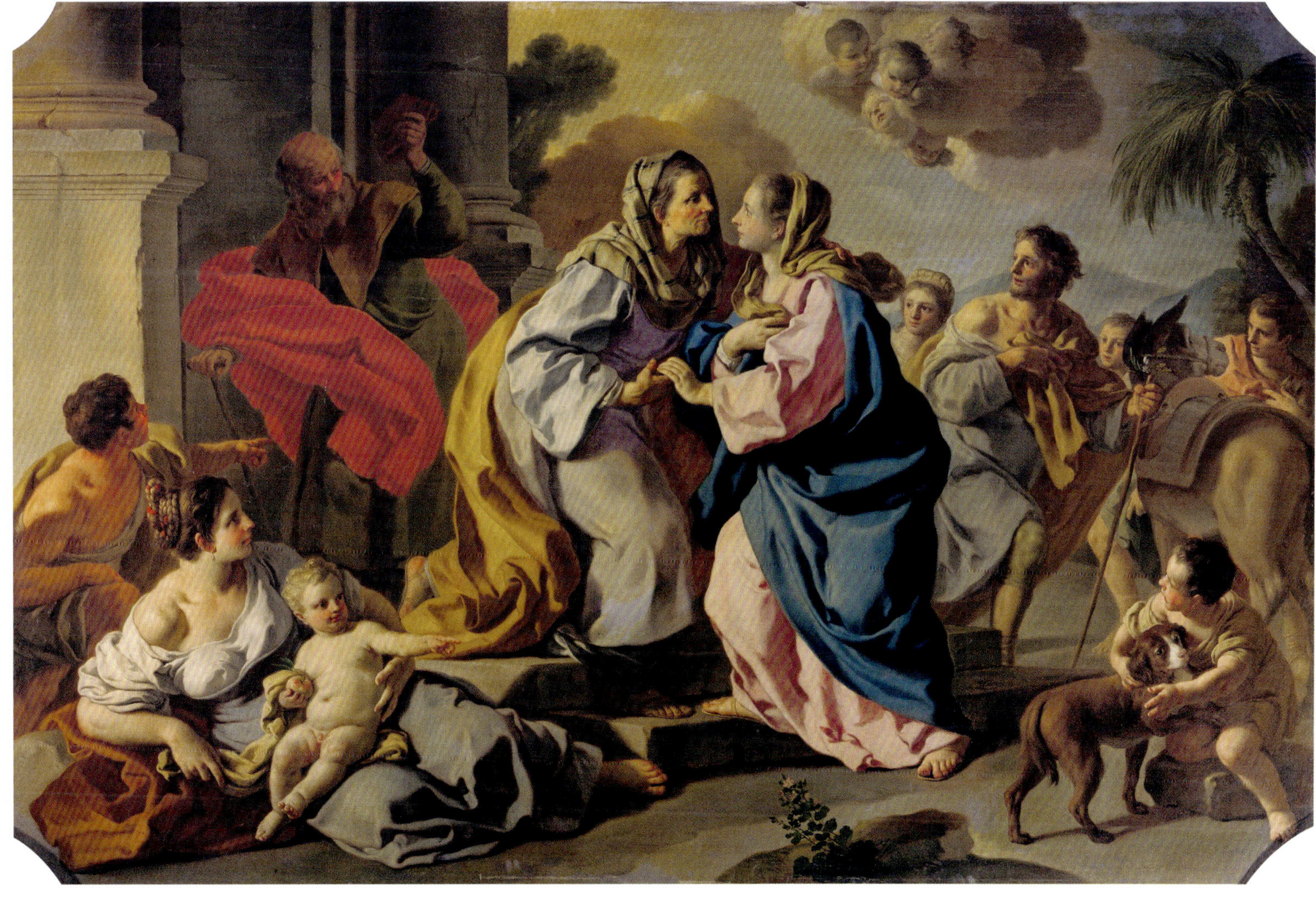

24

Francesco de Mura
Christ and the Woman of Samaria, 1752
Oil on canvas, 40¹⁵⁄₁₆ × 61⁷⁄₁₆ in. (104.2 × 156.3 cm)
Inscription on back of canvas (before relining): *FRANCISCUS DE MURO PINGBAT ANNO 1752*
Seattle Art Museum, gift of Dr. and Mrs. Richard E. Fuller, acc. no. 68.186

According to the Gospel of John (4:4–26), Jesus was traveling on the road through Samaria one day about noon when he stopped to rest at the well of Jacob the Patriarch. Jesus sat down and asked a Samaritan woman standing nearby for a drink of the well water, since he had no cup. The story is interpreted as Jesus' self-identification as the messiah, and his outreach to non-Jews (although the Samaritans considered themselves Jews, the Jews considered them gentiles) and to women in general, since he initiated the conversation with her.

Like *The Visitation* (cat. no. 23), with which this composition has much in common, De Mura visualized the New Testament story as if it takes place on a theatrical stage. The Samaritan woman, wearing a red Neapolitan hat, stands in profile by the ancient stone well (with putti, etc.), holding a wooden bucket with her right hand and grasping her yellow and blue overskirt with her left; her questionable morality (mentioned by John) is suggested by the exposed left shoulder, the lifted skirt, and bare feet. Her backward-leaning pose is the mirror opposite of Jesus'. Resting on a step next to the well and pointing to the water inside, Jesus also leans backward, tilting his haloed head, as his celestial blue mantle falls off his left shoulder. Jesus braces himself with his right hand, and his bent right leg creates an S-shape. The two are in a dance, much as Mary and Elisabeth are in *The Visitation*. Two dogs stop by Jesus' feet, one listening intently, and a red robe draped on the well's step unites the two spotlit actors. At stage left, we see Peter and three disciples returning from the market. They appear astonished, with hands lifted at Jesus' preaching. The center background (or theatrical backdrop) reveals three villagers pointing and looking doubtfully at Jesus, as do four others further into the scene.

The differences from an earlier version of the subject by the circle of Solimena[1] (fig. 69) are profound: rather than Solimena's simpler, sculptural, and heavy figures, De Mura presents bright, theatrically complex, and balletic figures. De Mura completed this work in 1752 during his work on the Nunziatella ceiling frescoes, and we see here the same light and airy figures as if viewed from below. This painting was designed for the ecclesiastical apartments of the Neapolitan church of Gesù Nuovo (where Solimena executed his *Expulsion of Heliodorus from the Temple* in 1725), as was De Mura's pendant (unlocated) of the related *Christ and the Woman Taken in Adultery*.[2] Earlier on, in 1735, De Mura executed another *Christ and the Samaritan Woman* that was destroyed in the bombing of Monte Cassino in 1944.[3]

1. This painting is a version of Solimena's *Christ and the Samaritan Woman* in the Pisani collection in Naples.
2. David Nolta, entry no. 37 in *A Taste for Angels*, 279–83.
3. *Ibid.*, fig. 120.

Provenance:
Ecclesiastical Apartments of church of Gesù Nuovo, Naples; private collection, Rome; Jack Baer, Hazlitt Gallery, London, to 1967; purchased from Hazlitt by Harry Brooks; M. Knoedler & Co., Inc., New York, inv. no. A9104, acquired Mar. 13, 1967; purchased by Dr. and Mrs. Richard E. Fuller and donated to Seattle Art Museum, July 18, 1968.

Exhibitions:
Art Institute of Chicago, Minneapolis Institute of Arts, Toledo Museum of Art, Ohio, *Painting in Italy in the Eighteenth Century: Rococo to Romanticism*, 1970–71, no. 99; Bellevue Art Museum, Wash., Oct. 30–Nov. 24, 1975, *17th-, 18th-, and* 19th-Century *Western Art*; Yale University Art Gallery, New Haven, Conn., John and Mable Ringling Museum of Art, Sarasota, Fla., Nelson-Atkins Museum of Art, Kansas City, Mo., Sept. 9, 1987–June 12, 1988, *A Taste for Angels: Neapolitan Paintings in North America, 1650–1750.*

Bibliography:
Seattle Art Museum, *Annual Report of the Seattle Art Museum* (Seattle: Seattle Art Museum, 1968), 45; John Maxon and Joseph J. Rishel, eds., *Painting in Italy in the Eighteenth Century: Rococo to Romanticism*, exhib. cat. (Chicago: Chicago Art Institute, 1970), 234–35 (ill.); Seattle Art Museum, *Engagement Book*, Oct. 11–17, 1970; Wilson, P. Boyd, article in *The Christian Science Monitor*, June 25, 1971, 10; Bellevue Art Museum, *17th-, 18th-, and 19th-Century Western Art*, exhib. brochure (Bellevue, Wash.: Bellevue Art Museum, 1975); *A Taste for Angels: Neapolitan Paintings in North America, 1650–1750*, exhib. cat. (New Haven: Yale University Art Gallery, 1987), 251–69, 278–83; Arthur R. Blumenthal et al., *Treasures of the Cornell Fine Arts Museum* (Winter Park, Fla.: Cornell Fine Arts Museum, Rollins College, 1993), 22–23, no. 11 (also used as exhib. cat.).

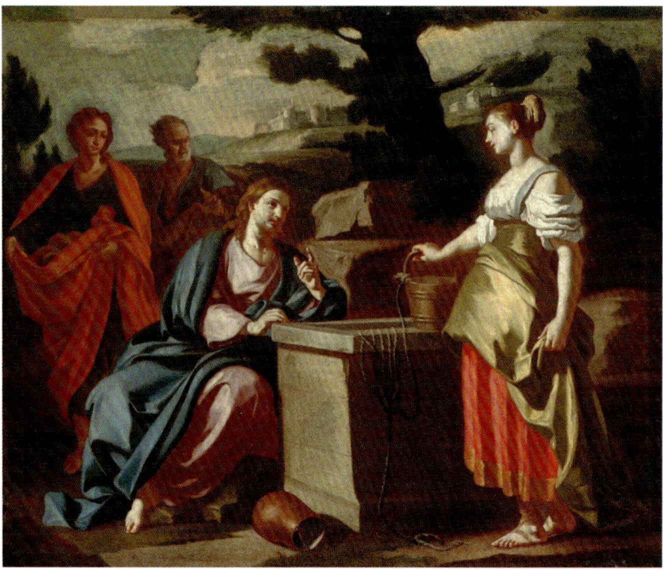

Fig. 69
Circle of Francesco Solimena, *Christ and the Samaritan Woman at the Well*, ca. 1725?, oil on canvas, private collection (after Solimena's work in the Pisani collection)

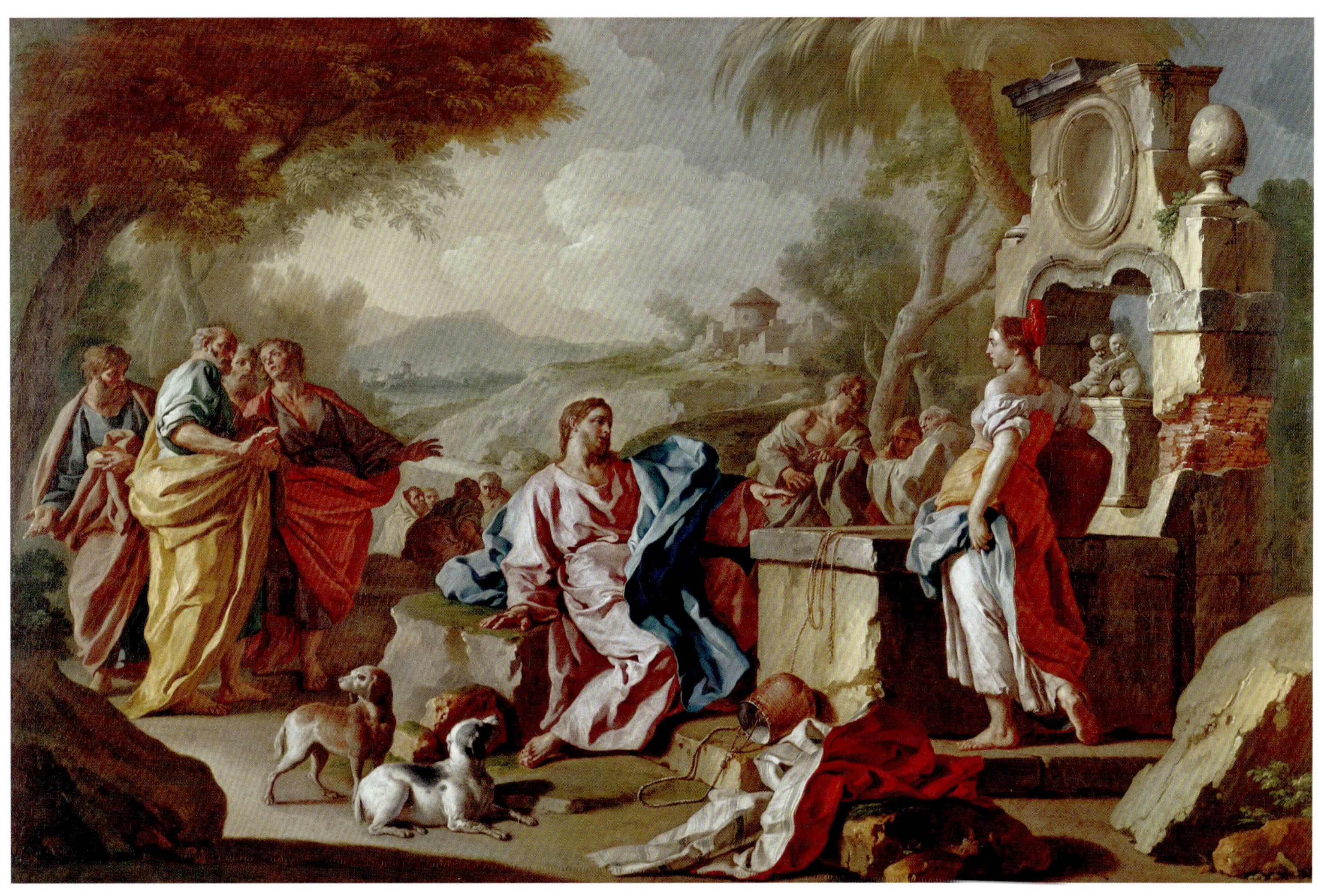

25

Francesco de Mura
Portrait of Count James Joseph O'Mahoney, Lieutenant-General in the Neapolitan
Service, Knight of St. Januarius, before June 1747
Oil on canvas, 39 × 28¾ in. (99 × 73 cm)
The Syndics of the Fitzwilliam Museum, University of Cambridge, U.K., acquired with
the assistance of the Friends of the Fitzwilliam Museum, the Victoria and Albert Museum
Purchase Grant Fund, and the National Art Collections Fund, acc. no. PD.4-1984

This superb work is one of the most powerfully incisive portraits of the
eighteenth century, demonstrating De Mura's extraordinary talent for
portraiture (see also cat. nos. 17 and 27). Count James Joseph O'Mahoney
(1699–1757), an Irish mercenary, was a celebrated lieutenant-general in
the service of Charles Bourbon, King of Naples (in 1759, King Charles III of
Spain). He was in charge of the Spanish troops in Italy and fought honorably
for the king. Completing his service in 1747, he commissioned a portrait of
himself from De Mura.

The artist has placed O'Mahoney before a charcoal-gray wall, all the
better to set off his gilded armor and royal-purple cape. The sitter stares
calmly at us, as if observing the artist at work; his right arm rests on his hip
with his hand turned inward and holding a wooden baton. His left hand rests
on a gilded helmet, which has been placed on a blue velvet cloth covering
a gilded pedestal. The Count's bright purple cape is joined on his shoulder
with a metal chain; its placement creates a sense of drama and movement,
opposing the straight lines of the sitter. De Mura's depiction of the intense
face is done with great empathy, the eyebrows suggesting an open inquisi-
tiveness, the eyes joining ours in an engaging gaze—all of which produce a
sense of aliveness.

At the time of this painting, De Mura's master Solimena, also a great
portraitist (see fig. 58), had just died on May 3, 1747, a few months shy of his
ninetieth birthday. De Mura had recently returned from one of his final trips
to the Palazzo Reale in Turin, and still had to complete the *St. Benedict* frescoes at Santi Severino e Sossio (see fig. 53). According to Spinosa, De Mura
executed this portrait before June of 1747,[1] during the Neapolitan sojourn of
the famous French painter Pierre Subleyras (1699–1749), who spent most
of his career in Rome. While De Mura painted Count O'Mahoney, Subleyras
painted a pendant *Portrait of Countess Anna Giustiniani O'Mahoney* (fig. 70).
Thus, the influence of the French artist on De Mura is possible, since he must
have known Subleyras during his own earlier sojourn in Rome.[2] In any event,
the brighter, lighter and more elegant portraiture of Subleyras, as seen in the
portrait of the countess, is also evident in this portrait of her husband. These
elements are also apparent in De Mura's magnificent *Self-Portrait* (cat. no.
17), in which the artist also assumes a similar pose to Count O'Mahoney's.

1. Spinosa, *Pittura napoletana del Settecento,* 2:152.
2. *Ibid.,* 1:160.

Provenance:
Durazzo-Pallavicini-Cambiaso-
Negrotto, from the Castle of
Borromeo Arese di Cesano
Maderno, Rome, Christie's,
Castello Borromeo Arese
Sale, Oct. 5–6, 1979, lot 535;
Colnaghi's, London, 1984;
acquired with assistance of
the Friends of the Fitzwilliam
Museum, 1984, with contribu-
tions from Victoria & Albert
Museum Grant-in-Aid and
National Art Collections Fund.

Exhibition:
National Portrait Gallery,
London, 1996, *The Art of the
Picture Frame.*

Bibliography:
Pierre Rosenberg, "Tre note
napoletane," in *Arti e civiltà
del Settecento a Napoli, Atti
del convegno,* ed. Cesare De
Seta (Rome: Laterza, 1982),
81–94; Nicola Spinosa, *Pittura
napoletana del Settecento,* vol.
1, *Dal barocco al rococò,* 2nd ed.
(Naples: Electa Napoli, 1993),
160–61, no. 257, fig. 306; Nicola
Spinosa, *Pittura napoletana del
Settecento,* vol. 2, *Dal Rococò al
Classicismo,* 2nd ed. (Naples:
Electa Napoli, 1993), 152, no.
253; National Art-Collections
Fund, *Annual Review* (London:
National Art-Collections
Fund, 1994), 151, no. 3104;
"Carving and Gilding a British
Rococo Frame," *The Frame
Blog,* May 17, 2003, http://
theframeblog.com/2013/05/17/
carving-gilding-a-british-
Rococo-frame/; Jacob Simon,
"The Italian Swept Frame," in
*The Art of the Picture Frame:
Artists, Patrons and the Framing
of Portraits in Britain,* exhib.
cat. (London: National Portrait
Gallery, 1996).

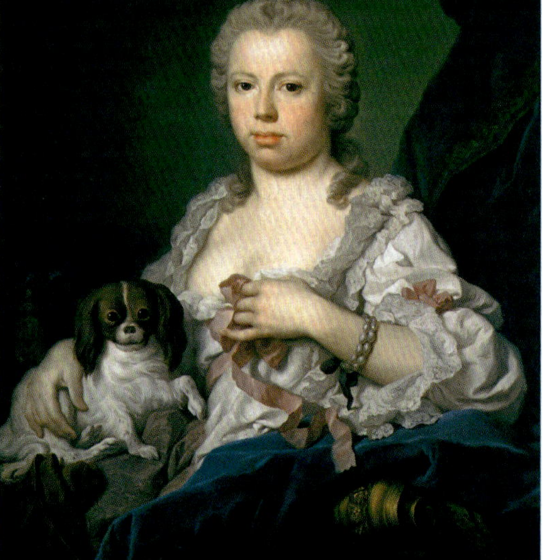

Fig. 70
Pierre Subleyras, *Portrait of Countess Anna
Giustiniani O'Mahoney,* ca. 1747–48, oil on
canvas, 39⅜ × 29⅜ in. (100 × 74.5 cm),
Musée des Beaux-Arts de Caen, France

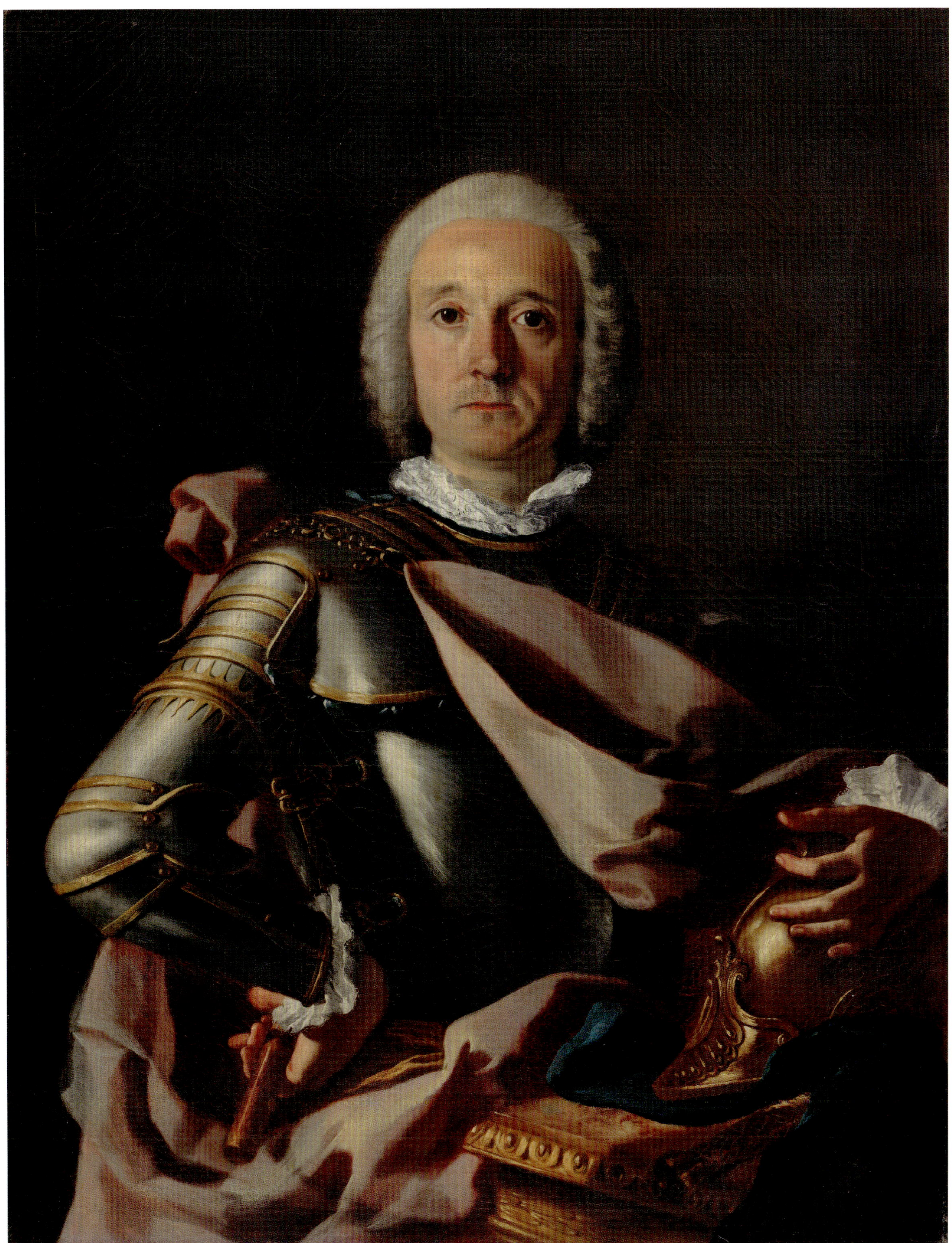

26

Francesco de Mura
Design for a Trophy Frame with a Portrait of a Nobleman
[*Count James Joseph O'Mahoney*?], ca. 1747–50
Brush and gray wash, pen and black ink, black chalk on paper, 14⅞ × 11 in. (37.8 × 27.9 cm)
Inscription on reverse in pen: *Fran di Mura*
Cooper Hewitt, Smithsonian Design Museum, Smithsonian Institution, Museum purchase through gifts of various donors and from Eleanor G. Hewitt Fund, acc. no. 1938-88-7068.

The *Portrait of Count James Joseph O'Mahoney* (cat. no. 25) is set in a gilded wooden frame designed and crafted in Italy around 1750 that De Mura himself may have designed (fig. 71).[1] In any case, De Mura created this extremely elaborate ink sketch of a trophy frame and included a faint chalk sketch of a sitter in armor similar in pose to Count O'Mahoney's, suggesting that this drawing was a design for a frame for the count's portrait. The oval shape in the center is trimmed with a laurel wreath, atop which is a lion-headed scroll. On each side of the oval are a dozen spears, and banners, drums, cannon, cannonballs, and helmets—all reflecting the sitter's distinguished military career. Two winged putti below support the oval frame as they perch on a ledge; below them are two acanthus-leaf swags. This beautiful design reminds us of De Mura's significant drafting skills, also seen in his lovely ink drawings from 1740 and 1750 (cat. nos. 14 and 20).

1. "Carving and Gilding a British Rococo Frame," *The Frame Blog*, May 17, 2003.

Provenance:
Giovanni Piancastelli (1845–1926), director of Galleria Borghese in Rome and major collector of Old Master drawings; purchased [from his estate sale?] by the Cooper-Hewitt in 1938.

Exhibitions:
Finch College Museum of Art, New York, Feb. 4–Mar, 20, 1970, *The Two Sicilies: Drawings from the Cooper-Hewitt Museum*, no. 37; The Metropolitan Museum of Art, New York, Jan. 30–Mar. 21, 1971, *Drawings from New York Collections: The Eighteenth Century in Italy*, no. 58; Detroit Institute of Arts, Art Institute of Chicago, Aug. 11, 1981–Mar. 8, 1982, *The Golden Age of Naples: Art and Civilization under the Bourbons, 1734–1805*, no. 8.

Bibliography:
Elaine Evans Dee, *The Two Sicilies: Drawings from the Cooper-Hewitt Museum*, exhib. cat. (New York: Finch College Museum of Art, 1970), 21, no. 37 (cover ill.); Jacob Bean and Felice Stampfle, *The Eighteenth Century in Italy*, Drawings from New York Collections 3, exhib. cat. (New York: Metropolitan Museum of Art and Pierpont Morgan Library, 1971), 41, no. 58; Renato Roli and Giancarlo Sestieri, *I disegni italiani del Settecento* (Treviso: Libreria Editrice Canova, 1981), 113, pl. 192; *The Golden Age of Naples: Art and Civilization under the Bourbons 1734–1805*, exhib. cat. (Detroit: Detroit Institute of Arts, 1981), 2:262, no. 8 (ill.); "Carving and Gilding a British Rococo Frame," *The Frame Blog*, May 17, 2003, http:// theframeblog.com/2013/05/17/ carving-gilding-a-british-rococo-frame/.

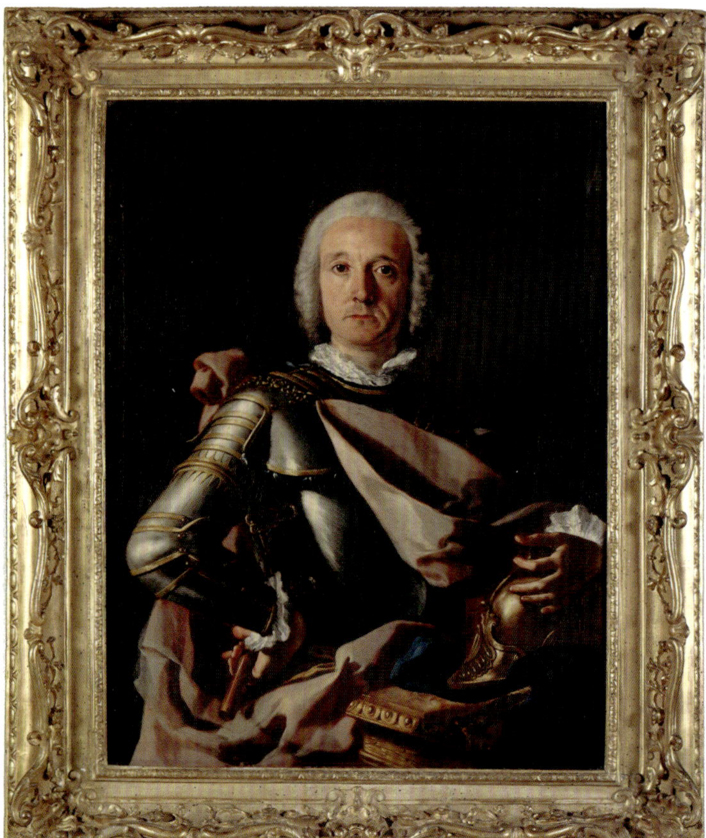

Fig. 71
Francesco de Mura, *Portrait of Count James Joseph O'Mahoney, Lieutenant-General in the Neapolitan Service, Knight of St. Januarius*, before June 1747, oil on canvas, in original frame (designed by the artist?), 50⅜ × 41 × 4⁵⁄₁₆ in. (120 × 104 × 11 cm), The Syndics of the Fitzwilliam Museum, Cambridge

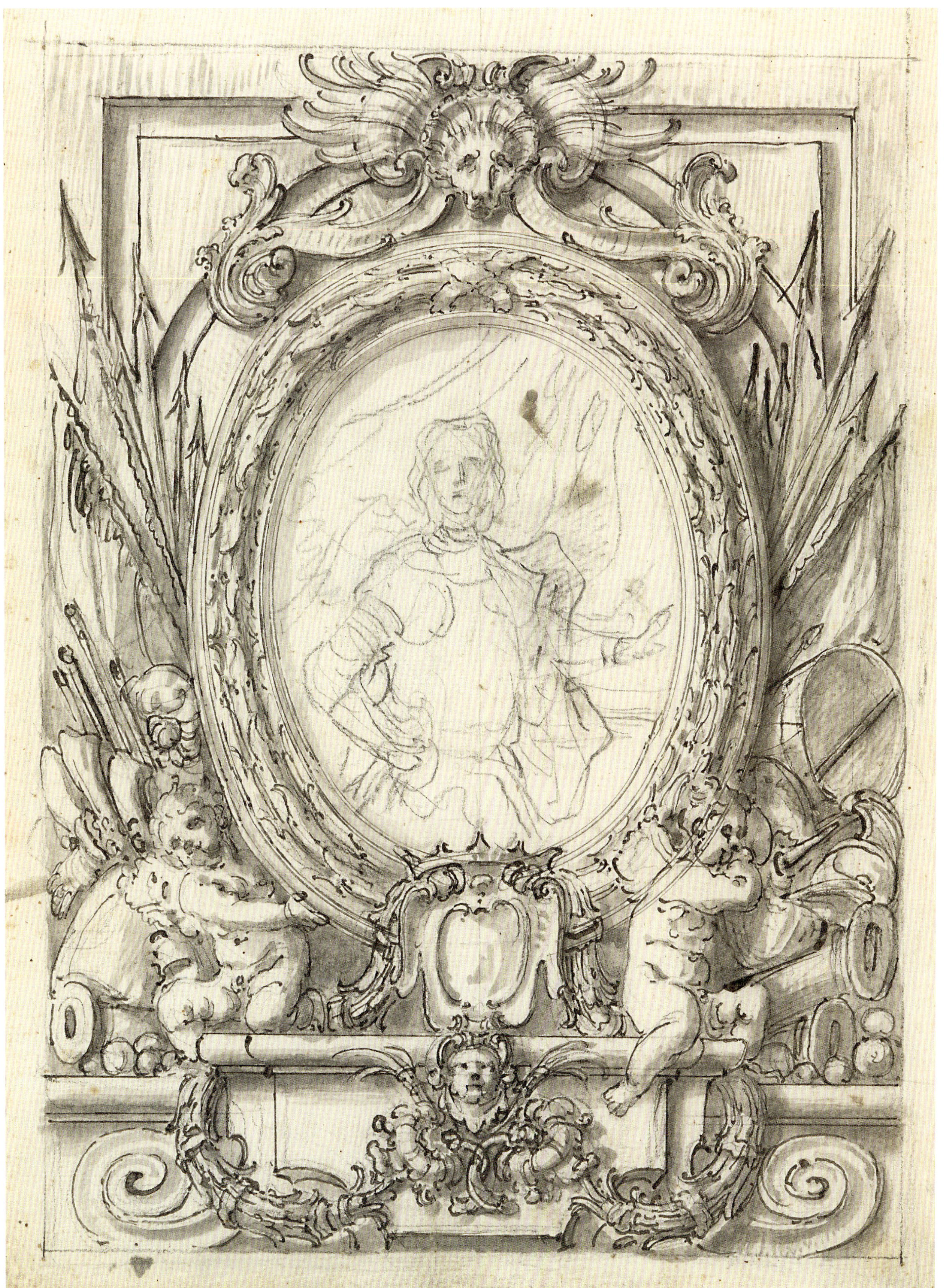

27

Francesco de Mura
Portrait of Cardinal Antonio Sersale, May 20, 1756
Oil on canvas, 34 × 28 in. (87 × 72 cm)
Inscription on reverse: *fatto in Napoli nel secondo anno della Nunziatura dal celebre pittore Francesco de Mura il 20 maggio 1756.*
Collection of Myron Laskin, Jr., on extended loan to the Milwaukee Art Museum, extended loan no. L138.1993

This striking portrait is of Cardinal Antonio (or Antonino) Sersale (1702–75), who became archbishop of Naples on February 11, 1754, and was elevated to cardinal a few months later, on April 22. Four weeks later, on May 20, he was installed as cardinal-priest of Santa Pudenziana, the cardinal titular church. Sersale rose rapidly in the church because of his powerful preaching, but he was also well known for his patronage of the arts. The cardinal was born into an aristocratic family and spent large sums to support and build seminaries and schools, and commissioned many silver ritual objects for Naples' cathedral of San Gennaro.[1] A skillful diplomat, the cardinal participated in the conclaves to choose a new pope in 1758, 1769, and 1774–75.

In 1756, the cardinal commissioned De Mura to paint his portrait, which the artist completed on May 20 (it is inscribed thus on the reverse), the second anniversary of Sersale's installation as cardinal-priest. The resulting painting is one of De Mura most magnificent works, on a par with his other splendid portraits (see cat. nos. 17 and 25), yet quite advanced and emotionally riveting.[2] The artist posed the refined Sersale as if the viewer has just entered the room and the cardinal is turning to see who is there. He removes his red hat with his right hand and fingers the black opal cross at his chest with his left (his ring seems also to be of black opal). Sersale wears a modest brown wig and a gray collar, and his sleeves are fashioned of red and white lace. As in the *Portrait of Count James Joseph O'Mahoney* (cat. no. 25), the emotional connection with the viewer is palpable, and here the cardinal's exquisitely painted hands add to the sense of aliveness and incipient movement. Light from an upper window brightens the right half of the cardinal's face, highlighting the elegant hands. Rich red color has been used to powerful effect by De Mura, creating a sense of understated drama.

On June 24, 1775, the cardinal died and was buried in the cathedral of San Gennaro in Naples. The famous Neapolitan sculptor Giuseppe Sanmartino (1720–93) created a portrait bust of Sersale in marble for his tomb (fig. 72).

1. Spinosa, entry 39 in *Golden Age of Naples*, 135.
2. *Ibid.*; "[This portrait] is even more elegant and intense than contemporary examples by Pompeo Batoni."

Provenance:
Patrick Mattiesen Gallery, London, to 1979; private collection, from 1979.

Exhibitions:
Palazzo Reale, Naples, Dec. 1979–Oct. 1980, *Civiltà del '700 a Napoli, 1734–1799*, no. 93; Detroit Institute of Arts, Art Institute of Chicago, Aug. 11, 1981–Mar. 8, 1982, *The Golden Age of Naples: Art and Civilization under the Bourbons, 1734–1805*, no. 39.

Bibliography:
Nicola Spinosa, *Civiltà del '700 a Napoli, 1734–1799*, exhib. cat. (Florence: Centro Di, 1979), 200, no. 93; Nicola Spinosa, entry no. 39 in *The Golden Age of Naples: Art and Civilization under the Bourbons, 1734–1805*, exhib. cat. (Detroit: Detroit Institute of Arts, 1981), 1:135; Nicola Spinosa, *Pittura napoletana del Settecento*, vol. 1, *Dal barocco al rococò*, 2nd ed. (Naples: Electa Napoli, 1993, 137, 161, color pl. 64, entry no. 263, pl. 64.

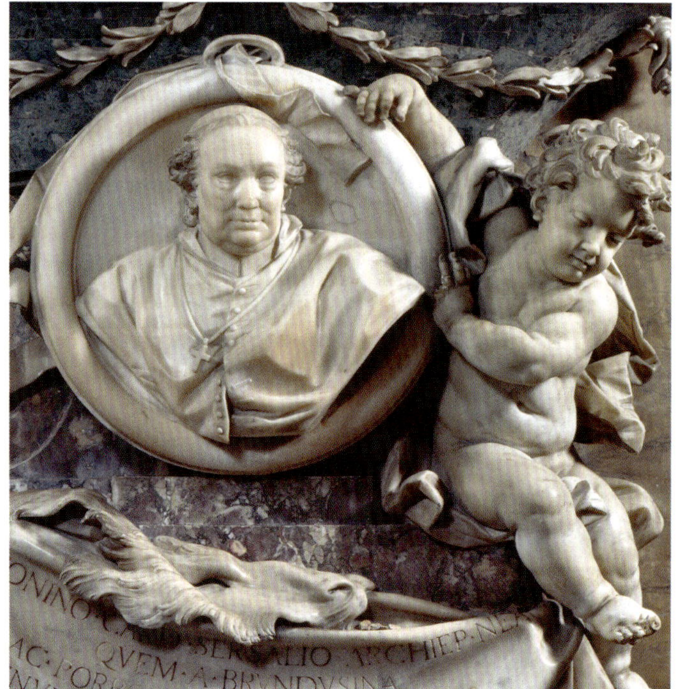

Fig. 72
Giuseppe Sanmartino, *Tomb of Archbishop Antonino Sersale* (detail), 1776–78, marble, cathedral of San Gennaro, Naples

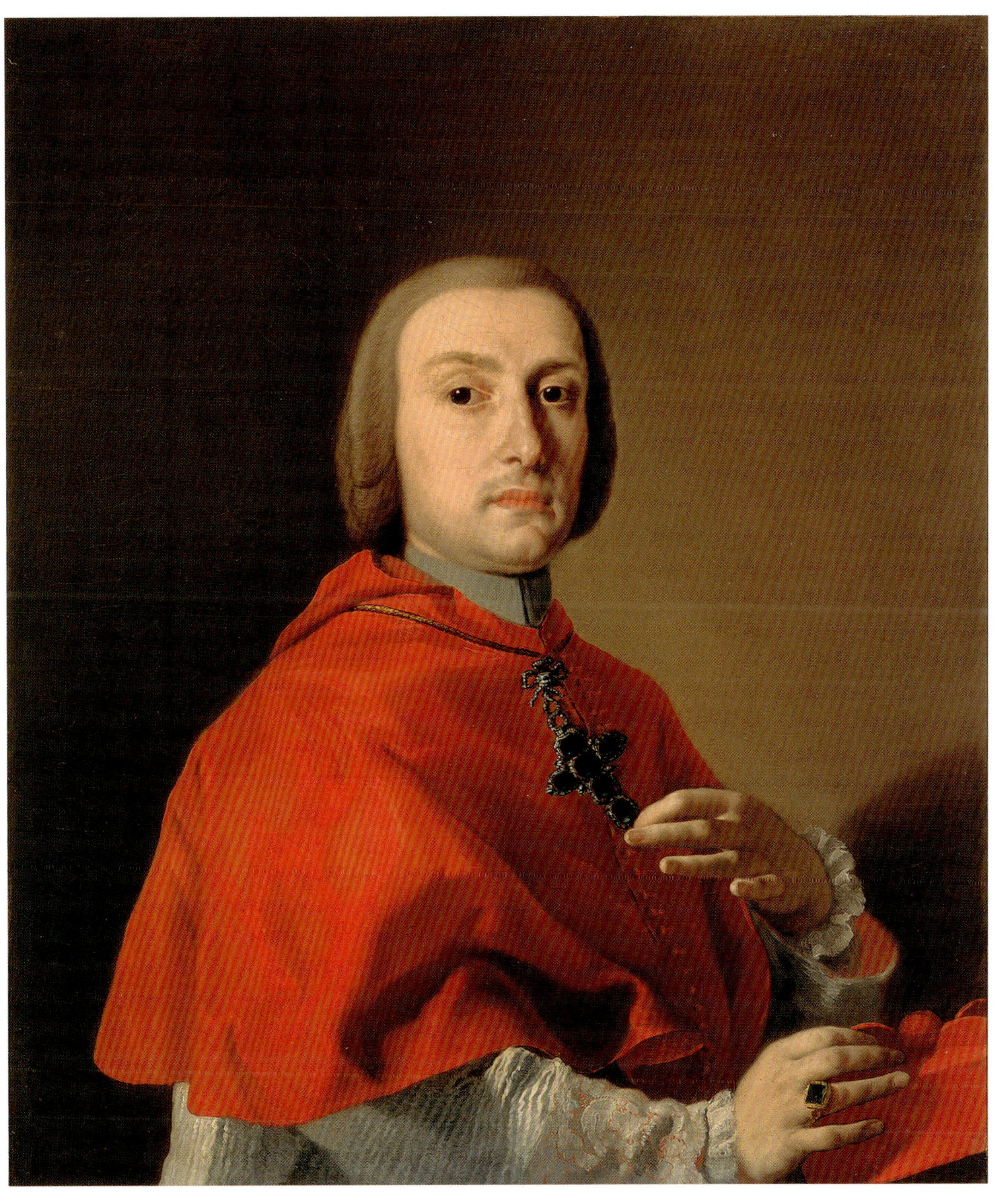

28

Francesco de Mura
Virgin in Glory Receiving St. Louis Gonzaga into Heaven, as Commended by
St. Louis King of France, ca. 1758
Oil on canvas, 60¾ × 40½ in. (159.9 × 103.3 cm)
John and Mable Ringling Museum of Art, the State Museum of Florida,
Florida State University, gift of John and Mable Ringling, acc. no. SN165

In this rich depiction of the canonization of the Jesuit St. Luigi (Aloysius) Gonzaga (1568–91), the Virgin Mary sits on a cloud in the upper left of this composition, pointing to a sphere in the distance and holding out her right hand in a gesture of welcome. The saint, dressed in a surplice and holding a crucifix in his hand, is lifted by two angels and a putto as he gazes beatifically at the Virgin. An angel to the right of the Virgin holds a lily and rosary to place over Gonzaga's head. Kneeling on the ground is the young, pious, and studious saint Louis IX, King of France (1214–70); he wears a brilliant crimson robe thrown over his shoulders and is supported by an angel. St. Louis is surrounded by his fellow students, and nearby lie his armor, royal robes, and books. The charitable St. Louis is commending his namesake Luigi for sainthood.

Luigi Gonzaga was born to a famous noble family. In 1584, when he was sixteen, he joined the Jesuits in Rome and became widely known for his piety; he died of the plague at the age of twenty-three in 1591. Soon after his death, people elevated him to the status of patron saint of plague victims. In 1726, Luigi Gonzaga was canonized, and, in 1729, Pope Benedict XIII declared him patron saint of students, four of whom we see kneeling in this painting. (In the twentieth century, for his compassion in facing an incurable disease, Luigi became the patron saint of AIDS victims.)

Around 1758, De Mura was commissioned for this work by the Jesuit priests of the church of Gesù Vecchio, for the main altar.[1] The painting is a small *ricordo* of the church's enormous canvas, which measures 14¼ × 7½ feet, or 4.5 × 2.2 meters (fig. 73). A more finely executed *bozzetto* for the work can be found in the Museo di Capodimonte. The Ringling work shows the strong chiaroscuro of Solimena, although it is from De Mura's mature period. The sober, elegant, and beautifully drawn figures remind us of Solimena, but they are more typical of De Mura's work after 1745, when he returned to Naples from Turin. The painting has a powerfully clear narrative, showing a graceful harmony in its gesticulating figures. The kneeling students look upward toward St. Luigi on the right, who himself gazes further upward to Mary. The Virgin points to the Jesuit monogram in the center distance—all of this creating an energetic zigzag up and into the composition's center. The dazzling reds, blues, and pinks underscore the movement in this complex scene. De Mura painted a stylistically similar subject and composition in 1758, *The Madonna and Child Appearing to Various Jesuit Saints* (signed and dated), for the chapel in the Palazzo di Via Nilo, 34 (now in the Real Monte Manso di Scala in Naples, fig. 74).[2]

1. Spinosa, *Pittura sacra a Napoli nel '700*, 52.
2. *Reale Monte Manso di Scala* (Naples: Arte Tipografica, 2001), 55 (ill.). One of the Jesuits shown in that painting is the Blessed Francesco de Gerolomo, who was beatified in 1758, when De Mura completed the work.

Provenance:
Art market, Boston, late 1920s; acquired by John Ringling (1866–1936), Sarasota, Fla., in 1928; bequest to Ringling Museum of Art in 1936 (attributed to Solimena).

Exhibition:
McMullen Museum of Art, Boston College, Feb. 1–May 24, 1999, *Saints and Sinners: Caravaggio and the Baroque Image.*

Bibliography:
William E. Suida, *A Catalogue of Paintings in the John and Mable Ringling Museum of Art* (Sarasota, Fla.: John and Mable Ringling Museum of Art, 1949), 143; Peter Tomory, *Catalogue of the Italian Paintings before 1800* (Sarasota, Fla.: John and Mable Ringling Museum of Art, 1976), 174–75 (as copy "after Francesco de Mura"); Burton B. Frederickson and Federico Zeri, *Census of Pre-Nineteenth-Century Italian Paintings in North American Public Collections* (Cambridge, Mass.: Harvard University Press, 1972), 202 (as Francesco de Mura); Nicola Spinosa, *Pittura sacra a Napoli nel '700*, exhib. cat. (Naples: Società Editrice Napoletana, 1980), 52, no. 18 (as *ricordo* or copy of De Mura).

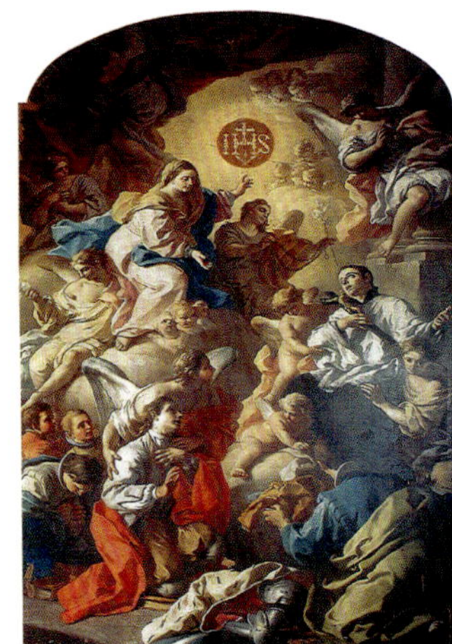

Fig. 73
Francesco de Mura, *Virgin in Glory Receiving St. Lugi Gonzaga*, ca. 1758, oil on canvas, 177⅛ × 86½ in. (450 × 219.7 cm), sacristy of the church of Gesù Vecchio, Naples

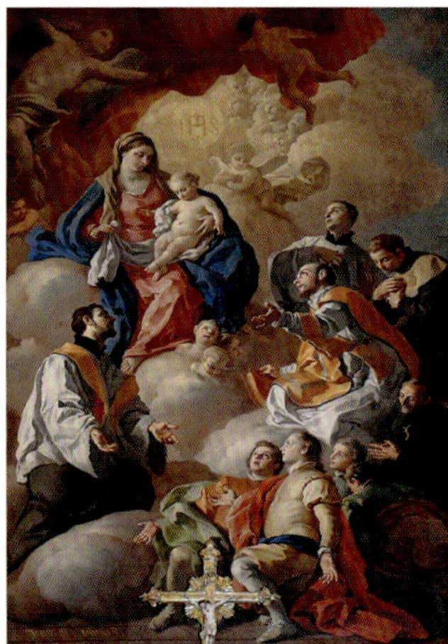

Fig. 74
Francesco de Mura, *Madonna and Child in Glory Receiving Saints*, signed and dated 1758, oil on canvas, Real Monte Manso di Scala, Naples (painted for the chapel, Palazzo di Via Nolo)

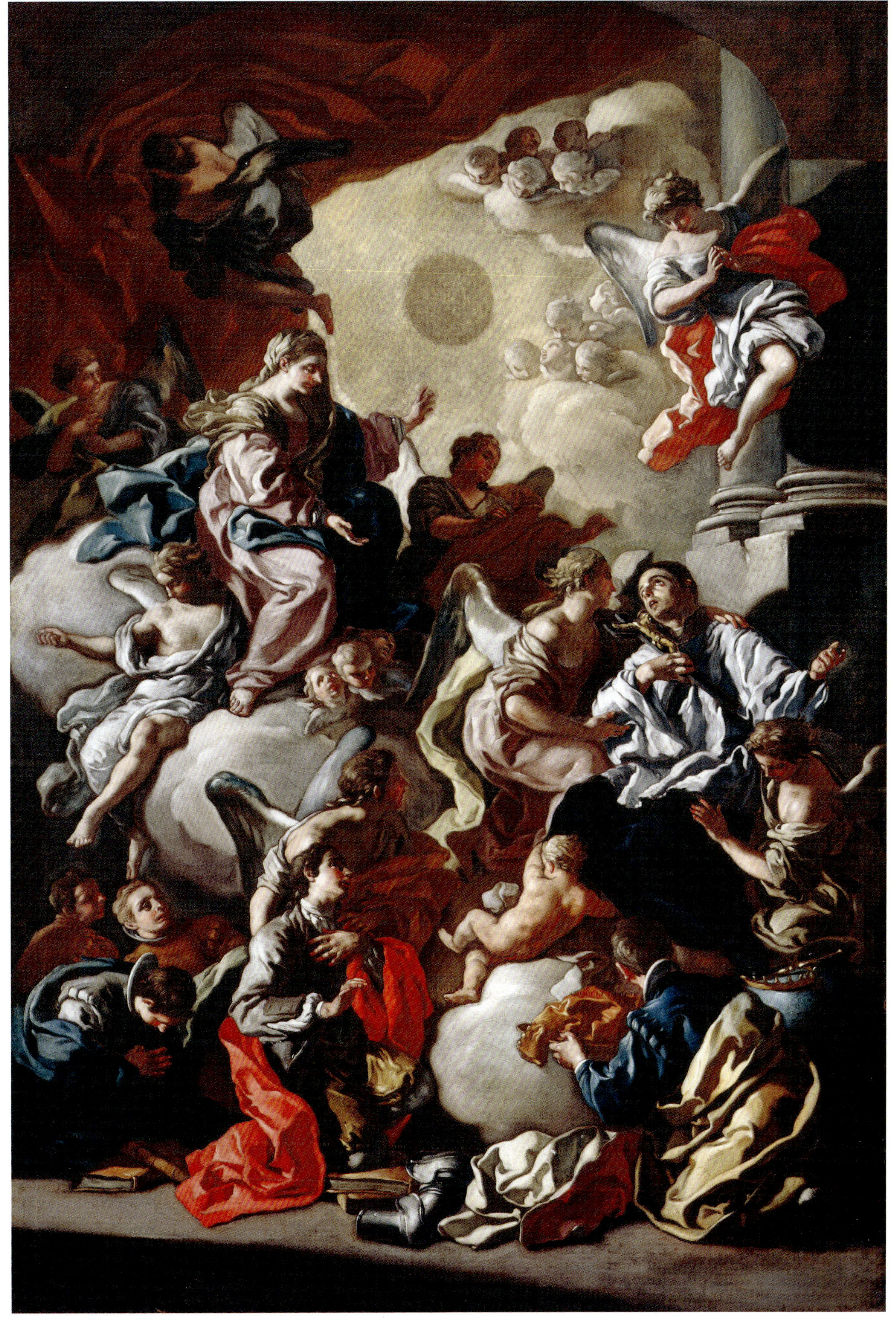

29

Francesco de Mura
Madonna and Child with the Infant St. John the Baptist, ca. 1745–50
Oil on copper (oval), 12 × 9½ in. (30.5 × 24.1 cm)
Inscription on reverse: *Fiore Romolo/21 Novembre, 1888*
Collection of Federico Castelluccio

This lovely small oval oil painting on copper depicts the Virgin Mary with her head turned to her left and down as she gazes at the baby Jesus. Her exquisitely painted right hand rests on her chest, as if she is about to nurse her child; her rich brown headscarf covers the back of her head, leaving her fine auburn hair exposed. Mary's sapphire-blue robe (the color reminding us of her role as Queen of Heaven) has slipped from her left shoulder, as if she is preparing to nurse, and her pale rose blouse covers a white undergarment. The naked Christ Child lies on a white pillow and white blanket, bracing himself on his left elbow. The baby looks at us and points with his right hand to his mother, who is the focus of the painting and the viewer's devotions. In shadow on the left, behind Mary, is Jesus' little cousin, John the Baptist, dressed in animal skins and carrying a bamboo cross, as he, too, gazes upon the Madonna and Child.

Small images of the Madonna and Child were popular for private devotions in one's home in seventeenth- and eighteenth-century Naples, and De Mura painted dozens of them (see cat. nos. 30, 31, and 32). He painted his Madonnas with a warmth and tenderness not usually found in Neapolitan Baroque Madonnas. Spinosa dates this work to the 1740s,[1] and, indeed, it has a close relationship with Chicago's superb *Allegory of Maternal Love*, painted ca. 1743–44 (see cat. no. 19). The figures in Castelluccio's painting, even the infant John the Baptist, are similar to the mother and children in *Maternal Love*, and De Mura used a pyramidal configuration in composing both works. The artist was able to give a sense of "monumentality" *and* intimacy even to this small work on copper.

This particular depiction of the Madonna and Child was repeated numerous times by De Mura and his followers—an indication of its popularity. One of the most famous versions—in its original elaborately gilded frame—is in the Palacio Real in Madrid.[2]

1. Nicola Spinosa, letter to Federico Castelluccio, Jan. 13, 2014: "[This painting] is a secure work by Francesco de Mura [done] between 1740 to 1750."
2. Teodoro Fittipaldi, "Un inedito di Francesco de Mura ed alcuni dipinti in Terra di Spagna," *Atti della Accademia pontaniana* 30 (1981): 139, fig. 5. A larger variation of Castelluccio's *Madonna and Child* was in the Pence estate auction in Kansas City, Mo., on May 3, 2008; it measures 16 × 13½ in. (40.6 × 34.3 cm). De Mura's student Pietro Bardellino painted a larger and stiffer version of this oval painting on canvas, sized 29⅞ × 24⅞ in. (75.5 × 63 cm) (formerly at auction; see "*Madonna con Bambino* by Pietro Bardellino on artnet," Artnet, accessed Dec. 8, 2015, http://www.artnet.com/artists/pietro-bardellino/madonna-con-bambino). There are many eighteenth-century copies of the Castelluccio painting.

Provenance:
Fiore Romolo, 1888; English private collection?; Finchelini Art and Antiques, North End Road, London; on eBay online in United Kingdom, Oct. 11, 2013, item no. 271288847245 (as "1700 Baroque Madonna Baby & John Baptist Italian Old Master Oil Copper Painting").

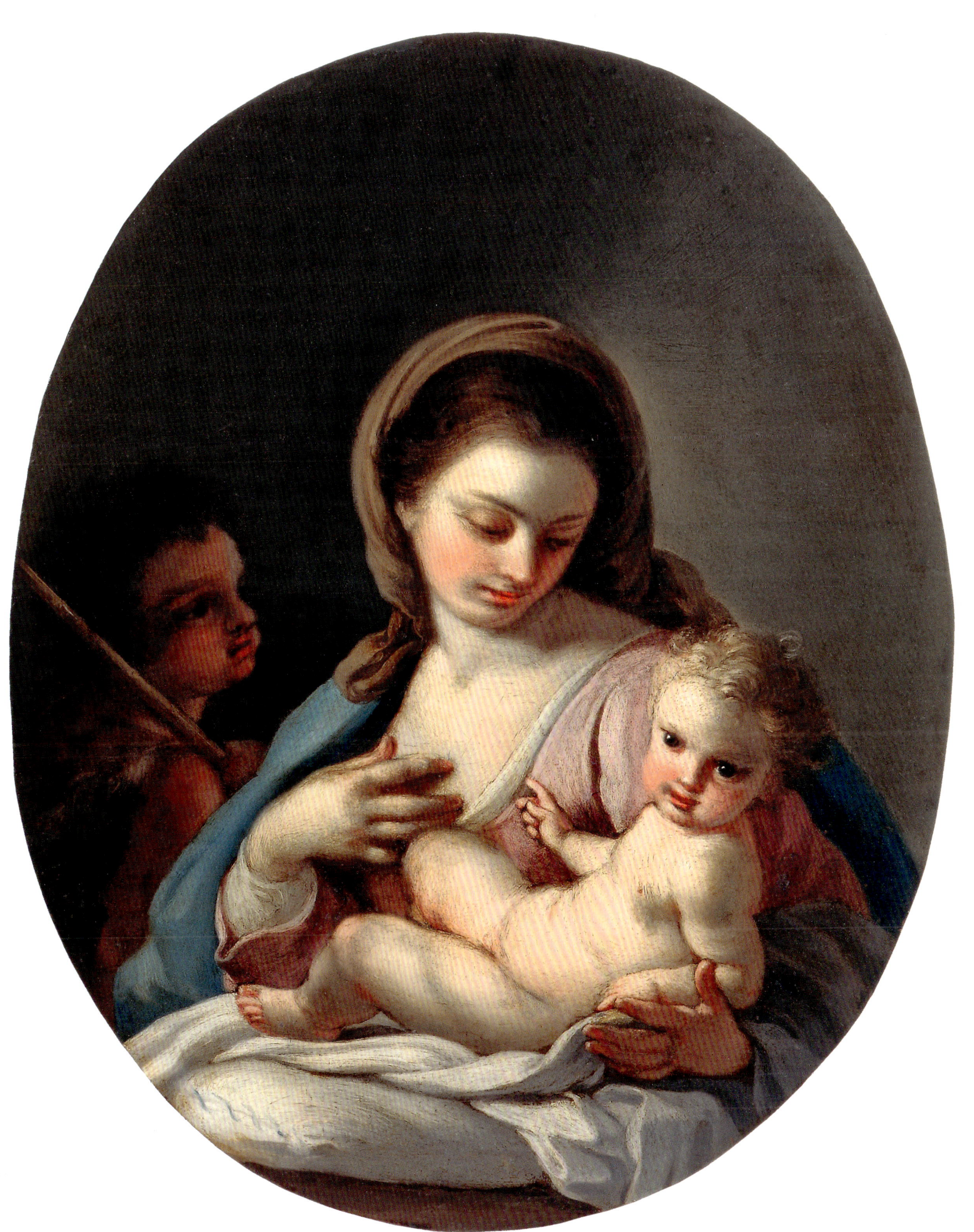

30

Francesco de Mura
Madonna and Child with the Infant St. John the Baptist, ca. 1752
Oil on copper with silver, silver gilt and gilt bronze frame, 10¼ × 8 in. (26.04 × 20.32 cm)
The Minneapolis Institute of Art, purchased with funds from the John R. Van Derlip Fund,
acc. no. 69.94

This lovely oval composition shows the Virgin Mary embracing a blond
Christ Child as he looks out at us and raises his right hand in a blessing.
Painting in oil on copper dates back to the mid-sixteenth century, when
European artists discovered that the smooth surfaces of thin sheets of
copper lent themselves to fine workmanship, were easy to handle, and gave
a luminous shine to the paint. They also were easier to preserve than works
on wood or canvas.[1] Because of the weight of copper, most oil paintings on
copper are small, just the right size for personal devotions at home.

Mary props up Jesus on a pillow as the little John the Baptist, clutching
a scarlet cape around him, gazes at his cousin. The grace and sweetness of
this grouping has a refinement typical of De Mura's best work. And, indeed,
the oval painting seems to have been created during the early 1750s when
De Mura was deeply involved with painting the fresco ceiling of the church
of the Nunziatella (see fig. 65), his greatest surviving achievement on a
large scale. Another example of a Madonna and Child painted at this time is
found in De Mura's *Adoration of the Shepherds* in the Southampton City Art
Gallery (fig. 75), where we see much the same colors and figural style as in
this Minneapolis work. The original elaborate Neapolitan frame—crafted of
silver, silver gilt, and gilt bronze—is typical of Rococo decorative arts of the
mid-1700s.

1. See *Copper as Canvas: Two Centuries of Masterpiece Paintings on Copper, 1575–1775*
   (New York: Oxford University Press), 1999.

Provenance:
Probably the Gallery
Pericle Rosio; M. & C.
Sestieri, Rome, by 1969;
purchased by Minneapolis
Institute in 1969.

Bibliography:
"Catalogue of Accessions,"
*The Minneapolis Institute
of Arts Bulletin* 58 (1969):
90–117 (ill. p. 98).

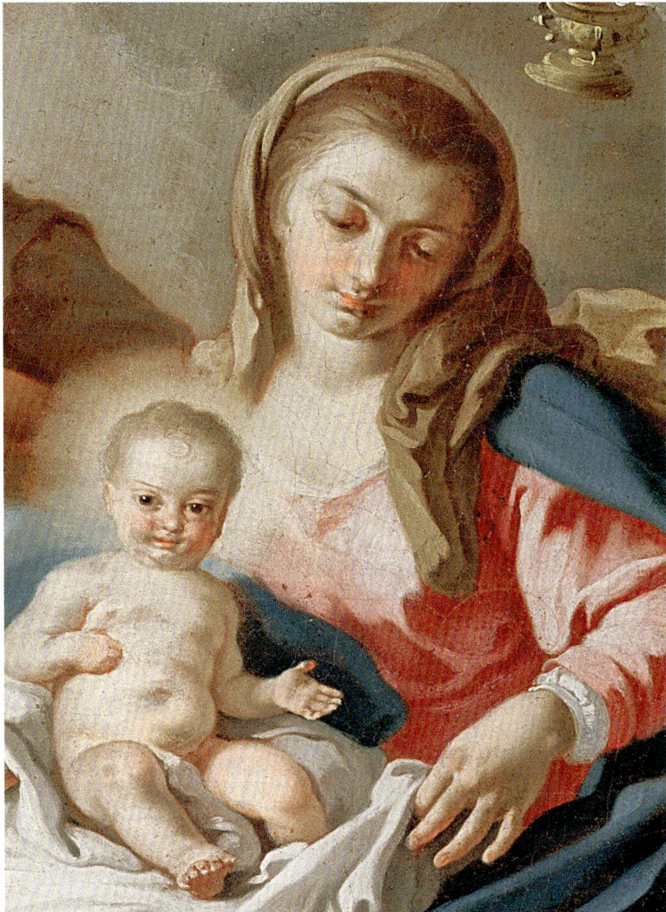

Fig. 75
Francesco de Mura, *The Adoration
of the Shepherds* (detail), ca. 1750–52,
oil on canvas, entire painting
54¾ × 39³⁄₁₆ in. (139.1 × 99.6 cm),
Southampton City Art Gallery,
Hampshire, U.K.

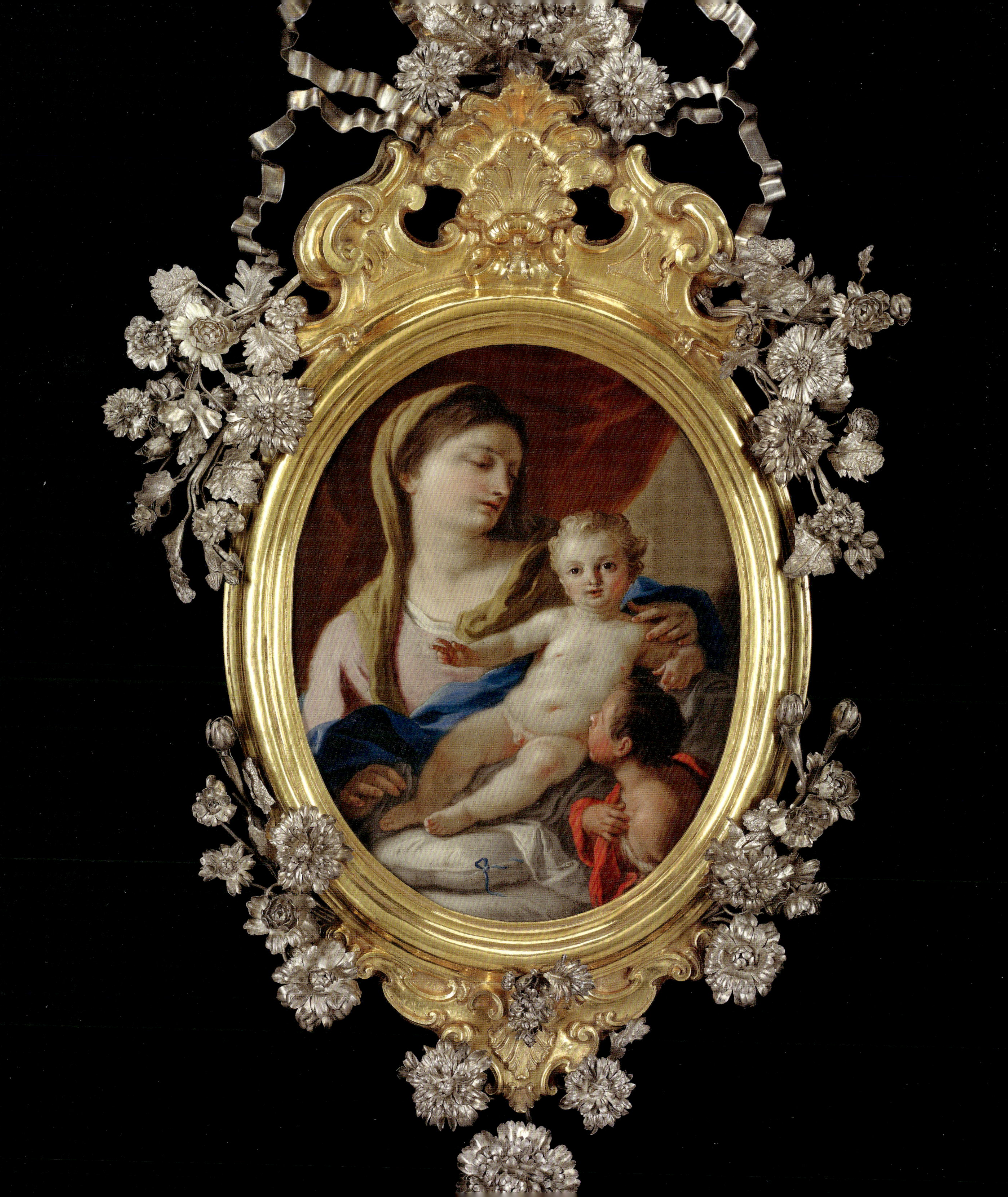

31

Francesco de Mura
Madonna and Child with the Infant St. John the Baptist, ca. 1740s
Oil on canvas (oval), 12⅝ × 10½ in. (31.1 × 26.7 cm)
Museo de Arte de Ponce, gift of the Luis A. Ferré Foundation, Inc.,
acc. no. 64.0469

This elegant image of the Madonna and Child with the infant John the Baptist, beautifully composed in a small oval, reveals the baby Jesus smiling at us as he points his right index finger heavenward, the direction of salvation and to where our prayers should be directed. In the very center of this work, meant for a home and personal devotions, is the Virgin Mary, in profile tilting her head to the right, facing left, and gazing sadly at her son—a hint of her foreknowledge of his crucifixion. Jesus' cousin, John the Baptist, stands behind him, holding a bamboo cross and banner. Mary gently lifts her son's left foot while bracing his outstretched arm; he rests on a white pillow covered with a golden cloth and pulls down on his mother's head covering. We sense the sweet, intimate relationship between Jesus and Mary and the light flooding the scene implies the presence of the Divine. The artist achieved a dramatic effect with the red drapery behind Mary (and in the lower left). The small unguent container by Jesus' right foot foretells the spice container that Mary Magdalene would bring to Jesus' tomb to anoint his body after his death.

The refined and delicate drawing style suggests De Mura's contact with the contemporary Neapolitan artist Corrado Giaquinto (see cat. nos. 44 and 45), as well as with such French artists as Pierre Subleyras (see fig. 70). But this work from Ponce—one of the most beautifully conceived of all De Mura's versions of this subject—also relates to his *Allegory of Modesty* (fig. 76) of the 1740s, in the pose of the female figure in profile and the images of the putti.[1]

1. Compare also De Mura's *Madonna and Child with the Infant John the Baptist* in the Pio Monte della Misericordia in Naples, no. 119, illustrated in Raffaello Causa, *Opere d'arte nel Pio Monte della Misericordia a Napoli* (Cava dei Tirreni: Mauro, 1970), 113, fig. 41: "This composition, repeated by De Mura many times, must have been very successful and very much valued."

Provenance:
Dr. Carl Gaber, Vienna; Dr. Adalbert Nemere, Vienna, sold at Dorotheum on March 17, 1964, color plate 111, lot 68.

Bibliography:
Museo de Arte de Ponce, Guide (Ponce, P.R.: Museo de Arte de Ponce, 1965), pl. 39; Burton B. Fredericksen and Federico Zeri, *Census of Pre-Nineteenth Century Italian Paintings in North American Collections* (Cambridge, Mass.: Harvard University Press, 1972), 146 (as Francesco de Mura); Julius Held, *Catalogue of the Museo de Arte Collection* (Ponce, P.R.: Museo de Arte de Ponce, 1984); David Nolta, "Francesco de Mura: Lives and Works" (Ph.D. diss., Yale University, New Haven, Conn., 1989), vol. 1: 298 ("later perhaps than 1752, lovely, genuine").

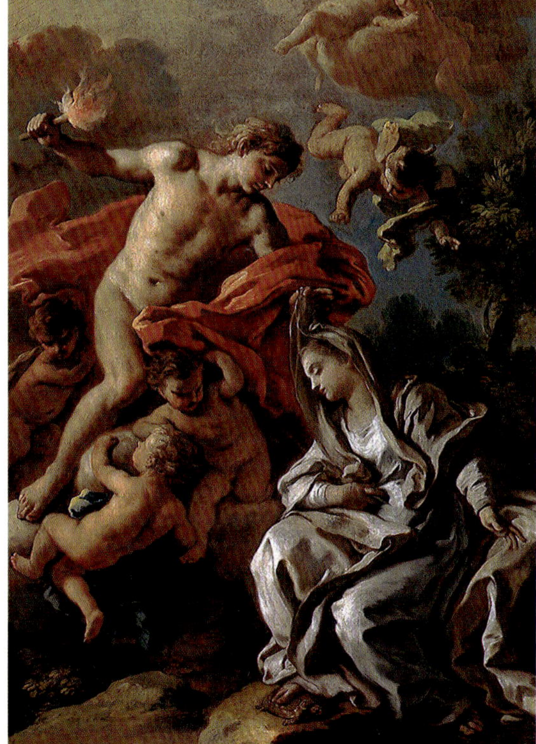

Fig. 76
Francesco de Mura, *Allegory of Modesty*, 1740s, oil on canvas, 28⅜ × 17⅜ in. (72 × 44 cm), Museo e Gallerie Nazionali di Capodimonte, Naples, inv. no. Q 1930-…, n. 227

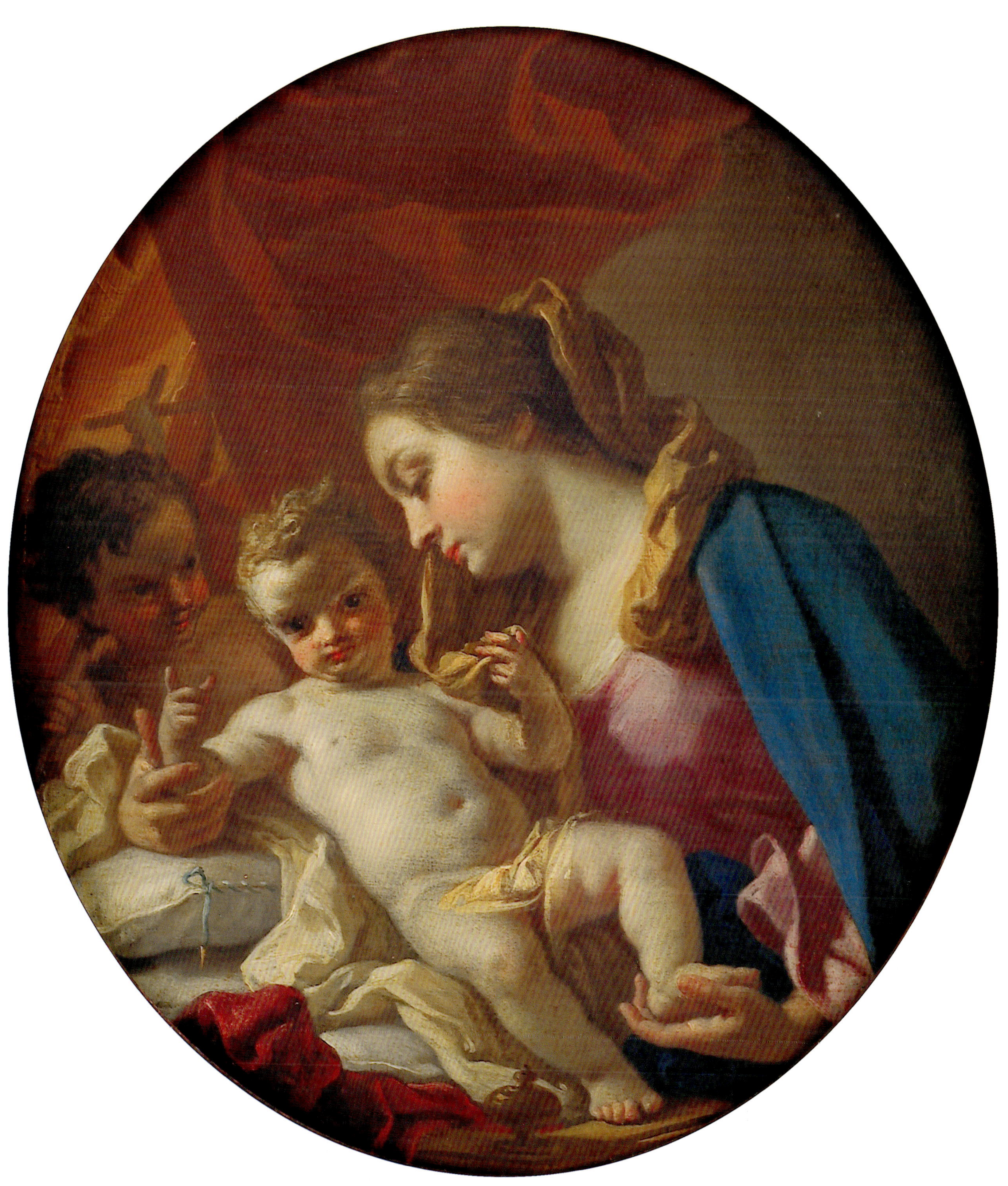

32a

Francesco de Mura
Madonna and Child with the Infant St. John the Baptist, 1760s
Oil on canvas, 30¾ × 25⅗ in. (78.1 × 64.5 cm)
Hearst San Simeon State Historical Monument, purchased by
W. R. Hearst in 1922, acc. no. 529-9-6178

32b

Francesco de Mura
Madonna and Child with Infant St. John the Baptist, ca. 1765
Oil on canvas, 14½ × 11½ in. (36.8 × 29.2 cm)
Collection of Federico Castelluccio

Both of these paintings were meant for private devotions in the home. Unlike other small images of the Madonna and Child by De Mura (see cat. nos. 29 and 30), both of these works are in oil on canvas, and both are considerably larger than the similar paintings on copper. Each composition depicts a luminous Virgin Mary looking up to heaven, tears in her eyes, as she braces a blond Christ Child with her right hand. The Child sits on a golden pillow and gestures with his outstretched hand. The Madonna's heavenly gaze demonstrates her divine role as our intermediary to heaven, beseeching God on behalf of all humanity. In shadow behind Jesus we see his young cousin, John the Baptist, with a bamboo cross—in the Hearst work (cat. no. 32a), the cross has a banner affixed: *ECCE AGNUS DEI*, "Behold the Lamb of God." Also in the Hearst version, Mary, Jesus, and the cherubs form a strong diagonal from lower left to upper right. In the Castelluccio version (cat. no. 32b), Jesus looks tenderly at his mother, holding out his left hand as if beseeching us to pray to her.

In the Hearst work, Jesus looks out at us, leaning forward while raising two fingers of his right hand in a blessing. On the brown table below are three red cherries, symbolizing the fruit of heaven (where all are exempt from sin), and a single apple, recalling the Original Sin of Adam eating the fruit of the Tree of Knowledge.

These two fine works have been compared to De Mura's manner of the 1760s, when he often returned to the style of Solimena.[1]

1. Nicola Spinosa examined the Castelluccio *Madonna and Child* in 2012 and dated it to De Mura's late work of the 1760s.

32a
Provenance:
Purchased by W. R. Hearst at auction, American Art Galleries, New York, *One Hundred Ancient Paintings of the Italian, Dutch, Flemish and French Schools*, March 22, 1922, lot 115 (as by Claudio Francesco Beaumont, 1694–1766); donated to the Hearst Corporation to the State of California in 1972.

Bibliography:
Burton B. Fredericksen and Federico Zeri, *Census of Pre-Nineteenth Century Italian Paintings in North American Collections* (Cambridge, Mass.: Harvard University Press, 1972), 634 (as Francesco de Mura); Burton B. Fredericksen, *Handbook of the Paintings in the Hearst San Simeon State Historical Monument* (California: Delphinian Publications in cooperation with the California Dept. of Parks and Recreation, 1977), no. 50 (as Francesco de Mura; ill.).

32b
Provenance:
Bonham's, London, April 13, 1999, sale 28,872, lot 55 (as "Follower of Francesco de Mura").

Cat. 32a

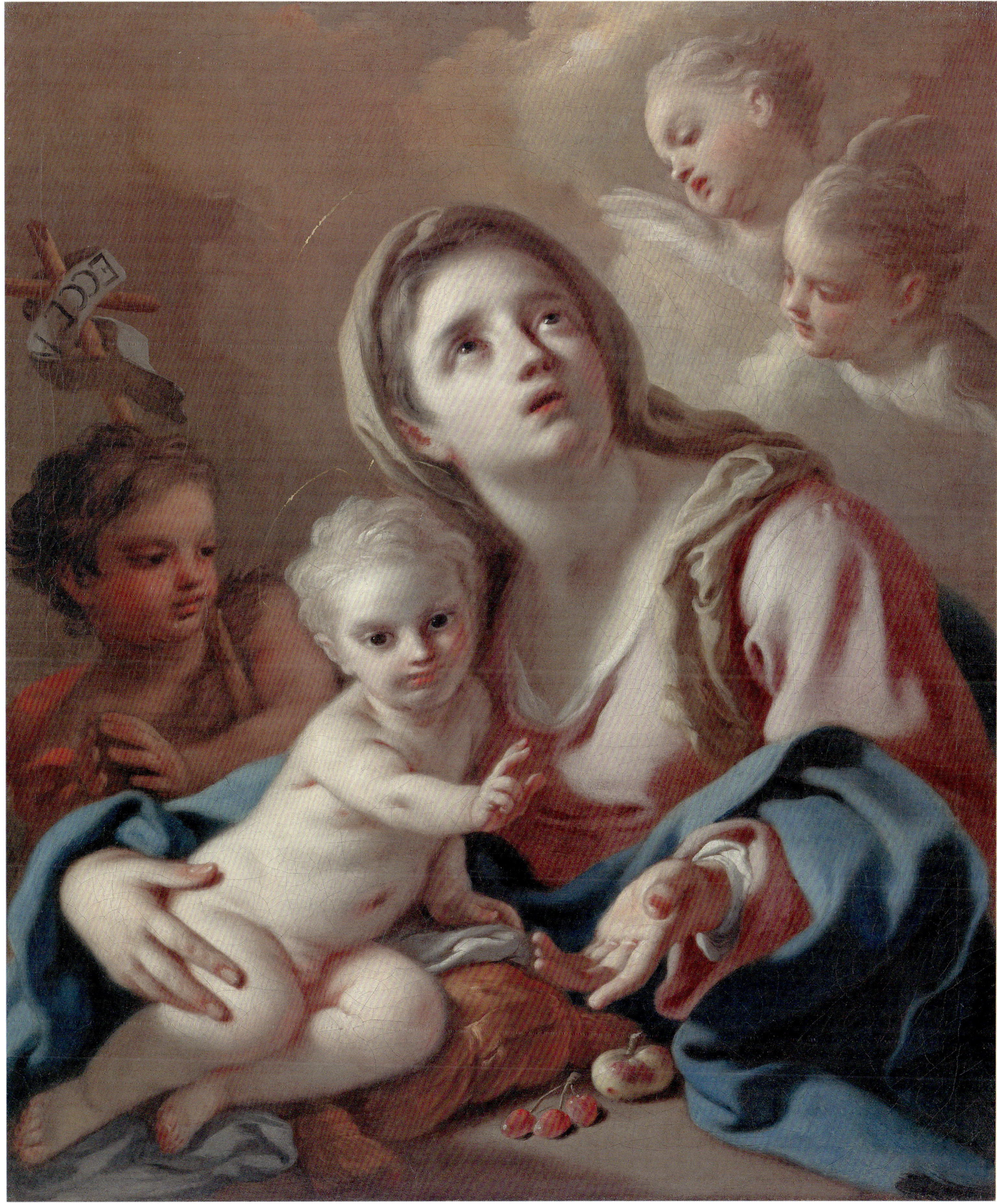

32 — continued

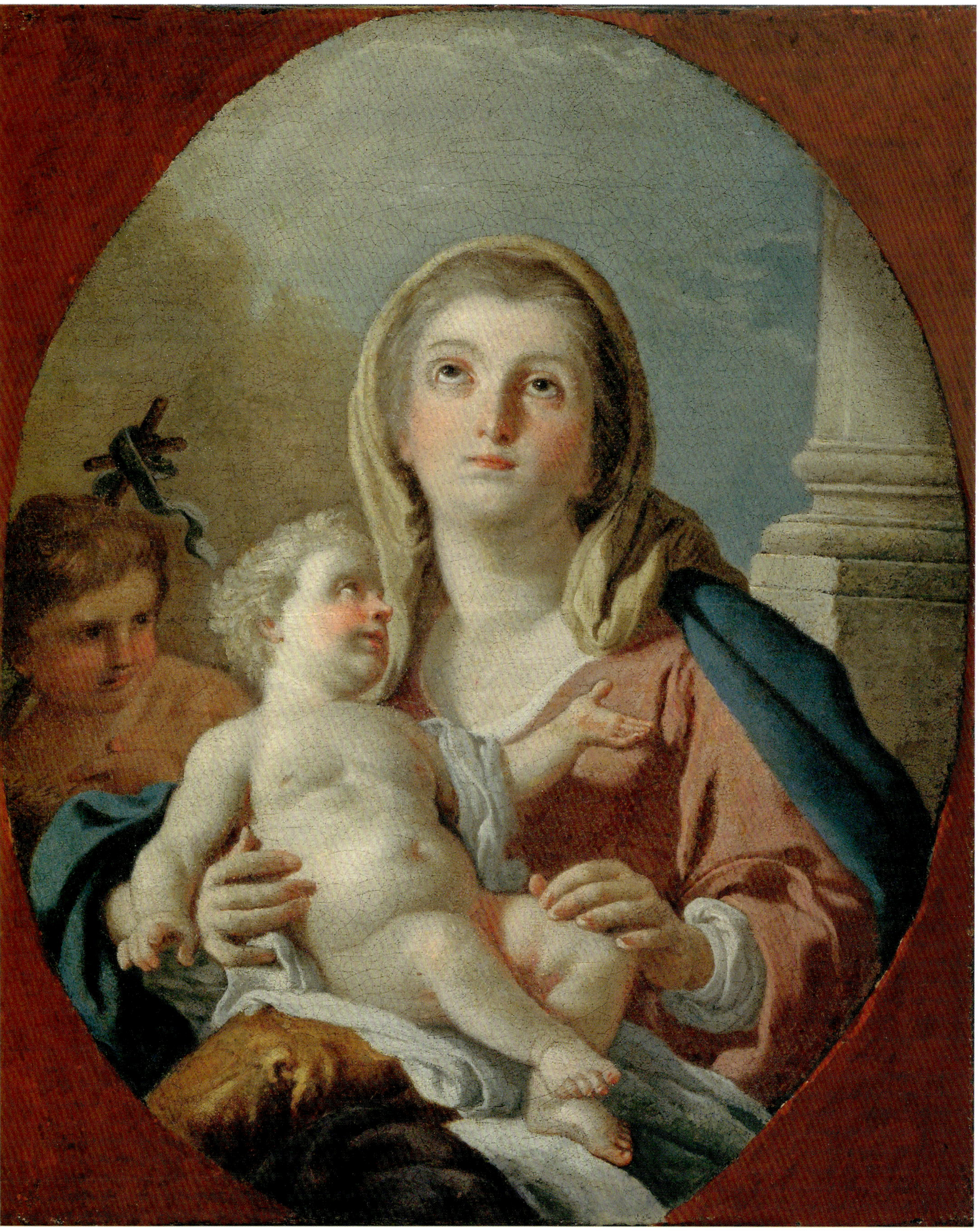

Cat. 32b

33

Francesco de Mura
Allegory of Spring, 1759
Oil on canvas, 40½ × 51 in. (102.9 × 129.5 cm)
Inscription on reverse: *Franc. de Mura ping./1759*
Also inscribed in Latin with the first three stanzas of an ode to Spring by
Horace: *"SOLVITUR ACRIS HIEMS..."* etc.
Toledo Museum of Art, purchased with funds from the Libbey Endowment,
gift of Edward Drummond Libbey, acc. no. 1979.79

Catalogue only.

This Allegory of Spring is one of a series of "The Four Seasons" by De Mura;
his Allegory of Autumn, entitled *The Procession of Bacchus*, is today in
the Gemäldegalerie, Staatliche Museen, in Berlin (fig. 77). This work was
destined for the apartments of King Carlo di Borbone (Charles Bourbon)
in the Palazzo Reale in Naples. Inscribed on the reverse is a quote from the
Odes of Horace, the ancient Roman poet, describing Spring's renewal as told
through the stories of the Roman gods.[1]

On a mythical shoreline near Naples, half a dozen nymphs surround
Venus in her conch-shell chariot as she arrives from the sea. Venus, who
stares serenely at the viewer, was the Roman goddess of love, beauty, and
nature; April, the beginning of Spring, was her month. In the temple of Venus
in nearby Pompeii, Romans worshipped her as creator and mother of the
universe. Here, she wears a flower crown, as do the nymphs as they dance
the Tarantella, smashing cymbals, clicking castanets, blowing horns, and
(presumably) singing a lovely refrain. Winged Cupid, the god of love and son
of Venus, stands at Venus' foot, showing her his bow and arrow. The shade
at the lower left reveals a shepherd dozing as his flock rests nearby. Above
the nymphs, in clouds descending from the heavens, winged putti fly, some
holding torches of love, others bows and arrows and flowers. At the extreme
right, three muscular men pull their boat from the bay, while on the left a
satyr sits on a rock talking to another shepherd. In the far background, Mount
Vesuvius erupts, emitting fire and smoke; in a cutaway view of the mountain's
depths, we see Venus' husband Vulcan and his assistants forging armor.

As Nicola Spinosa has pointed out, this is more a genre or pastoral
scene "translated into an idealized Demurian Arcadia."[2] In fact, De Mura
painted a number of allegorical pastoral scenes with shepherds and
shepherdesses. Similarly, the composition relates to the pastoral *presepio*
figurines of a Nativity. The beautiful image of Venus staring at the viewer
was used earlier by the artist in his *Allegory of Innocence* in the Museo di
Capodimonte (fig. 78).

1. A. E. Housman's 1910 English translation of the Latin ode by Horace (1.4.7) begins:
   "The snows are fled away...and grasses in the mead renew their birth.../The Nymphs
   and Graces there put off their fear and unapparelled in the woodland play..." For an
   illustration of the ode on the reverse, see D'Alessio, "Nuove osservazioni," 79, fig. 22.
2. Spinosa, *Pittura napoletana del Settecento*, 1:165, no. 276.

Provenance:
Royal Commission in 1759;
Colnaghi's, London, to 1979,
when acquired by the Toledo
Museum of Art.

Bibliography:
"La chronique des arts," *Gazette des Beaux-Arts* 77, no. 1334
(March 1980); Toledo Museum
of Art, "1979 Annual Report,"
Museum News 21, no. 4 (1979):
84 (ill.); Nicola Spinosa, *Pittura napoletana del Settecento*, vol. 1,
Dal barocco al rococò (Naples:
Electa Napoli, 1986), 165, 357,
no. 276, fig. 333; Nicholas H. J.
Hall, ed., *Colnaghi in America*
(New York: Colnaghi, 1992), 133
(listed); Gino D'Alessio, "Nuove
osservazioni sulle committenze
reali per Francesco de Mura
tra Napoli, Torino e Madrid,"
Prospettiva, no. 69 (1993):
78–79, figs. 21–22; Victoria
C. Gardner Coates, *The Last
Days of Pompeii: Decadence,
Apocalypse, Resurrection* (Los
Angeles: J. Paul Getty Museum,
2012), 17, fig. 1 (ill. p. 16).

33 — continued

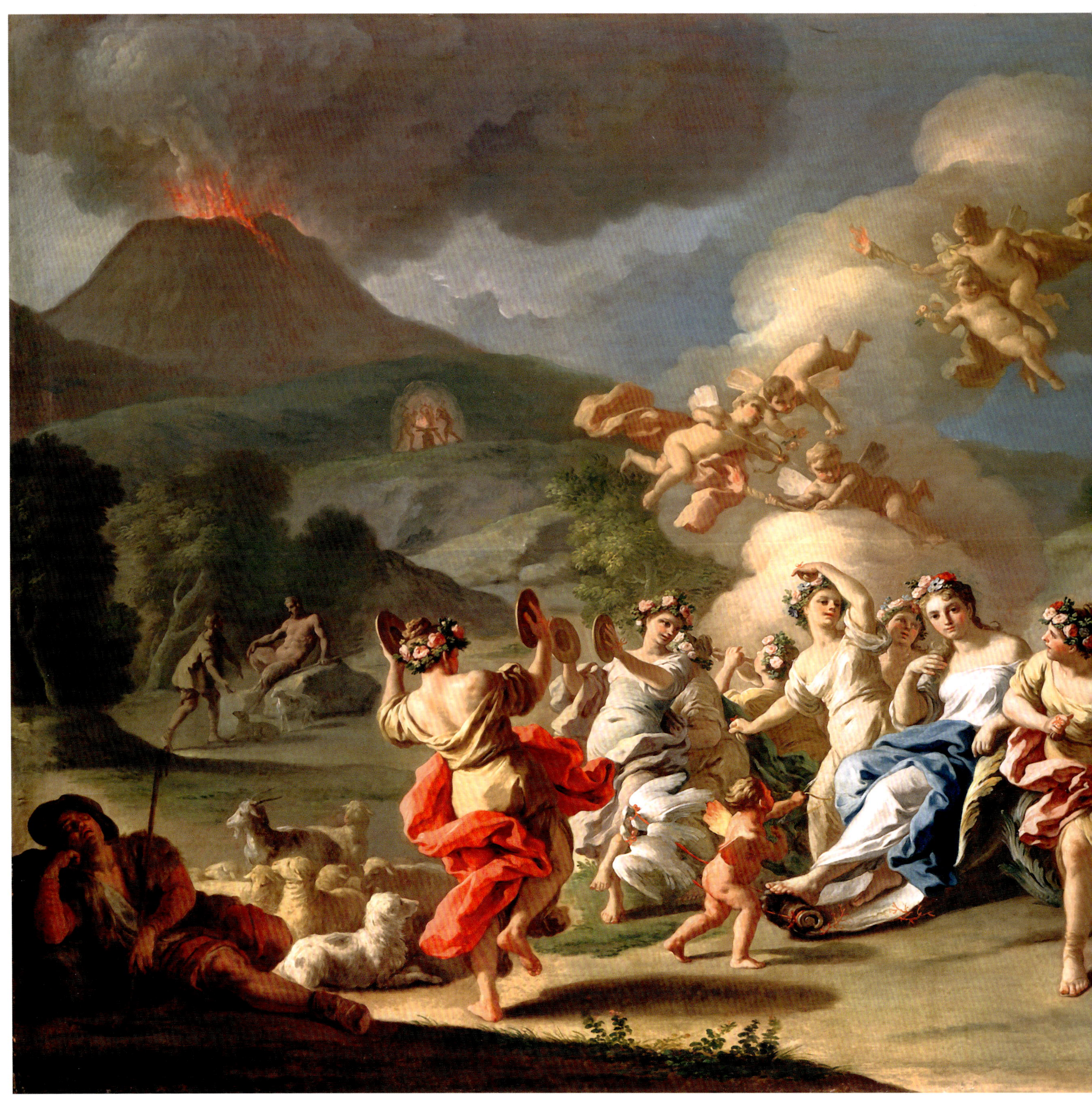

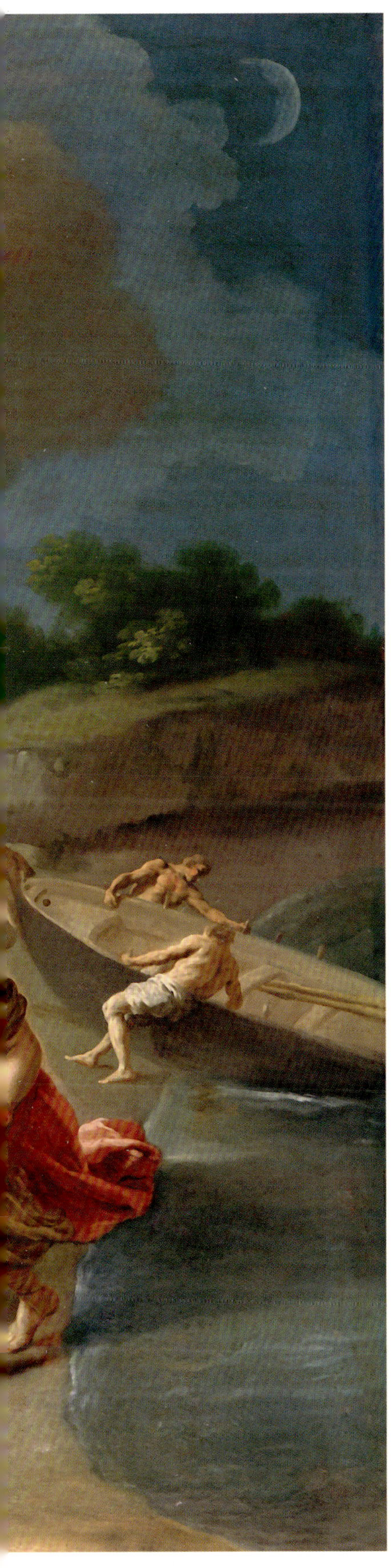

Cat. 33

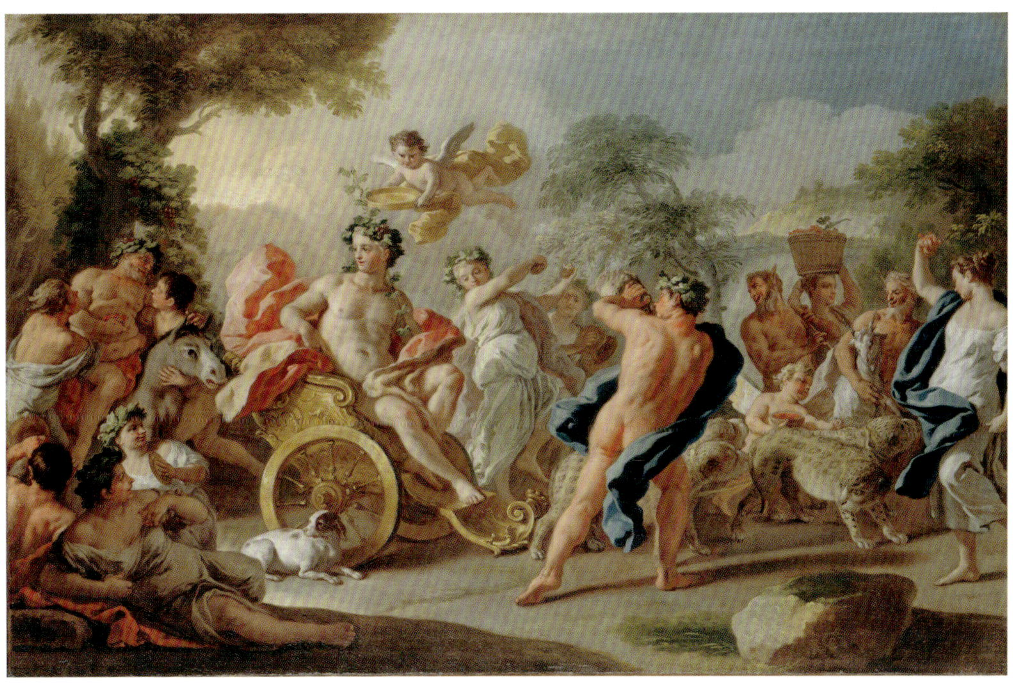

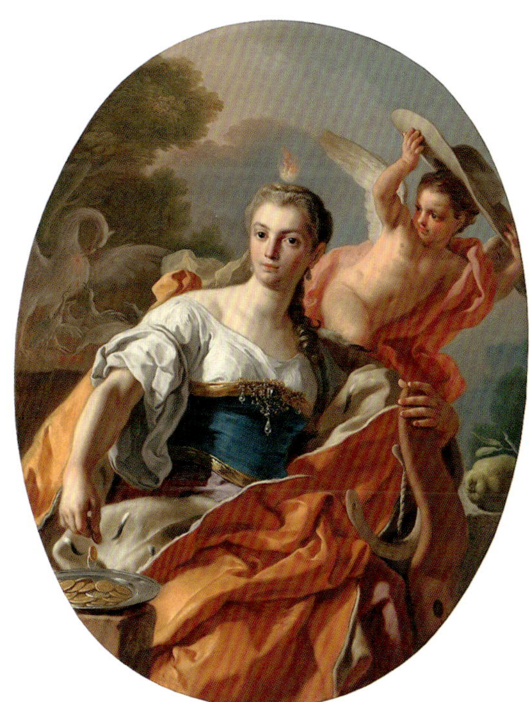

Fig. 77
Francesco de Mura, *The Procession of Bacchus*, ca. 1760, oil on canvas, 30½ × 45⁹⁄₁₆ in. (77.4 × 115.8 cm), Gemäldegalerie, Staatliche Museen, Berlin

Fig. 78
Francesco de Mura, *Allegory of Innocence* (detail), ca. 1758?, oil on canvas, Museo e Gallerie Nazionali di Capodimonte, Naples

34

Francesco de Mura
The Trinity, ca. 1763
Oil on canvas, 30½ × 25¼ in. (77.5 × 64.1 cm)
Collection of Federico Castelluccio

De Mura's extraordinary sense of color is seen in this strikingly beautiful work depicting a scene in heaven of the three persons of the Godhead—God the Father, his son Jesus, and the Holy Spirit—forming the Trinity ("threefold"), one God in three expressions. Jesus appears as the central figure, seated on a cloud and holding in his right hand the two tree trunks that form his cross. An angel on the left, propped on a cloud and swathed in a bright crimson cloth, helps support the cross while looking down at earth below. Jesus' eyes appear closed, his chest bared, and his lap covered in a brilliant aquamarine robe that exposes the wound in his right foot. In his left hand, we see the globe of the universe, and a second angel in shadow beneath it. Cherubs abound and putti float at top left and right. God the Father flies into the scene from the right, wearing a triangular halo and pale, flowing robes reminiscent of the figure of God creating Adam by Michelangelo in the Sistine Chapel.

Another version of this work can be found in the Galleria Nazionale d'arte antica in Palazzo Barberini in Rome (fig. 79). There are significant variations from the Castelluccio painting: it is horizontally composed and missing the upper portion of the scene and the four cherubs below Jesus; its colors are distinctly more subdued (though this is difficult to judge since it is covered by a yellowed varnish), Jesus' cross is composed of wood planks rather than tree trunks, and the figures are more meticulously drawn. Mario Alberto Pavone identifies this work as a *bozzetto* for De Mura's lost painting of *The Trinity*, which once hung over the main altar of the parish church of San Sossio in Frattamaggiore, about 9 miles (15 kilometers) north of Naples. On the reverse is an inscription stating that it was a "*macchia di un quadro sopra l'altare maggiore della parrocchiale chiesa di Frattamaggiore. Francesco de Mura P[inxit]. Marzo An[no]. 1763*" ("an oil sketch for a painting above the main altar of the parish church [of San Sossio] in Frattamaggiore/Francesco de Mura painted it/March 1763").[1]

Both versions of the *Trinity* have also been thought to be studies for a detail from De Mura's cupola ceiling fresco of *Christ Receiving St. Joseph into Heaven with the Madonna and Saints* done around 1741 for the church of San Giuseppe dei Ruffi in Naples, a *bozzetto* for which exists in the Pio Monte della Misericordia in Naples (cat. no. 13). But there are significant variations between the Pio Monte *bozzetto* and the two *Trinity* paintings in the Castelluccio and Barberini collections. A comparison seems to suggest that these two images of the *Trinity* were done much later than the San Giuseppe dei Ruffi painting, which is darker, more naturalistically drawn, and different in the positions of the major figures. Thus, this may be a study for the 1763 painting, as it seems close to a God the Father in a *bozzetto* of *The Death of St. Joseph* in the Museo di Capodimonte that Spinosa dates to about 1760–65 (fig. 80).[2]

1. Mario Alberto Pavone, "San Sossio di Miseno: da seguace a protagonista," *teCla*, July 27, 2010, http://www.unipa.it/tecla/rivista/10_rivista_pavone.php.
2. Nicola Spinosa, ed., *Museo e Gallerie Nazionali di Capodimonte: Dipinti del XVIII secolo; La scuola napoletana* (Naples: Electa Napoli, 2010), 60–61, no. 60.

Provenance:
Otto Naumann Gallery, New York; Robert Simon Gallery, New York.

Fig. 79
Francesco de Mura, *The Trinity*, 1763, oil on canvas, Palazzo Barberini, Rome

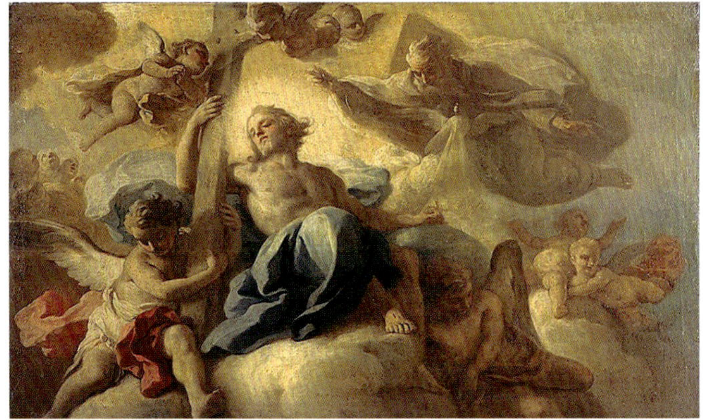

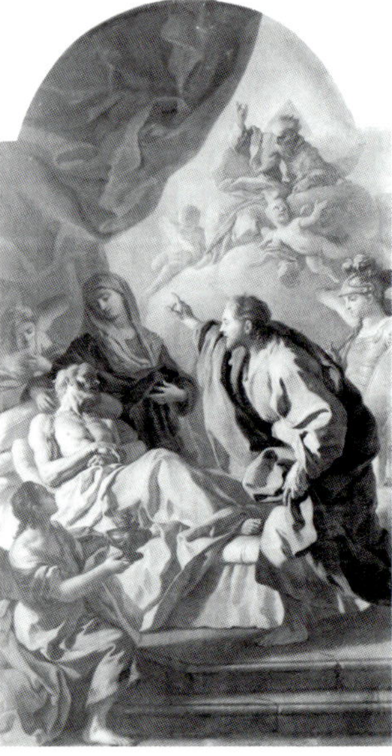

Fig. 80
Francesco de Mura, *The Death of St. Joseph*, ca. 1760–65, oil on canvas, 115⅝ × 63 in. (293 × 160 cm), Museo e Gallerie Nazionali di Capodimonte, Naples

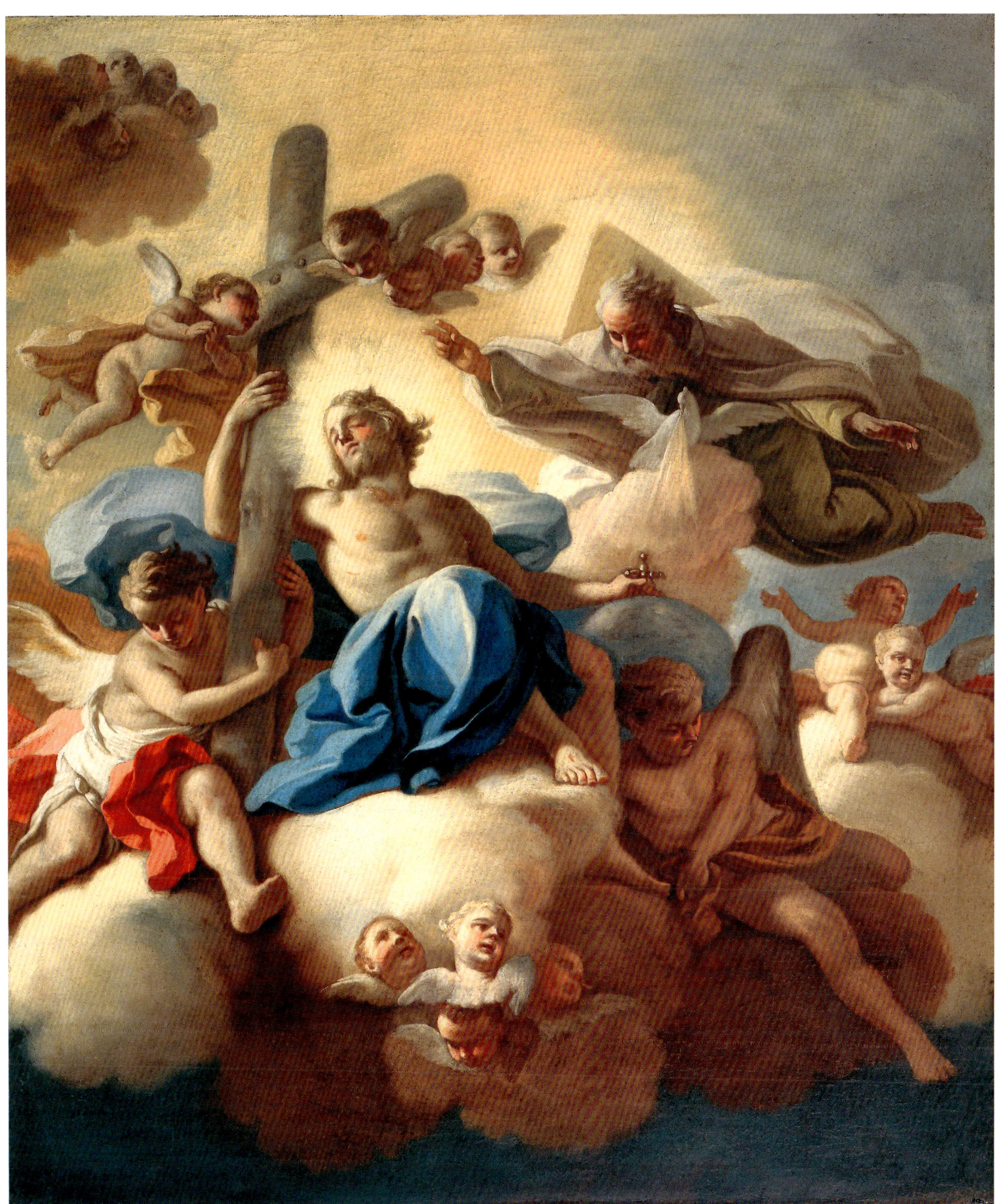

35

Francesco de Mura
The Glory of the Princes or *Allegory of the Virtues of King Carlo di Borbone*, ca. 1763
Oil on canvas, 28¾ × 38½ in. (73 × 98 cm)
Pio Monte della Misericordia, inv. no. 104

Pio Monte della Misericordia owns two versions of this energetic, crowded scene depicting an *Allegory of the Virtues of King Carlo di Borbone* (Charles Bourbon); the other version is considerably larger than this (fig. 81). Nicola Spinosa found documents that identify these two works as *bozzetti* created around 1763 for the frescoed ceiling of the king's dressing room (or Room of the Belvedere) next to his bedroom at the Palazzo Reale in Naples.[1] (The final ceiling paintings may have been destroyed in 1943 in the war, or possibly ca. 1810 during renovations.)

On a cloud, King Carlo di Borbone stands in profile to the left of the female personification of Strength, who leans on the large obelisk in the center, itself a symbol of strength, unity, and courage. Five angels above blow trumpets of Fame, while two others hold laurel wreaths. Roman gods represent Carlo's virtues: Minerva (Athena to the Greeks), goddess of wisdom, sits to the right of the obelisk and to her right, Mercury, god of financial gain, as Mars, god of war, rushes in (note the nearby cannon). Below Mars we see Diana (and a deer), goddess of celestial harmony, seated behind Hercules (strongest of all mortals) with the Nemean lion. In the center of the cloud, Fame and a group of angels support an oval plaque revealing the floor plan of the Palazzo Reale. In the lower left, an angel in a scarlet cloak points to a group of nude men who personify the enemies of peace, expelling them from the clouds.

At one time, this work was connected to the *bozzetto* for the *Allegory of Royal Genius with the Apotheosis of the House of Bourbon*, a ceiling De Mura painted for the Palacio Real in Madrid between 1737 and 1738. Although we see superficial similarities to the Spanish subject and composition, the *Virtues of King Carlo di Borbone* shows figures less sharply defined and smaller, and a composition that is not as darkly shadowed, static, and heavy as the earlier work, which remains still rather Solimenesque. Instead, this *bozzetto*, created twenty-six years later, is light in color and highly animated in movement. It is only an idea for the ceiling, yet De Mura reveals major stylistic connections—in color, figures, etc.—to his *bozzetto* of *Aurora and Tithonius* (cat. no. 36), which is securely dated to the 1760s.[2]

1. Spinosa, *Pittura napoletana del Settecento*, 1:167, entry no. 280: "In a letter of Sept. 6, 1763, that the Prince of Sannicandro, tutor of the very young Ferdinando IV, wrote to Carlo di Borbone in Madrid, reference is made to a series of projects that De Mura would have been involved in at the Palazzo Reale for just a few days, and specifically in the vault of the King's 'dressing room' of the bedroom, also called 'Room of the Belvedere.'" In many earlier publications (see, e.g., Giuseppe Ceci, "Lo 'Studio' di Francesco de Mura"; Raffaello Causa, *Opere d'arte*; and David Nolta, "Francesco de Mura," in *Taste for Angels*, 1987), this work was dated to 1738 and erroneously connected to the royal wedding of that year.
2. *Ibid.*

Provenance:
Studio of the artist, to 1782; bequest of Francesco de Mura in 1782.

Bibliography:
Giuseppe Ceci, "Lo 'Studio' di Francesco de Mura," *Rassegna storica napoletana*, nos. 2–3 (1933): 16; Raffaello Causa, *Opere d'arte nel Pio Monte della Misericordia a Napoli* (Cava dei Tirreni: Mauro, 1970), 73–74, 110–11, pl. 33–34; Nicola Spinosa, *Civiltà del '700 a Napoli, 1734–1799*, exhib. cat. (Florence: Centro Di, 1979), 1:202–3; *Il secolo d'oro della pittura napoletana*, Athens, exhib. cat., Naples, 1984, p. 66; Nicola Spinosa, *Pittura napoletana del Settecento*, vol. 1, *Dal barocco al rococò* (Naples: Electa Napoli, 1986), 167, no. 280, fig. 337; David Nolta, "Francesco de Mura," in *A Taste for Angels: Neapolitan Painting in North America, 1650–1750*, exhib. cat. (New Haven: Yale University Art Gallery, 1987), 257–58; Gino D'Alessio, "Nuove osservazioni sulle committenze reali per Francesco de Mura tra Napoli, Torino e Madrid," *Prospettiva*, no. 69 (1993): 80–81; Gino D'Alessio, essay in *Capolavori in Festa*, ed., exhib. cat. (Naples: Electa Napoli, 1997), 204–5; Lilia Rocco, entry on this work in *Luigi Vanvitelli e la sua cerchia*, ed. Cesare de Seta, exhib. cat. (Naples: Electa Napoli, 2000), 201–3; Nicola Spinosa, "Francesco de Mura al Pio Monte," in *Il Pio Monte della Misericordia di Napoli nel Quarto Centenario*, ed. Mario Pisani Massamormile (Naples: Electa Napoli, 2003), 191–211; Loredana Gazzara, "Note e documenti inediti per lo studio delle collezioni della Quadreria del Pio Monte della Misericordia (I)," *Napoli Nobilissima*, 5th ser., 9 (May–Aug. 2008): 160–79; Nicola Spinosa, "Francesco de Mura al Pio Monte della Misericordia," *FMR*, no. 29 (Jan.–Feb. 2009): 24–48.

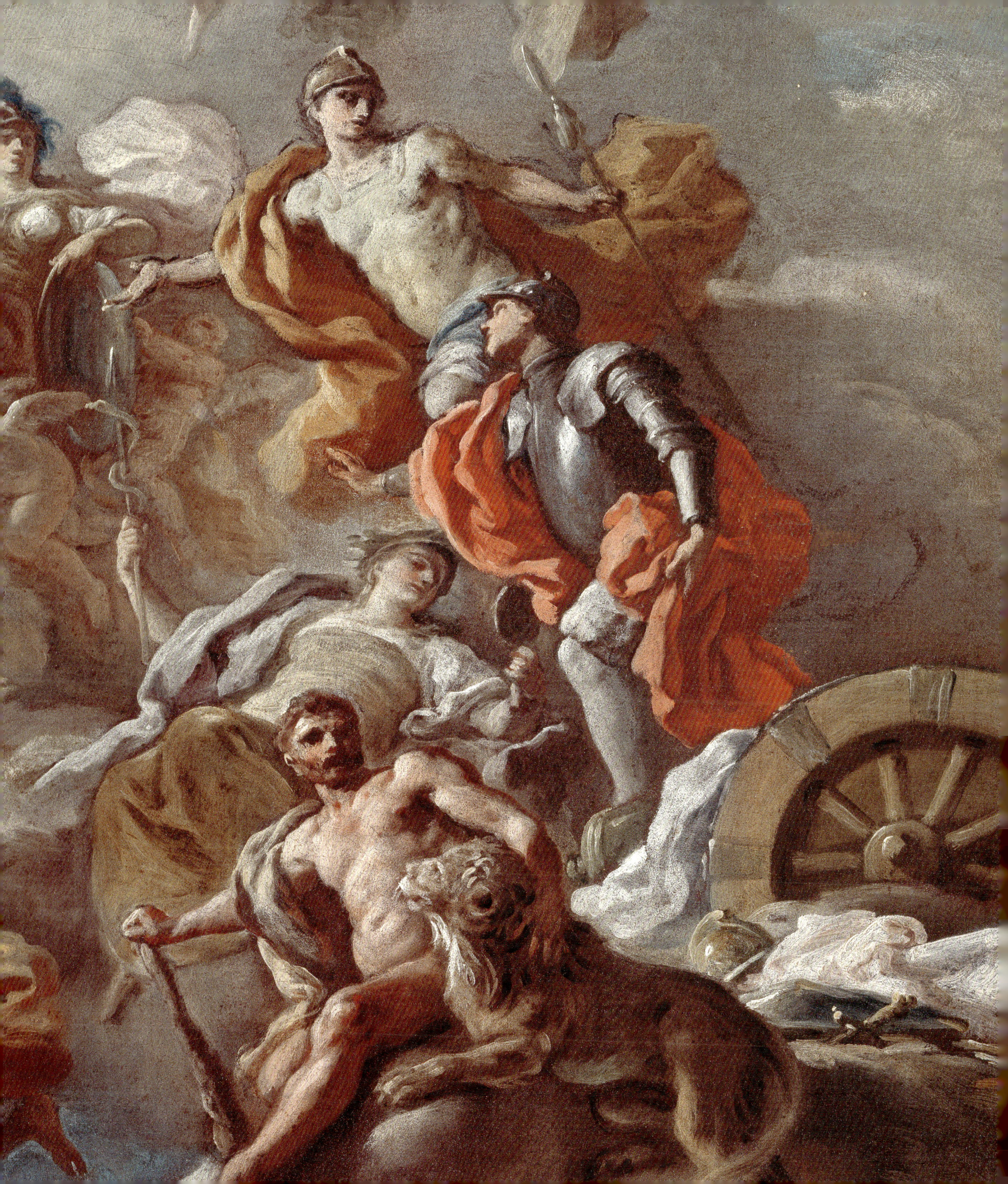

35 — continued

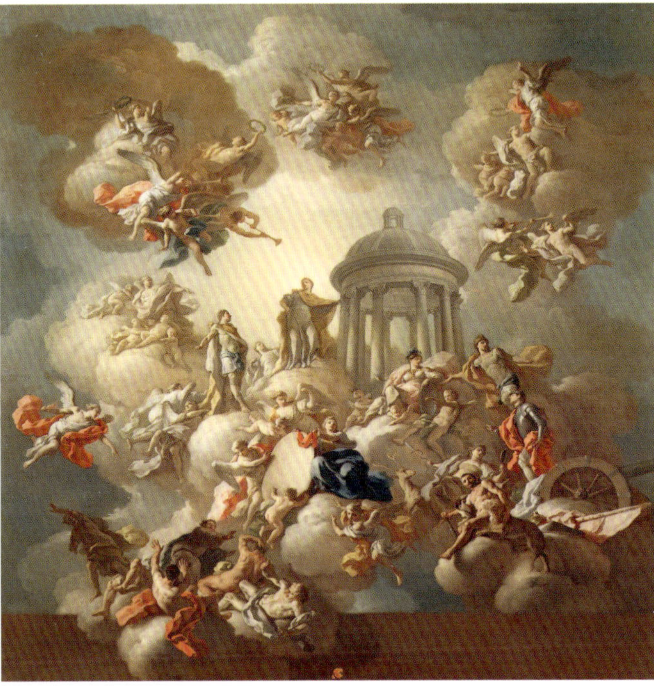

Fig. 81
Francesco de Mura, *The Glory of the Princes*,
ca. 1763, oil on canvas, 59 × 61 in. (150 × 155
cm), Pio Monte della Misericordia, Naples

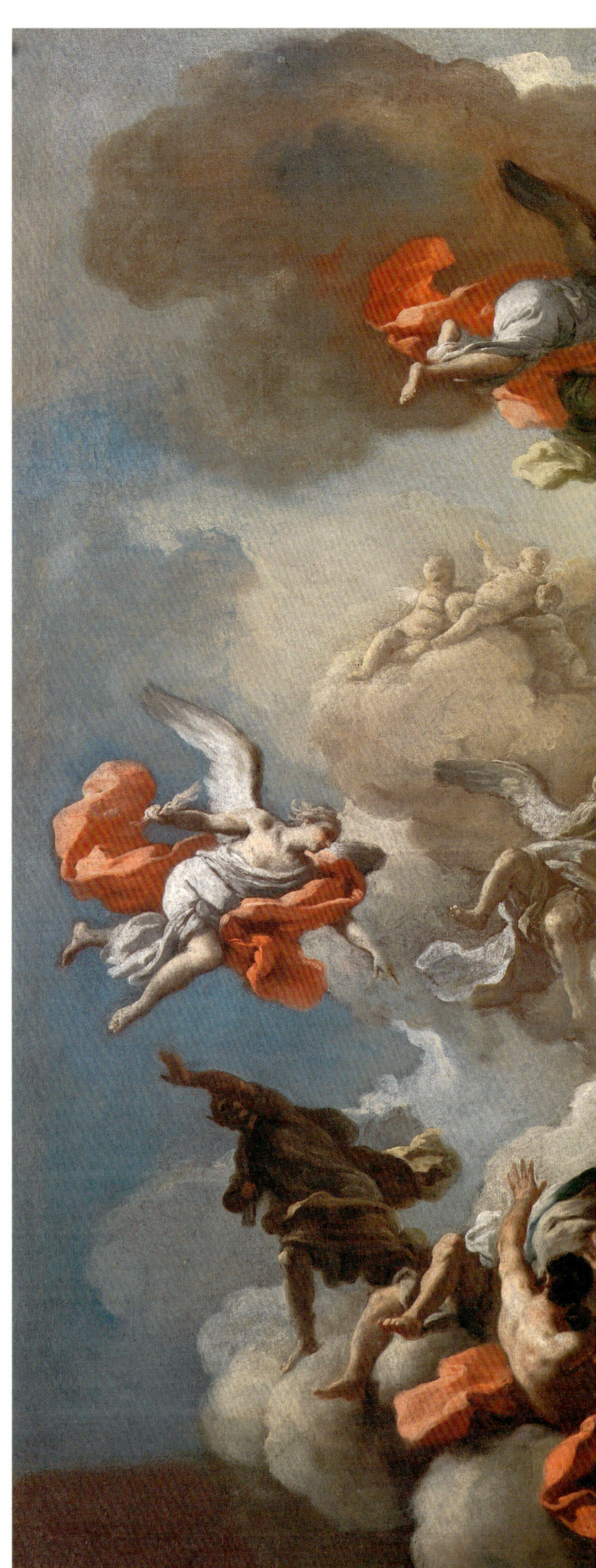

Cat. 35

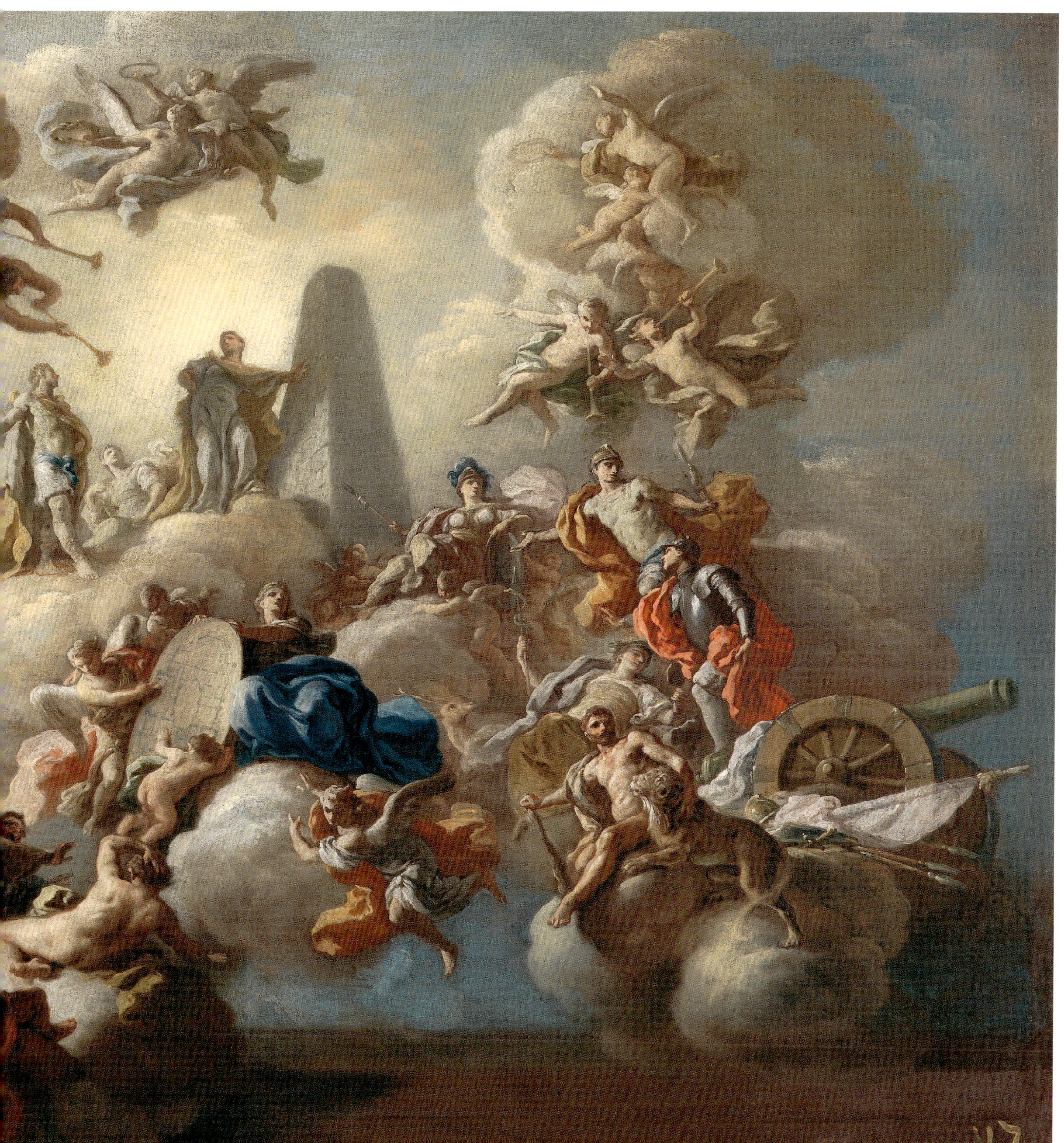

36

Francesco de Mura
Aurora, Goddess of the Dawn, and Her Husband, Tithonus, Prince of Troy,
ca. 1763–65
Oil on canvas, 50 × 60 in. (128 × 153 cm)
Museo e Gallerie Nazionali di Capodimonte, inv. De Rin. 526

This bright and elegant composition, an autograph replica by De Mura
of an earlier version, is a design for a 1762 ceiling fresco destined for the
bedroom of the young King Ferdinando IV in the Palazzo Reale in Naples
(these frescoes were destroyed during World War II). Aurora, goddess of the
Dawn, fell in love with a handsome young mortal, Tithonus, Prince of Troy,
and married him. She begged Jupiter, king of the gods, to make Tithonus
immortal. But she forgot to ask that the prince remain eternally young and
handsome. After many years, her handsome husband grew old and his hair
turned white, at which point she left him, but he continued to live in the goddess' palace. Over many decades, he became paralyzed in his legs and arms,
so she locked him in his bedroom, where he continually moaned. Upset with
this, Aurora at last turned Tithonus into a grasshopper.

The artist has composed an Allegory of the Eternal Rising of the
Morning Sun.[1] The celestial scene is set at the break of day; the flame of the
sun's light, which Aurora hands to a servant, brightens every corner. Aurora's
winged minions fly over the clouds about to crown her with roses and place
a bouquet in her lap. The goddess, who sits on a cloud with her head turned
in profile, looks down despairingly at her aging husband, Tithonus, whom
a putto has awakened from a deep sleep by drawing the red curtain. Lying
unclothed on his pillowed bed, he shields his eyes from the blinding light.

De Mura painted other versions of this subject (fig. 82), which are
quite beautiful but even more in the Rococo style. De Mura's pendant of
this work, *Diane and Endymion*, is in the Museo di San Martino in Naples.
De Mura modeled the blond-haired Aurora after the Louvre's dark-haired
woman personifying the Arts (fig. 23), which helps us date this work to the
1760s. Nicola Spinosa has pointed out how mythological scenes such as this
were inspired by the classical dramas of Pietro Metastasio (1698–1782).[2] In
addition, in the 1750s, De Mura was exposed to the classicism of artists in
Rome, such as Pompeo Girolamo Batoni (1708–87), and was influenced by
the Roman architects Luigi Vanvitelli (1700–1773) and Ferdinando Fuga
(1699–1782), who were working in Naples. Although late in his career, the
artist still looked forward, to the newer forms of Neoclassicism. In sixty
years, De Mura had progressed from Solimena's high Baroque (fig. 83),[3] to
the Rococo, and finally, to the burgeoning Neoclassical.

1. The title might be *Allegory of Summer (Ceres) Giving Way to Autumn (Bacchus),* as in
   a similar work by De Mura's close follower Giacinto Diano; see "Mostra Antiquariato
   Napoli 1988," *EosArte,* accessed Dec. 8, 2015, http://www.eosarte.it/Amarcord_tutti/
   Amarcord%20Napoli%201988.htm.
2. Nicola Spinosa, ed., *Museo e Gallerie Nazionali di Capodimonte: Dipinti del XVIII
   secolo; La scuola napoletana* (Naples: Electa Napoli, 2010), 62, no. 63, notes the
   academicizing quality of this work.
3. De Mura chose elements of Solimena's *Aurora Taking Leave of Tithonus* (fig. 83 in
   this volume) of 1704 (in the Getty Museum), but omitted the ponderous, dark monumentality of the Baroque for the bright colors and classical poses of the Neoclassical.

Provenance:
Targiani collection, Naples, to
1811; Real Museo Borbonico;
Museo Nazionale (before 1930);
handed over to Istituto Italiano
di Numismatica, Rome, to 1998.

Exhibitions:
Palazzo Reale, Caserta, Dec.
16, 2000–Mar. 16, 2001, *Luigi
Vanvitelli e la sua cerchia,*
no. 11; National Gallery of
Australia, Canberra, Melbourne
Museum, Mar. 28–Oct. 6, 2002,
*The Italians: Three Centuries
of Italian Art,* no. 70; Museo
Nacional de Bellas Artes,
Havana, Nov. 23, 2002–Feb. 15,
2003, *I tre secoli d'oro della pit-
tura napoletana da Battistello
Caracciolo a Giacinto Gigante.*

Bibliography:
Eduardo Dalbono, *Relazione
sul riordinamento della
Pinacoteca di Napoli letta alla
R. Accademia…* (Naples, 1906),
22 (as Giacinto Diano); Aldo
de Rinaldis, *Guida illustrata
del Museo Nazionale di Napoli,*
Parte seconda: Pinacoteca
(Naples: Richter, 1911), 479,
no. 526; Franco Strazzullo, ed.,
*Le lettere di Luigi Vanvitelli
della Biblioteca Palatina di
Caserta* (Galatina: Congedo,
1977), 3:662 (as Francesco
de Mura); Arnaldo Rocco, entry
on Francesco de Mura in *Luigi
Vanvitelli e la sua cerchia,*
ed. Cesare de Seta, exhib. cat.
(Naples: Electa Napoli, 2000),
202–3, no. 11; A. Confalone,
entry on Francesco de Mura in
*The Italians: Three Centuries
of Italian Art,* ed. Gilberto
Algranti, exhib. cat. (Milan:
Skira, 2002), 192, no. 70; Nome
De Rosa, entry on Francesco
de Mura in *I tre secoli d'oro
della pittura napoletana da
Battistello Caracciolo a Giacinto
Gigante,* ed. Nicola Spinosa,
exhib. cat. (Naples: Voyage
Pittoresque à Naples, 2002), 92.

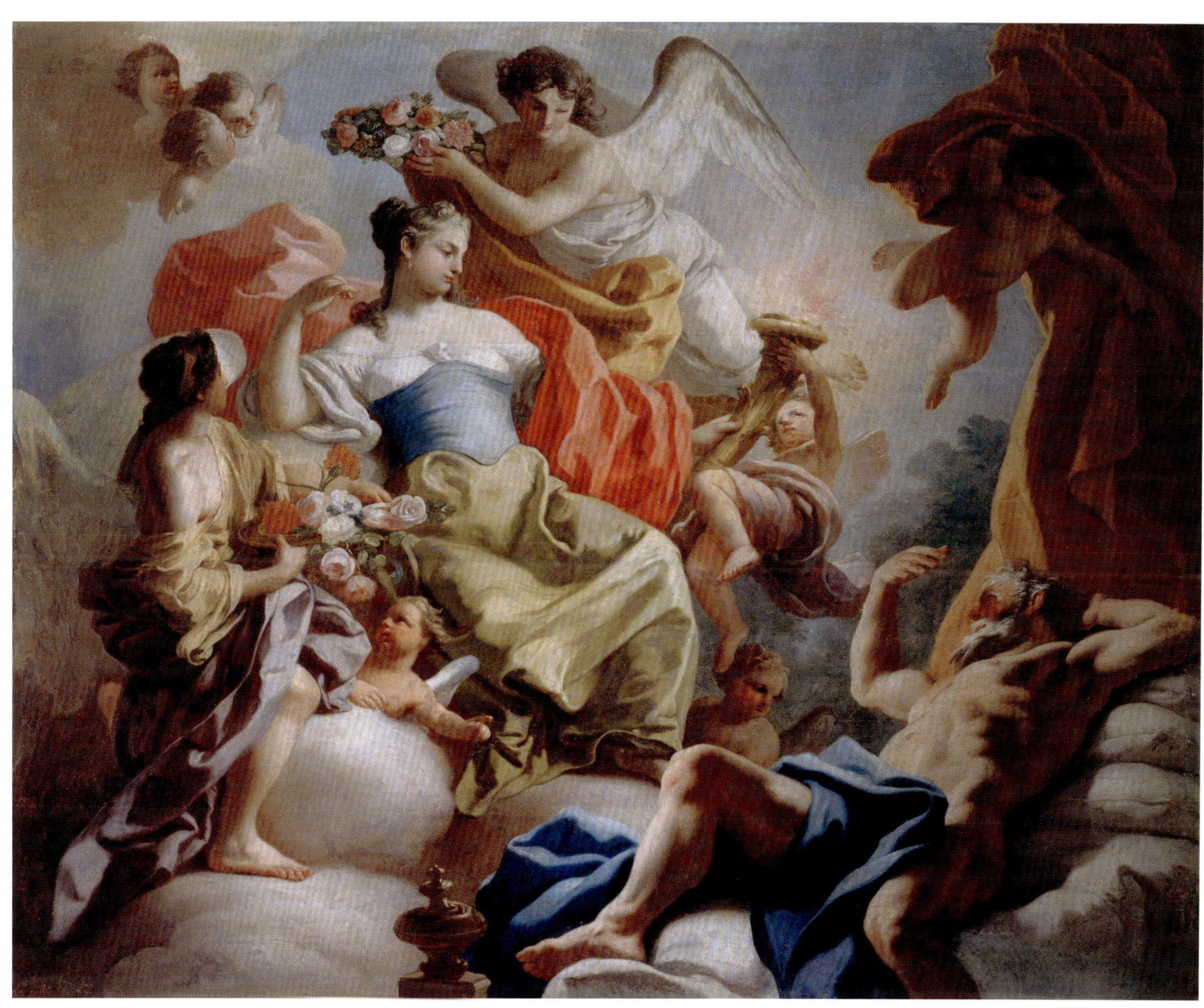

36 — continued

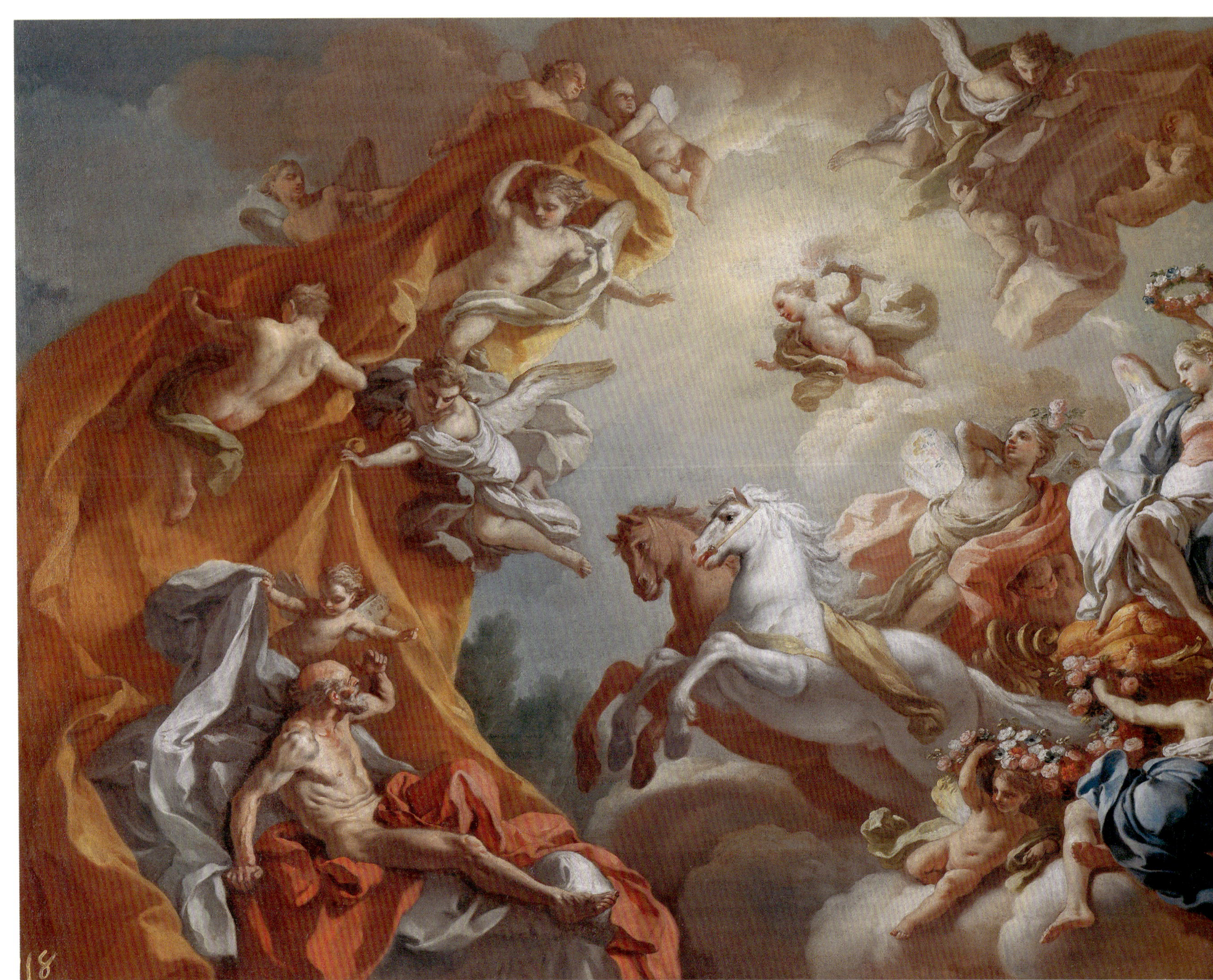

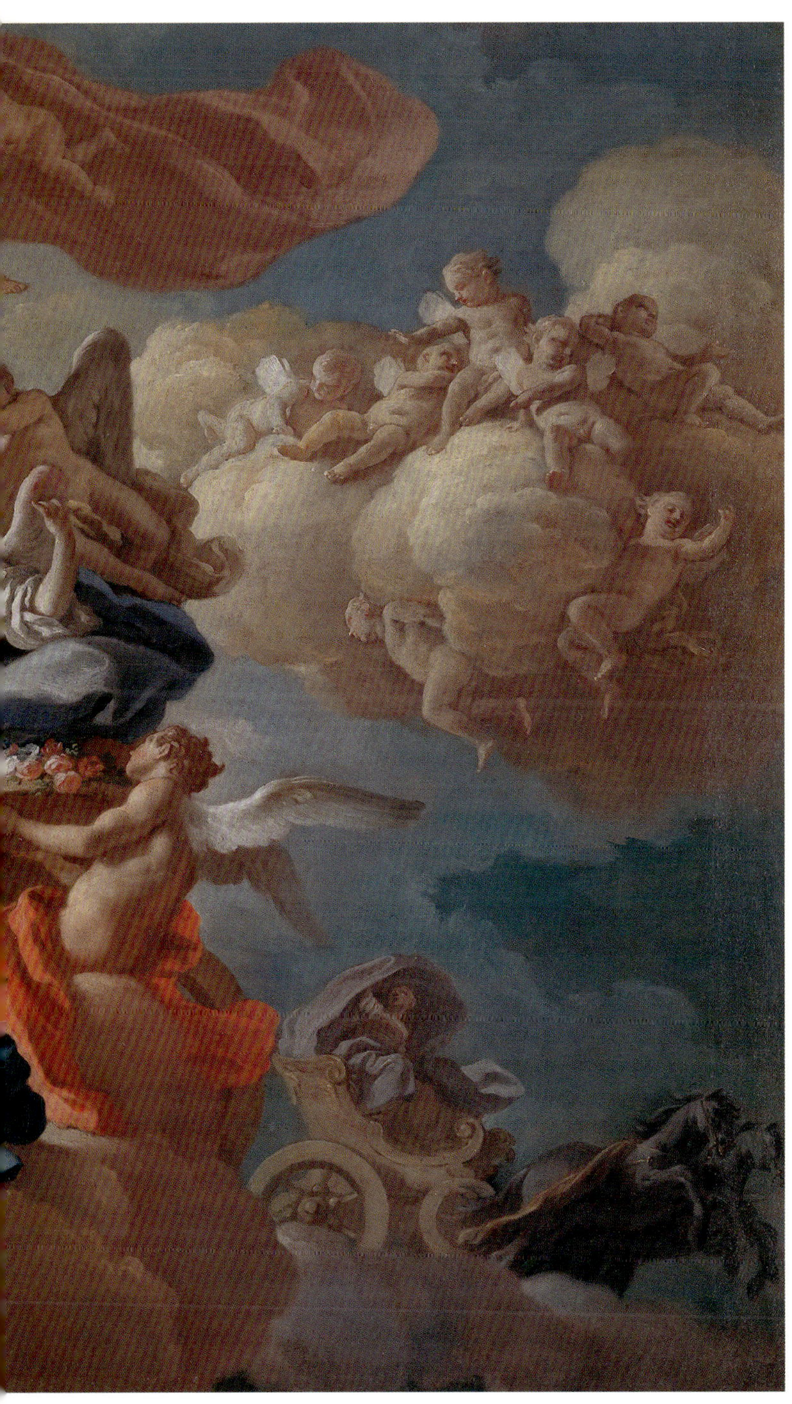

Fig. 82
Francesco de Mura, *Aurora and Tithonus*, ca. 1760s, oil on canvas, 38⅛ × 71⅝ in. (97 × 182 cm), Pio Monte della Misericordia, Naples

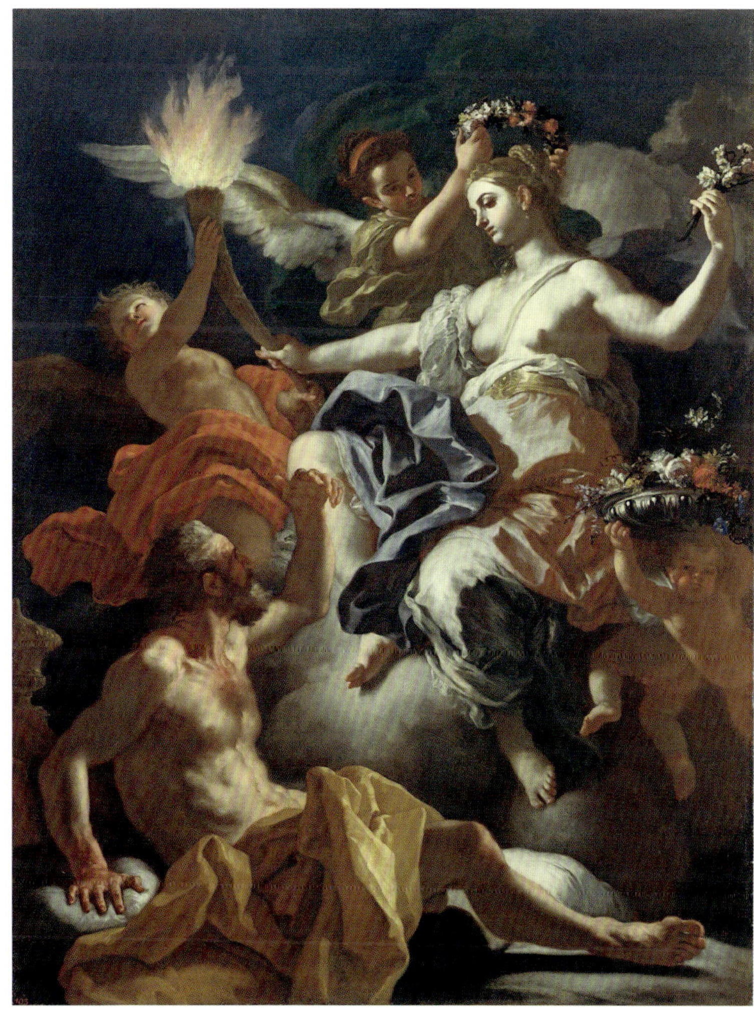

Fig. 83
Francesco Solimena, *Aurora Taking Leave of Tithonus*, 1704, oil on canvas, 79½ × 59¾ in. (201.9 × 151.8 cm), J. Paul Getty Museum, Los Angeles

37

Francesco de Mura
Bacchus and Ceres, ca. 1763
Oil on canvas, 82 × 61 in. (208 × 154.8 cm)
The Snite Museum of Art, University of Notre Dame, purchased from the
Lewis J. Ruskin fund, acc. no. 1972.2

The subject of this extremely large and beautiful painting was inspired by
a line by the Roman comic poet Terence (d. 159 BC): *"sine cerere et libero
friget venus"* (without Ceres and Bacchus, Venus would freeze)—that is,
without food and drink, love is impossible. The setting is Arcadia; Ceres,
goddess of the Harvest, gives her sheaf of wheat to a little winged Cupid,
god of love, as she accepts a wine bowl from her son, Bacchus, god of wine
and frivolity. With a grape-wreath on his head and glazed eyes, he swivels
on his stone bench to look up at Ceres, offering her the wine bowl. A small
satyr with his back to us holds down Bacchus' leopard. A strong diagonal
is created from lower left to upper right (forming a right-angle triangle),
and the swirl of drapery and the huge, full-bodied figures remind us of the
heroic-monumental images of De Mura's master, Solimena.

Even so, De Mura seems here to anticipate aspects of Neoclassicism,
with its simplicity of bright colors and large forms that recall polished
Roman statues. As Nicola Spinosa has noted, De Mura, at this point close
to seventy, exhibits his classicist approach powerfully with an "expressive
naturalness and visible concreteness."[1] David Nolta points out that the
narrative here "is not so much about activity as it is about technical grace
and harmony."[2]

This work, which may have been done for a Neapolitan palace or
villa, is stylistically close to the *Allegory of the Four Parts of the World* for
the Palazzo Chiablese in Turin that documents date to 1763, as well as to
allegories of three of the four classical elements—*Allegory of Earth, Allegory
of Fire,* and *Allegory of Water.*[3] De Mura executed around 1765 a variation
of his *Bacchus and Ceres* that was on sale in London in 1989 (fig. 84). The
powerful female figure in the Louvre's *Allegory of the Arts* (see fig. 23), now
dated ca. 1758–62, appears here in the image of Ceres, in mirror reversal
(also in *Aurora,* cat. no. 36).

Spinosa compares *Bacchus and Ceres* with De Mura's proto-classicistic
sovrapporta (overdoor) of *Dido and Aeneas* in the Palazzo Reale in Turin (fig.
85, an autograph replica in the Banca Commerciale), usually dated about
1758, but which he dates closer to 1763, when De Mura executed the Notre
Dame work.[4]

1. Spinosa, *Pittura napoletana del Settecento,* 1:164, no. 266, fig. 319.
2. Nolta, "Francesco de Mura" in *A Taste for Angels*]," 284.
3. Spinosa, *Pittura napoletana del Settecento,* 1:164, no. 265.
4. *Ibid.,* no. 267.

Provenance:
Private collection, Germany;
Heim Gallery, London, to
1971; purchased by the Snite
Museum in 1972.

Exhibition:
Heim Gallery, London, 1971,
*Fourteen Important Neapolitan
Paintings,* no. 131; Palazzo
Reale, Naples, Dec. 1979–
Oct. 1980, *Civiltà del '700 a
Napoli, 1734–1799,* no. 96;
Yale University Art Gallery,
New Haven, Conn., John and
Mable Ringling Museum of Art,
Sarasota, Fla., Nelson-Atkins
Museum of Art, Kansas City,
Mo., Sept. 9, 1987–June 12, 1988,
*A Taste for Angels: Neapolitan
Painting in North America,*
no. 3.

Bibliography:
Nicola Spinosa, *Civiltà del '700
a Napoli, 1734–1799,* exhib.
cat. (Florence: Centro Di,
1979), 1:204, no. 96 (ill.); Nicola
Spinosa, *Pittura napoletana del
Settecento,* vol. 1, *Dal barocco al
rococò* 2nd ed. (Naples: Electa
Napoli, 1993), 164, no. 266, fig.
319; David Nolta, "Francesco
de Mura," in *A Taste for Angels:
Neapolitan Painting in North
America,* exhib. cat. (New
Haven: Yale University Art
Gallery, 1987), 284–87, no. 3.

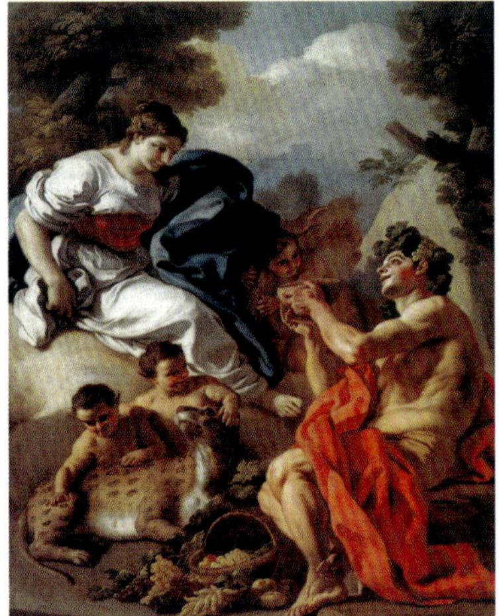

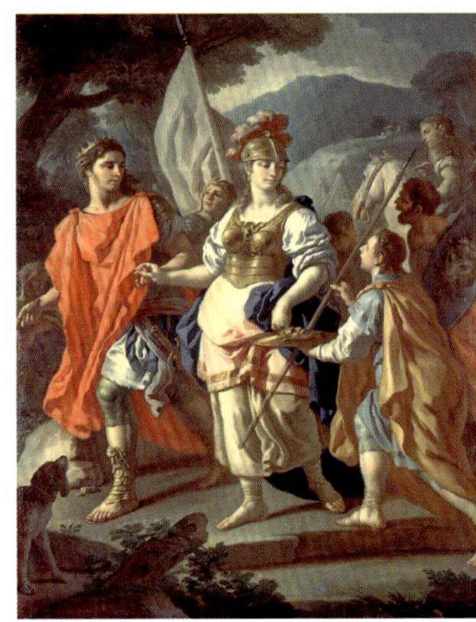

Fig. 84
Francesco de Mura, *Bacchus and
Ceres,* ca. 1765, oil on canvas, 82 × 61 in.
(208 × 155 cm), Sotheby's, London,
April 19, 1989, lot 16

Fig. 85
Francesco de Mura, *Dido and Aeneas
(?),* or *Agreement between Camilla and
Turnus,* or *Sisygambis, Wife of Darius,
Mistaking Haephestion for Alexander
the Great,* 1758 or 1765, oil on canvas,
93 x 74½ in. (236 x 189 cm), Banca
Commerciale Italiana, Eboli

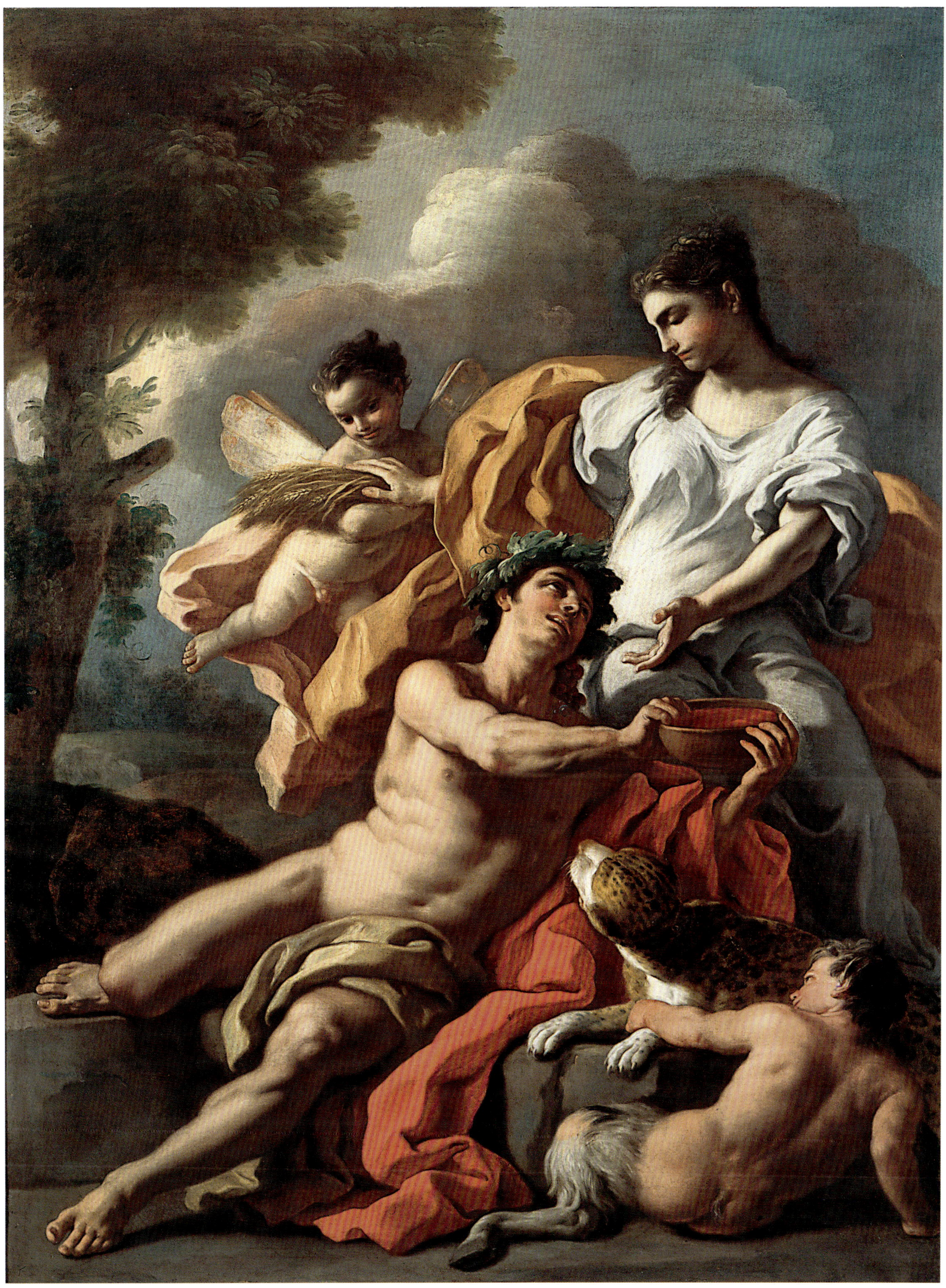

38

Francesco de Mura
Alexander Condemning False Praise [Scene from the Life of Alexander],
ca. 1768?
Oil on canvas, 29¹⁵⁄₁₆ × 24¹⁵⁄₁₆ in. (76 × 63.4 cm)
National Gallery of Art, Washington, D.C., Joseph F. McCrindle Collection,
acc. no. 2010.93.43

According to the Roman historian Marcus Justinius (fl. ca. 230–70),
Alexander the Great (336–323 BC) was a conqueror, but not a great man;
Alexander's arrogance (*insolentia*) and false pride (*tumor animi*) were
characteristic of him. Justinius tells the doubtful story of Alexander's
ordering his generals to worship him as a god. "Alexander, devoured by the
vanity of false pride, which invariably attend early popularity and elevation,
sunk him into the basest selfishness…"[1] The unusual title of this late work by
Francesco de Mura—*Alexander Condemning False Praise*—was attached to
it when Joseph McCrindle gave it to the National Gallery of Art in 2010. The
title may have rather been meant to be "Alexander *Showing* False Pride."

Alexander, a laurel wreath on his head, sits enthroned in a golden chair,
his head propped up by his left hand, his right hand folded into a fist that he
presses on his lap; his sword rests nearby, and, at his feet, are a faithful dog
and a book. On the left, a dark-haired, mustachioed general in armor (with
a red cape) stands before Alexander, both hands raised in surprise. Next to
him, another general points down to the floor (where one would bow down)
and steps forward in disbelief. Three other men in armor (two with spears)
look aghast at the generals; Alexander's companion Hephaestion, looking
concerned, stands behind him. Near the fluted columns in the background, a
statue of a goddess may indicate the entrance to a temple. In the upper right
corner, a large curtain is pulled back, revealing the scene.

This small *bozzetto* may have served as a model for a tapestry at the
Neapolitan Royal Tapestry Factory.[2] Other ancient Roman themes appear in
De Mura's work in the late 1750s and into the 1760s (figs. 86 and 87; see also
fig. 85). (He sent his *Dido and Aeneas* to the Palazzo Reale in Turin in 1758.)
This was no doubt because the Neapolitan clientele for paintings with clas-
sical subjects was growing rapidly, as was the desire to emulate the ancient
Greeks and Romans in all areas. Even more important was the stirrings of
Neoclassicism in France, which would explode in 1784 with Jacques-Louis
David (1748–1825) and his *Oath of the Horatii*.

Nicola Spinosa summed up the late paintings of Francesco de Mura,
which are often considered less interesting than his earlier work: "The
strongly stated classicism and refined and subtle grace [of the late paintings]
document the aging painter's continued determination to lift Neapolitan art
into the broader cultural spectrum of the European Enlightenment."[3]

1. Solomon Southwark, *Five Lessons for Young Men* (Albany, N.Y., 1837), 111.
   See also W. W. Tarn, *Alexander the Great* (Cambridge: Cambridge University Press,
   1948), 2:122.
2. Spinosa, *Pittura napoletana del Settecento*, 1:167, no. 282.
3. Spinosa, entry 282 on Francesco de Mura in *The Golden Age of Naples: Art and
   Civilization under the Bourbons, 1734–1805*, vol. 1, exhib. cat. (Detroit: Detroit
   Institute of Arts, 1981), 128. A larger variation of the Washington painting
   (55⅛ x 47¼ in.; 140 x 120 cm) is in a convent near Brescia, according to
   Superintendent Angelo Loda.

Provenance:
Hazlitt, Gooden & Fox, London,
by 1962; Sotheby's, New York,
June 6, 1985; purchased by
Joseph F. McCrindle [1923–
2008]; bequest to National
Gallery of Art.

Exhibition:
Hazlitt Gallery, London, 1962,
*Baroque and Rococo: Paintings
and Oil Sketches*, no. 7 (as *A
Scene from Roman History*).

Bibliography:
Nicola Spinosa, *Pittura napoletana del Settecento*, vol. 1, *Dal barocco al rococò* (Naples: Electa
Napoli, 1986), 167, no. 282, fig.
339; Margaret M. Grasselli
and Arthur K. Wheelock, Jr.,
eds., *The McCrindle Gift: A
Distinguished Collection of
Drawings and Watercolors*,
exhib. cat. (Washington, D.C.:
National Gallery of Art, 2012),
19, (ill. p.185).

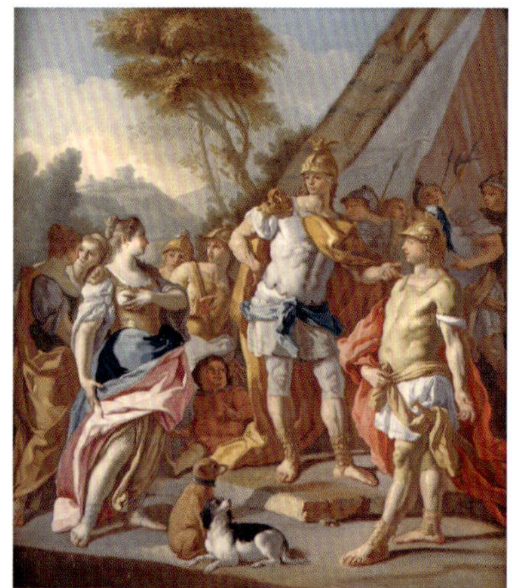

Fig. 86
Francesco de Mura,
*Sisygambis, Wife of Darius,
Mistaking Hephaestion for
Alexander the Great*,
ca. 1755, oil on canvas,
private collection

Fig. 87
Francesco de Mura, *Death
of Verginia*, ca. 1760, oil
on canvas, 35⅝ × 56⅞ in.
(90.5 × 144 cm), Manchester
Art Gallery, U.K.

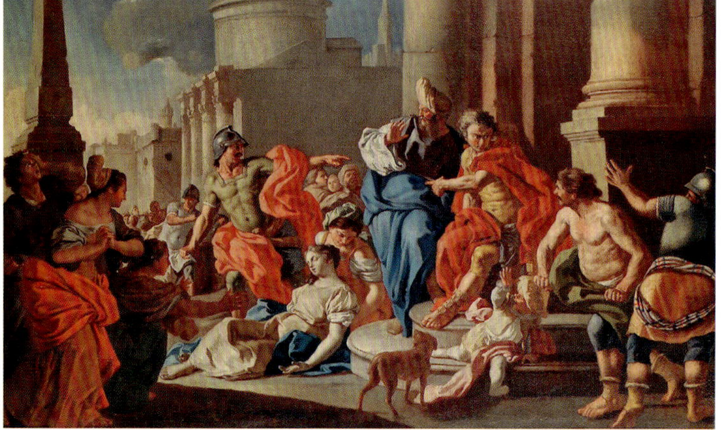

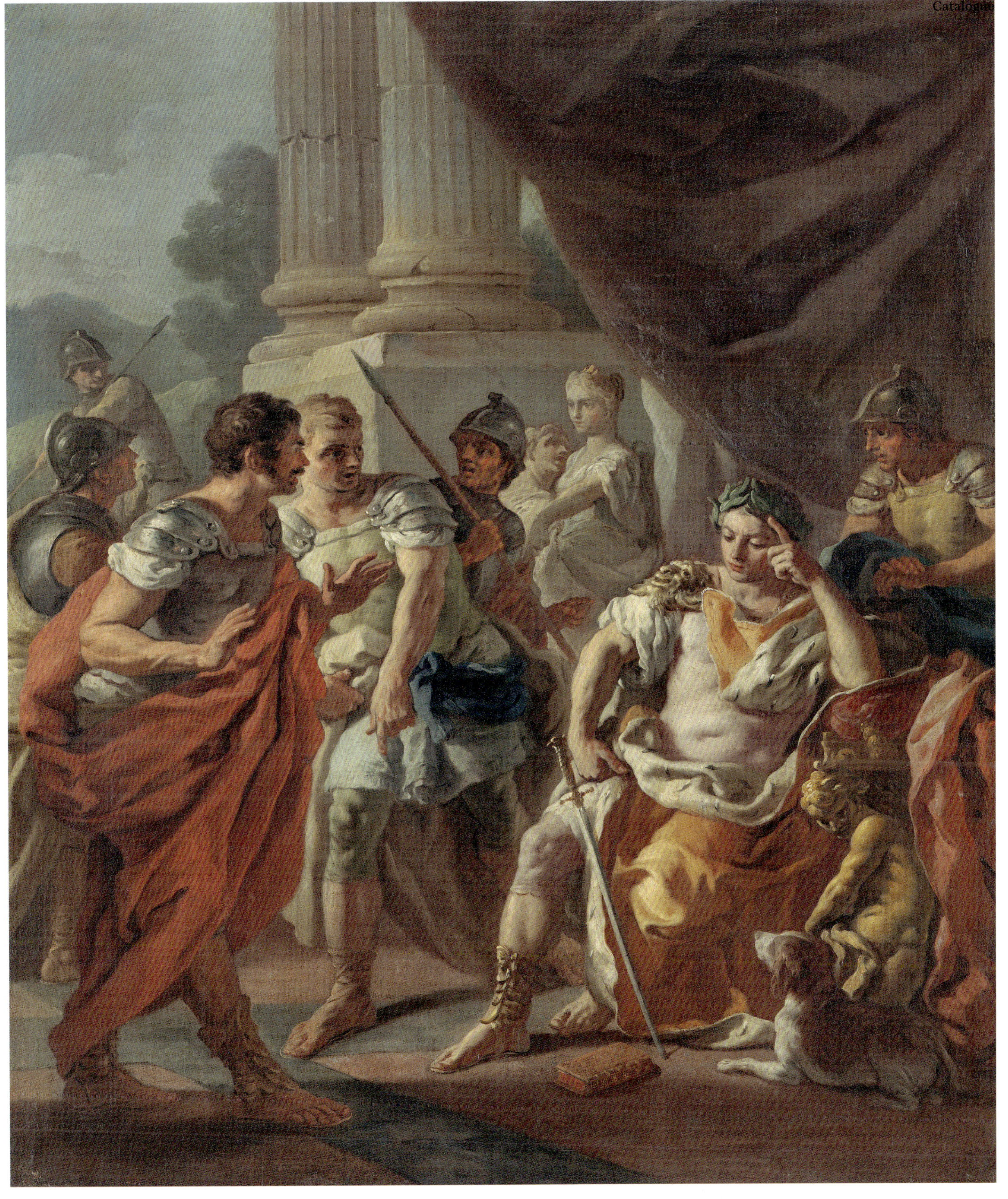

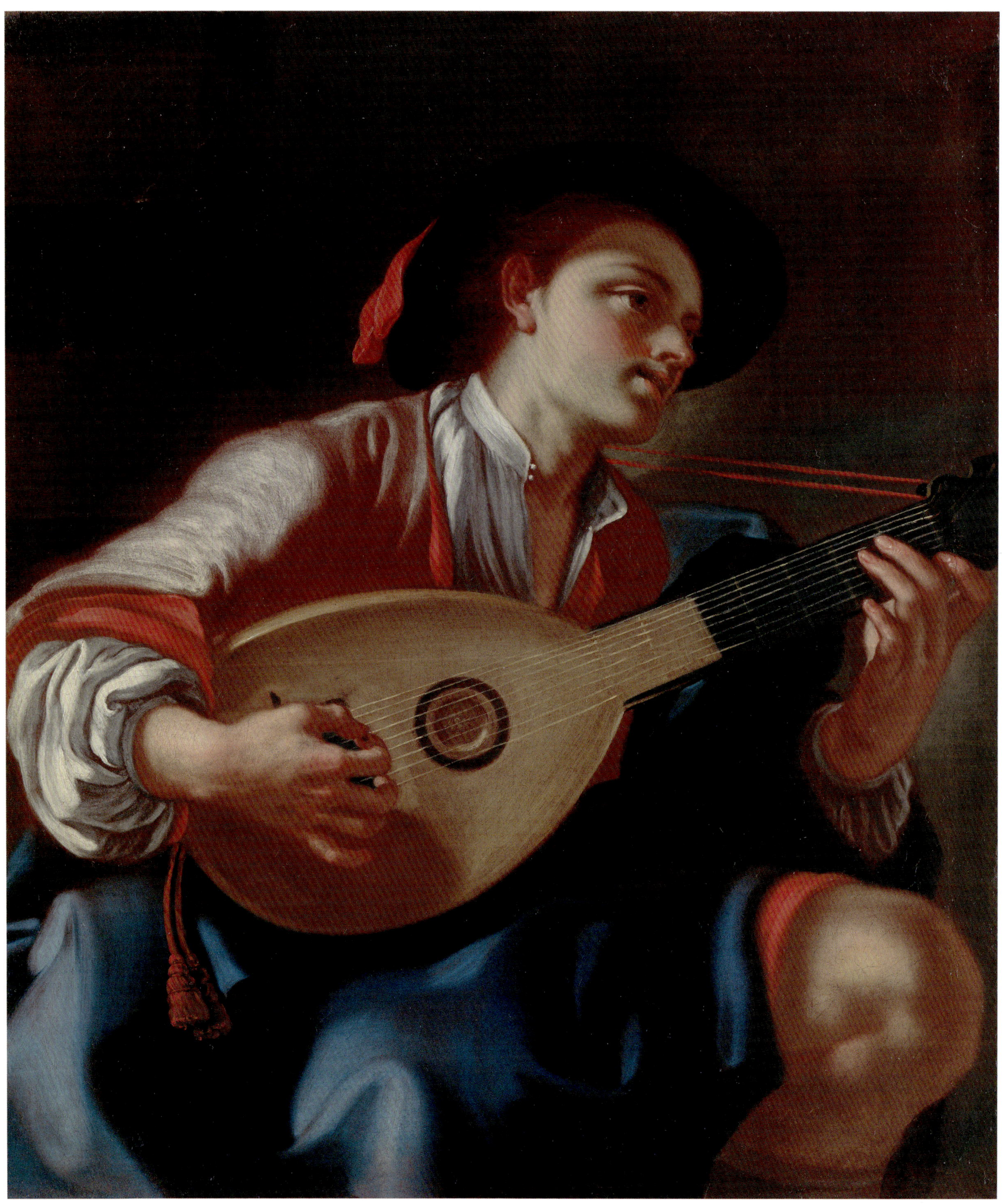

39

Francesco de Mura
Allegory of Summer or *Allegory of Music*, ca. 1770?
Oil on unlined canvas, 29¹⁄₂ × 24⁵⁄₈ in. (75 × 62.5 cm)
Inscription on reverse: *Francesco de Mura / ritratto di Agnellus Nobilone*
Collection of Clovis Whitfield

This painting and the one following (cat. no. 40) are a pair, an *Allegory of Summer* and its pendant, an *Allegory of Autumn*. This painting, also referred to as *Allegory of Music,* appears to be a *bozzetto* for a series of four allegories of the seasons, of which De Mura painted several versions. There is another *Allegory of Summer* (a *ricordo*?) of nearly the same measurements, formerly in the Santangelo collection in Naples.[1]

Clovis Whitfield, owner of these two allegories, also owns a second, much smaller pair of almost identical allegories of Summer and Autumn (figs. 88 and 91);[2] both are signed by De Mura on the reverse and *Summer* has an inscription that identifies the work as a portrait of "Agnellus Nobilone" (the smaller version of *Autumn*, cat. no. 40, is also signed on the reverse and inscribed as a portrait of Signora Nobilone). The Nobilone were a well-known family in Sorrento.

On a warm summer evening in the country, it is time to sing. With his right hand, a young peasant (*contadino*) strums a Neapolitan (or round-backed) mandolin, the soprano of the mandola, which is held in place by a red cord over his shoulder. He faces right, leaning forward while singing to an unseen person or persons. His white shirt is open at the neck, and his red-lined jacket is unbuttoned, the sleeve tassels swinging. The young man has spread a blue cloth over his lap (his left knee and red britches are exposed), and he wears a black-brimmed hat with a red kerchief attached.

This is a work of De Mura's later years, after 1770 probably, when he painted genre scenes and pastorals and composed single figures in deep Solimenesque chiaroscuro on small canvases, as in this example and another at the Galerie Canesso in Paris (fig. 89). Most likely, this was not painted or drawn from life, but was pulled from a stock of studio images of many figure types the artist had collected as *ricordi* or references over the years. It is an indication of his Neapolitan clientele's taste for an idealized countryside and images of country folk. This interest in the common man shows up also in the charming *contadini* figurines that Giuseppe Sanmartino and others, such as Matteo Bottiglieri, sculpted for the Christmas *presepi* (Nativity scenes; fig. 90), and may have also inspired De Mura's art.

1. Spinosa, *Pittura napoletana del Settecento*, 1:168
2. Each of Whitfield's smaller second pair of *Allegories* measures 11⁷⁄₈ × 9¹⁄₂ in. (30 × 24 cm). This smaller pair appears to be the same pair formerly in the Santangelo collection in Naples.

Provenance:
Romani collection, Florence.

Bibliography:
Nicola Spinosa, *Pittura napoletana del Settecento*, vol. 1, *Dal barocco al rococò*, 2nd ed. (Naples: Electa Napoli, 1993), 168, mentioned in entry no. 287.

Fig. 88
Francesco de Mura, *Allegory of Summer or Allegory of Music*, ca. 1770?, oil on canvas, 11⁷⁄₈ × 9¹⁄₂ in. (30 × 24 cm), collection of Clovis Whitfield, London

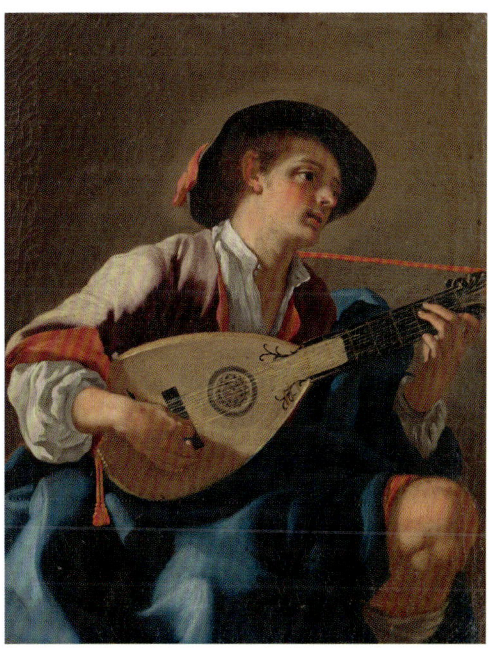

39 — continued

Fig. 89
Francesco de Mura, *Three Musicians*,
ca. 1765–70, oil on canvas, 13¼ × 16⅛ in.
(33.5 × 41 cm), Galerie Canesso, Paris

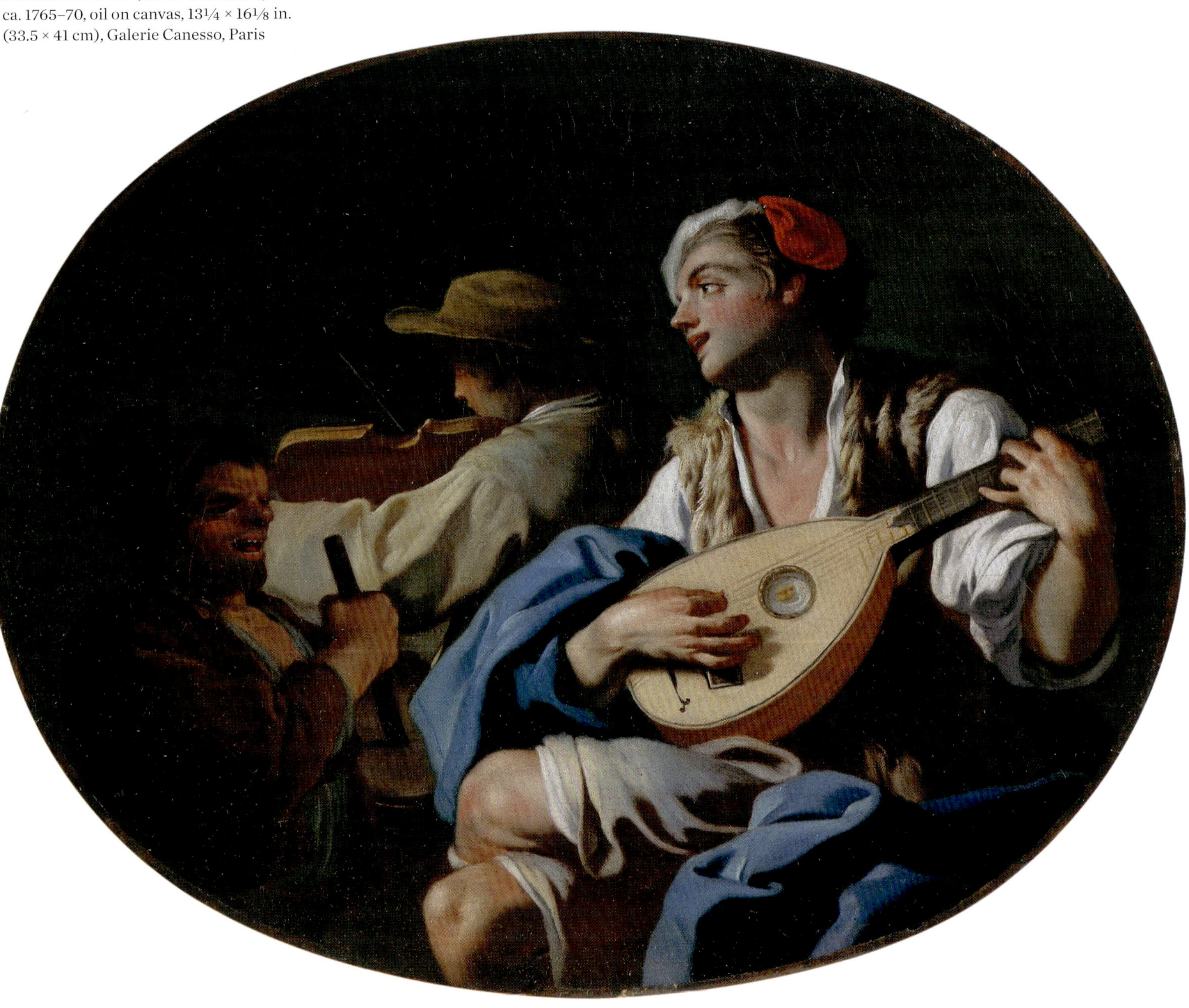

Fig. 90
Matteo Bottiglieri, *Mandolin Player*, ca. 1750, from a *presepio*, terracotta, glass, wood, wire, fabric, and metal, ca. 6 in. (15 cm) high, private collection

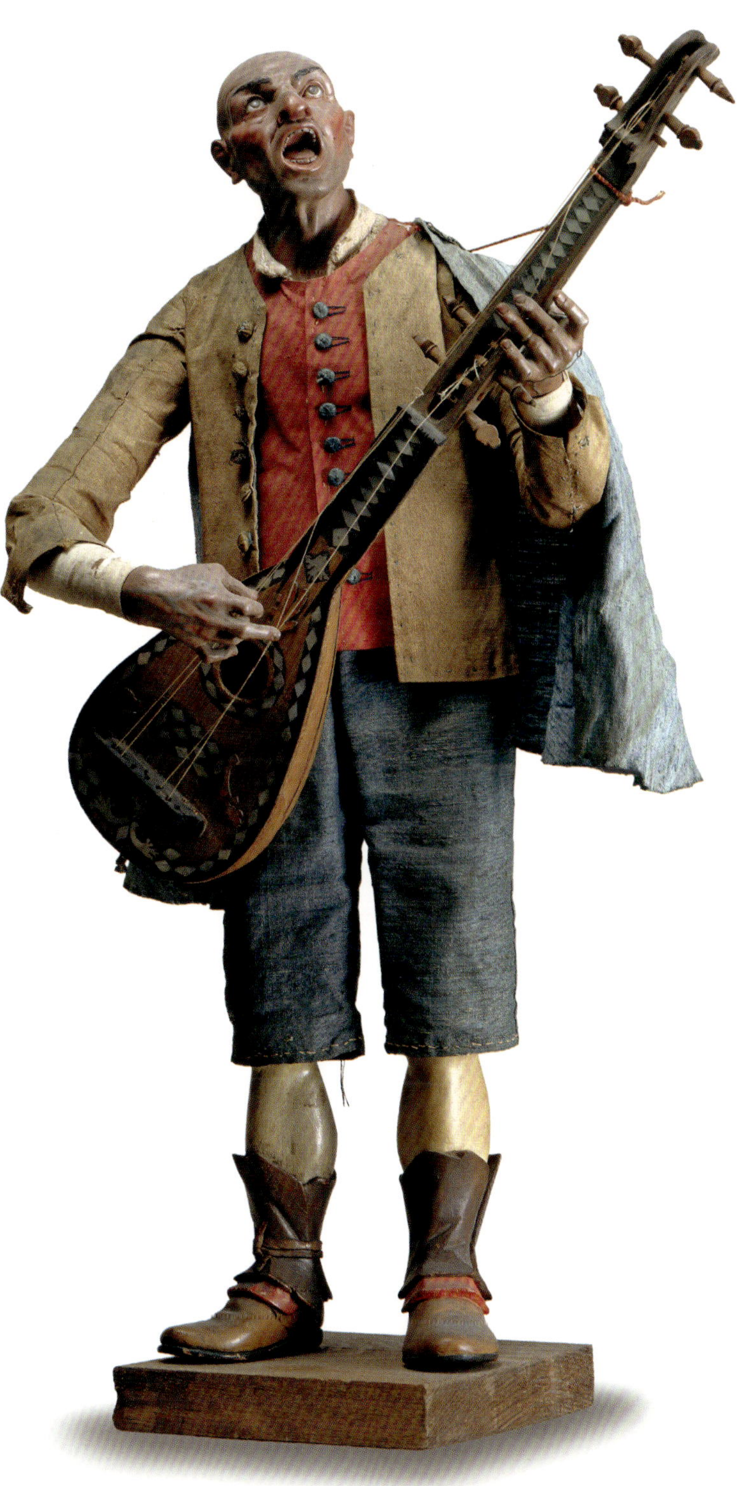

40

Francesco de Mura
Allegory of Autumn, ca. 1770?
Oil on unlined canvas, 29½ × 24⅝ in. (75 × 62.5 cm)
Inscription on reverse: *Francesco de Mura*
Collection of Clovis Whitfield

A young peasant woman, representing the season of Autumn, fills the entire composition and sweetly smiles at us. With her right hand, she offers us a bunch of freshly picked green grapes. Her body is facing left, as she turns her head left to gaze our way. She wears crystal earrings and a gold silk headdress with crimson ribbons in her hair. Her bodice (decorated with bows) and skirt are a red-orange or salmon color (a color De Mura often used). Her underskirt is a blue-green satin, striped with gold at the edges. She holds a gold platter in her lap, filled with autumn fruit—apples, purple grapes, small yellow squash, and figs. In the left background, a vine of blue morning glory springs from a branch. As with the *Allegory of Summer* (cat. no. 39), our *contadina* has been drawn from a prototype, and not from life (as the woman's rubbery left arm testifies)—an ideal of a peasant, not the reality of one (despite an inscription on Whitfield's second, smaller version, fig. 91, stating that it is a portrait of Signora Nobilone).

Provenance:
Romani collection, Florence.

Bibliography:
Nicola Spinosa, *Pittura napoletana del Settecento*, vol. 1, *Dal barocco al rococò*, 2nd ed. (Naples: Electa Napoli, 1993), 168, mentioned in entry no. 287.

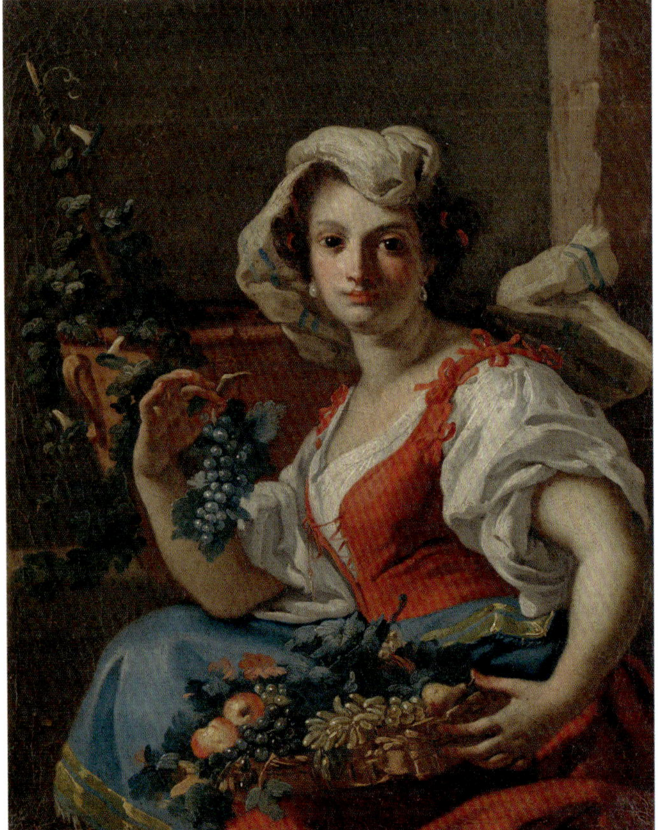

Fig. 91
Francesco de Mura, *Allegory of Autumn*, ca. 1770?, oil on canvas, 11⅞ × 9½ in. (30 × 24 cm), collection of Clovis Whitfield, London

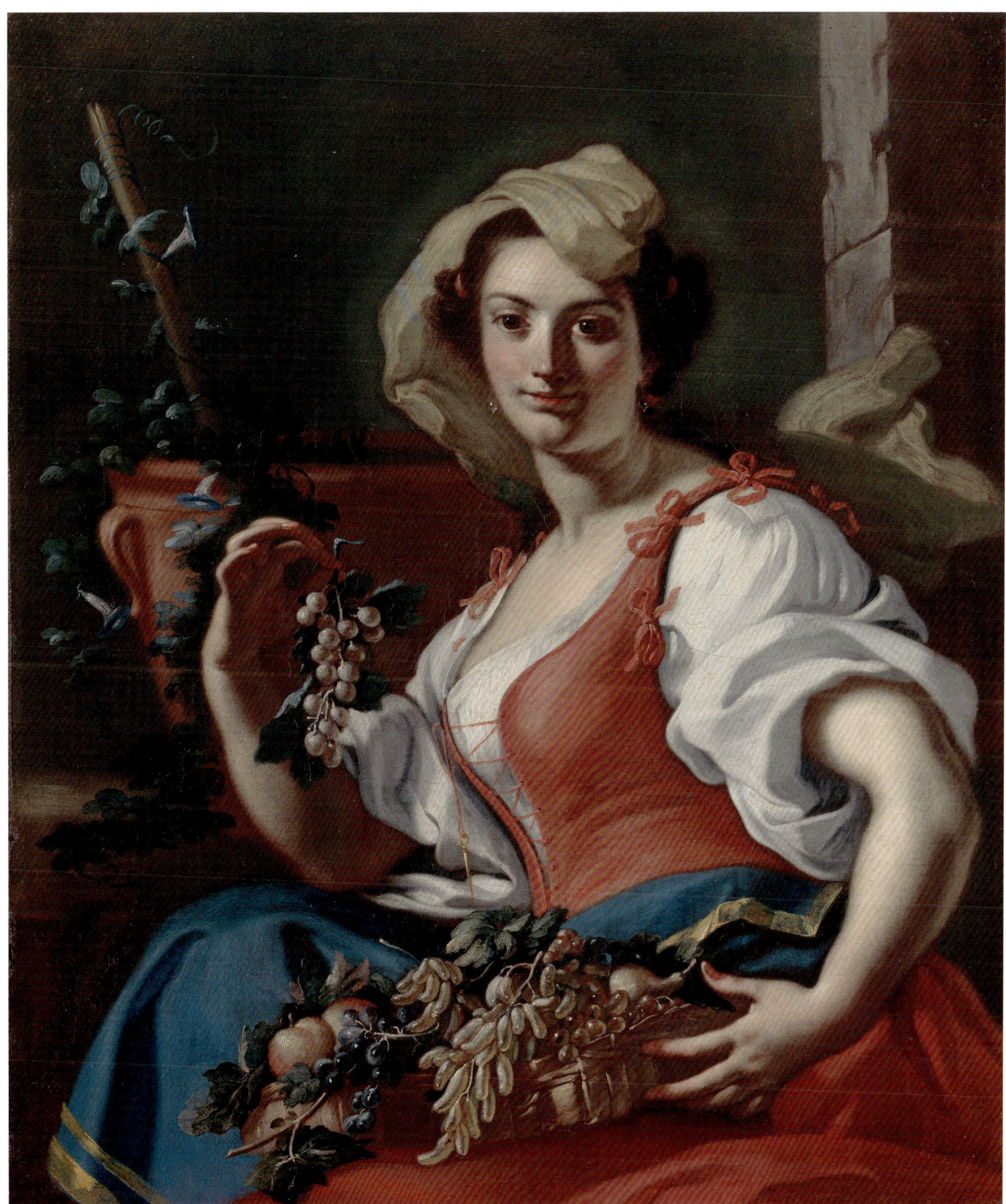

41

Francesco Solimena
St. Francis Xavier Baptizing Indians in Bombay, ca. 1680–90
Oil on canvas, 19⅜ × 25 in. (48.5 × 63.5 cm)
Cornell Fine Arts Museum, purchased with funds from the Michel Roux
Acquisitions Fund, in honor of Kenneth Murrah, acc. no. 2014.5

When he sketched this scene, Solimena was in his late twenties and very
much under the sway of Luca Giordano (1634–1705), the greatest Neapolitan
artist of the *seicento*. The dark chiaroscuro and the rapid brush strokes,
reminiscent of the Caravaggist master Mattia Preti (1613–99), indicate that
this is not a final study but an idea for an unidentified composition.[1]

Francis Xavier (1506–52), a co-founder (with Ignatius Loyola) of
the Society of Jesus, was born in Xavier, in Navarre, now part of Spain. As
organizer, he led a large Christianizing mission to Asia, in particular to India,
in the Portuguese colony of Goa and in Bombay (now Mumbai). Francis
devoted three years to preaching in southern India and Ceylon (Sri Lanka),
converting almost as many as St. Paul the Apostle.

Standing in the center of a primitive Bombay church, Francis Xavier,
clothed in the white robe and gold stole of a priest, pours a pitcher of holy
water over the bald head of a kneeling Indian man. The man's bare back and
head capture the brightest spots in the narrative—emphasizing the story's
essence. The newly baptized man wears a red cape over his left shoulder and a
skirt of peacock feathers, his feathered cap resting on the floor. (The feathers
indicate, perhaps, the artist's confusion between the garb of East Indians and
American Indians.) A kneeling altar boy, also dressed in white robes, gazes at
the Indian man while holding a tall cross. Francis gracefully points to the cross
with his raised left hand. Kneeling behind the man is a woman in profile, with
a feathered cap and an exposed shoulder, crossing her hands over her chest,
awaiting her turn. Next to her is an elaborate ceremonial pitcher on a table; on
the right side, another kneeling Indian man (with earrings and a white turban)
looks down and raises his right hand in amazement. The light wall behind
Francis underscores his central role; a small angel with a censor flies in a cloud
of incense in the upper left, emphasizing the holiness of the tableau.

This sketch may have been for a painting for the chapel of St. Francis
Xavier in the Neapolitan church of Gesù Nuovo, or for a chapel in the church
of San Ferdinando, which opened in 1665. Nicola Spinosa has related it
stylistically to Solimena's paintings of the *Life of St. Francis of Assisi* in the
choir of the Neapolitan church of Santa Maria Donnaregina. The figure of the
kneeling altar boy relates to the kneeling angel in Solimena's *Nativity* (fig.
92), from about 1695.

1. Nicola Spinosa, in "More Unpublished Works by Francesco Solimena," *The
   Burlington Magazine* 121, no. 913 (April 1979): 212: "Around 1695, Solimena returned
   to a style reminiscent of Mattia Preti...to the vigorously luministic and naturalistic aspects of Preti's Baroque style." Spinosa attributed this work to Francesco
   Solimena, and has indicated that he will include it in his forthcoming monograph on
   Solimena. In a written communication of Dec. 11, 2013, he characterized this work
   as a "notable example of Solimena's early years, in which the influence of Pietro da
   Cortona [1596–1669] and Luca Giordano is evident." John T. Spike has also, verbally
   and independently, confirmed the attribution to Solimena.

Provenance:
Christie's, New York, Old
Master Paintings, no. 2817, part
1, Wed., Jan. 29, 2014, lot 34;
after-sale in June 2014; pur-
chased by the Cornell Fine Arts
Museum with funds from the
Michel Roux Acquisition Fund.

Fig. 92
Francesco Solimena, *Christchild in a Manger
Adored by Angels*, ca. 1695–1710, oil on canvas,
88½ × 78¾ in. (225 × 200 cm), formerly
Gallery Fischer, Lucerne

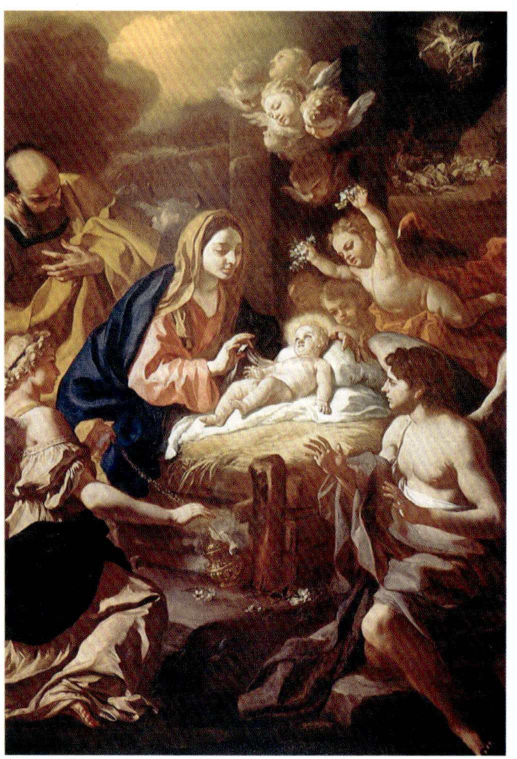

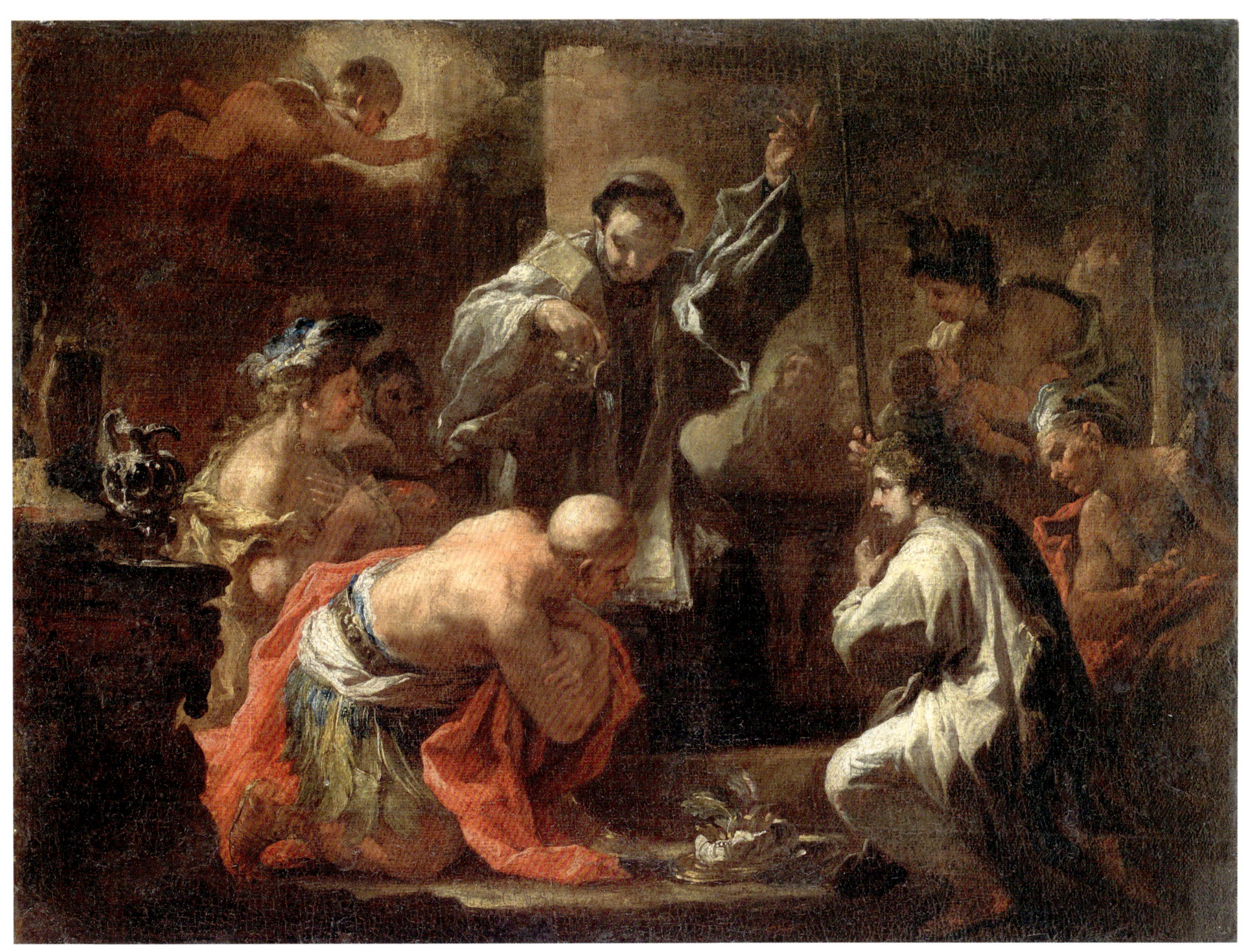

42

Francesco Solimena
Adoration of the Shepherds, ca. 1688 or ca. 1692
Oil on canvas, 54¾ × 71½ in. (139 × 181.6 cm)
Chazen Museum of Art, University of Wisconsin–Madison,
Thomas E. Brittingham Fund purchase, acc. no. 70.8

This powerful, large painting by Francesco Solimena (1657–1747) depicts the arrival of the shepherds in the barn where the baby Jesus had been placed in a manger filled with straw.[1] The Adoration of the Shepherds, according to the Gospel of Luke (2:15–20), took place immediately following Jesus' birth in Bethlehem. An angel announced the birth to shepherds in nearby fields, and they rushed into town to locate a manger with a baby in it. Finding the manger, they praised God that they were present at the birth of the messiah.

On the left, Mary, looking like a portrait bust of a Roman matron, sits next to the manger. She leans forward, one arm around the haloed infant lying on his back on top of white swaddling. Mary wears a striking cape of sapphire blue, symbol of her role as queen of heaven. At the foot of the manger shepherds have placed their offerings, including a trussed lamb (symbol of Jesus), chickens, and a lone rooster. Behind Mary stands Joseph, clad in a yellow garment (the color of loyalty), talking to a shepherdess in shadow on the far left. In the upper left corner, cherubs fly in thick clouds, and rays of moonlight flood the scene. On the right, a bearded and dark-haired shepherd kneels, arms spread in amazement. In this quiet drama, Mary and the kneeling shepherd are the lead characters, as both are the largest and most articulated figures. Next to the shepherd, a blond shepherdess kneels, inclining her head to the baby, arms crossed over her chest. Behind the kneeling shepherd stands another in a blue robe, smiling as he respectfully lifts his red cap and holds his offering over his shoulder. Next to him is another kneeling figure with a laurel wreath, and in the distance we see more shepherds arriving.

This work has been called "Solimena's parting fling with Giordanism."[2] And, indeed, this painting was at one time attributed to Luca Giordano. Another example from this early period of Solimena's career is *The Birth of the Virgin* (fig. 93) at the Metropolitan Museum; it, too, has close connections to Giordano, who was still alive and working in Naples. A comparison to a Giordano version of *The Adoration of the Shepherds* (fig. 94), done also around 1690, reveal their similarities in composition and rapid brush strokes. Over all, however, Solimena's beautifully drawn figures have a sculptural solidity, realism, and sobriety that distinguish his work.

1. In this work, the manger—an animal feeding trough or crib—is made of wood logs, and at the proper height for a nearby cow to feed.
2. Bambach, "Francesco Solimena," 172.

Provenance:
Private collection of English dealer/connoisseur and *marchand amateur*; P. & D. Colnaghi & Co., Ltd., London, to 1967–68; purchased with funds from Thomas E. Brittingham Fund on June 7, 1970, by Millard F. Rogers, Jr., Director 1967–78.

Exhibitions:
P. & D. Colnaghi & Co., London, 1967, *Paintings by Old Masters*; Wildenstein Galleries, New York, Columbus Museum of Art, Ohio, Oct. 3, 1973–Apr. 27, 1975, *Paintings from Midwestern University Collections: Seventeenth–Twentieth Centuries*.

Bibliography:
P. & D. Colnaghi & Co., *Paintings by Old Masters*, exhib. cat. (London: P. & D. Colnaghi & Co., 1967); *Elvehjem Art Center Bulletin—Annual Report 1970–71*, 46, (ill. p. 9); "Recent Accessions of American and Canadian Museums," *Art Quarterly* 34, no. 1 (1971): 131; Committee on Institutional Cooperation, *Paintings from Midwestern University Collections: Seventeenth–Twentieth Centuries*, exhib. cat. (Evanston, Ill.: Committee on Institutional Cooperation, 1973), 38–39; Elvehjem Art Center, *Handbook of the Collection of the Elvehjem Art Center* (Madison: University of Wisconsin–Madison, 1974), 32; Millard F. Rogers, Jr., "Paintings at the Elvehjem Museum of Art, University of Wisconsin," *Antiques* 108, no. 6 (Dec. 1975): 1146–55; James Watrous, *A Century of Capricious Collecting 1877–1970: From the Gallery in Science Hall to the Elvehjem Museum of Art* (Madison, Wisc.: Elvehjem Museum of Art, 1987); Elvehjem Museum of Art, *Handbook of the Collection* (Madison: University of Wisconsin–Madison, 1990); Carmen Bambach, "Francesco Solimena," in *A Taste for Angels: Neapolitan Painting in North America 1650–1750*, exhib. cat. (New Haven: Yale University Art Gallery, 1987), 171–72.

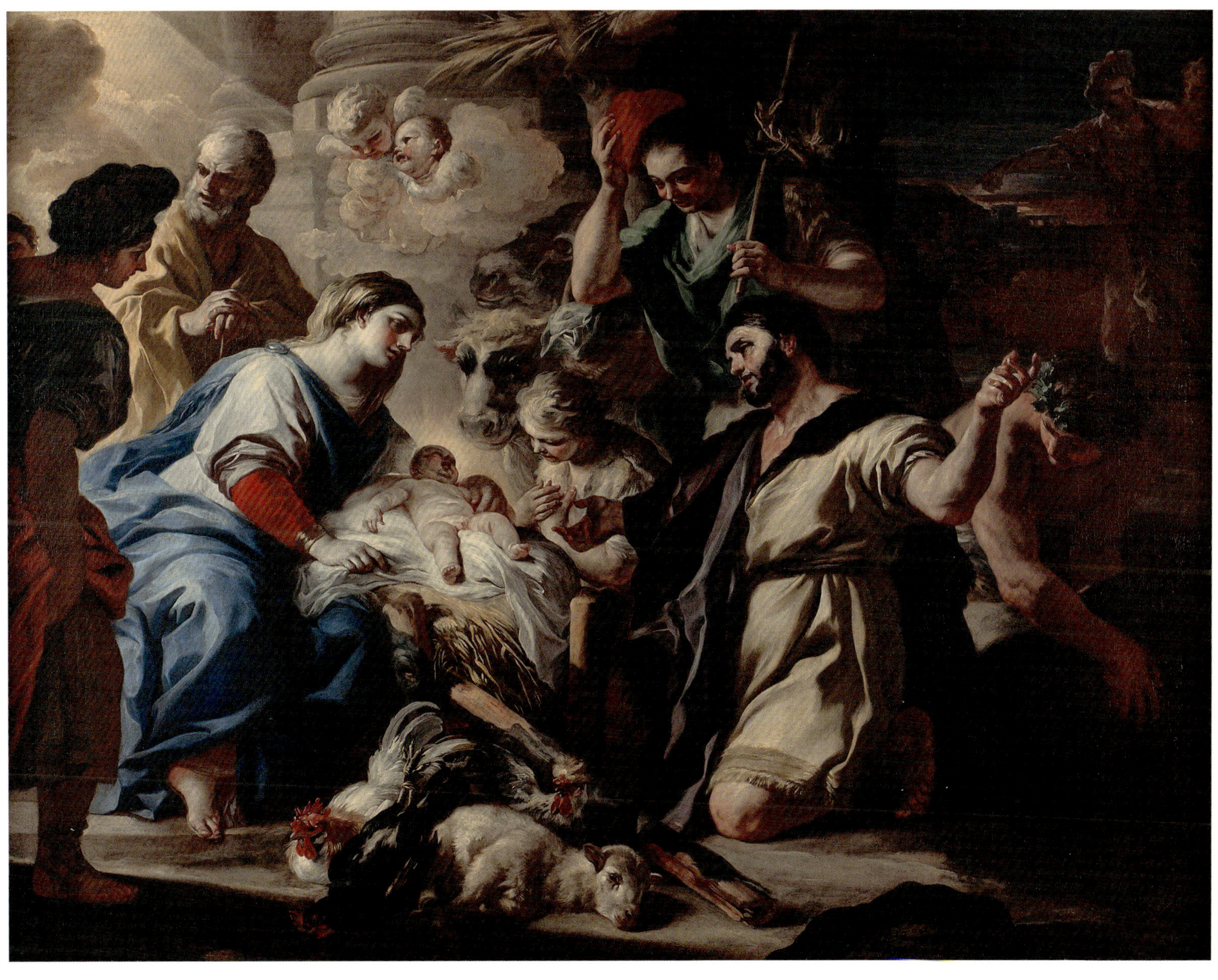

42 — continued

Fig. 93
Francesco Solimena, *The Birth of the Virgin*,
ca. 1690, oil on canvas, 80½ × 67¼ in.
(204.5 × 170.8 cm), The Metropolitan
Museum of Art, New York

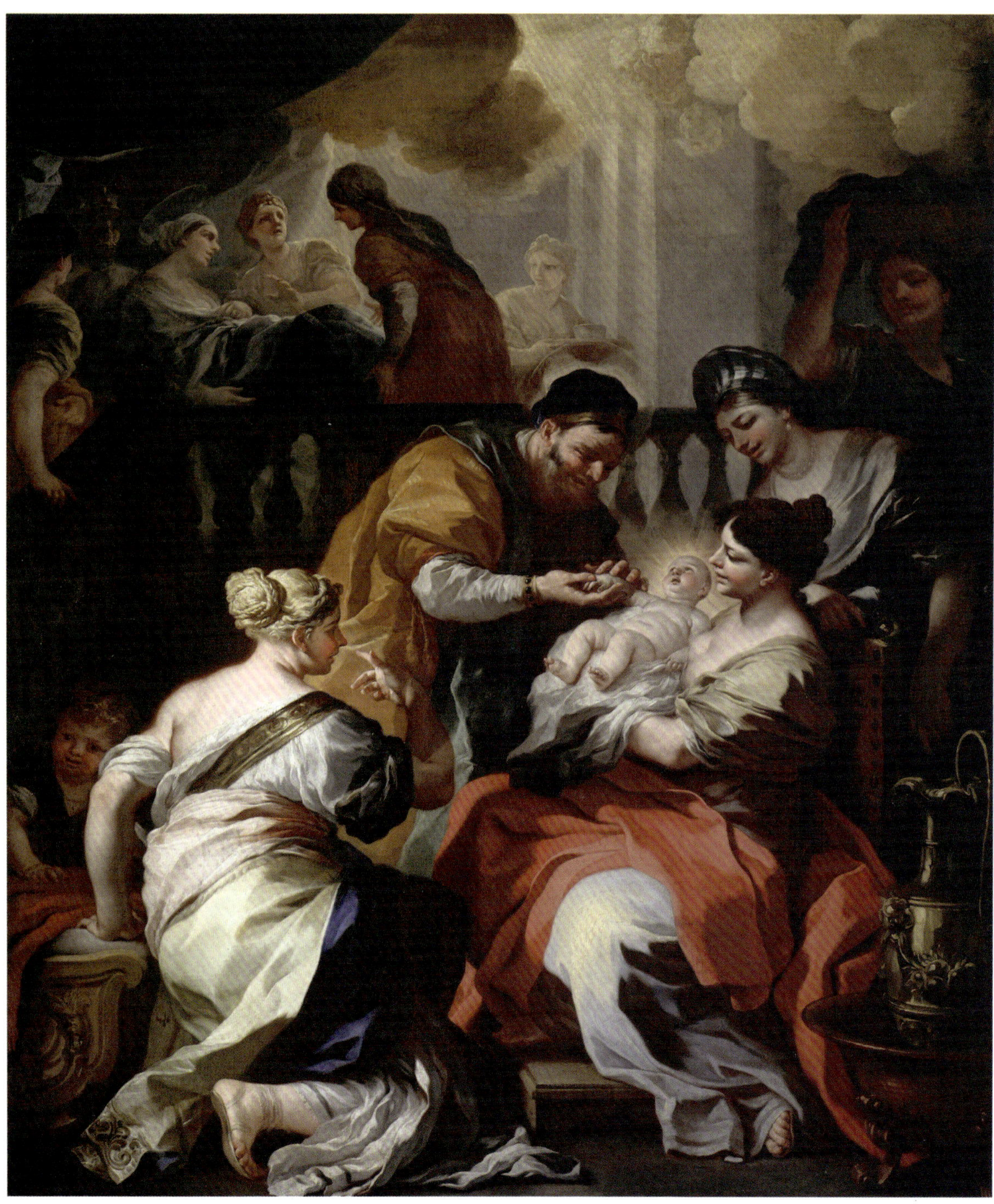

Fig. 94
Luca Giordano, *The Adoration of the Shepherds*, ca. 1688, oil on canvas, 45¼ × 53½ in. (115 × 136 cm), Musée du Louvre, Paris

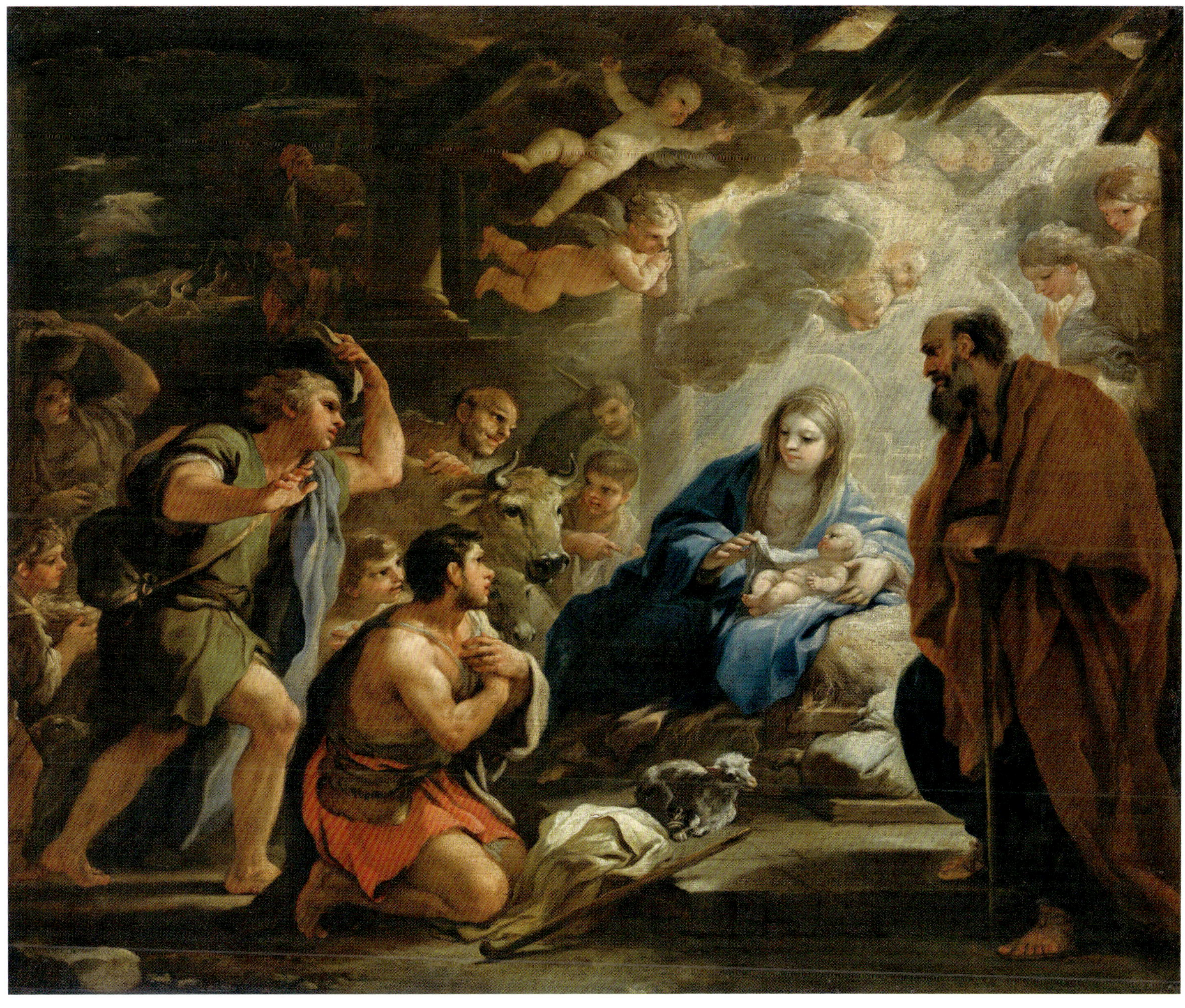

43

Giacinto Diano
The Apparition of the Virgin Mary to the Dominican Monk of Soriano, 1759
Oil on canvas, 30³⁄₁₆ × 30³⁄₁₆ in. (76.8 × 76.8 cm)
Museum of Fine Arts, Boston, gift of Azita Bina and Elmar W. Seibel,
acc. no. 2006.2064

In 1530, a Dominican monk of Soriano (in Calabria) prayed to the Virgin
Mary for a portrait of St. Dominic, the founder of his order. A day later, he
had a vision of the Virgin handing him an oil portrait of St. Dominic. The
portrait traditionally identified as the gift of the Virgin to this monk is today
housed in the monastery of Soriano.

We are looking at this rounded composition from below (*di sotto
in su*). In the lower left, the Virgin Mary, at the top of a series of steps in
a heavenly palace, hands the portrait of St. Dominic (depicted standing,
with a lily in his hand) to the Dominican monk, who kneels and spreads his
arms wide in gratitude. To the right of the Virgin are St. Mary Magdalene
and St. Catherine of Siena. At Mary's feet is a putto/angel gazing at us, and
below him, a large gold urn. In the upper heavenly sphere—accompanied by
numerous angels large and small—God the Father (triangular halo on his
head; see also cat. no. 34) gazes down at the monk.

When the Museum of Fine Arts in Boston acquired this work, it had
an attribution to Francesco de Mura, something that remained for many
decades (see Provenance). Nicola Spinosa identified this work in 2013 (in
a written communication to the author) as a *bozzetto* for the ceiling fresco
in the church of San Pietro Martire in Naples, which is signed by Giacinto
Diano (1731–1803) and dated 1759 (fig. 95).[1] The works of Diano and De Mura
are often confused, since he was the closest to De Mura in his studio, and
the fresco in San Pietro Martire was Diano's first major commission. The
overall design of this work closely relates to De Mura's ceiling fresco of *The
Assumption of the Virgin* of 1727 in Airola, which has the same curved format
and a very similar composition (see fig. 63). Diano painted with elements
from De Mura's repertoire, but also with hints of Corrado Giaquinto (see cat.
nos. 44–45), as Spinosa has pointed out.[2] We can also compare this work to
Diano's oval *bozzetto* of *The Madonna and Child Appearing to St. Dominic* in
Odessa (see fig. 54), which may relate to the Boston *bozzetto*, since both are
about St. Dominic.

From the 1740s till his death in 1782, De Mura was the most important
artist in Naples. Although Diano was his closest follower, Jacopo Cestaro
(1718–78) was another artist close to De Mura and whose works are sometimes mistaken for the master's (see Cestaro's *Circumcision*, fig. 43). Other
close followers of De Mura were Pietro Bardellino (1728–1819) and Fedele
Fischetti (1732–92), both of whom created for Pio Monte della Misericordia
the 1782 inventory of De Mura's bequest.

1. Nicola Spinosa, *Pittura napoletana del Settecento*, vol. 2, *Dal Rococò al Classicismo*,
   2nd ed. (Naples: Electa Napoli, 1993), 116, no. 136, fig. 167.
2. *Ibid.*

Provenance:
De Biase collection, Naples (?);
Pasquale Falanga, Milan art
dealer (?); "property of a lady,"
Sotheby's, London, May 23, 1986,
lot 50 (as "Francesco de Mura");
Azita Bina and Elmar W. Seibel
collection, Boston, to 2006.

Fig. 95
Giacinto Diano, *The Miracle of the Image
of St. Dominic Soriano*, 1759, fresco, ceiling
vault, church of San Pietro Martire, Naples

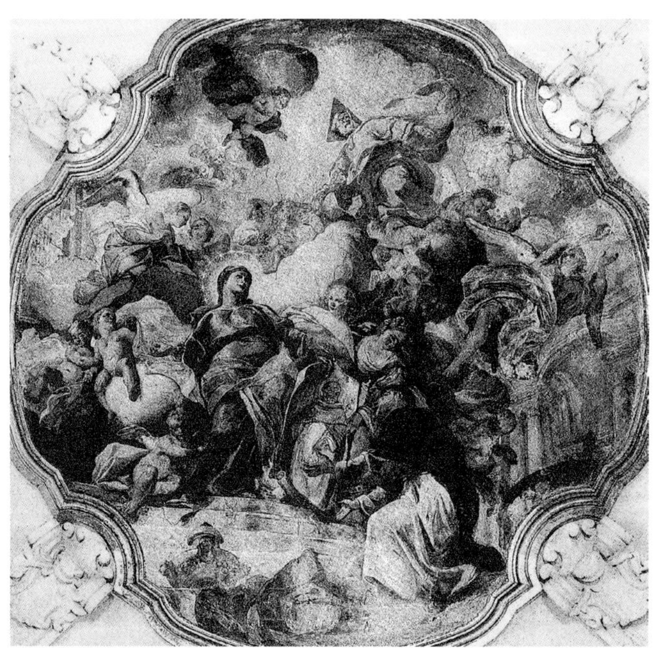

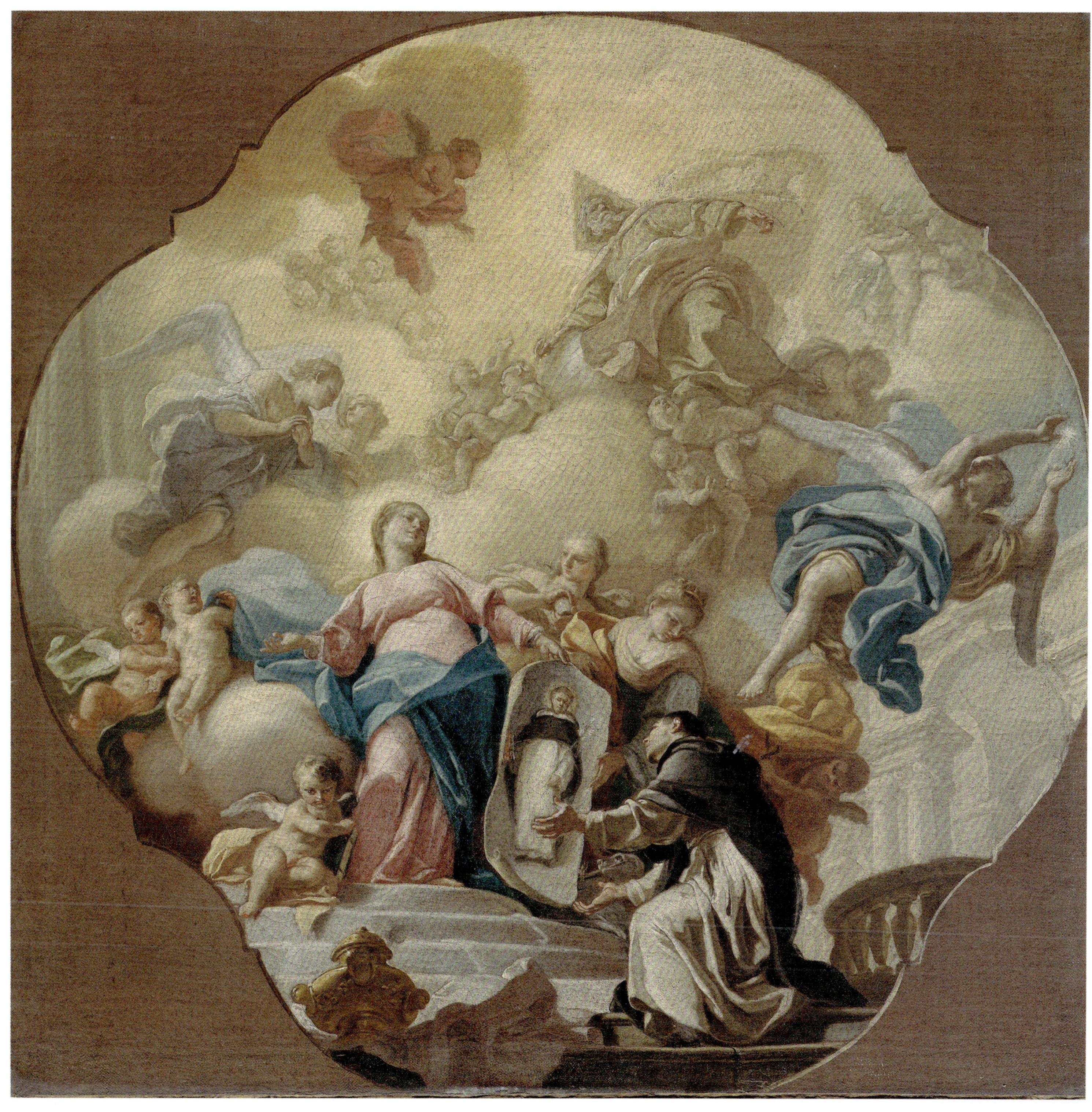

44

Corrado Giaquinto
Madonna and Child Appearing in Glory to Sts. Peter, Abercius, Stephen, and Benedict, 1750s
Oil on canvas, 19⅛ × 8⅞ in. (48.7 × 22.7 cm)
Frances Lehman Loeb Art Center, Vassar College, purchased with funds from the Louise Woodruff Johnson, class of 1922, Fund, acc. no. 1969.9

This small work may have been meant for personal devotions in the home, or may be a *bozzetto* for an unknown composition. The Madonna and Christ Child appear to four adoring saints in a celestial vision: Mary, assisted by an angel, holds up the Child, who sits on a bright white cloth covering a small cloud. The Child stretches his hand to bless the saints and the viewer; rays of light create haloes behind the heads of both figures. An enormous moon surrounded by ghostly angels shines in the background, and more light appears from the upper left. Mary, in a beautiful satin-blue robe, sits on a larger cloud and holds her hand up to her child, as if presenting him. Below Mary's cloud, above the Earth, four male saints—Apostle Peter, Greek Bishop Abercius, Martyr Stephen, and Monk Benedict—stand, kneel and bow, and a fifth female martyr saint, in the light behind the Virgin, sits with a palm frond.

This work was created, during his Spanish period, by Corrado Giaquinto (1703–65)—De Mura's colleague in the Solimena workshop from 1719 to 1723. Later, in the 1740s, both artists worked in creating paintings for the Palazzo Reale in Turin. It was in Turin that De Mura seems to have been influenced by Giaquinto's lighter palette, looser brushwork, and smaller, more animated figures (see cat. nos. 18, 19, and 23).

A mirror-reversal painting of this composition (of nearly the same dimensions) is in the National Galleries of Scotland (formerly in the Denis Mahon collection; fig. 96). Significant differences exist between the two versions, such as the absence of St. Peter. The small size of both may indicate that Giaquinto was quickly sketching ideas (easier to do in a small format).[1]

1. A drawing related to this painting, with all four saints, but reversed, is in the Museo della Certosa di San Martino in Naples. See Luigi Dania, "Inediti di Corrado Giaquinto," *Paragone* 20, no. 235 (Sept. 1969): 63–68, pl. 52; "La Chronique des Arts," *Gazette des Beaux-Arts* 75 (Feb. 1970): 69, no. 318 (ill.).

Provenance:
Count de Pret Roose de Ballesberg, Antwerp; Don Gorge Diaz-Alvarez, Madrid; Jose Castillo, Madrid; Guilliermo Bernstein, Madrid; P. & D. Colnaghi, London; F. Kleinberger & Co., New York; purchased by Vassar Art Gallery in 1969.

Exhibitions:
Yale University Art Gallery, New Haven, Conn., John and Mable Ringling Museum of Art, Sarasota, Fla., Nelson-Atkins Museum of Art, Kansas City, Mo., Sept. 9, 1987–June 12, 1988, *A Taste for Angels: Neapolitan Painting in North America 1650–1750*, no. 46; Smith College Museum of Art, Northampton, Mass., June 20, 1991–May 6, 1993; Loeb Art Center, Vassar College, Poughkeepsie, N.Y., Nov. 7–Jan. 4, 2008, *Revealed Anew: Selections from the Permanent Collection.*

Bibliography:
La peinture italienne au XVIIIe siècle, exhib. cat. (Paris: Musée du Petit Palais, 1961), no. 8 (*Madonna and Child with Three Saints*, Denis Mahon collection, London—another version of this work); George Hersey, entry no. 46 in *A Taste for Angels: Neapolitan Painting in North America, 1650–1750*, exhib. cat. (New Haven: Yale University Art Gallery, 1987), 320–22 (ill.); Richard Spear, "Review of *A Taste for Angels*," *The Burlington Magazine* 140, no. 1138 (Jan. 1988): 62; Luigi Dania, "Intorno a Corrado Giaquinto," in *Per Luigi Grassi: Disegno e Disegni*, ed. Anna Forlani Tempesti and Simonetta Prosperi Valenti Rodinò (Rimini: Galleria Editrice, 1998), 450–57, fig. 3.

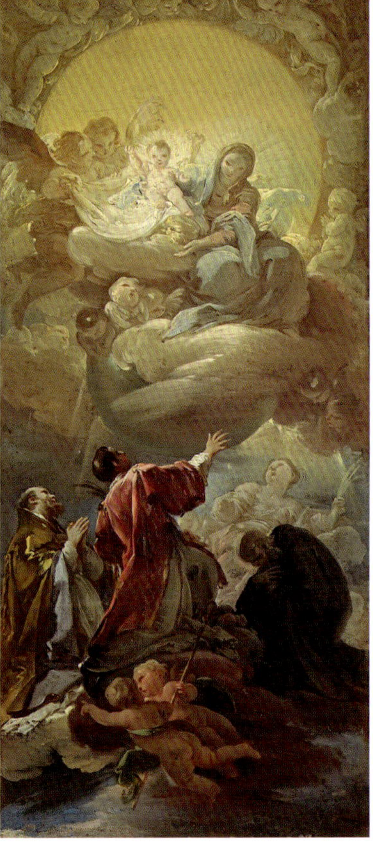

Fig. 96
Corrado Giaquinto, *Madonna and Child in Glory Appearing to St. Stephen and Three Other Saints*, ca. 1755–65, oil on canvas, 18⅞ × 8⅛ in. (47.5 × 20.7 cm), National Galleries of Scotland, Edinburgh (formerly collection of Denis Mahon)

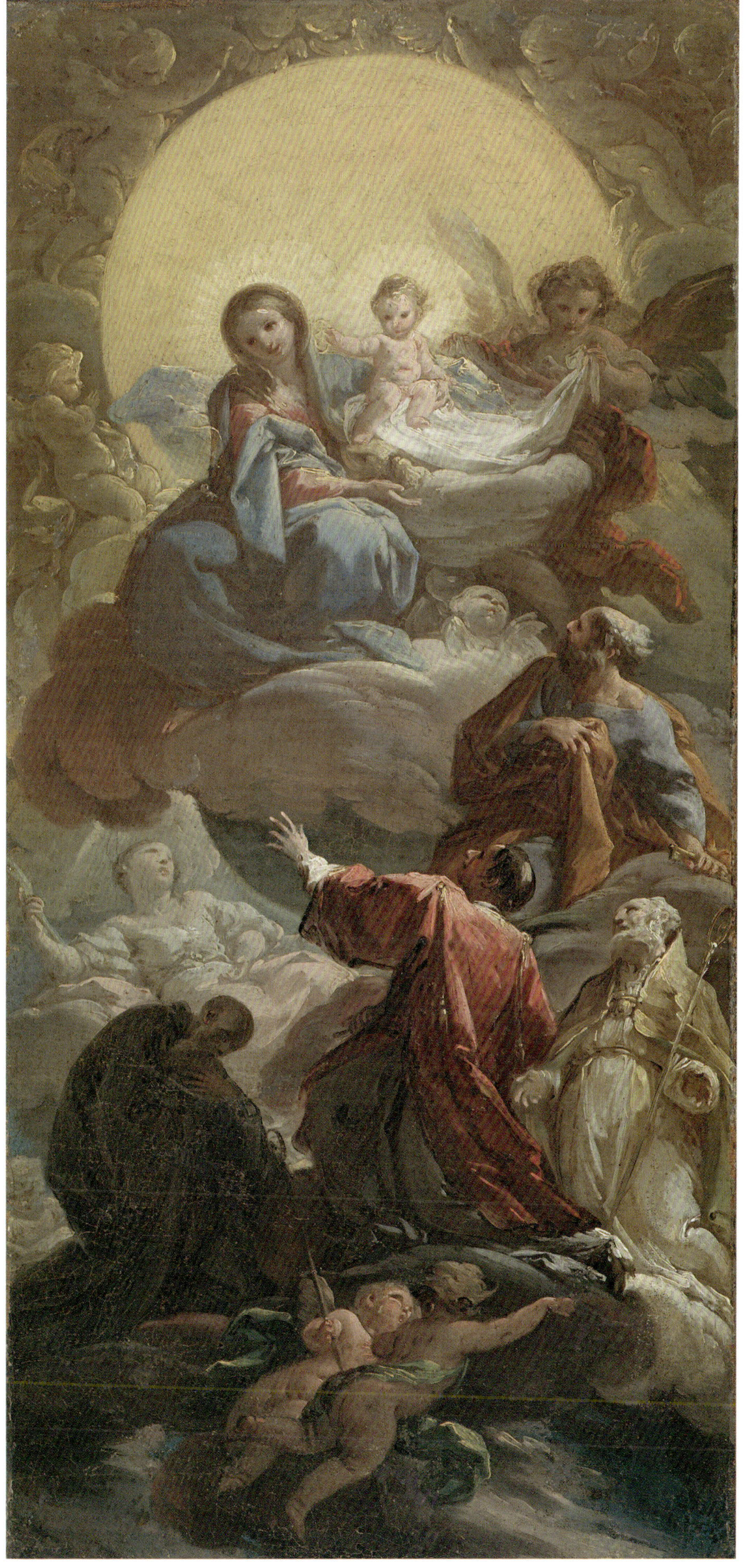

45

Corrado Giaquinto
Paradise: The Madonna and Child in Glory, 1749
Oil on canvas, 16½ × 38½ in. (42 × 98 cm)
Signed and dated on reverse: *C. Giaquinto/Roma 1749*
Museo e Gallerie Nazionali di Capodimonte,
inv. no. Q 1930-…, no. 1728

This is one of six paintings in the Museo di Capodimonte that are preparatory studies for the frescoes in the dome and spandrels of the chapel of Santa Maria del Popolo in the cathedral of Cesena, in Emilia-Romagna, painted by Giaquinto in Rome in 1749. The artist divided the Genealogy of the Virgin into six parts, with a different set of Mary's ancestors in each spandrel. Even though these are quick preliminary studies, they show finesse in their execution, with fast and free brushwork, using a golden coloring that suits Giaquinto's Rococo style.[1]

    Paradise: The Madonna and Child in Glory is the first in the series. The scene is in heaven, with the Madonna and Child placed in the center of the lunette-shaped space, with God the Father and the Holy Spirit hovering above them. Mary's ancestors from the Old Testament occupy clouds on either side. Angels in *grisaille* fill the upper corners. Giaquinto's light and airy style perfectly captured the sensibilities of the time, so much so that he might be called the Italian François Boucher, after the French artist who epitomized the Rococo. An oil sketch by Giaquinto of a *Rest on the Flight into Egypt* (fig. 97) has a similarly posed Madonna and Child. We see the influence of Giaquinto on De Mura's color and figure style in *The Trinity* (cat. no. 34) and *The Glory of the Princes* (cat. no. 35), among other examples.

1. Fiorentino, entry no. 72a in *Museo e Gallerie Nazionali di Capodimonte*, 82–83.

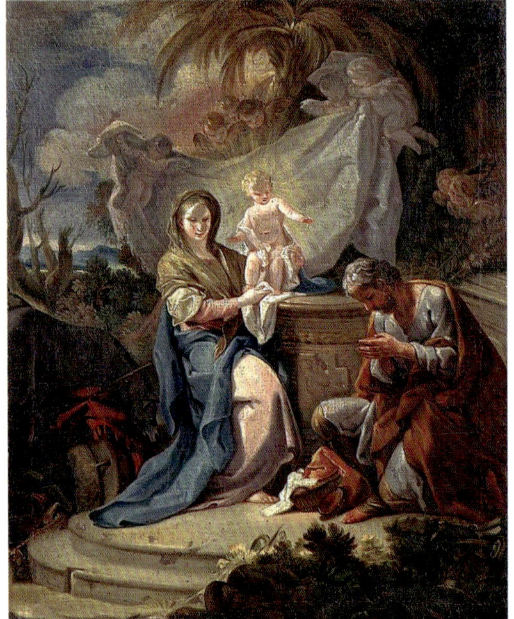

Fig. 97
Corrado Giaquinto, *Rest on the Flight into Egypt*, ca. 1760, oil on canvas, 24⅞ × 19⅞ in. (63 × 50 cm), private collection (*bozzetto* for a painting in the Detroit Institute of Arts)

Provenance:
A. Lisi collection, Bologna, to 1953; Museo Nazionale, Naples, until 1957; Museo Nazionale di Capodimonte (stored at the Museo Duca di Martina, Villa Floridiana), since 1974.

Exhibitions:
Naples, 1956; Rome, 1959, no. 260; Leningrad, Moscow, Warsaw, 1974, no. 7; Cesena, 2005.

Bibliography:
For bibliography before 1969, see Katia Fiorentino, entry no. 72a in *Museo e Gallerie Nazionali di Capodimonte: Dipinti del XVIII secolo; La scuola napoletana*, ed. Nicola Spinosa (Naples: Electa Napoli, 2010), 82–83; Luigi Dania, "Inediti di Corrado Giaquinto," *Paragone* 20, no. 235 (Sept. 1969): 63–69; Raffaello Causa, ed., *Le collezioni del Museo di Capodimonte* (Milan: Touring club italiano, 1982), 148 (ill. p. 110); George Hersey, entry no. 46 in *A Taste for Angels: Neapolitan Painting in North America, 1650–1750*, exhib. cat. (New Haven; Yale University Art Gallery, 1987), 320; Edith Gabrielli, entry in *Giaquinto: Capolavori dalle corti in Europa*, exhib. cat. (Milan: Charta, 1993), 50, 64–65, note 148; A. Confalone, essay in *The Italians: Three Centuries of Italian Art*, ed. Gilberto Algranti, exhib. cat. (Milan: Skira, 2002), 194, no. 71; Katia Fiorentino, entry 17 in *Corrado Giaquinto: Il cielo e la terra*, ed. Michela Scolaro, exhib. cat. (Bologna: Minerva, 2005), 216, pl. 27; Katia Fiorentino, entry 7 in *Corrado Giaquinto y España*, exhib. cat. (Madrid: Patrimonio Nacional, 2006), 144–45, no. 22.

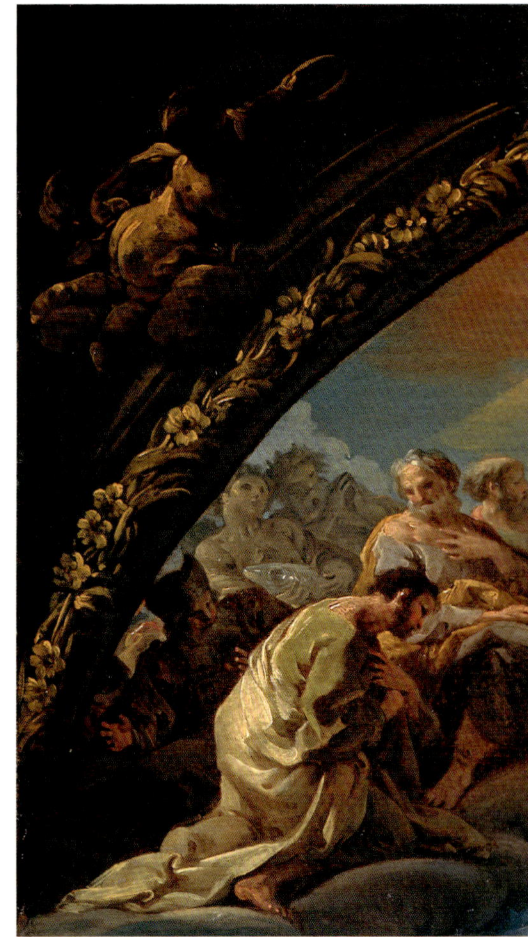

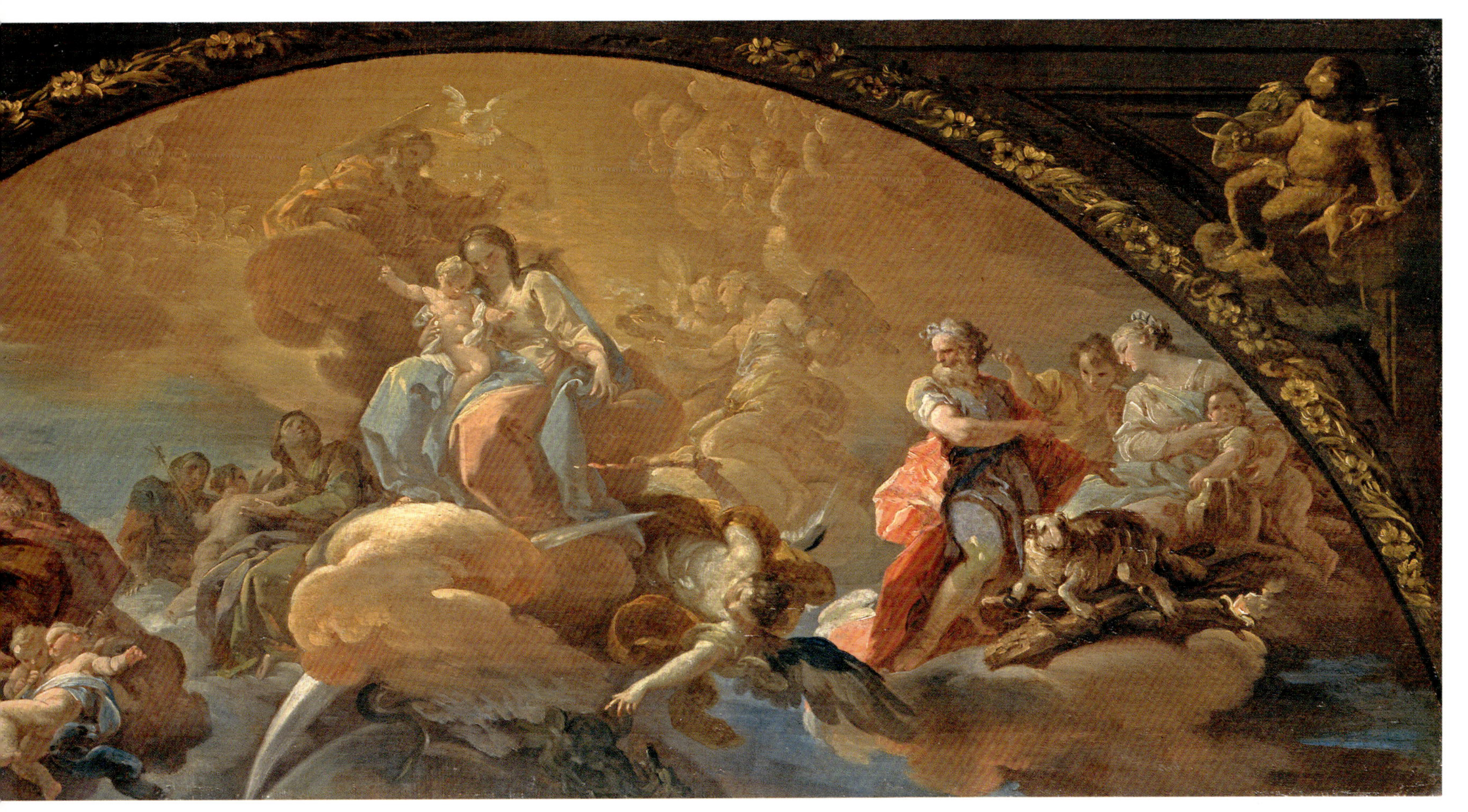

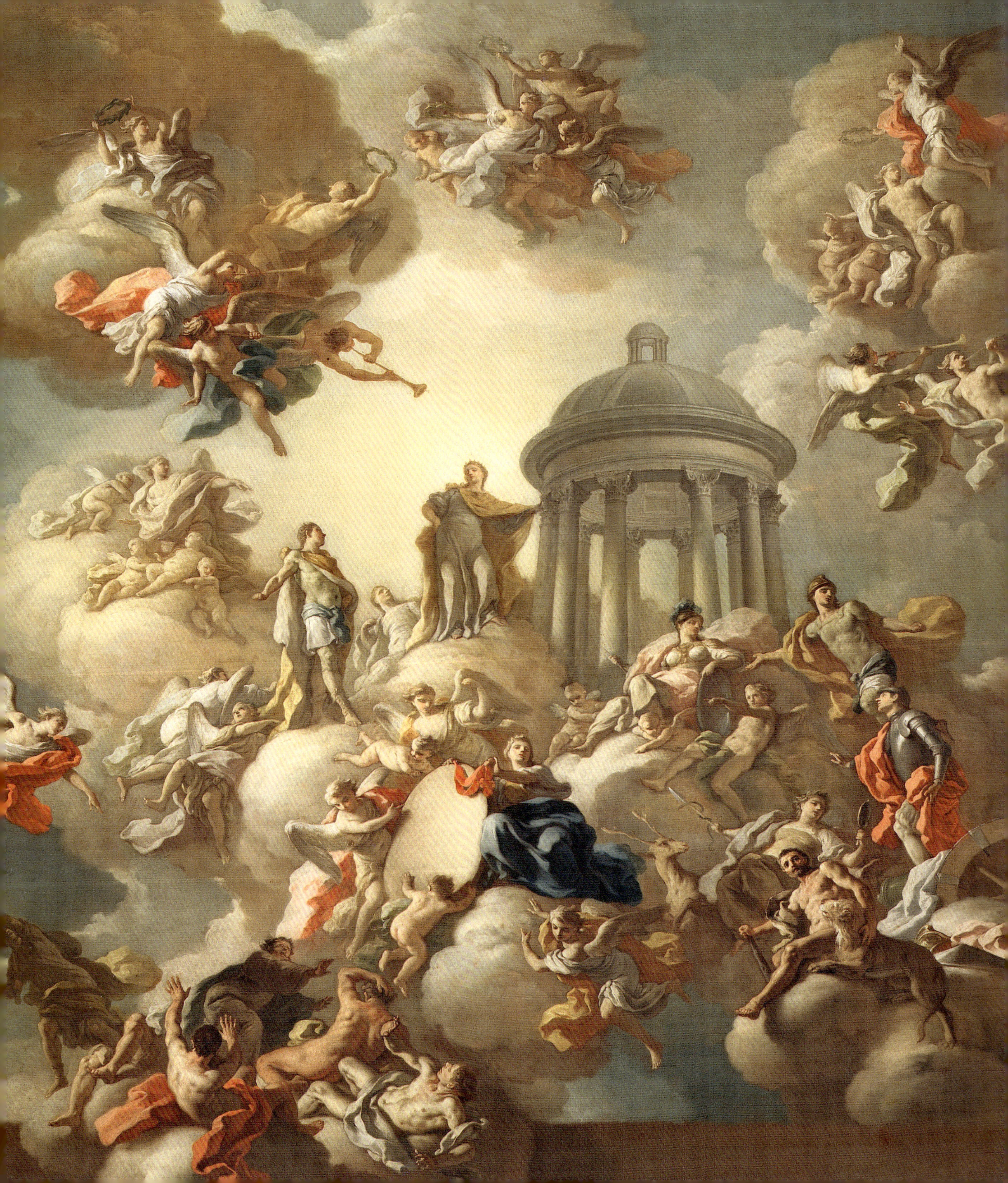

Selected Bibliography

Causa, Raffaello. *Opere d'arte nel Pio Monte della Misericordia a Napoli*. Cava dei Tirreni: Mauro, 1970.

D'Alessio, Gino. "Nuove osservazioni sulle committenze reali per Francesco de Mura tra Napoli, Torino e Madrid." *Prospettiva*, no. 69 (1993): 80–81.

Engass, Robert. "Francesco de Mura alla Nunziatella." *Bollettino d'arte* 49 (1964): 133–35.

Fredricksen, Burton B., and Federico Zeri, *Census of Pre-Nineteenth Century Italian Paintings in North American Public Collections*. Cambridge, Mass.: Harvard University Press, 1972.

Gazzara, Loredana. "Note e documenti inediti per lo studio delle collezioni della Quadreria del Pio Monte della Misericordia (I)." *Napoli Nobilissima*, 5th ser., 9 (May–Aug. 2008): 160–79, 175, 179.

The Golden Age of Naples: Art and Civilization under the Bourbons, 1734–1805. Vol. 1. Essay and entries by Nicola Spinosa. (Detroit: Detroit Institute of Arts, 1981). Exhib. cat., published in conjunction with the exhibition of the same name, shown at the Detroit Institute of Arts, Aug. 1981–Mar. 1982, and the Art Institute of Chicago, Dec. 24, 1981–Mar. 8, 1982.

Lorenzetti, Costanza. "La pittura napoletana del secolo XVIII." In *La mostra della pittura napoletana dei secoli XVII, XVIII, XIX*, ed. Sergio Ortolani and Maria Biancale. Naples, F. Giannini, 1938. Exhib. cat.

Maxon, John, and Joseph J. Rishel, eds. *Painting in Italy in the Eighteenth Century: Rococo to Romanticism* (Chicago: Art Institute of Chicago, 1970). Exhib. cat., published in conjunction with the exhibition of the same name, shown at the Art Institute of Chicago, Sept. 19–Nov. 1, 1970, Minneapolis Institute of Arts, Nov. 24, 1970–Jan. 10, 1971, and Toledo Museum of Art, Ohio, Feb. 7–Mar. 21, 1971.

Nolta, David. "Francesco de Mura: Lives and Works." 2 vols. Ph.D. diss. Yale University, New Haven, Conn., 1989.

Nolta, David. "Francesco de Mura." In *A Taste for Angels: Neapolitan Painting in North America, 1650–1750*. New Haven: Yale University Art Gallery, 1987. Exhib. cat., published in conjunction with the exhibition of the same name, shown at Yale University Art Gallery, New Haven, Conn., Sept. 9–Nov. 29, 1987, John and Mable Ringling Museum of Art, Sarasota, Fla., Jan. 13–Mar. 13, 1988, and Nelson-Atkins Museum of Art, Kansas City, Mo., Apr. 30–June 12, 1988.

Scolaro, Michaela, ed. *Corrado Giaquinto: Il cielo e la terra*, exhib. cat. Bologna: Minerva, 2005.

Spinosa, Nicola, ed. *Civiltà del '700 a Napoli, 1734–1799*. Vol. 1. Florence: Centro Di, 1979. Exhib. cat.

Spinosa, Nicola. "Francesco de Mura al Pio Monte." In *Il Pio Monte della Misericordia di Napoli nel Quarto Centenario*, edited by Mario Pisani Massamormile, 194–95. Naples: Electa Napoli, 2003.

Spinosa, Nicola. "Francesco de Mura al Pio Monte della Misericordia." *FMR*, no. 29 (Jan.–Feb. 2009): 24–48.

Spinosa, Nicola. "Mura, Francesco de." In *Dizionario enciclopedico Bolaffi dei pittori e degli incisori italiani dall'11º al 20º secolo*, vol. 10, 51–54. Turin: G. Bolaffi, 1976.

Spinosa, Nicola. "Neapolitan Painting in the Holy Land." In *Baroque Art from the Holy Sepulchre: The Image of Jerusalem in the Pre-Alps*: 59–73. Edited by Manuela Kahn-Rossi and Chiara Naldi. Lugano: Galleria Canesso, 2014. Exhib. cat.

Spinosa, Nicola. *Pittura napoletana del Settecento*. Vol. 1, *Dal barocco al rococò*. Naples: Electa Napoli, 1986.

Spinosa, Nicola, ed. *Pittura sacra a Napoli nel '700*. Naples: Società Editrice Napolentana, 1980. Exhib. cat.

Spinosa, Nicola. Entries in *Museo e Gallerie Nazionali di Capodimonte: Dipinti del XVIII secolo; La scuola napoletana*. Naples: Electa Napoli, 2010.

Spinosa, Nicola. "Francesco de Mura." In *Settecento napoletano: sulle ali dell'aquila imperiale, 1707–1734*. Naples: Electa Napoli, 1994. Exhib. cat., published in conjunction with the exhibition of the same name, shown at Kunstforum der Bank Austria, Vienna, Dec. 10, 1993–Feb. 20, 1994, and Castel Sant'Elmo, Naples, Mar. 19–July 24, 1994.

Photographic Credits

Copyright information and photographic credits of works included in this catalogue are below.
Images without specific credit are courtesy of the lending institution. Every effort has been made
to credit the photographers and sources of all illustrations in this volume.

Pages 6–7, 151, 152: © The Fitzwilliam Museum, Cambridge.
Pages 8, 9, 21, 22, 25, 26, 28, 29, 39, 50, 52, 71, 110–11, 112–13, 114–15, 122, 124–25, 126–27, 141, 154, 173: © Archivio dell'Arte
Pages 14, 139: © Art Gallery of Ontario
Pages 17, 54: © RMN-Grand Palais/Art Resource, NY
Pages 20, 128, 161: Photo: Minneapolis Institute of Art
Pages 26, 135, Back cover: Photography © The Art Institute of Chicago
Page 30 (left): Detroit Institute of Arts, USA/Founders Society Purchase, Henry Ford II Fund/Bridgeman Images
Page 36: Photo: The Montreal Museum of Fine Arts, Christine Guest
Page 46: Kimbell Art Museum, Fort Worth, Texas/Art Resource, NY
Pages 47, 49: De Agostini Picture Library/Bridgeman Images
Pages 76–77, 168: © The Toledo Museum of Art
Page 78 (bottom): Cobbe Collection, Hatchlands Park/United Agents LLP
Pages 81, 90, 98: © Molinari Pradelli Collection
Pages 82–83: Archives Charmet/© Bridgeman Images
Pages 88, 148, 182 (top): Photo © Christie's Images/Bridgeman Images
Page 91: © Bonhams, London, UK/Bridgeman Images
Page 101 (left): Photo Credit: bpk, Berlin/Staatsgaleri/Art Resource, NY
Page 101 (right): © Philadelphia Museum of Art
Page 107: © 2016. The Philbrook Museum of Art, Inc., Tulsa, Oklahoma
Pages 108 (bottom), 118, 132, 136: Zeri Photo Archive
Page 116: © Compton Verney
Pages 119, 137, 194: © The Metropolitan Museum of Art, Image source: Art Resource, NY
Pages 130 (right), 131 142, 147, 169, 174, 202: De Agostini Picture Library/ Bridgeman Images
Page 134: Bibliothèque Sainte-Geneviève, Paris, France/Archives Charmet/Bridgeman Images
Pages 149, 205: © Seattle Art Museum
Page 153: Copper Hewitt, Smithsonian Design Museum/Art Resource, NY
Page 156 (bottom): © Marco Maraviglia
Page 157: © The John and Mable Ringling Museum of Art
Page 160: Southampton City Art Gallery, Hampshire, UK/Bridgeman Images
Page 165: © Hearst Castle®/CA State Parks
Page 179: Digital image courtesy of the Getty's Open Content Program.
Page 180 (bottom): © Banca Commerciale Italiana, Eboli
Page 195: © Musée du Louvre, Dist. RMN-Grand Palais/Art Resource, NY
Page 196: © Kunsthistorisches Institut, Florence
Page 197: Photograph © 2016 Museum of Fine Arts, Boston

Photographer credits

Pixel Acuity, Florida: Front cover, front jacket; pp. 144–45, 191, 205
Robert Lorenzson: Frontispiece; pp. 79, 159, 166, 171
Luciano Pedicini: Back jacket; pp. 8, 9, 21, 22, 25, 26, 28, 29, 39, 50, 52, 71, 110–11, 112–13, 114–15, 122, 124–25, 126–27, 139, 154, 176
Christine Guest: p. 36
Erich Lessing: pp. 47, 195
Paola Tufo: pp. 59, 62, 65, 68, 69, 71, 72, 73
Lambert Photo: pp. 89, 143
Carlo Vanni and L. Landi: pp. 90, 98
Charles Benton: p. 97
A. Dagli Orti: pp. 130, 147, 169 (bottom), 174, 202
Victoria Garagliano: p. 165
Jörg P. Anders: p. 169 (top)

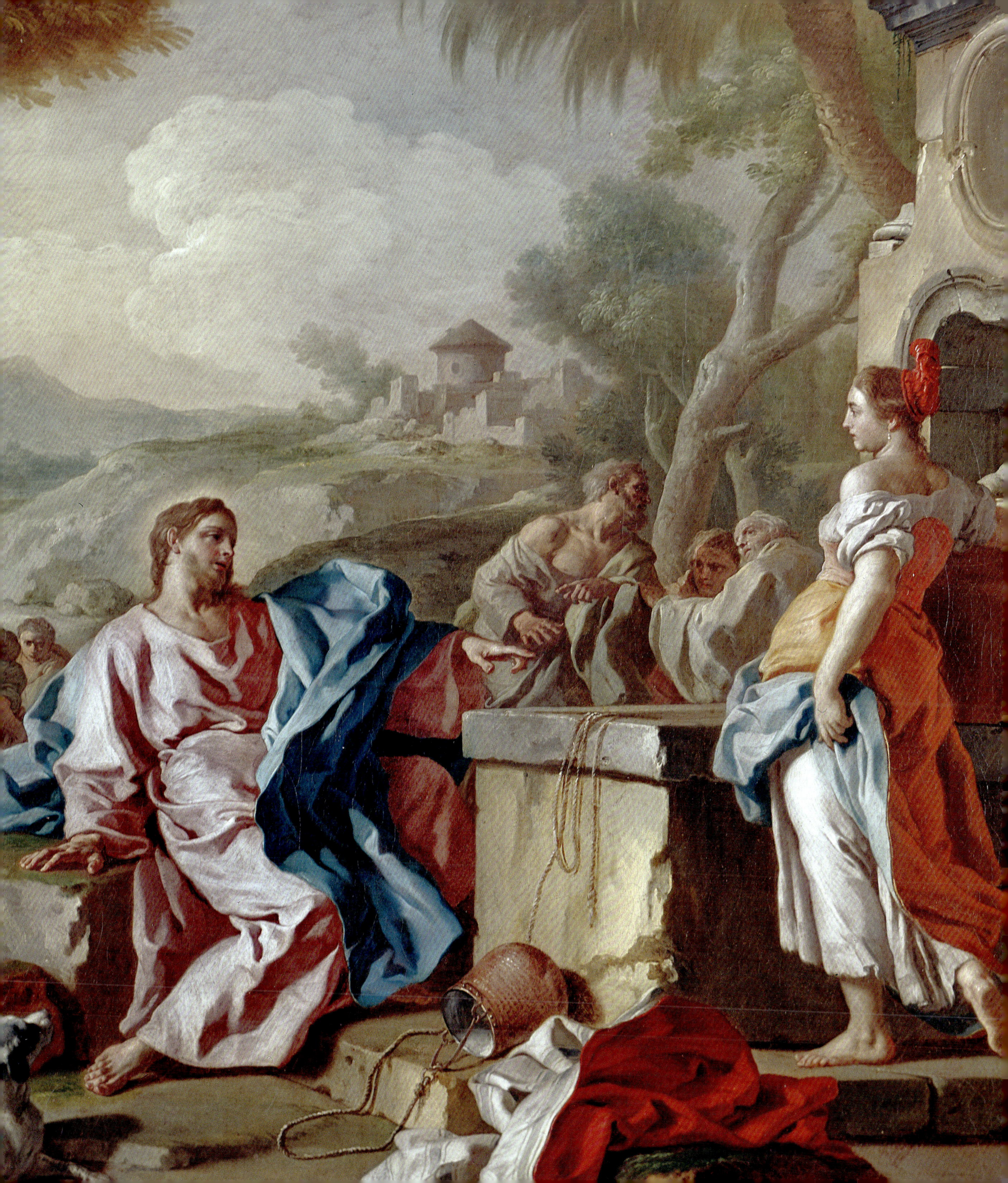

Index

Page numbers in *italics* refer to the illustrations.